Legal Writing
for the
Undergraduate

Legal Writing *for the* Undergraduate

ANTONIO ELEFANO
Associate Professor (Teaching) of Writing
University of Southern California

Wolters Kluwer

Copyright © 2022 CCH Incorporated.

Published by Wolters Kluwer in New York.

Wolters Kluwer Legal & Regulatory U.S. serves customers worldwide with CCH, Aspen Publishers, and Kluwer Law International products. (www.WKLegaledu.com)

No part of this publication may be reproduced or transmitted in any form or by any means, electronic or mechanical, including photocopy, recording, or utilized by any information storage or retrieval system, without written permission from the publisher. For information about permissions or to request permissions online, visit us at www.WKLegaledu.com, or a written request may be faxed to our permissions department at 212-771-0803.

Cover image: iStock.com/Trout55

To contact Customer Service, e-mail customer.service@wolterskluwer.com, call 1-800-234-1660, fax 1-800-901-9075, or mail correspondence to:

> Wolters Kluwer
> Attn: Order Department
> PO Box 990
> Frederick, MD 21705

Printed in the United States of America.

1 2 3 4 5 6 7 8 9 0

ISBN 978-1-5438-5022-2

Library of Congress Cataloging-in-Publication Data

Library of Congress Cataloging-in-Publication Data application is in process.

About Wolters Kluwer Legal & Regulatory U.S.

Wolters Kluwer Legal & Regulatory U.S. delivers expert content and solutions in the areas of law, corporate compliance, health compliance, reimbursement, and legal education. Its practical solutions help customers successfully navigate the demands of a changing environment to drive their daily activities, enhance decision quality and inspire confident outcomes.

Serving customers worldwide, its legal and regulatory portfolio includes products under the Aspen Publishers, CCH Incorporated, Kluwer Law International, ftwilliam.com and MediRegs names. They are regarded as exceptional and trusted resources for general legal and practice-specific knowledge, compliance and risk management, dynamic workflow solutions, and expert commentary.

For Lourdes and Tony Elefano,
who gave me everything I needed
to get everything I wanted

Summary Table of Contents

Table of Contents		xi
Preface		xv
Acknowledgments		xxv
chapter 1	Unpacking the Hierarchy of U.S. Law	1
chapter 2	Close Reading a Statute	9
chapter 3	Applying Law to Facts	13
chapter 4	Reading and Briefing a Case	19
chapter 5	Anticipating How a Court Will Rule	49
chapter 6	Legal Writing Fundamentals	97
chapter 7	Introduction to Legal Memoranda	105
chapter 8	One-Case Memorandum Assignments	123
chapter 9	Three-Case Memorandum Assignment	163
chapter 10	Five-Case Memorandum Assignments	171
chapter 11	Workshopping Legal Writing	253
chapter 12	Basic Legal Research	259
chapter 13	Introduction to Appellate Briefs	265
chapter 14	Getting into Law School	317
chapter 15	Practical Advice for Law School and Beyond, or What I Wish I'd Known When I Started Law School	323
Glossary		329
Index		333

Table of Contents

Preface — xv
Acknowledgments — xxv

chapter 1 Unpacking the Hierarchy of U.S. Law — 1
  Holdings and Dicta — 5

chapter 2 Close Reading a Statute — 9
  Introduction to Statutes — 9
  Statutory Construction — 11

chapter 3 Applying Law to Facts — 13
  Issues of Fact — 13
  Assignment 1: Bullying Policy Advice — 14

chapter 4 Reading and Briefing a Case — 19
  Reading the Case — 19
  Understanding Citations — 20
  Crafting the Brief — 21
    Case Name and Citation — 21
    Facts — 22
    Procedural History — 22
    Issues or Questions Presented — 23
    Holdings or Answers — 24
    Reasoning — 24
    Concurrence(s) — 25
    Dissent(s) — 25
  Sample Brief for *J.S. v. Blue Mountain School District* — 26

	Assignment 2: *DeShaney v. Winnebago County Department of Social Services* Case Brief	29
	Deshaney v. Winnebago County Department of Social Services	29
	Sample Brief for *DeShaney v. Winnebago County Department of Social Services*	44
chapter 5	**Anticipating How a Court Will Rule**	**49**
	Intrepreting Law	49
	Predicting Future Court Decisions Based on Prior Precedent	50
	Assignment 3: *Doe v. Covington County School District* Case Brief	51
	Doe v. Covington County School District	51
	Assignment 4: *Estate of Brown v. Cypress Fairbanks Independent School District* Case Brief	87
	Estate of Brown v. Cypress Fairbanks Independent School District	87
	The Power of Stare Decisis	95
chapter 6	**Legal Writing Fundamentals**	**97**
	Efficiency, Focus and Formality	97
	Writing Effectively	98
	Build Your Argument	99
	Craft Your Sentences	99
	Be Concise	100
	Be Concrete	100
	Cite Everything	101
	Adhere to Accepted Formats	101
	Stay Close to the Law	102
	Avoid Repetition	102
	Write. Rewrite. Repeat.	103
chapter 7	**Introduction to Legal Memoranda**	**105**
	Getting the Assignment	105
	Knowing Your Audience	106
	Formatting the Memorandum	106
	Crafting the Heading	107
	Crafting the Issue(s) Presented	108
	Crafting the Brief Answer(s)	108
	Crafting the Statement of Facts	109

Crafting the Discussion		110
Issue		110
Rule		110
Application		111
Conclusion		112
Crafting the Memo's Conclusion		113
Case Citations		113
Sample Memorandum: First Amendment Rights at Kinnear High		115
chapter 8	**One-Case Memorandum Assignments**	**123**
Assignment 5: Religious Liberty Memorandum		123
In re Garcia		126
Assignment 6: Copyright Infringement Advice Memorandum		135
Henley v. DeVore		138
chapter 9	**Three-Case Memorandum Assignment**	**163**
Assignment 7: Substantive Due Process Memorandum		164
chapter 10	**Five-Case Memorandum Assignments**	**171**
Assignment 8: First Amendment Rights at Morning Glory High Memorandum		171
Tinker v. Des Moines Independent Community School District		176
Bethel School District No. 403 v. Fraser		190
Wisniewski ex rel. Wisniewski v. Board of Education of the Weedsport Central School District		204
Mahanoy Area School District v. B. L.		210
B.H. ex rel. Hawk v. Easton Area School District		218
Assignment 9: First Amendment Rights at Kinnear High Memorandum		248
chapter 11	**Workshopping Legal Writing**	**253**
Assignment 10: Peer Critique		254
Sample Student Peer Critique		256
chapter 12	**Basic Legal Research**	**259**
Familiarizing Oneself with an Area of Law		259
Confirming the Currency and Validity of Particular Laws		260

	Searching for Specific Law in Targeted Jurisdictions	262
	Some Final Advice on the Research Process	263
chapter 13	**Introduction to Appellate Briefs**	**265**
	Getting Started	265
	Conducting Research	266
	Outlining Your Argument	267
	Formatting Your Brief	268
	Crafting the Statement of the Case	271
	Crafting the Summary of the Argument	272
	Crafting the Argument	275
	Concluding the Brief	276
	Attaching Appendices	276
	Sample Appellant Brief: *Jeremiah Smith v. LoanMe, Inc.*	277
	Appellate-Style Oral Argument	289
	Assignment 11: *In re Gallagher* Appellate Brief	291
	In re Taylor	292
	In re Gallagher	311
chapter 14	**Getting into Law School**	**317**
	Assignment 12: Personal Statement	317
	Letters of Recommendation	321
	Diversity Statements	322
	Resumes/CVs	322
	Addenda	322
chapter 15	**Practical Advice for Law School and Beyond, or What I Wish I'd Known When I Started Law School**	**323**
	Choosing Law as a Field	323
	Choosing a Law School	324
	Preparing for Law School	324
	Starting Law School	325
	Working During Law School	326
	Working After Law School	326
	Closing Statement	327
	Glossary	329
	Index	333

Preface

The Case for Undergraduate Legal Writing

I started college in 1999 as a political science major. I made the choice not because history and government were my favorite classes in high school, but because I was planning on going to law school one day. Before my first day of college, however, I attended a session with Texas A&M's pre-law advisor, the wonderful Karen Severn. Karen told me that law schools didn't care what I majored in as long as I did well in whatever I chose. Following her guidance, I switched to English. Over the next three years, I became a sharper writer and a better critical thinker, and I got to do it while reading Ernest Hemingway, Virginia Woolf and John Guare. Law schools don't expect you to know the law before you arrive, Karen told me; they're happy to take care of that themselves.

I did take one law-related class as an undergraduate: in the spring semester of my freshman year, I signed up for U.S. Constitutional Development. On my first midterm I got a lower grade than I expected; worse yet, I didn't understand *why* I'd gotten the lower grade. So I visited the professor during office hours to inquire. He reviewed my exam in front of me. I remember him saying that everything I'd written was correct and that I'd captured the substance from both the casebook and our class discussions perfectly. I was feeling pretty good at that point. He'd made a mistake, I thought, and was on the precipice of correcting it. But then, he asked a question that would haunt the rest of my undergraduate days. After he I admitted that I'd reproduced everything that had been given to me, he looked me in the eye and said, "But Antonio, where's the work?"

The difference between high school and college is simple. In high school, it's often enough just to remember what happened ("The Civil War started in the year 1861.") or to recognize concepts within fixed works ("Write a five-paragraph paper discussing three literary elements in *The Scarlet Letter*."). But in college, one is expected not just to regurgitate a body of knowledge but to contribute to it. College, more than anything, teaches one how to arrive at an original thought. I'm not sure how much U.S. Constitutional Development helped me in my law school Constitutional Law class. But it did make me a better thinker and defter college student. That said, after my three years at A&M, I felt as if I understood how to approach most theoretical problems and how to communicate my thoughts clearly and cogently. But I wasn't sure I had anything worth saying yet. So in fall 2002, I started my 1L year at Yale Law School.

At 21, I was one of the youngest people in my class, and when I looked around the room at my cohort—filled mostly with Ivy League-educated scholars—I felt thoroughly outclassed. But I was there, and I was determined. I worked harder than I'd ever worked and relied on the one skill that had set me apart as a high schooler and undergraduate. I was a writer. My senior year of high school, I was the state champion in ready writing (an impromptu essay competition). In college, I'd won top honors for my fiction and playwriting. It helped that writing is a big part of both law school and legal practice, and it really helped that my professor in the subject was Robert Harrison. Robert had a reputation as the most caring, sincere professor at Yale Law. He more than lived up to his reputation. My time at Yale was the most rigorous and formative of my academic career. I met the smartest and kindest people I'd ever met in my life, and I was challenged in a way I'd never been challenged before. Law school was also where I finally discovered what was worth saying and what was worth fighting for. Law school gave me the skills, not just to understand the world, but to advocate and effect change within it. In the spring of 2005, I graduated from Yale and accepted an offer to work in New York at Kaye Scholer LLP (now Arnold & Porter Kaye Scholer LLP) the following fall.

I worked as a corporate litigator at Kaye Scholer for five years and confirmed what I'd been told for years: that the vast majority of work for a litigator happened not in a courtroom but on a page. I wrote countless memos and motions and the occasional brief. I remember the thrill when the first motion I was ever asked to draft on my own, a motion everyone expected to lose based on the precedent case law, resulted in an unexpected win. Life at a law firm is taxing, however, and is only sustainable for a precious few. The more senior I became at Kaye Scholer, the less time I had to devote to anything other than work, including fiction and playwriting. So in 2010, I left my practice and accepted one of ten spots as a Master of Fine Arts fiction candidate at Boston University. My new professors and classmates not only made me a much better fiction writer, they taught me how to teach writing. Post-graduation, I taught at BU, then at the University of Houston for two years, until finally finding my home in 2014 at the University of Southern California.

I was hired by USC to replace my eventual mentor at the university, the late Dr. James Brecher. James had been teaching legal writing to undergraduates for over a decade and was about to retire, so the Writing Program needed a new specialist. When I was assigned my first undergraduate legal writing courses, I asked James for guidance. He handed me a 500-page course packet, filled with law review articles, classic law school opinions (like the 1928 New York case, *Palsgraf v. Long Island Railroad Co.*) and assignments (I remember one involved a contract dispute and another a landlord/tenant issue). I knew I couldn't just adopt the same packet—I always hated *Palsgraf* and contracts was my least favorite class 1L year—so I took a couple of the articles from James's packet and started almost entirely from scratch.

I'll admit: I was apprehensive about teaching legal writing to undergraduates. To teach a junior or senior in college how to refine their thinking and writing is already a tall task. Was it really possible to convert my legal argumentation training into something an undergraduate could absorb? Well, the existence of this book should tell you the answer to that question, but I imagine you might have other worthy queries, such as:

Why Should an Undergraduate (or Any Non-lawyer) Learn Legal Writing?

When I started teaching legal writing at USC, I assumed that all my students would be pre-law. After all, my course was titled Advanced Writing for Pre-Law Students. My university offered a myriad of advanced writing courses (a prerequisite for graduation), including courses in the arts and humanities, the social sciences and the natural sciences. In those courses, students write traditional academic essays and research papers but often have broad discretion on the topics of those papers. The idea is that by the end of one's undergraduate career, students should have the freedom to explore the specific subjects they're most interested in or that are most relevant to their future careers. It's the instructor's duty to help refine their students' voices and prepare them for life beyond the academy.

Advanced Writing for Pre-Law Students, which I teach as an Introduction to Legal Writing, gives very little freedom to students to explore their research interests. There's hardly any research at all. Instead, my students are given a series of cases — closed case universes revolving around particular legal issues — and assignment prompts that invite students to apply a set of law to a set of facts. My thought process was simple: who, other than a prospective law student, would be interested in developing such a specialized skill?

Let's start with the obvious population: actual pre-law students. In my view, the most important function of undergraduate legal writing isn't preparing students for law school; it's providing a means for pre-law students to determine if law school is right for them or not. Most representations of law in the news and in popular culture focus on the courtroom: opening and closing statements, direct and cross-examinations, Johnny Cochran and Atticus Finch. Trial advocacy, however, is just a small part of lawyering, even for litigators. Most matters, in fact, never make their way to trial. During my years as a corporate litigator, the vast majority of my time was spent researching and writing. Yet to this day, pre-law students imagining their futures envision themselves delivering impassioned pleas to juries and judges. How can undergraduate legal writing fill the gap between expectation and reality?

In my undergraduate legal writing class, students act like members of a law firm, tasked with the same kinds of work that young associates often do. Early in the semester, students interview a distressed client (played by me) for an advice memo they eventually craft. In so doing, they are forced to gauge that client's knowledge and state of mind and adjust their questions accordingly. Later in the semester, they write a legal memorandum pitched to a fellow attorney discussing possible litigation strategies for a fictitious case. Students get to do the kind of work that lawyers do and hopefully gain insight into how they might one day fit into this profession. This kind of knowledge is important, especially if the student is unsure about the investment that three years of law school represents.

For students who ultimately decide to take the law school plunge, undergraduate legal writing provides them an invaluable head start on their law school career. Students learn how to read a case, how to engage in a Socratic dialogue, how to structure an argument and how to predict legal outcomes despite contradictory precedent. Former students who go to law school frequently tell me that legal writing was their first year's highest grade — an expected outcome perhaps, as practice and comfort in anything often breed good results. But undergraduate legal writing does more than just teach the conventions of a new style of writing; it prepares students for a new mode of thinking that carries over to other law school courses as well.

The benefits of undergraduate legal writing, however, extend beyond just pre-law students or students toying with the idea of law school. When I started teaching legal writing at USC, I was surprised by the number of people that took my course who were not considering law school at all. In the spring of 2017, for example, USC offered 136 sections of advanced writing. Of these, only seven were pre-law and three of the seven were mine (the only three taught as an intensive legal writing practicum).

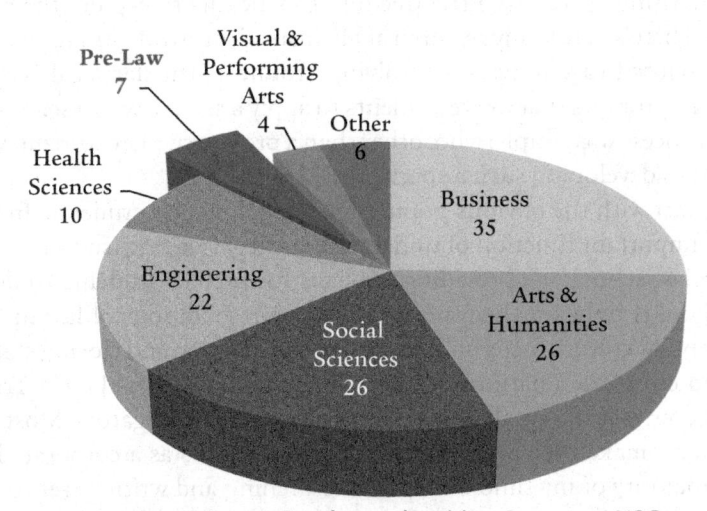

Exhibit P.1: Spring 2017 Advanced Writing Courses at USC

Prospective law students can of course come from any discipline, so in the spring of 2017, I asked my students the following question: "Are you actually considering law school?" The result (polling 52 students): 65 percent yes; 35 percent no. This proportion was in line with what I'd observed in previous classes and what I've observed since. It begs the question: why is such a sizeable portion of my students who aren't even thinking about law school subjecting themselves to the very individual challenges of legal reading and writing? Here are the conclusions I've come to:

1. Students Learn How to Read and Synthesize the Law

How many of us when confronted with a contract or terms of agreement feel our eyes glaze over? As dense and sometimes incomprehensible as these documents can be, they enumerate important rights and responsibilities. Legal writing's first task is issue spotting: can a student locate the facts that potentially trigger a given law? Do they understand how to interpret that law through different lenses and perspectives? Even though legal writing classes focus primarily on case law, the skills gleaned from unpacking those cases can apply to statutes, contracts, handbooks and other kinds of legal writing.

The major most often represented in my classes is business, and while some of those business majors are thinking about law school, there is a large proportion who just want to understand the law better, so that they aren't puzzled or intimidated by its often-strange language. Making the strange — if not quite familiar — at least a little less strange can be quite the advantage in any professional setting.

2. Students Learn How to Write Professionally

Many of the documents lawyers write — memos, client letters, summaries — are documents that other professionals write as well. The class accordingly has utility beyond just the specific back-and-forth of a law firm or court. The substance may be focused but the utility for students is expansive. Former business students have used writing samples from my class when trying to get a job. A former journalism student was given a plum legal reporting assignment at NBC News because of her unique ability to understand, analyze and interpret case law. Legal writing is audience-centered; one writes differently when writing to a judge versus a fellow attorney versus a client. That kind of rhetorical dexterity is useful outside of the law as well, both in industry and even personal communication.

3. Students Learn How to Write Persuasively

Legal writing is the art of convincing another, of confronting opposition and persuading an arbiter that your position is superior. Students must understand who the arbiter is and what criteria that person is applying to their argument. They must have a command of the hierarchy of law to understand what is binding and what is merely persuasive to the deciding party. They must anticipate the opposing side's arguments and craft counterarguments. An awareness of audience and the interplay of argument and counterargument are hardly new concepts to any student who's taken a traditional composition course, but their practical application to law and the performance of lawyering gives these concepts added vitality, highlighting their real-world significance.

Advanced composition classes often task students with writing for academic, professional and lay audiences. The rhetorical strategies are different, and the rewards for success are often amorphous. Legal writing has very specific objectives: win this for your client; get this complaint dismissed. This kind of functional, results-driven approach to rhetoric is useful in circumstances ranging from trying to get a raise at work to convincing your cell phone carrier to honor the discount they promised.

4. Students Learn How to Become More Effective Self-Advocates

It is one thing to know one's rights, but what legal writing teaches is how to fight for them. During my first semester teaching legal writing, a student driving to campus was pulled over for an illegal turn. To contest the ticket, he wrote a five-page traffic court brief detailing his understanding of the applicable law and the facts at issue. To understand the law, to know enough to demand that its application makes sense, can be an empowering feeling. People often hire lawyers not because they're not invested enough in a conflict to fight for themselves, but because they lack the vocabulary and command of the issues to advocate confidently. When an issue is complex, hiring an attorney is the safest course, but for simple issues—drafting a basic will, for example—self-education and some practical guidelines for analysis and writing may be sufficient.

In addition, legal writing classes often teach oral argument skills, using the appellate-style model whereby judges engage with the advocate directly, asking questions as the arguer presents their case. So often in academia, oral presentations are one-direction affairs: one person talks; everyone else listens. But appellate-style oral arguments invite a conversation, requiring that the presenting student both listen closely and speak carefully. At first glance, this may appear to be about the ability to speak extemporaneously, but it's also about reading a judge's questions, anticipating their concerns, and being prepared enough to handle the myriad of issues that a single case can pose.

In the end, students come away from my courses able to deliver thoughtful and polished arguments—both at the podium and on the page. They learn to respect opposing viewpoints and to adjust their own thinking accordingly. They learn how to situate themselves within a society of laws and how to protect their own rights.

The skills above are essential for lawyers, but they're equally essential to many other professions, which brings me to the next question:

Who Is This Book Designed to Serve?

While the title is *Legal Writing for the Undergraduate,* I've crafted this textbook with the following populations in mind:

- Undergraduate legal writing students
- Undergraduate legal studies students
- Master of Legal Studies/Law/Jurisprudence students
- Summer pre-law program students
- Undergraduate moot court competitors
- Students taking classes where law plays a secondary role: e.g., business and law or engineering and law
- Admitted law students preparing for 1L year

My goal in writing this book was to provide enough guidance and scaffolding so that any person unfamiliar with the law could learn how to read and analyze cases and how to formulate basic legal arguments. I teach a version of my Introduction to Legal Writing class to high school students every summer, and after a mere four-week session, even at that level my students can produce credible legal memoranda.

Will Reading This Book Make Me Equivalent to a Lawyer?

While experience has proven that even teenagers can master the basic tenets of legal reasoning and argumentation, it's important to recognize the limitations of this text. *Legal Writing for the Undergraduate* is an introduction to American law and legal writing, a way to make one less afraid of reading legal documents and writing about legal issues. It's easy to be intimidated by everything from leases to case law, but at the end of the day, law is just language, and this book will make that language more accessible. But lawyers learn more than just how to write in law school. The first year of law school is all about setting a substantive foundation in legal precedent: torts, procedure, contracts, etc. This textbook utilizes several closed universes of cases, allowing you to focus on the provided law to apply to the assignments. Real lawyers, of course, must be responsible for all the relevant precedent that binds a given court; wading through thickets of statutes, regulations and opinions to discern what's relevant and what's not takes time and experience. Additionally, while this book provides the basic structures for legal memoranda and appellate briefs, it does not go into the same level of detail or nuance as an equivalent text intended for law students.

There are three basic hallmarks of legal writing that I hope you'll absorb over the course of this text: **efficiency**, **focus** and **formality**. Many lawyers bill their clients by five- or six-minute increments. As time is literally money in this industry, lawyers must be efficient both with their time and with their work product. If a client asks for a memorandum detailing their chances of winning their lawsuit against their neighbor, they likely don't want you to spend hours providing them pages and pages of background about famous court cases involving next-door neighbors. In your high school courses, there may have been times when adding these kinds of flourishes and details was rewarded. But in a field where every task is billed, you're discouraged from assuming more work than you've been asked to do.

Related to that, your work product should be as focused as possible on the task you've been given. If you've been asked to opine on the likely success of a copyright infringement suit, don't spend half your memorandum talking about the possible defamation suit that you also see in the fact pattern. As you'll soon see, almost all legal writing follows a basic structure that requires you to first reveal the law you're applying and then connect that law to the applicable facts of the case. Adherence to that structure will keep you from straying beyond the scope of the assignment. If the law you've been asked to apply is copyright infringement, isolate your analysis to that cause of action. Too often, when faced with a complex factual scenario, students want to point out every instance of wrongdoing they see. But lawyers don't sue for violations of vague moral boundaries; they sue for violations of law. Whenever you argue, stay close to the law you've been asked to apply and you'll rarely go astray.

Finally, as law is a professional service industry, you should always try to err on the side of formality in your rhetoric. Even the aesthetic of the documents you produce will be judged. Imagine the difference between getting a letter from your attorney on sleek letterhead with a courteous greeting versus a handwritten note on the back of a piece of scrap paper. Which seems more professional? Remember that the client paid for the crafting of that note.

Your language, too, should be appropriate for a formal advisor. This doesn't mean that you shouldn't be clear and concise: formal language doesn't mean thesaurus language. But avoid overly aggressive or casual language ("We're going to rip the other side apart!"). It's good to be confident when there's reason for confidence, but it's wiser to be conservative in your expectations and then over-deliver when talking to a client ("Given the precedent case law, we have a high likelihood of success."). When talking to a fellow lawyer in an interoffice memorandum, you can be blunter, especially regarding a difficult or likely losing claim ("Based on how the statute has been interpreted over the past 20 years, we will almost certainly be unsuccessful raising suit on this issue.").

How Is the Book Structured?

I've structured the book to follow the steps I take in teaching my two-course legal writing progression at USC: from Introduction to Legal Writing (which typically culminates in mastery of the legal memorandum) to Advanced Legal Writing (which typically culminates in mastery of the appellate brief). I start with my Five Steps to Turn Any Novice into a Legal Writer:

1. Unpack the Hierarchy of U.S. Law
2. Close Read a Statute
3. Apply Law to Facts
4. Read and Brief a Case
5. Anticipate How a Court Will Rule

Through the first five chapters of this textbook, you'll get a basic overview of the U.S. legal system. You'll learn how to break down a law and then apply it to varying situations. You'll read your first case and learn how to properly summarize case law. Finally, you'll learn how to use precedent cases to predict how courts will rule in future cases.

After that, I'll turn to the fundamentals of legal writing and then to specific forms of legal writing. I'll offer a number of assignments to practice those forms. I'll offer advice on how to workshop legal writing, a key part of my pedagogy that I borrowed from my years leading fiction workshops. I will also offer an introduction to basic legal research. To close, I'll lend some practical advice for law school and beyond.

Tips for Navigating *Legal Writing for the Undergraduate*

1. Be patient. What you're learning is normally reserved for first-year law students. Not only are law students committed to learning law, their study of legal writing is supported by simultaneous doctrinal courses (like contracts, procedure and torts) that reinforce their legal reasoning and argumentation skills.
2. Pay close attention to language. Law is a field where the choice of conjunction ("and" versus "or") or even punctuation in a legal standard can win or lose your case. Accordingly, your own choice of language must be sharp as well.
3. Don't try to write like a Supreme Court justice. Many undergraduates start their college careers trying to sound smart instead of actually saying smart things; they consult the thesaurus instead of refining their argument. Clarity is key in legal writing. The law is complicated, so keep your prose simple.
4. Know the source of your law. As you'll soon read, not all law in America is treated with equal weight. You must always cite the source of a given standard, and be mindful of where that source fits within the hierarchy of law.
5. Be an active reader. If you're not highlighting and jotting notes all over this book, you're not treating it right.
6. Be courageous in your Socratic dialogue. The first time I got called on in law school, I froze. A saintly classmate named Rafael Mason jumped in and saved the day. I was humiliated and it only augmented my feeling of imposter syndrome. The truth is, however, that no one other than you will remember your wrong answers in class. One of my favorite students once said during a class discussion, "I'm not sure I have this right, so I want to try." That's the spirit! What you're learning is hard, and your success is just as dependent on error as it is on affirmation.
7. Don't be intimidated by impressive peers. Pre-law students can't help but try to measure themselves against their classmates. But just because someone always sounds like a Rhodes Scholar doesn't mean their writing is amazing. (And even if it is amazing, you get the benefit of their brilliance, too, by sharing a class with them).

Acknowledgments

I grew up in a small town in Texas just outside a larger town that in 2014 *Forbes* called the "least educated city in America." Personally, I loved growing up there. But it's not lost on me how unlikely it is that the son of two Filipino immigrants from Port Neches, Texas got to be the author of the book you now hold. For that, I have many people to thank, starting with my wonderful team at Wolters Kluwer. Managing editor Stacie Goosman plucked my query out of the slush pile and got me a contract in record time. My developmental editor, Betsy Kenny, steered me from first draft to instructor's guide with unparalleled proficiency and kindness. My manuscript editor, Tom Daughhetee, ably and generously guided me through multiple rounds of copy editing as copy editor Renee Cote sharpened my prose with wit and grace. Thanks also to the compositors at Newgen for typesetting the pages, to proofreader Paul Butters, and the Wolters Kluwer marketing team.

This textbook is the result of many years of trial and error, experimentation and refinement—the work of a teacher trying every semester to get through to his students better and better. I owe so much gratitude to my many pupils over the years. In particular, I must thank my intrepid and tireless teaching assistants over the past seven years, especially Trenton Stone (who crafted the index), Adrika Yousuf, Vibhav Laud (who crafted the glossary), Ben Rosenthal and Grace McMahon, who all contributed directly to this work. The TAs before them were just as important at helping set the foundation for this text: Michael Jeung, Kasia Rudnicki, Evan Walike and Cyrus Mann.

Thanks, also, to the all-star student writers who generously gave me permission to include excerpts of their work product in this text and in the instructor's manual: Blake Andersen, Lauren Andrews, Ariana Arzani, Shauli Bar-On, Jake Bubman, Tim Buchanan, Andrea Capone, Stuart Carson, Stefan Catana, Julie Chandler, Giulia Corno, Abigail Drood, Maya Fransz-Myers, Harmon Gill, Andy Gu, Tim Guiteras, Jonas Guan, Colin Heath, Noah Hellum, Matt Ingraham, Michael Jeung, Lucia Jiang, Jack Kimble, Dylan Lee, Frank Lee, Sarah Leitner, Mazen Loan, Ellory Longdon, George MacCabe, Grace McMahon, Cyrus Mann, Shala Munn, Michaela Murphy, Shyann Murphy, Isabelle Nazha, Katie Negroni, Robert Ota, Maya Prakash, Philine Qian, Coby Rabushka, Ben Rosenthal, Polly Roth, Kasia Rudnicki, Sonali Seth, Lindsey Sloan, Ted Steinberg, Trenton Stone,

Jesse Stricof, Jeffrey Tan, Dan Toomey, and Adrika Yousuf. You all were the kind of students who make professors want to teach.

Thanks, also, to my mentors, teachers and institutional support at Port Neches-Groves High School, Texas A&M University, Yale Law School, Boston University and the University of Houston: specifically, Erma Richter, Cheryl Hancock, Kathy Hanlon, Susan Wisenbaker, Karen Severn, Victoria Rosner, Donnalee Dox, Kenji Yoshino, Deborah Cantrell, Harlon Dalton, Rob Harrison, Leslie Epstein, Ha Jin, Allegra Goodman, Paul Butler, Nathan Shepley and James Zebroski. Working with all of you has shaped my entire academic career. A special thank you to my wonderful colleagues at the University of Southern California; I've never felt so simultaneously supported and inspired at work, especially by Norah Ashe, Jeffrey Chisum, Mariko Zare, James Brecher, Tammara Anderson, Cory Nelson, Jennifer Bankard, Daniel Pecchenino and Brian Raphael (who was especially helpful in crafting the Legal Research chapter).

Thanks to the many friends and colleagues across the country who offered their aid and insight as I dove into my first textbook: specifically, Nicole Estey, Wynne Beers, Kabrina Kau, Brianne Gorod, Steven Wu, Tina Charoenpong, Barney Eskandari, Paula Levy, Pamela Carter, Chris Jeu, Abja Midha, Jeffrey Wu, James Grimmelmann, Tim Schnabel, Michael Epstein, Robert Mena, Jackson Tobin, Erin Chack, Alijah Case, Lindsay Head, Lisa-Jane Klotz, Brian Larson, Phillip Mink, Chris Soper, Christine Coughlin and Genelle Belmas.

Thanks especially to my wonderful family for ceding me for months as I worked on this project: my lovely and amazing wife, Jeanine, and my two endlessly clever sons, Elijah and Gabriel. It takes a village to raise children, and we're so lucky to have my sister, Kathy Elefano, close by, as well as Cynthia Coronel, Tess Coronel, Menchie Coronel, Cristeta and Lito Cabrera, Nini and Mike Flores, Boy and Sally Coronel, Noel and Emily Coronel, Sito and Luz Coronel, and Belen and Lucy Japlit. Your constant support and love has made Los Angeles home.

Finally, I dedicate this book to the two greatest parents a man could ask for. When I was growing up in Port Neches, every morning started with a freshly cooked breakfast by my mom, an ICU nurse who worked every weeknight until 11:30 p.m. Every night ended with a goodnight kiss on the forehead from my dad, a food service director at the local hospital. My entire childhood was nestled between those two gestures of love. There is no greater gift you can give someone than the certainty of their parents' devotion. Mom and Dad, you gave me that and so much more. I love you always, and I thank you for always loving me.

Legal Writing *for the* Undergraduate

chapter 1

Unpacking the Hierarchy of U.S. Law

Not all law in the United States is equal. There are many sources of law and they all exist within a hierarchy. Understanding that hierarchy is essential to gauge the strength of any legal argument.

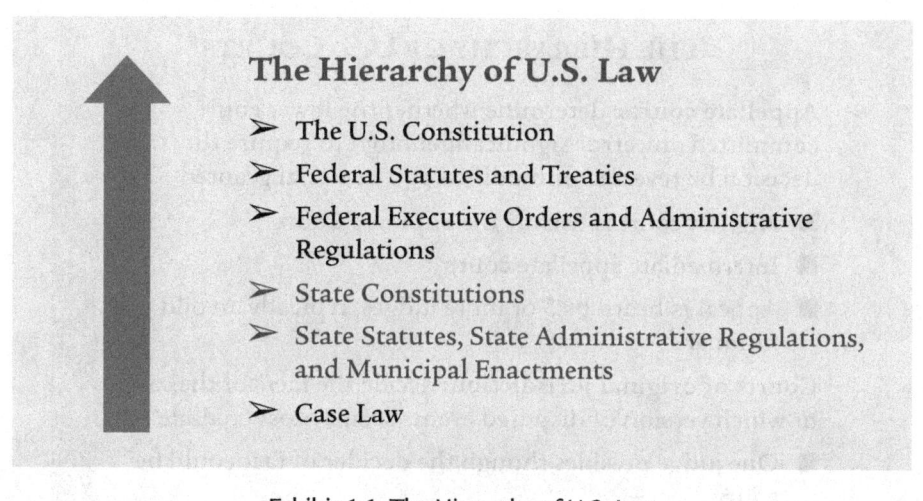

The Hierarchy of U.S. Law
- The U.S. Constitution
- Federal Statutes and Treaties
- Federal Executive Orders and Administrative Regulations
- State Constitutions
- State Statutes, State Administrative Regulations, and Municipal Enactments
- Case Law

Exhibit 1.1. The Hierarchy of U.S. Law

As you can see from Exhibit 1.1, there is no higher source of law in the United States than the U.S. Constitution. Federal statutes, or laws passed by Congress, have the next highest precedential value. And generally speaking, under the Supremacy Clause of the Constitution, federal law takes precedence over state law. The most important interplay to keep in mind, however—whether you're in the federal system of law or a parallel state system—is that constitutions come first, statutes second, and at the very bottom of the hierarchy is case law.

Just because case law is at the bottom of the hierarchy doesn't mean that it isn't important. Not every dispute in the United States triggers a provision of the Constitution. The same goes for statutory codes. The United States has a *common law* legal system, in which judges create their own body of law. Judge-made law, however, can't run afoul of the Constitution or statutory law. At the same time, because the United States has a system of checks and balances in which each branch of government (the executive, which includes the President; the legislative, which includes Congress; and the judiciary, which includes the Supreme Court) can limit the power of other branches, the judiciary can decide whether, for example, a legislative statute violates the U.S. Constitution. Such a decision would render the statute invalid entirely or in part.

When a judge is faced with an issue where no constitutional provision or statute applies, earlier cases decided in the applicable court dictate the applicable rule. Even when the Constitution or a statute *does* apply, you should still check the case law in your jurisdiction (more on that in a bit) to see how the applicable court has interpreted the given constitutional provision or statute.

Even within the court system, there is a hierarchy in which higher courts' decisions have more precedential weight than lower courts' decisions (see Exhibit 1.2).

THE HIERARCHY OF U.S. COURTS

➤ **Appellate courts:** determine whether the lower court committed any error significant enough to require the decision be reversed or modified or a new trial granted
- Highest court is usually the Supreme Court
- Intermediate appellate court
- Appeal is heard by 3 or more judges, typically an odd number

➤ **Courts of original jurisdiction:** decide the facts of the case, or which version of disputed events seems most credible
- One judge presides though the decider of fact could be a jury
- Usually courts of general jurisdiction, meaning they can hear cases of all subject matters: civil and criminal

➤ **Courts of inferior jurisdiction:** hear limited types of cases; some examples include:
- Traffic
- Family Law
- Small Claims
- Juvenile

Exhibit 1.2. The Hierarchy of U.S. Courts

TABLE 1.1 COMPARISON OF FEDERAL AND STATE COURT SYSTEMS

Federal Court System	State Court System
◆ **Highest court:** U.S. Supreme Court	◆ **Highest court:** depending on the state, either a Supreme Court (e.g., the Florida Supreme Court) or Court of Appeals (e.g., New York Court of Appeals)
◆ **Intermediate courts:** U.S. Courts of Appeal, divided into 13 Circuits	◆ **Intermediate courts:** 41 of the 50 states have some intermediate court or courts between trial courts and courts of last resort (e.g., the Texas Court of Appeals)
◆ **Trial courts:** district courts	◆ **Trial courts:** e.g., California Superior Court or Colorado District Court

Courts of inferior jurisdiction hear cases within a limited subject matter. The majority of these matters are decided without a trial, and if there is a trial or hearing, it is often decided more rapidly than in a court of general jurisdiction. The vast majority of inferior jurisdiction decisions do not result in full written opinions. The judge decides who prevails and what penalties, if any, apply. None of the cases you'll read in this textbook will come from courts of inferior jurisdiction.

Courts of original or general jurisdiction are what most Americans think of when they think of the U.S. court system. In these courts, questions of fact — such as whether defendant X ran a red light — are decided. Testimony may be taken from the affected drivers and observers. Attorneys on both sides will have an opportunity to directly examine their witnesses and cross-examine the opposing side's witnesses. In the end, the arbiter of fact — a judge in a bench trial or a jury in a jury trial — will determine culpability based on their findings of fact applying the relevant law.

If a party loses at the trial stage, they have the right to appeal that decision. If an appeals court grants review of the case, the appeals court won't retry the entire case. They won't recall all the witnesses from the trial and re-take their testimony. Instead, the job of an appeals court, whether it's an intermediate appeals court or the jurisdiction's highest court (or court of last resort), is to determine whether the court below made an error that requires that decision to be reversed or remanded back to the lower court for further proceedings. If the appeals court finds no such error, the decision below will be affirmed. This layered court hierarchy exists for both federal and state courts in the United States.

Exhibit 1.3 shows a map of the federal circuits:

Geographic Boundaries
of United States Courts of Appeals and United States District Courts

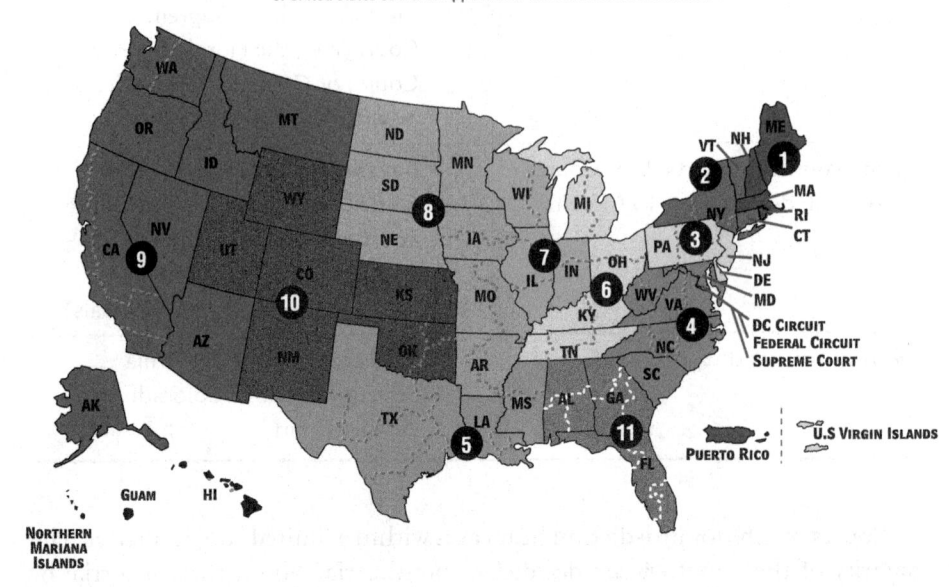

Exhibit 1.3. U.S. Courts of Appeal

The reason these hierarchies are important is because of the most important concept you need to understand about U.S. law: *stare decisis*. Stare decisis is Latin for "to stand by things decided." Basically, the principle boils down to courts needing to follow their own precedent and the precedent of courts higher than them in the hierarchy of law. Cases decided by courts that do not bind are persuasive authority only. They can still be cited as probative precedent, but you must be careful to make clear that the decision is persuasive only and not binding.

With regard to the hierarchy of law under both the federal and state systems:

- The decisions of the highest court in both systems are binding on both intermediate courts and trial courts below.
- The decisions of any intermediate courts in both systems are binding on themselves and the trial courts below but are not binding on parallel intermediate courts. For example, the decisions of the Fifth Circuit Court of Appeals in the federal system do not bind the Ninth Circuit Court of Appeals.
- Similarly, the decisions of trial courts in both systems are binding on themselves only and not binding on parallel trial courts.

As for which system, federal or state, is appropriate for a given case, federal jurisdiction is appropriate for cases involving federal law and cases involving citizens of different states (the latter is called diversity jurisdiction). In diversity suits, the federal court will apply state law and follow the state courts' decisions on state law questions. Most other matters will be handled by state courts.

As the hierarchy above might indicate, court decisions are primarily undone when a higher court disagrees with a decision below: an intermediate appellate court reverses a trial court, or a court of last resort reverses an intermediate appellate court. Occasionally, however, courts may choose to overrule their own precedent. The reasons for this may be because:

- The earlier decision has become outdated because of changed circumstances.
- The existing rule has produced undesirable results.
- The prior decision was based on what has been revealed as poor logic or reasoning.
- Subsequent legislation has rendered the previous decision moot. (Remember that in the hierarchy of law, both in the federal and state systems, statutes always take precedence over case law.)

HOLDINGS AND DICTA

Before leaving the subject of hierarchies, there's one last hierarchy to consider: the hierarchy of reasoning *within* a given case. Unlike statutes, where even the punctuation must be viewed as meaningful and intentional, not every sentence or word in a judicial opinion has the same precedential force. Imagine there's a patent infringement case where in the middle of the opinion, the judge goes off on a tangent about immigration law. Has that case now set precedent in both the realm of patent infringement *and* immigration law? The answer is no. In the United States, under Article III, Section 2 of the Constitution, judges can only decide the specific case or controversy brought before them for resolution. The judge's decision in resolving that case or controversy and the reasoning that leads to that resolution is the *holding* of the case. In other words, the holding is the legal principle that animates the court's final decision.

Anything else a judge may say in their opinion—any statement or observation that is not an essential part of the legal reasoning necessary to resolve the case—is called *dicta*. Dicta is not binding on subsequent courts. Dicta can still be cited, but only as persuasive authority.

One last observation about holdings: just as statutes can be interpreted in myriad ways, so can a court's holding. Let's say I told an associate at my law firm, Jack, to go into my home while I was out of town to retrieve an important file. I tell him where to find the spare key, and he enters my house and finds the file. But before Jack reaches the front door, my black and white bulldog, Hattie, runs in front of him and starts growling. Now, Jack has always had a fear of dogs, so, clutching the file, he retreats to a corner and hopes that Hattie will go away. She doesn't. And Jack, thinking he was only coming inside the house for a few minutes, left his phone in his car. It's not until eight hours later, when Hattie finally dozes off, that Jack is finally able to leave. Imagine Jack then sues me for false imprisonment and wins.

Six months later, almost exactly the same situation occurs, but this time the employee is paralyzed by fear of a loose turtle rather than a black and white bulldog. The plaintiff in this case attempts to use Jack's case against me as precedent. The plaintiff claims that the case involving Jack and me, which is binding precedent as it was decided by the same court, held that anytime an unrevealed household pet effectively confines a houseguest against their will, that constitutes false imprisonment. That's how the plaintiff interprets the holding of the precedent case.

The defense, however, has a different interpretation. They believe that Jack's case against me stands for the proposition that when an unrevealed dog or potentially vicious animal confines a houseguest against their will, that constitutes false imprisonment. Because the current case involves a turtle, an animal no reasonable person would consider to be a threat, the precedential case offers no help to the plaintiff's argument. The defense, in other words, argues for a narrower holding of *Jack v. Elefano*.

The question of which interpretation makes the most sense—the broader household pet standard or the narrower vicious animal standard—is a question of law. It's not a question about what happened between the parties in the case, which would be a question of fact, but about what rule to apply in the situation.

The line between holdings and dicta will become clearer as you move through the textbook and read your first court cases. And the ability to interpret holdings in multiple ways will be helpful later in the book when you start positing arguments for your first legal memorandum.

Finally, below are some definitions of common terms you'll encounter in the cases in this book:

- *Civil action:* lawsuit where one person files a complaint against another asking the court to order the other side to pay money or to stop doing something
  - *Damages:* an award of money
  - *Injunction:* an order to do something
- *Criminal action:* proceeding where the plaintiff is a government prosecutor (the United States in federal cases and a state in state cases) asking the court to punish a defendant with jail time or a fine
- *Appellant* or *Petitioner:* party who petitions an appellate court after losing in a lower court
- *Appellee* or *Respondent:* party defending the lower court's decision in an appeal
- An appellate court can take any of the following actions in deciding a case:
  - *Affirm:* uphold the lower court's ruling
  - *Reverse:* hold in favor of the losing party from the lower court proceeding
  - *Vacate:* wipe out the lower court opinion entirely, often necessitating a:
  - *Remand:* send the case back to the lower court for further proceedings, often with specific instructions or legal clarifications to guide the lower court

Questions Regarding the Hierarchy of Law

1. Cases in intermediate appellate courts are generally heard by multiple judges, typically an odd number of them. Why do you think an odd number is important?
2. There are 13 federal circuits in the United States, but the map in this chapter only shows numbers 1 through 11. Can you figure out where the twelfth and thirteenth circuits are?
3. In the turtle hypothetical above, where the defendant's attorney argued for a narrower holding for *Jack v. Elefano,* why didn't the attorney argue for an even narrower holding: e.g., "*Jack v. Elefano* merely stands for the proposition that if a vicious, black and white bulldog confines a houseguest against their will, that constitutes false imprisonment"? What might be a problem with such an argument?

chapter 2

Close Reading a Statute

Now that you understand the hierarchy of law and how to prioritize its different sources, it's time to dive deeper into one of those sources: statutes. A *statute* is a law passed by a legislature, either Congress or its equivalent on the state level. When people talk about laws being passed, they're typically referring to statutes. Unlike case law, where not every sentence holds equal force, everything down to the word and even the punctuation has force in a statute.

INTRODUCTION TO STATUTES

Statutes are supposed to be written in plain language, such that those governed by the statute can understand what is expected of them. In interpreting statutes, judges will often try to honor the statute's original intent. They will apply the usual and ordinary meanings of the words chosen. Statutes should be written consistently: if a word has one meaning in one part of the statute, it should have the same meaning in a different part of the statute. If analyzing a statute using the language's plain meaning fails to produce a clear interpretation, courts may then look at the law's *legislative history* (the committee reports, hearings and debates preceding a law's enactment) to determine the statute's original intent. The process of determining what a statute means so that a court can interpret it correctly is called *statutory construction*. Anyone advocating under statutory law must learn how to interpret statutory law just as a judge would.

Below is an excerpt of a section in Texas's Education Code that defines bullying in schools. One might think that "bullying" is a relatively easy concept to understand; it's certainly not a legal term of art. Compare Merriam-Webster's dictionary definition of bullying ("abuse and mistreatment of someone vulnerable by someone stronger, more powerful, etc.") to the Texas Education Code's:

> **Sec. 37.0832. Bullying Prevention Policies and Procedures.**
>
> (a) In this section:
> (1) "Bullying":

(A) means a single significant act or a pattern of acts by one or more students directed at another student that exploits an imbalance of power and involves engaging in written or verbal expression, expression through electronic means, or physical conduct that satisfies the applicability requirements provided by Subsection (a-1), and that:

(i) has the effect or will have the effect of physically harming a student, damaging a student's property, or placing a student in reasonable fear of harm to the student's person or of damage to the student's property;

(ii) is sufficiently severe, persistent, or pervasive enough that the action or threat creates an intimidating, threatening, or abusive educational environment for a student;

(iii) materially and substantially disrupts the educational process or the orderly operation of a classroom or school; or

(iv) infringes on the rights of the victim at school; and

(B) includes cyberbullying.

(2) "Cyberbullying" means bullying that is done through the use of any electronic communication device, including through the use of a cellular or other type of telephone, a computer, a camera, electronic mail, instant messaging, text messaging, a social media application, an Internet website, or any other Internet-based communication tool.

(a-1) This section applies to:

(1) bullying that occurs on or is delivered to school property or to the site of a school-sponsored or school-related activity on or off school property;

(2) bullying that occurs on a publicly or privately owned school bus or vehicle being used for transportation of students to or from school or a school-sponsored or school-related activity; and

(3) cyberbullying that occurs off school property or outside of a school-sponsored or school-related activity if the cyberbullying:

(A) interferes with a student's educational opportunities; or

(B) substantially disrupts the orderly operation of a classroom, school, or school-sponsored or school-related activity.

If the above seems like rhetorical overkill, keep in mind that laws are meant to regulate the conduct of people to whom those laws apply. This particular law would apply to millions of Texas students from elementary to high school. Imagine if the dictionary definition were adopted as Texas's legal definition:

"abuse and mistreatment of someone vulnerable by someone stronger, more powerful, etc."

Begin by asking: what constitutes "abuse"? What constitutes "mistreatment"? How are they different? Drafters of laws avoid verbal surplusage; accordingly, when interpreting a law, one should assume that every rhetorical choice was made purposefully. That means "abuse" and "mistreatment" can't be mere synonyms, and given the conjunction between them ("and"), both are necessary elements.

What makes someone "vulnerable"? What makes someone "stronger"? What makes someone "more powerful"? Does the comma in between the two phrases indicate that both conditions are necessary? In other words, does a bully have to be both stronger and more powerful? And who knows what to do with the etcetera at the end?

STATUTORY CONSTRUCTION

Statutory drafting is one of the most demanding and complicated skills in legal writing (and will not be covered in this text). But statutory construction is a basic prerequisite for any legal writer. In looking at the statute above and even the dictionary definition, the choice of conjunction, in particular, is significant.

Compare two prospective definitions of a "balanced meal":

1. a fruit, a vegetable, a dairy product, a grain **or** a protein.
2. a fruit, a vegetable, a dairy product, a grain **and** a protein.

Only one word is changed between definition 1 and definition 2, and yet the resulting meals would be much different. An apple alone would satisfy definition 1. But for definition 2, an apple only gets you one-fifth of the way to the goal.

Now let's look at the first part of the bullying definition, (a)(1)(A), ignoring its sub-elements for the moment. Let's break it down to its necessary components (as signified by the conjunction "and"):

1. **single significant act** OR a **pattern of acts**
2. by **one** OR **more students**
3. **directed at another student**
4. that **exploits** an **imbalance of power** and
5. involves engaging in **written or verbal expression, expression through electronic means**, or **physical conduct**
6. that **satisfies** the applicability requirements provided by **Subsection (a-1)**, and that . . .

Section (a)(1)(A) of the statute continues with four conditions, one of which must be met, but before we even get to those, there are already six conditions that must be met first. And while this definition is more precise than the dictionary equivalent, there are still ambiguities. For example:

- What makes an act "significant"? Its impact? If so, its impact on whom? The school? The victim(s)?
- How is "power" defined? Is it social power? Physical power? Intellectual power? All the above?

Think also about the *burden of proof*, or what is necessary for the person trying to prove a violation of the law. Ambiguity in the law's language can be advantageous if the ambiguity allows for more opportunities to meet one's burden. Numerous necessary elements, however, favor the party without the burden of proof. If there are, for example, 12 necessary elements for a plaintiff to prove their case, then the defendant only needs to disprove one of those 12 to prevail.

> **Questions Regarding Section 37.0832**
>
> 1. Section 37.0832(a)(1)(A) includes four sub-elements, only one of which must be met to fulfill the definition of bullying. Based only on the plain language of the four sub-elements, which do you think would be the most difficult to prove? The least difficult?
> 2. Under Section 37.0832(a-1)(3)(A), what kinds of facts might be probative in proving interference with a student's educational opportunities?
> 3. Under Section 37.0832(a-1)(3)(B), what kinds of disruption can you imagine rising to the level of a substantial disruption to the orderly operation of a classroom?

chapter 3

Applying Law to Facts

What follows is an assignment memorandum where you'll have your first opportunity to apply a law (the bullying law from Chapter 2) to varying sets of facts. Before moving to that exercise, it's worth explaining what an issue of fact is. Imagine an automobile collision at a busy intersection where one driver T-bones another. One driver then accuses the other of running a red light; the other driver insists that the light was yellow. The legal issue is clear: red lights mean stop. So if the case went to trial, the only remaining issue is which driver is telling the truth. Each of the two drivers involved would likely want to testify. But any finder of fact—a jury in a jury trial or a judge in a bench trial—would realize that both drivers were highly incentivized to present a version of the events that favored their side.

What additional evidence might be probative? Other witnesses, people with no affiliation to either party, would presumably be more objective. Surveillance camera footage capturing the moments leading up to the collision would obviously be best, and if the footage were clear enough, it's highly unlikely that a case like this would get to trial at all.

ISSUES OF FACT

An issue of fact in a legal dispute is a question of what happened between the parties in the case. A *material fact* is a fact relevant to the underlying legal claim. For example, in a dispute about a car accident, a material factual issue might be whether one of the drivers was wearing their glasses or not at the time of the accident. This is because the ability to see clearly can affect the quality of one's driving. Whether that same driver was employed or not at the time of the accident would not be material to any relevant legal question and accordingly would be a non-material fact. The process of finding answers to material factual questions is called *discovery*. Parties might exchange sets of questions, called *interrogatories*, to the other side. They might take relevant testimony in a deposition. In the assignment memorandum below, you're given three sets of facts and asked to apply law that's much more ambiguous and complicated than "Don't run a red light." You

13

might find yourself wishing you knew more facts to make the legal argument. Since you don't have the luxury of an actual discovery process, feel free to make reasonable factual assumptions, but label those assumptions clearly.

ASSIGNMENT 1: BULLYING POLICY ADVICE

Learned Foot, LLP

Memorandum

To: Associates

From: [Your Professor/Supervising Partner]

Date: [Month] [Date], 20___

Subject: Bullying Policy Advice for the Port Harmon Independent School District

Background:

We represent the Port Harmon Independent School District (PHISD) of Port Harmon, TX. The Port Harmon school board has recently come under fire because of allegations of bullying in its junior high and high school. Three incidents in particular, detailed below, have caused much consternation. As a result, the PHISD has asked for our firm's assistance in revising their bullying policy. Specifically, they want to ensure that their policy complies with Texas law.

Applicable Law:

The applicable Texas law is Tex. Educ. Code § 37.0832: Bullying Prevention Policies and Procedures. The law was enacted in 2011, revised in 2017 and as of today, no Texas court has had occasion to interpret its language. The relevant text of the law is excerpted below:

Sec. 37.0832. Bullying Prevention Policies and Procedures.

(a) In this section:
 (1) "Bullying":
  (A) means a single significant act or a pattern of acts by one or more students directed at another student that exploits an imbalance of power and involves engaging in written or verbal expression, expression through electronic means, or physical conduct that satisfies the applicability requirements provided by Subsection (a-1), and that:
   (i) has the effect or will have the effect of physically harming a student, damaging a student's property, or placing a student in

reasonable fear of harm to the student's person or of damage to the student's property;

(ii) is sufficiently severe, persistent, or pervasive enough that the action or threat creates an intimidating, threatening, or abusive educational environment for a student;

(iii) materially and substantially disrupts the educational process or the orderly operation of a classroom or school; or

(iv) infringes on the rights of the victim at school; and

(B) includes cyberbullying.

(2) "Cyberbullying" means bullying that is done through the use of any electronic communication device, including through the use of a cellular or other type of telephone, a computer, a camera, electronic mail, instant messaging, text messaging, a social media application, an Internet website, or any other Internet-based communication tool.

(a-1) This section applies to:

(1) bullying that occurs on or is delivered to school property or to the site of a school-sponsored or school-related activity on or off school property;

(2) bullying that occurs on a publicly or privately owned school bus or vehicle being used for transportation of students to or from school or a school-sponsored or school-related activity; and

(3) cyberbullying that occurs off school property or outside of a school-sponsored or school-related activity if the cyberbullying:

(A) interferes with a student's educational opportunities; or

(B) substantially disrupts the orderly operation of a classroom, school, or school-sponsored or school-related activity.

Enacted by Acts 2011, 82nd Leg., ch. 776 (H.B. 1942), § 7, effective June 17, 2011; am. Acts 2017, 85th Leg., ch. 522 (S.B. 179), §§ 2, 15, effective September 1, 2017.

Issues Presented:

The PHISD would like more guidance on the definition of bullying under the above statute. PHISD's current bullying policy, contained in the PHISD Code of Conduct (CoC), covers most traditional bullying (e.g., schoolyard taunting and physical threats) but has not been revised in over a decade and does not adequately cover contemporary forms of bullying (e.g., cyberbullying). The PHISD realized that its policies needed to be updated after the three aforementioned incidents.

Though the matters below have already been handled under the current CoC, in anticipation of future problems, **the PHISD would like to know whether the following acts constitute "bullying" under Tex. Educ. Code § 37.0832.** Prepare what you believe to be the most likely interpretation under the law (be ready to point me and the client to the specific applicable statutory language) and also prepare counterarguments, anticipating any opposing perspectives. If you believe you require more facts to apply the law, craft whatever questions you'd like me to ask the client to clarify the issue.

Incident 1: The Jilted Quarterback

T-Roy Weiss played quarterback for the Port Harmon Panthers. After a morning pep rally, he asked out fellow student, Shyann Gragg, on a date. He asked her to dinner in the middle of a busy hallway, and she promptly rebuffed him, kindly but unmistakably. Embarrassed, he retreated to his study hall and tweeted the following from his personal cell phone: "Shyann Gragg is a lesbian."

Shyann Gragg is, in fact, a lesbian, though by Weiss's own admission, he did not know this at the time. Ms. Gragg did not keep her sexuality a secret and had come out two years before to family and friends. Would Weiss's posting constitute "bullying" under Texas law?

Incident 2: The Toilet Photo

Stuart "Flash" Myers was the star running back of the Port Harmon Panthers. Though popular in school and among his teammates, he frequently butted heads with fullback Andres Pilar. One day during practice, Pilar took advantage of an under-the-weather Myers, humiliating him during a routine drill. Incensed, Myers took revenge by snapping a photograph of Pilar while he was perched on a locker room toilet. Pilar was naked at the time, though in the photograph in question, his genitalia were not visible.

Pilar then tried to gain possession of Myers's phone, which he eventually did, but not before Myers texted the photo to Pilar's ex-girlfriend, Erica Stone. Upon receiving the photograph, Stone "laughed [her] ass off" and then proceeded to text the photo to 30 of her classmates. Would Myers's actions constitute "bullying" under Texas law? What about Stone's?

Incident 3: Poor Prom Queen

Sydney Sinwell was the head cheerleader of the Port Harmon Panthers as well as the president of the student council and prom queen. Joey Jeung was an honor roll student, president of the Dungeons and Dragons league, and member of a Christian a cappella group called Crooners for Christ. By her own admission, Sinwell had taunted Jeung for years, dating back to grade school, calling him a "pasty troll" and "mega-geek," among other things.

One day, however, Jeung saw an envelope on Sinwell's desk and opened it. The contents included Sinwell's practice S.A.T. grade, in which she scored a composite placing her in the 69th percentile. Jeung then coined a new nickname for Sinwell: "Sydney 69." For over six months, he called her this, and others in the school joined in as well, before Sinwell filed a complaint with the Port Harmon High School principal, Jackson Tobin. Under Texas law, do Jeung's actions constitute "bullying"?

> **Tips for Bullying Policy Advice for the Port Harmon Independent School District**
>
> 1. Start by breaking down Section 37.0832 into its necessary and optional elements.
> 2. Even when you see one road to meeting your burden of proof, if there are alternate possibilities, consider arguing in the alternative in case a judge disagrees with one version of your argument.
> 3. Remember that the task isn't to identify culpable behavior generally but to determine violations of one law, Section 37.0832. Make sure your arguments are relevant to that law.

chapter 4

Reading and Briefing a Case

Judicial opinions are explanations of a judge's or judicial panel's decision in a case. Some opinions are short; some are expansive. But having a command over cases relevant to your legal issue is essential in building an effective legal argument. To avoid having to reread lengthy opinions over and over again, law students and lawyers draft summaries of cases called case briefs. If you're going to be working with a set of case law for an extended period of time—as part of a curriculum or as research for a piece of writing—it makes sense to brief those cases so that you don't have to constantly hunt for the relevant language. If you will be the only one using your case briefs, you may tailor them to your own habits of mind, considering what you're likely to remember over time. If others will be using your case briefs, you may want to be more exhaustive (though not inefficient) in your notes.

READING THE CASE

Before starting your brief, it's a good idea to read the entire case first. If the source of your case is an online database like LexisNexis, note that the introductory sections—like Headnotes and Summary—are not part of the official text of the decision and should not be cited in your brief or in any writing that uses the case. The official text of the court's opinion will often be preceded by the author of that opinion ("Opinion By") and then a heading labeled, appropriately enough, "Opinion."

If you're briefing the case with particular objectives in mind (if, for example, you're writing a memorandum on a specific issue), then review those objectives before reading. Read with a highlighter in hand to mark the most important parts of the decision. The act of briefing is, as the name implies, converting a long text into something shorter. Highlighting starts the process of narrowing the prose.

Reading the entire opinion before briefing enables you to understand the full scope of the court's decision and the web of its reasoning before you winnow it to its essence. And if there are parts of the opinion that seem hazy after one read, the act of briefing can help clarify your understanding.

Remember that briefing is not just copying and pasting the most notable parts of an opinion (the kind of brief that often results from simultaneously briefing and reading for the first time). Briefing requires you to synthesize the prose and to learn its logic—converting a judge's thinking through the prism of your own. Those are the kind of notes that will ultimately prove most useful to you.

UNDERSTANDING CITATIONS

Court opinions are often reprinted by different reporting publications. In the LexisNexis reproduction of the Supreme Court opinion, *DeShaney v. Winnebago Cnty. Dep't of Soc. Servs.*, for example, you would find the following citations on the header of every page of the case:

> 489 U.S. 189, *; 109 S. Ct. 998, **;
> 103 L. Ed. 2d 249, ***; 1989 U.S. LEXIS 1039

These four citations represent four different reporters:

1. The United States Reports, the official publication of the United States government
2. The Supreme Court Reporter, an unofficial Supreme Court reporter that is updated more quickly than the United States Reports
3. The United States Supreme Court Reports, Lawyers' Edition, another unofficial Supreme Court reporter that is updated more quickly than the United States Reports
4. The LEXIS database

The general format of this kind of header citation is:

> **[VOLUME] [ABBREVIATION FOR REPORTER] [PAGE NUMBER WHERE THE CASE BEGINS IN REPORTER].**

The exception to this is the LEXIS database cite, which uses the year the case was decided in place of VOLUME, an abbreviation of the court in place of ABBREVIATION FOR REPORTER and a document number in place of a FIRST PAGE NUMBER.

The asterisks following each citation in the header align with the subsequent page numbers or "pincites" for that reporter's version of the case throughout the rest of the opinion. Typically, in a legal document, you'd only need to cite to one reporter for a case, preferably the official reporter if that version is available. In *DeShaney*, for example, that would mean you'd cite the U.S. Report (489 U.S. 189), which would start with page 189, and then you'd follow only the pincites in the document that are bracketed and attached to one asterisk. They should follow in sequence: [*189], [*190], [*191], etc. You would accordingly ignore all pincites with two or three asterisks. (Throughout this text, I've only included pincites to one reporter — the official reporter if available — to simplify your process.) If you were citing a quote on page 195 of *DeShaney* in the United States Reports, it would look like this:

DeShaney v. Winnebago Cnty. Dep't of Soc. Servs., 489 U.S. 189, 195 (1989).

Note the parenthetical at the end of the citation, which includes the year the case was decided. Most citations, however, would include in the parenthetical the name of the court as well as the year it was decided: e.g., (9th Cir. 2001) for a Ninth Circuit case decided in 2001 or (E.D. Pa. 2018) for an Eastern District of Pennsylvania case decided in 2018. For the *DeShaney* citation above, however, the United States Reports only publishes Supreme Court cases, so the name of the court in that particular parenthetical is unnecessary.

As you brief your case, especially as you find notable passages in the reasoning that feed into the court's ultimate holdings, you should consider including the pincites in your notes so that you don't have to hunt for them later. The purpose of a brief is to write a document that:

1. Gets to the heart of a court's ruling as efficiently as possible, but that also
2. Includes enough relevant information and reasoning so that you don't have to reread the full-text case again.

CRAFTING THE BRIEF

Case briefs generally have the following sections in the following order:

1. Case Name and Citation
2. Facts
3. Procedural History
4. Issues or Questions Presented
5. Holdings or Answers
6. Reasoning
7. Concurrence(s)
8. Dissent(s)

Case Name and Citation

The case name should be italicized with a *v.* (representing "versus") between the opposing parties. Long case names with multiple plaintiffs and defendants can generally be shortened to the last name of the first listed plaintiff and the last name of the first listed defendant, assuming the parties are individuals and not institutions.

As mentioned in the Understanding Citations section above, you should use an official report citation if one is available. Since you're citing the case as a whole at the top of the brief, there's no need for pincites yet, because a pincite is the specific page or page range that you're referring to within a case. Include the volume, the abbreviation for the reporter and the page in that reporter where the case begins. The parenthetical that follows should include an abbreviation for the name of the deciding court (unless the reporter already makes that clear) and the year the case was decided. The year of the decision is important because more recent authority is generally better than less recent (as the former will have presumably considered intervening binding cases in its reasoning).

Here is an example of another case name and citation:

J.S. v. Blue Mountain Sch. Dist., 650 F.3d 915 (3d Cir. 2011).

Facts

The Facts are an account of what happened between the litigants that led to the lawsuit, e.g., the weather and conditions of the road in a car accident case, the chain of communication in a contract dispute. Facts are often the first part of a classic Socratic presentation of a case, so you want to have the basic narrative of the matter down. But what's most important is how the court interprets those facts under the relevant law, which will come in the Reasoning section of the brief.

Consider bulleting the facts if it makes the presentation easier to read. Consider subheadings to separate discrete timelines. And make sure to include all facts you'll later refer to in your Reasoning. While you want the facts to be pithy, you're also setting the universe for the case; someone reading your brief shouldn't learn a new fact in the Reasoning.

Below is an example of Facts taken from the 2013 New Mexico Supreme Court case *Elane Photography, LLC v. Willock*, 309 P.3d 53 (N.M. 2013):

Facts

- In 2003, the New Mexico Human Rights Act (NMHRA) was amended to add "sexual orientation" as a class of persons protected from discriminatory treatment. 59.
- Vanessa Willock contacted Elane Photography to inquire whether it could photograph a same-sex commitment ceremony and was told it only served "traditional weddings." 59.

Sometimes the Facts will include the passage of a law, especially if that law was recently put into place. For a First Amendment violation, however, one wouldn't have to state the passage of the First Amendment in the Facts. Notice that after each bulleted fact is a number. That is the pincite, or the page number where the cited language can be found. One quick way to check the accuracy of a pincite is to look at the full citation: 309 P.3d 53. The 53 at the end indicates that this case starts on page 53 of the cited reporter. The pincite, accordingly, must be 53 or higher.

Procedural History

It's important to note what happened in the lower courts leading up to the case you're briefing. What was the outcome in the court(s) below? By what mechanism (e.g., summary judgment or a motion to dismiss) did the court decide the case? Start with the original court of jurisdiction. In federal courts, this will most often be a district court. If you're briefing a Supreme Court case that was not appealed directly from a district court, then you'll also likely need to include the intervening Circuit Court opinion. Explain whether that Circuit Court affirmed, reversed or vacated the decision below and to what extent. A case with four separate counts—alleging four independent offenses of law—could be affirmed on two counts and reversed on the other two. Briefly explain the court's basis (in a sentence or two if possible).

The Procedural History doesn't need to be as detailed as the brief of the opinion itself—after all, the higher court's opinion will ultimately control—but it does provide useful context for the reader. As with the Facts, consider presenting this in a bulleted list as well.

Below is the Procedural History for the *Elane* case cited above:

Procedural History

- Willock filed a discrimination complaint with the New Mexico Human Rights Commission for sexual orientation discrimination. 60.
- New Mexico Human Rights Commission decided for Willock on her sexual orientation discrimination claim under NMHRA. 60.
- The Second Judicial District Court of New Mexico affirmed the Commission's decision, granting summary judgment for Willock. 60.
- The Court of Appeals affirmed the District Court's decision in favor of Willock. 60.

This particular cause of action started at an administrative body, the New Mexico Human Rights Commission, before weaving its way through the New Mexico state court system. The district court decided the case on *summary judgment*. Summary judgment is judgment as a matter of law, and it resolves the matter in dispute without the benefit of a full trial. Denying a party their day in court is no small matter, and the burden to obtain a summary judgment is high. Remember that trial courts are where the material facts of the case are decided (e.g., Did Party X run a red light before crashing into Party Y?). Summary judgments are only appropriate when a judge is convinced that there is no genuine dispute as to any material fact in the case. In other words, even if Party X were to go to trial and every relevant factual dispute in the case were decided in their favor, if they still would lose the case as a matter of law, there's no reason to have a trial.

Trials are expensive and involve a lot of personnel (lawyers, judges, clerks, sometimes a jury); if a judge believes the outcome of a case would be no different with a trial than without, if the facts are essentially unimportant in the ultimate decision of the case, then the judge will issue a summary judgment.

Issues or Questions Presented

For a court to reach a judgment in a case, it must resolve particular legal issues. Any issue a court addresses (or question it answers) that is necessary to resolve the dispute should be included as an Issue or Question Presented. Part of the reason it makes sense to read an entire case before crafting a brief is so that you know what parts of the opinion are actually critical in building toward the court's holding(s). If there are multiple Issues or Questions Presented, consider numbering them and crafting a parallel holdings or answers list.

Below are the issues from the *Elane* case:

Issues

1. Whether a commercial photography business refusing services to a same-sex couple violates the NMHRA? 59.
2. Whether the NHMRA impermissibly compels a commercial photography business into speaking a government-mandated message or publishing the speech of another in requiring that business to cater to same-sex couples? 59.

Holdings or Answers

The section above framed the case in terms of its central questions. Here is where you provide the answers to those questions, as seen by a judge or majority of judges on the relevant court. Only a majority ruling (or judge's ruling at trial) has the force of law and the potential to set precedent for the future. Below are the Answers to the two issues above from *Elane:*

Held

1. Yes, the New Mexico Supreme Court affirmed the court below, finding that Elane Photography did violate the NHMRA when it refused to photograph a same-sex commitment ceremony on the same basis that it serves opposite-sex couples. 59.
2. No, the NHMRA does not violate free speech guarantees by forcing Elane Photography to speak a government-mandated message or publish another's speech. 59.

Reasoning

In the Reasoning section, which should be the longest section in the brief by far, you will unpack how the majority reached its ultimate holdings. What logic did it use? What legal precedent did it rely on? What facts did it apply? This is the section where it's most critical to quote exactly, when necessary, and to pincite, as it's this section you're most likely to draw from in memoranda and appellate briefs.

In a case dealing with multiple issues and holdings, consider dividing the Reasoning section using those same holdings. For example, if a case had two issues and answers, the skeleton of your Reasoning might look like this:

1. Your answer to the first issue
    a. The first step in the court's reasoning regarding the first issue

b. The second step in the court's reasoning regarding the first issue
   c. The third step . . .
2. Your answer to the second issue
   a. The first step in the court's reasoning regarding the second issue
   b. The second step in the court's reasoning regarding the second issue
   c. The third step . . .

Below is the Reasoning flowing from the first issue and answer of *Elane:*

Reasoning:

1. Elane Photography did violate the NHMRA when it refused to photograph a same-sex commitment ceremony on the same basis that it serves opposite-sex couples.
   a. Elane Photography argues that it does not discriminate because of sexual orientation but because it did not wish to endorse Willock's and Collinsworth's wedding. 61.
   b. However, "to allow discrimination based on conduct so closely correlated with sexual orientation would severely undermine the purpose of the NMHRA." 61.
   c. "Elane Photography's willingness to offer some services to Willock does not cure its refusal to provide other services that it offered to the general public." 62.

Concurrence(s)

When a judge or justice agrees with the outcome of a case (meaning they agree on which party should prevail) but disagrees with at least part of the majority's reasoning, they will craft a concurring opinion to offer their alternative logic for reaching the same outcome. Concurrences do not have the force of law—they have no precedential effect—but are still sometimes cited in memoranda and appellate briefs where binding authority may not be available.

Concurring opinions can be useful at showing a burgeoning sea change in the law (the concurring reasoning of today could become the majority holding of tomorrow) or more likely a potential alternative way of arguing for future litigants arguing similar, but slightly distinct, cases.

Every separately written concurrence (which can be joined by other judges or justices) should be handled distinctly, and you only need to note the unique reasoning that has compelled that judge or justice to write.

Dissent(s)

When a judge or justice disagrees with the outcome of a case (meaning they believe the party who lost under the majority opinion should have prevailed), they will craft a dissent. Like concurrences, dissents do not have the force of law. They are even less likely than concurrences to be cited in memoranda and appellate briefs, but a litigant may still draw from dissents, especially if they believe there's a strong indication a court may be willing to revisit or overrule an unpopular previous holding.

As with concurrences, every separately written dissent (which can also be joined by other judges or justices) should be handled distinctly. What specifically does the dissenting judge/justice believe the majority got wrong? What alternative reasoning leads them to the opposite conclusion?

SAMPLE BRIEF

Below is a sample brief for a 2011 Third Circuit First Amendment case:

J.S. v. Blue Mountain Sch. Dist., **650 F.3d 915 (3d Cir. 2011).**

Facts:

- One weekend, on a home computer, J.S. and K.L. created a MySpace profile making fun of their middle school principal. The profile contained adult language and sexually explicit content; the profile did not identify the principal by name, school or location. 920.
- The record indicates that the profile was so outrageous that no one took its content seriously, and J.S. testified that it was meant as a joke. 921.
- Initially, the profile was public, but one day later J.S. made the profile private after several students approached her at school. 921.
- The School District's computers block access to MySpace, so no Blue Mountain student was ever able to view the profile from school, but upon learning of the profile, the principal had a student bring a printout to campus. 921.
- The principal decided that the profile was a Level Four Infraction of the school's disciplinary code as a "false accusation about a member of the school" and a "copyright" violation of the computer use policy, for using the principal's photograph. 921.
- J.S. and K.L. were given ten days out-of-school suspension and were prohibited from attending school dances. 922.
- In terms of disruption in school, the district alleged the following: 922-23.
  - General rumblings
  - Students discussing the profile in class
  - A report from students to a teacher about the profile
  - The school counselor had to cancel appointments to attend a hearing

Procedural Posture:

- J.S. filed a § 1983 action against the School District alleging (1) violation of her First Amendment rights with the school acting outside its authority in punishing out-of-school speech, (2) violation of the parents' due process rights to raise their child, and (3) overbreadth and vagueness challenges against the school policies. 920.

- The district court granted the School District summary judgment on all claims, though it acknowledged that under *Tinker*, there had been no substantial and material disruption in school. 923.

Issues:

1. Whether a school can suspend a student for off-campus speech—a lewd, mocking online profile of her principal—that caused no substantial disruption in school and could not reasonably have led officials to forecast substantial disruption.
2. Whether the School District's punishment violated J.S.'s parents' due process rights to raise their child as they saw fit.
3. Whether Blue Mountain's Student-Parent Handbook is unconstitutionally overbroad and vague.

Held:

1. No, schools cannot "punish students for off-campus speech that is not school-sponsored or at a school-sponsored event and that caused no substantial disruption at school." 933. The district court's holding in favor of the school on this count was reversed and remanded.
2. No, "a decision involving a child's use of social media on the internet" is not a matter of great importance and the school's actions did not deprive the parents of their ability to reach their own disciplinary decision regarding their child. 934. The district court's holding in favor of the school on this count was affirmed.
3. No, the misinterpretation of policies by individuals does not make the policies themselves facially overbroad. 935. The district court's holding in favor of the school on this count was affirmed.

Reasoning:

1. Schools cannot "punish students for off-campus speech that is not school-sponsored or at a school-sponsored event and that caused no substantial disruption at school." 933.
   a. There was no substantial disruption here nor a reasonable forecast of disruption. 928. If Tinker's armband, from *Tinker v. Des Moines*, could not reasonably have led to a forecast of disruption, neither can J.S.'s profile. 929-30.
   b. The profile was created as a joke, it was eventually made private, it did not identify the principal by name, and the content was so juvenile that no reasonable person could take it seriously. 929.
   c. Additionally, Pennsylvania law barred the School District from punishing J.S. for off-campus speech. 929.
   d. The court distinguished other disruption cases on the grounds that in this case, the allegations were outrageous and that J.S. did not intend her speech to reach the school. 930.

e. Finally, the court found that *Fraser*'s "lewdness" standard could not be extended to speech outside the school, during non-school hours. 932.
2. "[A] decision involving a child's use of social media on the internet" is not a matter of great importance and the school's actions did not deprive the parents of their own disciplinary discretion. 934.
3. The misinterpretation of policies by individuals does not make the policies themselves facially overbroad. 935.
   a. The policies at issue were limited to in-school speech. 935.
   b. Just because the school misapplied the policies doesn't make the policies themselves overbroad. 935.

Concurrence (by Smith):

- Would hold that *Tinker* does not apply to off-campus speech and that the First Amendment protects students' off-campus speech in the same way that it protects adults. 936.
- The difficult question is what counts as on- or off-campus speech:
  ○ Speech directed toward a school should be considered on-campus. 940.
  ○ But speech originating off-campus does not mutate into on-campus speech simply because it foreseeably makes its way onto campus. 940.

Dissent (by Fisher):

- Agrees with majority's conclusion that off-campus student speech can rise to the level of substantial disruption but disagrees with the application of that rule to this case. 941.
- *Tinker* involved peaceful, nonintrusive political speech while this case was a targeted, lewd attack against a principal and his family. 943-44.
- Agrees that the facts fail to show substantial disruption but believes that the profile's *potential* to disrupt was reasonably foreseeable and thus sufficient. 945.
  ○ There was a threat of interference with the educational environment, undermining the principal's authority. 945.
  ○ There was a reasonably foreseeable threat of disrupting classroom operations. 945.
- The majority decision causes a split with the Second Circuit and its *Wisniewski v. Bd. of Educ. of Weedsport Cent. Sch. Dist.* holding. 950.

Tips for Reading and Briefing Cases

1. After reading the case one time through, your first and most critical task is determining what the Issues Presented are. Ask yourself what legal questions the court has to resolve in order to rule for one party over another.

> 2. As mentioned above, the Reasoning section should be the longest part of the brief and should only include the reasoning of the majority opinion.
> 3. Concurrences and dissents should be noted in your brief, but you don't have to summarize the entire argument for these sections; instead, it's often sufficient just to explain the main reasons why the judges/justices diverge from the majority.

ASSIGNMENT 2: *DESHANEY V. WINNEBAGO COUNTY DEPARTMENT OF SOCIAL SERVICES* CASE BRIEF

The first case in this textbook is the U.S. Supreme Court case *DeShaney v. Winnebago Cnty. Dep't of Soc. Servs.* Read the case in its entirety first, highlighting and marking the pages as you go, then try to brief the case using the format described above. As a reminder, these elements should be included:

1. Case Name and Citation
2. Facts
3. Procedural History
4. Issues or Questions Presented
5. Holdings or Answers
6. Reasoning
7. Concurrence(s)
8. Dissent(s)

After the case, there is a sample brief of *DeShaney*, but don't look at it until you've done your own brief. Then compare what you pulled from the case with the example.

DESHANEY v. WINNEBAGO COUNTY DEPARTMENT OF SOCIAL SERVICES

Supreme Court of the United States
November 2, 1988, Argued; February 22, 1989, Decided
No. 87-154
Reporter: 489 U.S. 189 *

Judges: Rehnquist, C.J., delivered the opinion of the Court, in which White, Stevens, O'Connor, Scalia, and Kennedy, JJ., joined. Brennan, J., filed a dissenting opinion, in which Marshall and Blackmun, JJ., joined, post, p. 203. Blackmun, J., filed a dissenting opinion, post, p. 212.

Opinion

[*191] CHIEF JUSTICE REHNQUIST delivered the opinion of the Court.

Petitioner is a boy who was beaten and permanently injured by his father, with whom he lived. Respondents are social workers and other local officials who received complaints that petitioner was being abused by his father and had reason to believe that this was the case, but nonetheless did not act to remove petitioner from his father's custody. Petitioner sued respondents claiming that their failure to act deprived him of his liberty in violation of the Due Process Clause of the Fourteenth Amendment to the United States Constitution. We hold that it did not.

I

The facts of this case are undeniably tragic. Petitioner Joshua DeShaney was born in 1979. In 1980, a Wyoming court granted his parents a divorce and awarded custody of Joshua to his father, Randy DeShaney. The father shortly thereafter moved to Neenah, a city located in Winnebago County, Wisconsin, taking the infant Joshua with him. There he entered into a second marriage, which also ended in divorce.

[*192] The Winnebago County authorities first learned that Joshua DeShaney might be a victim of child abuse in January 1982, when his father's second wife complained to the police, at the time of their divorce, that he had previously "hit the boy causing marks and [was] a prime case for child abuse." App. 152-153. The Winnebago County Department of Social Services (DSS) interviewed the father, but he denied the accusations, and DSS did not pursue them further. In January 1983, Joshua was admitted to a local hospital with multiple bruises and abrasions. The examining physician suspected child abuse and notified DSS, which immediately obtained an order from a Wisconsin juvenile court placing Joshua in the temporary custody of the hospital. Three days later, the county convened an ad hoc "Child Protection Team"—consisting of a pediatrician, a psychologist, a police detective, the county's lawyer, several DSS caseworkers, and various hospital personnel—to consider Joshua's situation. At this meeting, the Team decided that there was insufficient evidence of child abuse to retain Joshua in the custody of the court. The Team did, however, decide to recommend several measures to protect Joshua, including enrolling him in a preschool program, providing his father with certain counselling services, and encouraging his father's girlfriend to move out of the home. Randy DeShaney entered into a voluntary agreement with DSS in which he promised to cooperate with them in accomplishing these goals.

Based on the recommendation of the Child Protection Team, the juvenile court dismissed the child protection case and returned Joshua to the custody of his father. A month later, emergency room personnel called the DSS caseworker handling Joshua's case to report that he had once again been treated for suspicious injuries. The caseworker concluded that there was no basis for action. For the next six months, the caseworker made monthly visits to the DeShaney home, during which she observed a number of suspicious injuries on [*193] Joshua's head; she also noticed that he had not been enrolled in school, and that the girlfriend had not moved out. The caseworker dutifully recorded these incidents in her files, along with her continuing suspicions that someone in the DeShaney household was physically abusing Joshua, but she did nothing more. In November 1983, the emergency room notified DSS that Joshua had been treated once again for injuries that they believed to be caused by child abuse. On the caseworker's next two visits to the DeShaney home, she was told that Joshua was too ill to see her. Still DSS took no action.

In March 1984, Randy DeShaney beat 4-year-old Joshua so severely that he fell into a life-threatening coma. Emergency brain surgery revealed a series of hemorrhages caused by traumatic injuries to the head inflicted over a long period of time. Joshua did not die, but he suffered brain damage so severe that he is expected to spend the rest of his life confined to an institution for the profoundly retarded. Randy DeShaney was subsequently tried and convicted of child abuse.

Joshua and his mother brought this action under 42 U.S.C. § 1983 in the United States District Court for the Eastern District of Wisconsin against respondents Winnebago County, DSS, and various individual employees of DSS. The complaint alleged that respondents had deprived Joshua of his liberty without due process of law, in violation of his rights under the Fourteenth Amendment, by failing to intervene to protect him against a risk of violence at his father's hands of which they knew or should have known. The District Court granted summary judgment for respondents.

The Court of Appeals for the Seventh Circuit affirmed, 812 F.2d 298 (1987), holding that petitioners had not made out an actionable § 1983 claim for two alternative reasons. First, the court held that the Due Process Clause of the Fourteenth Amendment does not require a state or local governmental entity to protect its citizens from "private violence, or other [*194] mishaps not attributable to the conduct of its employees." *Id.*, at 301. In so holding, the court specifically rejected the position endorsed by a divided panel of the Third Circuit in *Estate of Bailey by Oare v. County of York*, 768 F.2d 503, 510-511 (1985), and by dicta in *Jensen v. Conrad*, 747 F.2d 185, 190-194 (CA4 1984), cert. denied, 470 U.S. 1052 (1985), that once the State learns that a particular child is in danger of abuse from third parties and actually undertakes to protect him from that danger, a "special relationship" arises between it and the child which imposes an affirmative constitutional duty to provide adequate protection. 812 F.2d, at 303-304. Second, the court held, in reliance on our decision in *Martinez v. California*, 444 U.S. 277, 285 (1980), that the causal connection between respondents' conduct and Joshua's injuries was too attenuated to establish a deprivation of constitutional rights actionable under § 1983. 812 F.2d, at 301-303. The court therefore found it unnecessary to reach the question whether respondents' conduct evinced the "state of mind" necessary to make out a due process claim after *Daniels v. Williams*, 474 U.S. 327 (1986), and *Davidson v. Cannon*, 474 U.S. 344 (1986). 812 F.2d, at 302.

Because of the inconsistent approaches taken by the lower courts in determining when, if ever, the failure of a state or local governmental entity or its agents to provide an individual with adequate protective services constitutes a violation of the individual's due process rights, see *Archie v. Racine*, 847 F.2d 1211, 1220-1223, and n. 10 (CA7 1988) (en banc) (collecting cases), cert. pending, No. 88-576, and the importance of the issue to the administration of state and local governments, we granted certiorari. 485 U.S. 958 (1988). We now affirm.

II

The Due Process Clause of the Fourteenth Amendment provides that "[n]o State shall . . . deprive any person of life, liberty, or property, without due process of law." Petitioners [*195] contend that the State[1] deprived Joshua of his liberty interest in "free[dom] from . . . unjustified intrusions on personal security," see *Ingraham v. Wright*, 430 U.S. 651, 673 (1977), by failing to provide him with adequate protection against his father's violence. The claim is one invoking the substantive rather than the procedural component of the Due Process Clause; petitioners do not claim that the State denied Joshua protection without according him appropriate procedural safeguards, see *Morrissey v. Brewer*, 408 U.S. 471, 481 (1972), but that it was categorically obligated to protect him in these circumstances, see *Youngberg v. Romeo*, 457 U.S. 307, 309 (1982).[2]

But nothing in the language of the Due Process Clause itself requires the State to protect the life, liberty, and property of its citizens against invasion by private actors. The Clause is phrased as a limitation on the State's power to act, not as a guarantee of certain minimal levels of safety and security. It forbids the State itself to deprive individuals of life, liberty, or property without "due process of law," but its language cannot fairly be extended to impose an affirmative obligation on the State to ensure that those interests do not come to harm through other means. Nor does history support such an expansive reading of the constitutional text. [*196] Like its counterpart in the Fifth Amendment, the Due Process

---

1. As used here, the term "State" refers generically to state and local governmental entities and their agents.

2. Petitioners also argue that the Wisconsin child protection statutes gave Joshua an "entitlement" to receive protective services in accordance with the terms of the statute, an entitlement which would enjoy due process protection against state deprivation under our decision in *Board of Regents of State Colleges v. Roth*, 408 U.S. 564 (1972). Brief for Petitioners 24-29. But this argument is made for the first time in petitioners' brief to this Court: it was not pleaded in the complaint, argued to the Court of Appeals as a ground for reversing the District Court, or raised in the petition for certiorari. We therefore decline to consider it here. See *Youngberg v. Romeo*, 457 U.S., at 316, n. 19; *Dothard v. Rawlinson*, 433 U.S. 321, 323, n. 1 (1977); *Duignan v. United States*, 274 U.S. 195, 200 (1927); *Old Jordan Mining & Milling Co. v. Societe Anonyme des Mines*, 164 U.S. 261, 264-265 (1896).

Clause of the Fourteenth Amendment was intended to prevent government "from abusing [its] power, or employing it as an instrument of oppression," *Davidson v. Cannon, supra,* at 348; see also *Daniels v. Williams, supra,* at 331 ("'"to secure the individual from the arbitrary exercise of the powers of government,"'" and "to prevent governmental power from being 'used for purposes of oppression'") (internal citations omitted); *Parratt v. Taylor,* 451 U.S. 527, 549 (1981) (Powell, J., concurring in result) (to prevent the "affirmative abuse of power"). Its purpose was to protect the people from the State, not to ensure that the State protected them from each other. The Framers were content to leave the extent of governmental obligation in the latter area to the democratic political processes.

Consistent with these principles, our cases have recognized that the Due Process Clauses generally confer no affirmative right to governmental aid, even where such aid may be necessary to secure life, liberty, or property interests of which the government itself may not deprive the individual. See, *e.g., Harris v. McRae,* 448 U.S. 297, 317-318 (1980) (no obligation to fund abortions or other medical services) (discussing Due Process Clause of Fifth Amendment); *Lindsey v. Normet,* 405 U.S. 56, 74 (1972) (no obligation to provide adequate housing) (discussing Due Process Clause of Fourteenth Amendment); see also *Youngberg v. Romeo, supra,* at 317 ("As a general matter, a State is under no constitutional duty to provide substantive services for those within its border"). As we said in *Harris v. McRae:* "Although the liberty protected by the Due Process Clause affords protection against unwarranted *government* interference . . . , it does not confer an entitlement to such [governmental aid] as may be necessary to realize all the advantages of that freedom." 448 U.S., at 317-318 (emphasis added). If the Due Process Clause does not require the State to provide its citizens with particular protective services, it follows that the State cannot **[*197]** be held liable under the Clause for injuries that could have been averted had it chosen to provide them.[3] As a general matter, then, we conclude that a State's failure to protect an individual against private violence simply does not constitute a violation of the Due Process Clause.

Petitioners contend, however, that even if the Due Process Clause imposes no affirmative obligation the State to provide the general public with adequate protective services, such a duty may arise out of certain "special relationships" created or assumed by the State with respect to particular individuals. Brief for Petitioners 13-18. Petitioners argue that such a "special relationship" existed here because the State knew that Joshua faced a special danger of abuse at his father's hands, and specifically proclaimed, by word and by deed, its intention to protect him against that danger. *Id.,* at 18-20. Having actually undertaken to protect Joshua from this danger—which petitioners concede the State played no part in creating—the State acquired an affirmative "duty," enforceable through

---

3. The State may not, of course, selectively deny its protective services to certain disfavored minorities without violating the Equal Protection Clause. See *Yick Wo v. Hopkins,* 118 U.S. 356 (1886). But no such argument has been made here.

the Due Process Clause, to do so in a reasonably competent fashion. Its failure to discharge that duty, so the argument goes, was an abuse of governmental power that so "shocks the conscience," *Rochin v. California*, 342 U.S. 165, 172 (1952), as to constitute a substantive due process violation. Brief for Petitioners 20.[4]

[*198] We reject this argument. It is true that in certain limited circumstances the Constitution imposes upon the State affirmative duties of care and protection with respect to particular individuals. In *Estelle v. Gamble*, 429 U.S. 97 (1976), we recognized that the Eighth Amendment's prohibition against cruel and unusual punishment, made applicable to the States through the Fourteenth Amendment's Due Process Clause, *Robinson v. California*, 370 U.S. 660 (1962), requires the State to provide adequate medical care to incarcerated prisoners. 429 U.S., at 103-104.[5] We reasoned [*199] that because the prisoner is unable "'by reason of the deprivation of his liberty [to] care for himself,'" it is only "'just'" that the State be required to care for him. *Ibid.*, quoting *Spicer v. Williamson*, 191 N.C. 487, 490, 132 S.E. 291, 293 (1926).

In *Youngberg v. Romeo*, 457 U.S. 307 (1982), we extended this analysis beyond the Eighth Amendment setting,[6] holding that the substantive component of the

---

4. The genesis of this notion appears to lie in a statement in our opinion in *Martinez v. California*, 444 U.S. 277 (1980). In that case, we were asked to decide, *inter alia*, whether state officials could be held liable under the Due Process Clause of the Fourteenth Amendment for the death of a private citizen at the hands of a parolee. Rather than squarely confronting the question presented here—whether the Due Process Clause imposed upon the State an affirmative duty to protect—we affirmed the dismissal of the claim on the narrower ground that the causal connection between the state officials' decision to release the parolee from prison and the murder was too attenuated to establish a "deprivation" of constitutional rights within the meaning of § 1983. *Id.*, at 284-285. But we went on to say:

"[T]he parole board was not aware that appellants' decedent, as distinguished from the public at large, faced any special danger. We need not and do not decide that a parole officer could never be deemed to 'deprive' someone of life by action taken in connection with the release of a prisoner on parole. But we do hold that at least under the particular circumstances of this parole decision, appellants' decedent's death is too remote a consequence of the parole officers' action to hold them responsible under the federal civil rights law." *Id.*, at 285 (footnote omitted).

Several of the Courts of Appeals have read this language as implying that once the State learns that a third party poses a special danger to an identified victim, and indicates its willingness to protect the victim against that danger, a "special relationship" arises between State and victim, giving rise to an affirmative duty, enforceable through the Due Process Clause, to render adequate protection. See *Estate of Bailey by Oare v. County of York*, 768 F.2d 503, 510-511 (CA3 1985); *Jensen v. Conrad*, 747 F.2d 185, 190-194, and n. 11 (CA4 1984) (dicta), cert. denied, 470 U.S. 1052 (1985)); *Balistreri v. Pacifica Police Dept.*, 855 F.2d 1421, 1425-1426 (CA9 1988). But see, in addition to the opinion of the Seventh Circuit below, *Estate of Gilmore v. Buckley*, 787 F.2d 714, 720-723 (CA1), cert. denied, 479 U.S. 882 (1986); *Harpole v. Arkansas Dept. of Human Services*, 820 F.2d 923, 926-927 (CA8 1987); *Wideman v. Shallowford Community Hospital Inc.*, 826 F.2d 1030, 1034-1037 (CA11 1987).

5. To make out an Eighth Amendment claim based on the failure to provide adequate medical care, a prisoner must show that the state defendants exhibited "deliberate indifference" to his "serious" medical needs; the mere negligent or inadvertent failure to provide adequate care is not enough. *Estelle v. Gamble*, 429 U.S., at 105-106. In *Whitley v. Albers*, 475 U.S. 312 (1986), we suggested that a similar state of mind is required to make out a substantive due process claim in the prison setting. *Id.*, at 326-327.

6. The Eighth Amendment applies "only after the State has complied with the constitutional guarantees traditionally associated with criminal prosecutions.... [T]he State does not acquire the

Fourteenth Amendment's Due Process Clause requires the State to provide involuntarily committed mental patients with such services as are necessary to ensure their "reasonable safety" from themselves and others. *Id.*, at 314-325; see *id.*, at 315, 324 (dicta indicating that the State is also obligated to provide such individuals with "adequate food, shelter, clothing, and medical care"). As we explained: "If it is cruel and unusual punishment to hold convicted criminals in unsafe conditions, it must be unconstitutional [under the Due Process Clause] to confine the involuntarily committed—who may not be punished at all—in unsafe conditions." *Id.*, at 315-316; see also *Revere v. Massachusetts General Hospital*, 463 U.S. 239, 244 (1983) (holding that the Due Process Clause requires the responsible government or governmental agency to provide medical care to suspects in police custody who have been injured while being apprehended by the police).

But these cases afford petitioners no help. Taken together, they stand only for the proposition that when the State takes a person into its custody and holds him there [*200] against his will, the Constitution imposes upon it a corresponding duty to assume some responsibility for his safety and general well-being. See *Youngberg v. Romeo, supra*, at 317 ("When a person is institutionalized—and wholly dependent on the State[,] . . . a duty to provide certain services and care does exist").[7] The rationale for this principle is simple enough: when the State by the affirmative exercise of its power so restrains an individual's liberty that renders him unable to care for himself, and at the same time fails to provide for his basic human needs—*e.g.*, food, clothing, shelter, medical care, and reasonable safety—it transgresses the substantive limits on state action set by the Eighth Amendment and the Due Process Clause. See *Estelle v. Gamble, supra*, at 103-104; *Youngberg v. Romeo, supra*, at 315-316. The affirmative duty to protect arises not from the State's knowledge of the individual's predicament or from its expressions of intent to help him, but from the limitation which it has imposed on his freedom to act on his own behalf. See *Estelle v. Gamble, supra*, at 103 ("An inmate must rely on prison authorities to treat his medical needs; if the authorities fail to do so, those needs will not be met"). In the substantive due process analysis, it is the State's affirmative act of restraining the individual's freedom to act on his own behalf—through incarceration, institutionalization, or other similar restraint of personal liberty—which is the "deprivation of liberty" triggering the protections of the Due Process Clause, not its failure to act to protect his liberty interests against harms inflicted by other means.[8]

---

power to punish with which the Eighth Amendment is concerned until after it has secured a formal adjudication of guilt in accordance with due process of law." *Ingraham v. Wright*, 430 U.S. 651, 671-672, n.40 (1977); see also *Revere v. Massachusetts General Hospital*, 463 U.S. 239, 244 (1983); *Bell v. Wolfish*, 441 U.S. 520, 535, n.16 (1979).

7. Even in this situation, we have recognized that the State "has considerable discretion in determining the nature and scope of its responsibilities." *Youngberg v. Romeo*, 457 U.S., at 317.

8. Of course, the protections of the Due Process Clause, both substantive and procedural, may be triggered when the State, by the affirmative acts of its agents, subjects an involuntarily confined

[*201] The *Estelle-Youngberg* analysis simply has no applicability in the present case. Petitioners concede that the harms Joshua suffered occurred not while he was in the State's custody, but while he was in the custody of his natural father, who was in no sense a state actor.[9] While the State may have been aware of the dangers that Joshua faced in the free world, it played no part in their creation, nor did it do anything to render him any more vulnerable to them. That the State once took temporary custody of Joshua does not alter the analysis, for when it returned him to his father's custody, it placed him in no worse position than that in which he would have been had it not acted at all; the State does not become the permanent guarantor of an individual's safety by having once offered him shelter. Under these circumstances, the State had no constitutional duty to protect Joshua.

It may well be that, by voluntarily undertaking to protect Joshua against a danger it concededly played no part in creating, the State acquired a duty under state tort law to provide [*202] him with adequate protection against that danger. See Restatement (Second) of Torts § 323 (1965) (one who undertakes to render services to another may in some circumstances be held liable for doing so in a negligent fashion); see generally W. Keeton, D. Dobbs, R. Keeton, & D. Owen, Prosser and Keeton on the Law of Torts § 56 (5th ed. 1984) (discussing "special relationships" which may give rise to affirmative duties to act under the common law of tort). But the claim here is based on the Due Process Clause of the Fourteenth Amendment, which, as we have said many times, does not transform every tort committed by a state actor into a constitutional violation. See *Daniels v. Williams*, 474 U.S., at 335-336; *Parratt v. Taylor*, 451 U.S., at 544; *Martinez v. California*, 444 U.S. 277, 285 (1980); *Baker v. McCollan*, 443 U.S. 137, 146 (1979); *Paul v. Davis*, 424 U.S. 693, 701 (1976). A State may, through its courts and legislatures, impose such affirmative duties of care and protection upon its agents as it wishes. But not "all common-law duties owed by government actors were . . . constitutionalized by the Fourteenth Amendment." *Daniels v. Williams, supra*, at 335. Because, as explained above, the State had no constitutional duty to protect

---

individual to deprivations of liberty which are not among those generally authorized by his confinement. See, *e.g., Whitley v. Albers, supra*, at 326-327 (shooting inmate); *Youngberg v. Romeo, supra*, at 316 (shackling involuntarily committed mental patient); *Hughes v. Rowe*, 449 U.S. 5, 11 (1980) (removing inmate from general prison population and confining him to administrative segregation); *Vitek v. Jones*, 445 U.S. 480, 491-494 (1980) (transferring inmate to mental health facility).

9. Complaint para. 16, App. 6 ("At relevant times to and until March 8, 1984, [the date of the final beating,] Joshua DeShaney was in the custody and control of Defendant Randy DeShaney"). Had the State by the affirmative exercise of its power removed Joshua from free society and placed him in a foster home operated by its agents, we might have a situation sufficiently analogous to incarceration or institutionalization to give rise to an affirmative duty to protect. Indeed, several Courts of Appeals have held, by analogy to *Estelle* and *Youngberg*, that the State may be held liable under the Due Process Clause for failing to protect children in foster homes from mistreatment at the hands of their foster parents. See *Doe v. New York City Dept. of Social Services*, 649 F.2d 134, 141-142 (CA2 1981), after remand, 709 F.2d 782, cert. denied sub nom. *Catholic Home Bureau v. Doe*, 464 U.S. 864 (1983); *Taylor ex rel. Walker v. Ledbetter*, 818 F.2d 791, 794-797 (CA11 1987) (en banc), cert. pending *Ledbetter v. Taylor*, No. 87-521. We express no view on the validity of this analogy, however, as it is not before us in the present case.

Joshua against his father's violence, its failure to do so — though calamitous in hindsight — simply does not constitute a violation of the Due Process Clause.[10]

Judges and lawyers, like other humans, are moved by natural sympathy in a case like this to find a way for Joshua and his mother to receive adequate compensation for the grievous [*203] harm inflicted upon them. But before yielding to that impulse, it is well to remember once again that the harm was inflicted not by the State of Wisconsin, but by Joshua's father. The most that can be said of the state functionaries in this case is that they stood by and did nothing when suspicious circumstances dictated a more active role for them. In defense of them it must also be said that had they moved too soon to take custody of the son away from the father, they would likely have been met with charges of improperly intruding into the parent-child relationship, charges based on the same Due Process Clause that forms the basis for the present charge of failure to provide adequate protection.

The people of Wisconsin may well prefer a system of liability which would place upon the State and its officials the responsibility for failure to act in situations such as the present one. They may create such a system, if they do not have it already, by changing the tort law of the State in accordance with the regular lawmaking process. But they should not have it thrust upon them by this Court's expansion of the Due Process Clause of the Fourteenth Amendment.

Affirmed.

Dissent by: Brennan; Blackmun

Dissent

Justice BRENNAN, with whom Justice MARSHALL and Justice BLACKMUN join, dissenting.

"The most that can be said of the state functionaries in this case," the Court today concludes, "is that they stood by and did nothing when suspicious circumstances dictated a more active role for them." *Ante* this page. Because I believe that this description of respondents' conduct tells only part of the story and that, accordingly, the Constitution itself "dictated a more active role" for respondents in the circumstances presented here, I cannot agree that respondents had no constitutional duty to help Joshua DeShaney.

---

10. Because we conclude that the Due Process Clause did not require the State to protect Joshua from his father, we need not address respondents' alternative argument that the individual state actors lacked the requisite "state of mind" to make out a due process violation. See *Daniels v. Williams*, 474 U.S., at 334, n. 3. Similarly, we have no occasion to consider whether the individual respondents might be entitled to a qualified immunity defense, see *Anderson v. Creighton*, 483 U.S. 635 (1987), or whether the allegations in the complaint are sufficient to support a § 1983 claim against the county and DSS under *Monell v. New York City Dept. of Social Services*, 436 U.S. 658 (1978), and its progeny.

It may well be, as the Court decides, *ante*, at 194-197, that the Due Process Clause as construed by our prior cases creates no general right to basic governmental services. That, [*204] however, is not the question presented here; indeed, that question was not raised in the complaint, urged on appeal, presented in the petition for certiorari, or addressed in the briefs on the merits. No one, in short, has asked the Court to proclaim that, as a general matter, the Constitution safeguards positive as well as negative liberties.

This is more than a quibble over dicta; it is a point about perspective, having substantive ramifications. In a constitutional setting that distinguishes sharply between action and inaction, one's characterization of the misconduct alleged under § 1983 may effectively decide the case. Thus, by leading off with a discussion (and rejection) of the idea that the Constitution imposes on the States an affirmative duty to take basic care of their citizens, the Court foreshadows—perhaps even preordains—its conclusion that no duty existed even on the specific facts before us. This initial discussion establishes the baseline from which the Court assesses the DeShaneys' claim that, when a State has—"by word and by deed," *ante*, at 197—announced an intention to protect a certain class of citizens and has before it facts that would trigger that protection under the applicable state law, the Constitution imposes upon the State an affirmative duty of protection.

The Court's baseline is the absence of positive rights in the Constitution and a concomitant suspicion of any claim that seems to depend on such rights. From this perspective, the DeShaneys' claim is first and foremost about inaction (the failure, here, of respondents to take steps to protect Joshua), and only tangentially about action (the establishment of a state program specifically designed to help children like Joshua). And from this perspective, holding these Wisconsin officials liable—where the only difference between this case and one involving a general claim to protective services is Wisconsin's establishment and operation of a program to protect children—would seem to punish an effort that we should seek to promote.

[*205] I would begin from the opposite direction. I would focus first on the action that Wisconsin *has* taken with respect to Joshua and children like him, rather than on the actions that the State failed to take. Such a method is not new to this Court. Both *Estelle v. Gamble*, 429 U.S. 97 (1976), and *Youngberg v. Romeo*, 457 U.S. 307 (1982), began by emphasizing that the States had confined J. W. Gamble to prison and Nicholas Romeo to a psychiatric hospital. This initial action rendered these people helpless to help themselves or to seek help from persons unconnected to the government. See *Estelle, supra*, at 104 ("[I]t is but just that the public be required to care for the prisoner, who cannot by reason of the deprivation of his liberty, care for himself"); *Youngberg, supra*, at 317 ("When a person is institutionalized—and wholly dependent on the State—it is conceded by petitioners that a duty to provide certain services and care does exist"). Cases from the lower courts also recognize that a State's actions can be decisive in assessing the constitutional significance of subsequent inaction. For these purposes, moreover,

actual physical restraint is not the only state action that has been considered relevant. See, *e.g., White v. Rochford*, 592 F.2d 381 (CA7 1979) (police officers violated due process when, after arresting the guardian of three young children, they abandoned the children on a busy stretch of highway at night).

Because of the Court's initial fixation on the general principle that the Constitution does not establish positive rights, it is unable to appreciate our recognition in *Estelle* and *Youngberg* that this principle does not hold true in all circumstances. Thus, in the Court's view, *Youngberg* can be explained (and dismissed) in the following way: "In the substantive due process analysis, it is the State's affirmative act of restraining the individual's freedom to act on his own behalf—through incarceration, institutionalization, or other similar restraint of personal liberty—which is the 'deprivation of liberty' triggering the protections of the Due Process **[*206]** Clause, not its failure to act to protect his liberty interests against harms inflicted by other means." *Ante*, at 200. This restatement of *Youngberg*'s holding should come as a surprise when one recalls our explicit observation in that case that Romeo did not challenge his commitment to the hospital, but instead "argue[d] that he ha[d] a constitutionally protected liberty interest in safety, freedom of movement, and training within the institution; and that petitioners infringed these rights *by failing to provide* constitutionally required conditions of confinement." 457 U.S., at 315 (emphasis added). I do not mean to suggest that "the State's affirmative act of restraining the individual's freedom to act on his own behalf," *ante*, at 200, was irrelevant in *Youngberg*; rather, I emphasize that this conduct would have led to no injury, and consequently no cause of action under § 1983, unless the State then had failed to take steps to protect Romeo from himself and from others. In addition, the Court's exclusive attention to state-imposed restraints of "the individual's freedom to act on his own behalf," *ante*, at 200, suggests that it was the State that rendered Romeo unable to care for himself, whereas in fact—with an I.Q. of between 8 and 10, and the mental capacity of an 18-month-old child, 457 U.S., at 309—he had been quite incapable of taking care of himself long before the State stepped into his life. Thus, the fact of hospitalization was critical in *Youngberg* not because it rendered Romeo helpless to help himself, but because it separated him from other sources of aid that, we held, the State was obligated to replace. Unlike the Court, therefore, I am unable to see in *Youngberg* a neat and decisive divide between action and inaction.

Moreover, to the Court, the only fact that seems to count as an "affirmative act of restraining the individual's freedom to act on his own behalf" is direct physical control. *Ante*, at 200 (listing only "incarceration, institutionalization, [and] other similar restraint of personal liberty" in describing relevant "affirmative acts"). I would not, however, give *Youngberg* **[*207]** and *Estelle* such a stingy scope. I would recognize, as the Court apparently cannot, that "the State's knowledge of [an] individual's predicament [and] its expressions of intent to help him" can amount to a "limitation . . . on his freedom to act on his own behalf" or to obtain help from others. *Ante*, at 200. Thus, I would read *Youngberg* and *Estelle* to stand for the much more generous proposition that, if a State cuts off private sources of aid and then refuses aid itself, it cannot wash its hands of the harm that results from its inaction.

Youngberg and *Estelle* are not alone in sounding this theme. In striking down a filing fee as applied to divorce cases brought by indigents, see *Boddie v. Connecticut*, 401 U.S. 371 (1971), and in deciding that a local government could not entirely foreclose the opportunity to speak in a public forum, see, *e.g., Schneider v. State*, 308 U.S. 147 (1939); *Hague v. Committee for Industrial Organization*, 307 U.S. 496 (1939); *United States v. Grace*, 461 U.S. 171 (1983), we have acknowledged that a State's actions—such as the monopolization of a particular path of relief—may impose upon the State certain positive duties. Similarly, *Shelley v. Kraemer*, 334 U.S. 1 (1948), and *Burton v. Wilmington Parking Authority*, 365 U.S. 715 (1961), suggest that a State may be found complicit in an injury even if it did not create the situation that caused the harm.

Arising as they do from constitutional contexts different from the one involved here, cases like *Boddie* and *Burton* are instructive rather than decisive in the case before us. But they set a tone equally well established in precedent as, and contradictory to, the one the Court sets by situating the DeShaneys' complaint within the class of cases epitomized by the Court's decision in *Harris v. McRae*, 448 U.S. 297 (1980). The cases that I have cited tell us that *Goldberg v. Kelly*, 397 U.S. 254 (1970) (recognizing entitlement to welfare under state law), can stand side by side with *Dandridge v. Williams*, 397 U.S. 471, 484 (1970) (implicitly rejecting idea that welfare is a fundamental right), and that *Goss v.* [*208] *Lopez*, 419 U.S. 565, 573 (1975) (entitlement to public education under state law), is perfectly consistent with *San Antonio Independent School Dist. v. Rodriguez*, 411 U.S. 1, 29-39 (1973) (no fundamental right to education). To put the point more directly, these cases signal that a State's prior actions may be decisive in analyzing the constitutional significance of its inaction. I thus would locate the DeShaneys' claims within the framework of cases like *Youngberg* and *Estelle*, and more generally, *Boddie* and *Schneider*, by considering the actions that Wisconsin took with respect to Joshua.

Wisconsin has established a child-welfare system specifically designed to help children like Joshua. Wisconsin law places upon the local departments of social services such as respondent (DSS or Department) a duty to investigate reported instances of child abuse. See Wis. Stat. § 48.981(3) (1987-1988). While other governmental bodies and private persons are largely responsible for the reporting of possible cases of child abuse, see § 48.981(2), Wisconsin law channels all such reports to the local departments of social services for evaluation and, if necessary, further action. § 48.981(3). Even when it is the sheriff's office or police department that receives a report of suspected child abuse, that report is referred to local social services departments for action, see § 48.981(3)(a); the only exception to this occurs when the reporter fears for the child's *immediate* safety. § 48.981(3)(b). In this way, Wisconsin law invites—indeed, directs—citizens and other governmental entities to depend on local departments of social services such as respondent to protect children from abuse.

The specific facts before us bear out this view of Wisconsin's system of protecting children. Each time someone voiced a suspicion that Joshua was being abused, that information was relayed to the Department for investigation and possible action. When Randy DeShaney's second wife told the police that he had "'hit the boy causing marks and [was] a prime case for child abuse,'" the police referred her [*209] complaint to DSS. Ante, at 192. When, on three separate occasions, emergency room personnel noticed suspicious injuries on Joshua's body, they went to DSS with this information. Ante, at 192-193. When neighbors informed the police that they had seen or heard Joshua's father or his father's lover beating or otherwise abusing Joshua, the police brought these reports to the attention of DSS. App. 144-145. And when respondent Kemmeter, through these reports and through her own observations in the course of nearly 20 visits to the DeShaney home, id., at 104, compiled growing evidence that Joshua was being abused, that information stayed within the Department—chronicled by the social worker in detail that seems almost eerie in light of her failure to act upon it. (As to the extent of the social worker's involvement in, and knowledge of, Joshua's predicament, her reaction to the news of Joshua's last and most devastating injuries is illuminating: "'I just knew the phone would ring some day and Joshua would be dead.'" 812 F.2d 298, 300 (CA7 1987).)

Even more telling than these examples is the Department's control over the decision whether to take steps to protect a particular child from suspected abuse. While many different people contributed information and advice to this decision, it was up to the people at DSS to make the ultimate decision (subject to the approval of the local government's corporation counsel) whether to disturb the family's current arrangements. App. 41, 58. When Joshua first appeared at a local hospital with injuries signaling physical abuse, for example, it was DSS that made the decision to take him into temporary custody for the purpose of studying his situation—and it was DSS, acting in conjunction with the corporation counsel, that returned him to his father. Ante, at 192. Unfortunately for Joshua DeShaney, the buck effectively stopped with the Department.

In these circumstances, a private citizen, or even a person working in a government agency other than DSS, would doubtless feel that her job was done as soon as she had reported [*210] her suspicions of child abuse to DSS. Through its child-welfare program, in other words, the State of Wisconsin has relieved ordinary citizens and governmental bodies other than the Department of any sense of obligation to do anything more than report their suspicions of child abuse to DSS. If DSS ignores or dismisses these suspicions, no one will step in to fill the gap. Wisconsin's child-protection program thus effectively confined Joshua DeShaney within the walls of Randy DeShaney's violent home until such time as DSS took action to remove him. Conceivably, then, children like Joshua are made worse off by the existence of this program when the persons and entities charged with carrying it out fail to do their jobs.

It simply belies reality, therefore, to contend that the State "stood by and did nothing" with respect to Joshua. *Ante*, at 203. Through its child-protection program, the State actively intervened in Joshua's life and, by virtue of this intervention, acquired ever more certain knowledge that Joshua was in grave danger. These circumstances, in my view, plant this case solidly within the tradition of cases like *Youngberg* and *Estelle*.

It will be meager comfort to Joshua and his mother to know that, if the State had "selectively den[ied] its protective services" to them because they were "disfavored minorities," *ante*, at 197, n. 3, their § 1983 suit might have stood on sturdier ground. Because of the posture of this case, we do not know why respondents did not take steps to protect Joshua; the Court, however, tells us that their reason is irrelevant so long as their inaction was not the product of invidious discrimination. Presumably, then, if respondents decided not to help Joshua because his name began with a "J," or because he was born in the spring, or because they did not care enough about him even to formulate an intent to discriminate against him based on an arbitrary reason, respondents would not be liable to the DeShaneys because they were not the ones who dealt the blows that destroyed Joshua's life.

[*211] I do not suggest that such irrationality was at work in this case; I emphasize only that we do not know whether or not it was. I would allow Joshua and his mother the opportunity to show that respondents' failure to help him arose, not out of the sound exercise of professional judgment that we recognized in *Youngberg* as sufficient to preclude liability, see 457 U.S., at 322-323, but from the kind of arbitrariness that we have in the past condemned. See, *e.g., Daniels v. Williams*, 474 U.S. 327, 331 (1986) (purpose of Due Process Clause was "to secure the individual from the arbitrary exercise of the powers of government" (citations omitted)); *West Coast Hotel Co. v. Parrish*, 300 U.S. 379, 399 (1937) (to sustain state action, the Court need only decide that it is not "arbitrary or capricious"); *Euclid v. Ambler Realty Co.*, 272 U.S. 365, 389 (1926) (state action invalid where it "passes the bounds of reason and assumes the character of a merely arbitrary fiat," quoting *Purity Extract & Tonic Co. v. Lynch*, 226 U.S. 192, 204 (1912)).

Youngberg's deference to a decisionmaker's professional judgment ensures that once a caseworker has decided, on the basis of her professional training and experience, that one course of protection is preferable for a given child, or even that no special protection is required, she will not be found liable for the harm that follows. (In this way, *Youngberg*'s vision of substantive due process serves a purpose similar to that served by adherence to procedural norms, namely, requiring that a state actor stop and think before she acts in a way that may lead to a loss of liberty.) Moreover, that the Due Process Clause is not violated by merely negligent conduct, see *Daniels, supra*, and *Davidson v. Cannon*, 474 U.S. 344 (1986), means that a social worker who simply makes a mistake of judgment under what are admittedly complex and difficult conditions will not find herself liable in damages under § 1983.

As the Court today reminds us, "the Due Process Clause of the Fourteenth Amendment was intended to prevent government **[*212]** 'from abusing [its] power, or employing it as an instrument of oppression.'" *Ante*, at 196, quoting *Davidson, supra*, U.S., at 348. My disagreement with the Court arises from its failure to see that inaction can be every bit as abusive of power as action, that oppression can result when a State undertakes a vital duty and then ignores it. Today's opinion construes the Due Process Clause to permit a State to displace private sources of protection and then, at the critical moment, to shrug its shoulders and turn away from the harm that it has promised to try to prevent. Because I cannot agree that our Constitution is indifferent to such indifference, I respectfully dissent.

Justice BLACKMUN, dissenting.

Today, the Court purports to be the dispassionate oracle of the law, unmoved by "natural sympathy." *Ante*, at 202. But, in this pretense, the Court itself retreats into a sterile formalism which prevents it from recognizing either the facts of the case before it or the legal norms that should apply to those facts. As Justice Brennan demonstrates, the facts here involve not mere passivity, but active state intervention in the life of Joshua DeShaney—intervention that triggered a fundamental duty to aid the boy once the State learned of the severe danger to which he was exposed.

The Court fails to recognize this duty because it attempts to draw a sharp and rigid line between action and inaction. But such formalistic reasoning has no place in the interpretation of the broad and stirring Clauses of the Fourteenth Amendment. Indeed, I submit that these Clauses were designed, at least in part, to undo the formalistic legal reasoning that infected antebellum jurisprudence, which the late Professor Robert Cover analyzed so effectively in his significant work entitled Justice Accused (1975).

Like the antebellum judges who denied relief to fugitive slaves, see *id.*, at 119-121, the Court today claims that its decision, however harsh, is compelled by existing legal doctrine. On the contrary, the question presented by this case **[*213]** is an open one, and our Fourteenth Amendment precedents may be read more broadly or narrowly depending upon how one chooses to read them. Faced with the choice, I would adopt a "sympathetic" reading, one which comports with dictates of fundamental justice and recognizes that compassion need not be exiled from the province of judging. Cf. A. Stone, Law, Psychiatry, and Morality 262 (1984) ("We will make mistakes if we go forward, but doing nothing can be the worst mistake. What is required of us is moral ambition. Until our composite sketch becomes a true portrait of humanity we must live with our uncertainty; we will grope, we will struggle, and our compassion may be our only guide and comfort").

Poor Joshua! Victim of repeated attacks by an irresponsible, bullying, cowardly, and intemperate father, and abandoned by respondents who placed him in a dangerous predicament and who knew or learned what was going on, and yet did essentially nothing except, as the Court revealingly observes, *ante*, at 193, "dutifully recorded these incidents in [their] files." It is a sad commentary upon American life, and constitutional principles — so full of late of patriotic fervor and proud proclamations about "liberty and justice for all" — that this child, Joshua DeShaney, now is assigned to live out the remainder of his life profoundly retarded. Joshua and his mother, as petitioners here, deserve — but now are denied by this Court — the opportunity to have the facts of their case considered in the light of the constitutional protection that 42 U.S.C. § 1983 is meant to provide.

> **Questions Regarding *DeShaney v. Winnebago County Department of Social Services***
>
> 1. In the majority opinion, Chief Justice Rehnquist says, "[N]othing in the language of the Due Process Clause requires the State to protect life, liberty, or property of its citizens against invasion by private actors." What is the policy reason for this interpretation? In other words, what is the risk if the Court finds the opposite?
> 2. Chief Justice Rehnquist's majority opinion opines that the state of Wisconsin's intervention in this case did not put Joshua DeShaney in a worse position than he was prior to the government's intervention? Do you agree?
> 3. Do you agree with Chief Justice Rehnquist's majority holding in this case? Or are you more convinced by the dissents of Justice Brennan and/or Justice Blackmun?

SAMPLE BRIEF FOR *DESHANEY v. WINNEBAGO COUNTY DEPARTMENT OF SOCIAL SERVICES*

DeShaney v. Winnebago Cnty. Dep't of Soc. Servs., 489 U.S. 189 (1989).

Facts:
Petitioner child was beaten several times by his father. Respondents, a county department of social services and several social workers, received abuse complaints and took steps to protect him but did not remove petitioner from the father's custody. Petitioner's father then beat him so severely that he suffered permanent brain damage.

- 1979: Joshua DeShaney was born
- 1980: Joshua's parents divorced and his father, Randy DeShaney, was awarded custody

This paragraph summarizes the most salient facts in the case on a macro-level. It's useful to have this bird's eye view, but the Reasoning that follows relies on factual details as well, which is why the timeline below is also included.

- 1982: Father's second wife reported abuse to Winnebago County authorities; the Department of Social Services (DSS) interviewed father, who denied allegations
- January 1983: Joshua admitted to hospital with bruises and abrasions; physician notified DSS and Joshua was placed in temporary custody of hospital
    - County convened an ad hoc "Child Protection Team," which decided there was insufficient evidence of abuse
    - The team, however, enrolled him in a preschool program, provided father with counselling services and encouraged girlfriend to move out of home
    - Randy DeShaney agreed to cooperate
- February 1983: Emergency room personnel called DSS about suspicious injuries; caseworker determined there was no basis for action
- For the next six months, the caseworker made monthly visits to the DeShaney home and observed suspicious injuries on Joshua's head, that Joshua was not enrolled in school and that the girlfriend had not moved out
- November 1983: ER notified DSS that Joshua was being treated for injuries consistent with child abuse; for caseworker's next two visits, she was told Joshua was too ill to see her; DSS took no action
- March 1984: Randy DeShaney beat 4-year-old Joshua so severely that he fell into a coma; he did not die but was expected to spend the rest of his life confined to an institution for the profoundly retarded
- DeShaney was subsequently tried and convicted of child abuse

> The last listed fact involves an entirely different cause of action (child abuse) handled by an entirely different court. Why is this potentially relevant in a substantive due process civil case? Because implicit in the Court's reasoning is the acknowledgment that there are alternative avenues for relief in this case.

Procedural Posture:
- Petitioner and his mother sued respondents under 42 U.S.C. § 1983, alleging that respondents had deprived petitioner of his liberty interest in bodily integrity, violating his substantive due process rights.
- The district court granted summary judgment for respondents.
- The Court of Appeals affirmed.

Issues:

1. Whether the Due Process Clause of the Fourteenth Amendment imposed a duty on government-employed social workers to protect a child brought to their attention from the violent acts of a third party? 193.
2. Whether the State's knowledge of a child's danger and the State's expression of willingness to protect him against that

danger established a "special relationship" giving rise to an affirmative constitutional duty to protect under the Due Process Clause? 193.

Held (Opinion by Rehnquist):

1. The Supreme Court affirmed the lower court's ruling. The Due Process Clause imposes no duty on the State to provide members of the general public with adequate protective services. The Clause is a limitation on the State's power to act, not a guarantee of certain minimal levels of safety and security.
2. The Supreme Court affirmed the lower court's ruling. Knowledge of a child's danger is not sufficient to a establish a "special relationship" under the Due Process Clause; an affirmative duty to protect only arises when the State actually limits the freedom of a person to act on his own behalf through imprisonment, institutionalization or other similar restraint on liberty.

Reasoning:

1. The Due Process Clause imposes no duty on the State to provide members of the general public with adequate protective services. The Clause is a limitation on the State's power to act, not a guarantee of certain minimal levels of safety and security.

    a. The Due Process Clause provides that "[n]o State shall . . . deprive any person of life, liberty, or property without due process of law." 194.
    b. "[N]othing in the language of the Due Process Clause requires the State to protect life, liberty, and property of its citizens against invasion by private actors." 195.
    c. The Clause is a limitation on the State's power to act, not a guarantee of certain minimal levels of safety and security. 195.
    d. "Its purpose was to protect the people from the State, not to ensure that the State protected them from each other." 196.
    e. Supreme Court precedent has recognized that due process does not confer an "affirmative right to governmental aid, even where such aid may be necessary to secure life, liberty, or property interests of which the government itself may not deprive the individual." 196.

2. Knowledge of a child's danger is not sufficient to establish a "special relationship" under the Due Process Clause; an affirmative duty to protect only arises when the State actually limits the freedom of a person to act on his own behalf through imprisonment, institutionalization or other similar restraint on liberty.
    a. Court rejects argument that the State's undertaking to protect Joshua from danger resulted in an affirmative due process "duty." 198.
    b. Court distinguished cases where State took person in custody against his will (through incarceration and institutionalization) and imposed a corresponding duty for the ward's safety and well-being. 199-200. In those cases, it is the "deprivation of liberty" that triggers due process, not the failure to act to protect a person's liberty against harms inflicted by other means. 200.
    c. Temporary custody is not sufficient; when DSS returned Joshua to his father, "it placed him in no worse position than that in which he would have been had [DSS] not acted at all." 200.

> Laws are often framed in terms of duties: certain actions trigger duties of parties toward other parties.

> Because courts are governed by stare decisis and because they are always striving for consistency in their decisions, courts and attorneys must often distinguish cases where the outcome went the opposite way.

Dissent (by Brennan, joined by Marshall and Blackmun):
- Disagrees with Court's decisive divide between action and inaction; believes "if a State cuts off private sources of aid and then refuses aid itself, it cannot wash its hands of . . . harm that results from its inaction." 207.
- Wisconsin law directs "citizens and other governmental entities to depend on local departments of social services . . . to protect children from abuse." 208.
- By relieving private citizens of the sense of obligation to intervene, Wisconsin's child-protection program "effectively confined Joshua DeShaney." 210.
- "My disagreement with the Court arises from its failure to see that inaction can be every bit as abusive of power as action, that oppression can result when a State undertakes a vital duty and then ignores it." 212.

> Concurrences and dissents aren't written the same way as majority opinions. The authors of concurrences and dissents assume you've already read the majority opinion and often write in dialogue with the majority. Majority opinions, in turn, often refer to concurrences and dissents in justifying their reasoning.

Dissent (by Blackmun):
Blackmun would adopt a "sympathetic" reading of the Due Process Clause, which comports with dictates of fundamental justice and recognizes that "compassion need not be exiled from the province of judging." 213.

chapter 5

Anticipating How a Court Will Rule

In the previous chapter, you learned how to read and summarize a case. In this chapter, you will learn how to use knowledge of precedent cases to predict the outcome of future cases. In Chapter 1, you were introduced to the concept of stare decisis. After a court decides a particular issue of law, the court's stance on that issue should remain consistent in future cases. Additionally, any courts below that deciding court in the hierarchy of law are also bound by the higher court's decision. So if the Second Circuit Court of Appeals rules on a particular issue of trademark law, all the district courts in the Second Circuit—those in New York, Connecticut and Vermont—are also bound by that ruling.

INTREPRETING LAW

This striving for consistency among courts over time makes predicting judicial outcomes more than just guesswork. That said, it's the rare case that aligns perfectly—both on issues of fact and of law—with a prior case. An attorney arguing for the opposite outcome from an unfavorable precedent will try to distinguish that unfavorable precedent by showing how their case is different. If more favorable precedent is available, they'll try to align their case with that precedent. For the majority of the assignments in this textbook, a grasp of stare decisis and the hierarchy of law will be sufficient for the predictive work you'll be asked to tackle. But because understanding how to argue under the law requires understanding how judges interpret the law, it's worth a moment to discuss a few of the most common methods of legal interpretation for constitutional law, as several of this book's assignments deal with constitutional questions.

Textualism focuses on the plain meaning of a legal document's text. If the meaning of the words is clear, a textualist judge goes no further.

Originalism focuses on the intent of the framers of the Constitution. An originalist believes that the language of the Constitution had an objective meaning at the time it was crafted and that meaning should not change over time. Accordingly, judges should always strive to construct a constitutional provision's original meaning when interpreting that provision.

While an originalist interpretation looks to the past for meaning, a *pragmatic* interpretation of the Constitution looks to the future. A pragmatist weighs the probable practical consequences of its interpretations—like a cost and benefit analysis—and then selects the interpretation they believe would lead to the best outcome.

Finally, a *moral reasoning* interpretation of the Constitution allows moral concepts and ideals to inform judges' interpretations.

While certain judges may sometimes be closely associated with one of the above modes of interpretation, many judicial opinions will exhibit a mix of the above, including the case you read in Chapter 4, *DeShaney v. Winnebago County*. Chief Justice Rehnquist's majority opinion, for example, points out that "nothing in the language of the Due Process clause requires the State to protect life, liberty, and property of its citizens against invasion by private actors." *DeShaney v. Winnebago Cnty. Dep't of Soc. Servs.*, 489 U.S. 189, 195 (1989). That attention to the plain meaning of the Clause's language is an example of a textual interpretation.

That textual interpretation, though, leads to a practical consideration of what the consequence would be for the government if the Constitution guaranteed minimal levels of safety and security to all its citizens. This consideration of the practical effects of a more expansive view of due process law is an example of pragmatic interpretation.

In Justice Blackmun's dissent, he begs for a "sympathetic" reading of the Due Process Clause, one that comports with his concept of fundamental justice and compassion. This is an example of a moral reasoning interpretation of the Clause.

PREDICTING FUTURE COURT DECISIONS BASED ON PRIOR PRECEDENT

For the purposes of this textbook, it's not important that you know the specific judicial philosophy of the judges whose opinions you'll read. But it's useful to understand the myriad ways in which judges may view the law, especially as you endeavor to predict future court decisions based on prior precedent.

As a Supreme Court case, *DeShaney v. Winnebago County*'s holdings and reasoning had a significant effect on substantive due process cases throughout the United States. The reasoning of the next two cases you'll read, *Doe v. Covington Cnty. Sch. Dist.* and *Estate of Asher Brown v. Cypress Fairbanks Indep. Sch. Dist.*, flow directly from *DeShaney*. As you read these cases, pay special attention to how the logic of *DeShaney* animates these subsequent decisions.

ASSIGNMENT 3: *DOE V. COVINGTON COUNTY SCHOOL DISTRICT* CASE BRIEF

Read the following case in its entirety first, highlighting and marking the pages as you go, then brief the case using the format you used for the *DeShaney* case brief.

Doe v. Covington Cnty. Sch. Dist. is a case from the Fifth Circuit Court of Appeals. What law is the Fifth Circuit bound to uphold? In your brief for this case, you should again note in the Procedural Posture the means by which the Court decides the case. A *12(b)(6) motion* is similar to a summary judgment in that it dispenses with a case without the benefit of a full trial. In this case, we have a 12(b)(6) failure to state a claim motion. Basically, what the moving party asserts is that the *complaint* (which is the legal argument submitted to a court to commence a lawsuit) is insufficient on its face and doesn't plead a claim that the court has the power to grant.

Qualified immunity, which will be mentioned in the case, is legal immunity for government officials against lawsuits suing them as individuals as opposed to suing the government body for which they work. For example, if a prison warden violated a prisoner's constitutional rights and the prisoner wanted to sue, qualified immunity might bar the prisoner from suing the individual warden but would not foreclose a suit against the prison itself.

En banc refers to a case heard by the full panel of court of appeals judges (or a representative critical mass) in a given jurisdiction, as opposed to a smaller panel. En banc proceedings often occur when the court believes there is a particularly significant issue at stake.

Finally, *de novo* means anew: when a court reviews an issue de novo, it reviews the issue as if it were the first court to do so, giving no deference to the lower court's decision on the same issue.

DOE v. COVINGTON COUNTY SCHOOL DISTRICT

United States Court of Appeals for the Fifth Circuit
March 23, 2012, Filed
No. 09-60406
Reporter: 675 F.3d 849 *

Judges: Before Jones, Chief Judge, and King, Jolley, Davis, Smith, Wiener, Garza, Benavides, Stewart, Dennis, Clement, Prado, Owen, Elrod, Southwick, Haynes, Graves, and Higginson, Circuit Judges. King, Circuit Judge, joined by Edith H. Jones, Chief Judge, E. Grady Jolly, W. Eugene Davis, Jerry E. Smith, Emilio M. Garza, Fortunato P. Benavides, Carl E. Stewart, Edith Brown Clement, Edward C. Prado, Priscilla Owen, Jennifer Walker Elrod, Leslie H. Southwick, Catharina Haynes, and James E. Graves, Jr., Circuit Judges. E. Grady Jolly, Circuit Judge, specially concurring. Higginson, Circuit Judge, concurring in the judgment. Wiener, Circuit Judge, joined by Dennis, Circuit Judge, dissenting.

Opinion (Edited for Content)

[*852] King, Circuit Judge, joined by Edith H. Jones, Chief Judge, E. Grady Jolly, W. Eugene Davis, Jerry E. Smith, Emilio M. Garza, Fortunato P. Benavides, Carl E. Stewart, Edith Brown Clement, Edward C. Prado, Priscilla Owen, Jennifer Walker Elrod, Leslie H. Southwick, Catharina Haynes, and James E. Graves, Jr., Circuit Judges:

For the third time, the en banc court is called upon to decide whether a public school student has stated a constitutional claim against her school for its failure to protect her from harm inflicted by a private actor. Relying on our prior en banc opinions, the district court found that she had failed to state a claim and dismissed her complaint. A panel of this court reversed in part, concluding that the student had a special relationship with her school under *DeShaney v. Winnebago County Department of Social Services*, 489 U.S. 189, 109 S. Ct. 998, 103 L. Ed. 2d 249 (1989), and that the school was therefore constitutionally obligated to protect her from acts of private violence. The panel nevertheless granted qualified immunity to those defendants sued in their individual capacities. We granted rehearing en banc, thereby vacating the panel opinion. We now hold that the student did not have a *DeShaney* special relationship with her school, and her school therefore had no constitutional duty to protect her from harm inflicted by a private actor. We also hold that the student has failed to state a claim under the state-created danger theory or under a municipal liability theory. We therefore affirm the judgment of the district court.

I. FACTUAL AND PROCEDURAL BACKGROUND

During the 2007-2008 school year, Jane Doe ("Jane") attended an elementary [*853] school in Covington County, Mississippi. She was nine years old at the time. At some point during the school year, Jane's guardians filled out a "Permission to Check-Out Form," on which they listed the names of the individuals with exclusive permission to "check out" Jane from school during the school day. On six separate occasions between September 2007 and January 2008,[1] school employees allowed a man named Tommy Keyes ("Keyes"), who allegedly bore no relation to Jane and was not listed on her check-out form, to take Jane from school. On these occasions, Keyes took Jane from school without the knowledge or consent of her parents or guardians, sexually molested her, and subsequently returned her to school. On the first five occasions, Keyes signed out Jane as her father. On the final occasion, he signed her out as her mother. The complaint alleges that Keyes was able to gain access to Jane because the policy promulgated by the various school officials permitted school employees to release Jane to Keyes without first verifying Keyes's identification or whether

---

1. The incidents occurred on September 12, September 27, October 12, November 6, December 11, 2007, and January 8, 2008.

he was among those people listed on her "Permission to Check-Out Form." The complaint contends that this policy created a danger to students and the implementation and execution of the policy constituted deliberate indifference towards the rights and safety of those students, including Jane. This policy is alleged to be the direct and proximate cause of Jane's injury.

The complaint thus assigns a passive role to school employees, alleging that the school violated Jane's constitutional rights by "*allowing* the Defendant, Tommy Keyes, to check the minor child out from school" without verifying his identity or his authorization to take the child. It also alleges that the school policy *permitted* school employees to release students to individuals without checking their identification or authorization, but did not *require* them to do so. The policy thus delegated to school employees the discretion to release a student without verifying an adult's identity or his authorization. Furthermore, the complaint does not claim that any school employee had actual knowledge that Keyes was not authorized to take Jane from school, only that the employees did not check Keyes's identification or verify that he was among the adults listed on Jane's check-out form.

Jane, her father, and her paternal grandmother (together, the "Does") sued the Covington County School District; the Covington County Superintendent of Education, I.S. Sanford, Jr., in his official and individual capacities; the Covington County School Board; and the President of the Covington County School Board, Andrew Keys, in his official and individual capacities (together, "Education Defendants"). The Does also named Keyes and other unnamed education defendants in their official and individual capacities. The Does asserted due process and equal protection claims under 42 U.S.C. §§ 1983, 1985, and 1986,[2] as well as various state law causes of action.

[*854] On the Education Defendants' motion, the district court dismissed the Does' federal claims for failure to state a claim and declined to exercise supplemental jurisdiction over the remaining state law claims. The court concluded that under the Supreme Court's decision in *DeShaney v. Winnebago County Department of Social Services*, 489 U.S. 189, 109 S. Ct. 998, 103 L. Ed. 2d 249 (1989), Jane had no constitutional right to be protected from harm inflicted by a private actor such as Keyes except under one of two narrow exceptions—the "state-created danger" theory and the "special relationship" exception. The district court assumed that the state-created danger theory was available in this circuit, but

---

2. As discussed further herein, the limited right to state protection from private violence arises out of the substantive due process component of the Fourteenth Amendment, not equal protection or procedural due process. *See DeShaney v. Winnebago County Department of Social Services*, 489 U.S. 189, 200, 109 S. Ct. 998, 103 L. Ed. 2d 249 (1989) ("In the substantive due process analysis, it is the State's affirmative act of restraining the individual's freedom to act on his own behalf . . . which is the 'deprivation of liberty' triggering the protections of the Due Process Clause . . . ."); *Walton v. Alexander*, 44 F.3d 1297, 1302-03 (5th Cir. 1995) (en banc). We therefore analyze Jane's cause of action as a substantive due process claim.

held that the Does had not sufficiently pleaded a due process violation based on that theory. The court thus determined that the "primary question" was whether the Does could state a claim based on a special relationship between Jane and the Education Defendants, and concluded that the claim was foreclosed by our precedent.

On appeal, a majority of a panel of this court reversed the district court's judgment in part. The majority found that the Does had pleaded a facially plausible claim that the school had violated Jane's substantive due process rights by virtue of its special relationship with her and its deliberate indifference to known threats to her safety. *Doe ex rel. Magee v. Covington Cnty. Sch. Dist. ex rel. Bd. of Educ.*, 649 F.3d 335, 353-54 (5th Cir. 2011). The panel majority, however, affirmed the district court's qualified-immunity dismissal of Jane's constitutional claim against those Education Defendants sued in their individual capacities. *Id.* We ordered rehearing en banc. *Doe ex rel. Magee v. Covington Cnty. Sch. Dist. ex rel. Bd. of Educ.*, 659 F.3d 358 (5th Cir. 2011). For the reasons set forth herein, we now affirm the judgment of the district court.

II. STANDARD OF REVIEW

We review a district court's dismissal under Rule 12(b)(6) de novo, "accepting all well-pleaded facts as true and viewing those facts in the light most favorable to the plaintiffs." *Dorsey v. Portfolio Equities, Inc.*, 540 F.3d 333, 338 (5th Cir. 2008) (citation and internal quotation marks omitted). To survive dismissal pursuant to Rule 12(b)(6), plaintiffs must plead "enough facts to state a claim to relief that is plausible on its face." *Bell Atl. Corp. v. Twombly*, 550 U.S. 544, 570, 127 S. Ct. 1955, 167 L. Ed. 2d 929 (2007); *see also Ashcroft v. Iqbal*, 556 U.S. 662, 129 S. Ct. 1937, 1949, 173 L. Ed. 2d 868 (2009); *Cornerstone Christian Schs. v. Univ. Interscholastic League*, 563 F.3d 127, 133 (5th Cir. 2009). "A claim has facial plausibility when the plaintiff pleads factual content that allows the court to draw the reasonable inference that the defendant is liable for the misconduct alleged." *Iqbal*, 129 S. Ct. at 1949 (citing *Twombly*, 550 U.S. at 556). Our task, then, is "to determine whether the plaintiff has stated a legally cognizable claim that is plausible, not to evaluate the plaintiff's likelihood of success." *Lone Star Fund V (U.S.), L.P. v. Barclays Bank PLC*, 594 F.3d 383, 387 (5th Cir. 2010) (citing *Iqbal*, 129 S. Ct. at 1949).

III. DISCUSSION

To state a claim under 42 U.S.C. § 1983, "a plaintiff must (1) allege a violation of a right secured by the Constitution or laws of the United States and (2) demonstrate that the alleged deprivation was committed by a person acting under color of state law." *James v. Tex. Collin Cnty.*, [*855] 535 F.3d 365, 373 (5th Cir. 2008) (citation and internal quotation marks omitted). The central issue here is whether the Does have in fact alleged the violation of a constitutional right.

Because we find that they have not, we affirm the district court's dismissal of this case.

A. *DeShaney* Special Relationship

Jane's constitutional claim against the Education Defendants is based not upon Keyes's molestation of Jane, but rather upon the school's allegedly deficient check-out policy, which allowed the molestation to occur.[3] Jane's constitutional claim can proceed, therefore, only if the Education Defendants had a constitutional duty to protect Jane from non-state actors. This duty, in turn, may exist if there is a special relationship, as contemplated by *DeShaney*, between Jane and her school. *See Walton v. Alexander*, 44 F.3d 1297, 1300-01 (5th Cir. 1995) (en banc). We begin by reviewing *DeShaney* and its progeny, then consider the application of this law in the context of this case.

1. DeShaney *Recognizes a Limited Duty to Protect*

DeShaney v. Winnebago County Department of Social Services, 489 U.S. 189, 109 S. Ct. 998, 103 L. Ed. 2d 249 (1989), arose out of the tragic case of young Joshua DeShaney, who had been placed in state custody after the Winnebago County Department of Social Services suspected his father of child abuse. The agency subsequently returned Joshua to his home after finding insufficient evidence of abuse. Once at home, Joshua continued to endure beatings from his father, and was ultimately left with severe brain damage. *Id.* at 191-93. Joshua DeShaney and his mother sued the Winnebago County Department of Social Services and various individual defendants, alleging that the Department and its employees had violated Joshua's substantive due process right by failing to protect him from his father's violence even though they knew that he faced a very real danger of harm. *Id.* at 193. The Supreme Court rejected this claim, and held that the plaintiffs could not maintain an action under § 1983 because there had been no constitutional violation. *Id.* at 202. The Court noted that the Fourteenth Amendment was enacted to "protect the people from the State, not to ensure that the State protect[] them from each other." *Id.* at 196. The Due Process Clause, the Court explained, "forbids the State itself to deprive individuals of life, liberty, or property without 'due process of law,' but its language cannot fairly be extended to impose an affirmative obligation on the State to ensure that those interests do not come to harm through other means." *Id.* at

---

[3]. Jane does not, and indeed cannot, state a substantive due process claim based upon the sexual molestation itself. Although we recognized a constitutional right to bodily integrity in *Doe v. Taylor Independent School District*, 15 F.3d 443 (5th Cir. 1994) (en banc), we found that this right is "necessarily violated when a *state actor* sexually abuses a schoolchild and that such misconduct deprives the child of rights vouchsafed by the Fourteenth Amendment." *Id.* at 451-52 (emphasis added). *Taylor* is inapplicable here because the actual violation of Jane's bodily integrity was caused by Keyes, a non-state actor.

195. Thus, the Court concluded that "a State's failure to protect an individual against private violence simply does not constitute a violation of the Due Process Clause." *Id.* at 197.

The Court noted that this categorical rule is subject to at least one very limited exception.[4] Under this exception, a state [*856] may create a "special relationship" with a particular citizen, requiring the state to protect him from harm, "when the State takes a person into its custody and holds him there against his will." *Id.* at 199-200. In such instances, "the Constitution imposes upon it a corresponding duty to assume some responsibility for his safety and general well-being." *Id.* at 200. That special relationship exists when the state incarcerates a prisoner, *Estelle v. Gamble*, 429 U.S. 97, 103-04, 97 S. Ct. 285, 50 L. Ed. 2d 251 (1976), or involuntarily commits someone to an institution, *Youngberg v. Romeo*, 457 U.S. 307, 315-16, 102 S. Ct. 2452, 73 L. Ed. 2d 28 (1982). The *DeShaney* Court reasoned that:

> when the State by the affirmative exercise of its power so restrains an individual's liberty that it renders him unable to care for himself, and at the same time fails to provide for his basic human needs—*e.g.*, food, clothing, shelter, medical care, and reasonable safety—it transgresses the substantive limits on state action set by the Eighth Amendment and the Due Process Clause.

DeShaney, 489 U.S. at 200. The Court stated that "[t]he affirmative duty to protect arises not from the State's knowledge of the individual's predicament or from its expressions of intent to help him, but from the limitation which it has imposed on his freedom to act on his own behalf." *Id.*

In addition to the circumstances of incarceration and involuntary institutionalization recognized by the Court in *DeShaney*, we have extended the special relationship exception to the placement of children in foster care. *Griffith v. Johnston*, 899 F.2d 1427, 1439 (5th Cir. 1990). We reasoned that the state assumes a constitutional duty to care for children under state supervision because "the state's duty to provide services stems from the limitation which the state has placed on the individual's ability to act on his own behalf." *Id.* We have not extended the *DeShaney* special relationship exception beyond these three situations, and have explicitly held that the state does *not* create a special relationship with children attending public schools.

2. Schools and the Special Relationship Exception in the Fifth Circuit

We have twice considered en banc whether the special relationship exception to the *DeShaney* rule applies in the context of public schools. *Doe v. Hillsboro Indep. Sch. Dist.*, 113 F.3d 1412 (5th Cir. 1997) (en banc); *Walton v. Alexander*, 44 F.3d

---

4. Several courts of appeals have recognized a second limited exception, the so-called "state-created danger" theory. We address this theory below.

1297 (5th Cir. 1995) (en banc). In both cases, we concluded that a public school does not have a special relationship with a student that would require the school to protect the student from harm at the hands of a private actor.

In *Walton v. Alexander*, the student plaintiff attended the Mississippi School for the Deaf, a residential public school, and was sexually assaulted by a fellow student. 44 F.3d at 1299. The student plaintiff brought suit under § 1983, based upon the special relationship exception. Even though the school was a residential school, and thus responsible for fulfilling most of the students' day-to-day needs, we held that the school had not created a special relationship with the student, because the student "attended [the] school voluntarily with the option of leaving at will." *Id.* at 1305. In so holding, we "strictly" construed *DeShaney* and explained that it is "important to apply *DeShaney* as it is written." *Id.* at 1303, 1305. **[*857]** We reasoned, "*DeShaney* emphasize[d] . . . that extending the Due Process Clause to impose on the state the obligation to defend and to pay for the acts of non-state third parties is a burden not supported by the text or history of the Clause, nor by general principles of constitutional jurisprudence." *Id.* at 1305. We concluded that "[s]uch an expansion of the state's liability for acts of third parties only can make constitutional sense . . . when the state has effectively taken the plaintiff's liberty under terms that provide no realistic means of voluntarily terminating the state's custody *and* which thus deprives the plaintiff of the ability or opportunity to provide for his own care and safety." *Id.* (emphasis in original). It is only under these "extreme circumstances that the state itself, by its affirmative act and pursuant to its own will, has effectively used its power to force a 'special relationship,' with respect to which it assumes a certain liability." *Id.*

We next addressed the special relationship exception in *Doe v. Hillsboro Independent School District*, where we likewise held that the exception did not apply in the context of a public school. 113 F.3d at 1415. The student plaintiff in that case was thirteen years old. She was "kept after school to do special work on her studies" and was sexually assaulted by a custodian (who was not alleged to have been acting under color of state law) when she was sent to an unoccupied area of the school to retrieve supplies for her teacher. *Id.* at 1414. We rejected the plaintiff's argument that a special relationship existed between the school and the student due to the fact that school attendance was required by state law, and declined "to hold that compulsory attendance laws alone create a special relationship giving rise to a constitutionally rooted duty of school officials to protect students from private actors." *Id.* at 1415. We reasoned that "[t]he restrictions imposed by attendance laws upon students and their parents are not analogous to the restraints of prisons and mental institutions" because "[t]he custody is intermittent," "the student returns home each day," and "[p]arents remain the primary source for the basic needs of their children." *Id.*

Numerous panel decisions have declined to recognize a special relationship between a public school and its students. *See, e.g., Doe v. San Antonio Indep. Sch. Dist.*, 197 F. App'x 296, 298-301 (5th Cir. 2006) (finding no special relationship between a school and a fourteen-year-old special education student when the student was allowed to leave with her "uncle," who later allegedly molested her); *Teague v. Tex. City Indep. Sch. Dist.*, 185 F. App'x 355, 357 (5th Cir. 2006) (finding no special relationship between a school and an eighteen-year-old special education student who was sexually assaulted by another special education student); *Johnson v. Dallas Indep. Sch. Dist.*, 38 F.3d 198, 199, 202-03 (5th Cir. 1994) (finding no special relationship between a high school and a student shot and killed in the school hallway during the school day by a boy who was not a student but had gained access to the school); *Leffall v. Dallas Indep. Sch. Dist.*, 28 F.3d 521, 522, 529 (5th Cir. 1994) (finding no special relationship between a high school and a student fatally wounded by a gunshot fired in the school parking lot after a school dance).

We reaffirm, then, decades of binding precedent: a public school does not have a *DeShaney* special relationship with its students requiring the school to ensure the students' safety from private actors. Public schools do not take students into custody and hold them there against their will in the same way that a state takes prisoners, involuntarily committed mental [*858] health patients, and foster children into its custody. See *DeShaney*, 489 U.S. at 199-200; *Griffith*, 899 F.2d at 1439. Without a special relationship, a public school has no *constitutional* duty to ensure that its students are safe from private violence. That is not to say that schools have absolutely no duty to ensure that students are safe during the school day. Schools may have such a duty by virtue of a state's tort or other laws. However, "[s]ection 1983 imposes liability for violations of rights protected by the Constitution, not for violations of duties of care arising out of tort law." *Baker v. McCollan*, 443 U.S. 137, 146, 99 S. Ct. 2689, 61 L. Ed. 2d 433 (1979).

Like our court, each circuit to have addressed the issue has concluded that public schools do not have a special relationship with their students, as public schools do not place the same restraints on students' liberty as do prisons and state mental health institutions. See, e.g., *Hasenfus v. LaJeunesse*, 175 F.3d 68, 69-72 (1st Cir. 1999) (fourteen-year-old student attempted suicide after being sent unsupervised to a locker room); *D.R. v. Middle Bucks Area Vocational Technical Sch.*, 972 F.2d 1364, 1366, 1370-73 (3d Cir. 1992) (en banc) (sixteen-year-old student was sexually assaulted by fellow students in a unisex bathroom and darkroom, both of which were part of a classroom where a teacher was present during the attacks); *Stevenson ex rel. Stevenson v. Martin Cnty. Bd. of Educ.*, 3 F. App'x 25, 27, 30-31 (4th Cir. 2001) (ten-year-old student assaulted by his classmates); *Doe v. Claiborne Cnty., Tenn.*, 103 F.3d 495, 500-01, 509-10 (6th Cir. 1996) (fourteen-year-old student sexually assaulted by an athletic coach off school grounds); *J.O. v. Alton Cmty. Unit Sch. Dist. 11*, 909 F.2d 267, 268, 272-73 (7th Cir. 1990) (teacher sexually molested two "school-age children"); *Dorothy J. v. Little Rock Sch. Dist.*, 7 F.3d 729, 731-34 (8th Cir. 1993) (intellectually disabled high school boy was sexually assaulted by another intellectually disabled student); *Patel v. Kent Sch. Dist.*, 648 F.3d 965, 968-69, 972-74 (9th Cir. 2011) (developmentally disabled high school student was sexually assaulted by a classmate when she was permitted to use restroom alone even though her parents specifically requested that she be under adult supervision at all times due to her disability); *Maldonado v. Josey*, 975 F.2d 727, 728, 729-33 (10th Cir. 1992) (eleven-year-old boy died of accidental strangulation in an unsupervised cloakroom adjacent to his classroom during the school day); *Wyke v. Polk Cnty. Sch. Bd.*, 129 F.3d 560, 563, 568-70 (11th Cir. 1997) (thirteen-year-old boy committed suicide a few days after unsuccessful attempts at school and school officials never told his mother of the attempts).

3. *No Special Relationship Exists Here*

Against this backdrop, and the many decisions to the contrary, the Does (together with our dissenting colleagues) argue that Jane had a special relationship with her school, and therefore a substantive due process interest. They contend that compulsory school attendance laws, combined with Jane's young age and the affirmative act of placing Jane into Keyes's custody (what the Does describe as the Education Defendants' "active, deliberatively indifferent, conduct"), created a special relationship in this case. None of these factors, however, provides a basis to conclude that the school assumed a constitutional duty to protect Jane. Instead, the Does' argument ignores the contours of the special relationship exception to create a cause of action where none exists.

a. Jane's Young Age

The Does (and the dissenters) rely largely upon Jane's young age to distinguish **[*859]** this case from the many others in which we have held that schools have no special relationship with their students. We do not find Jane's age to be a relevant distinguishing characteristic for purposes of the special relationship analysis.[5]

Although it is true that in our prior cases we have dealt with children older than Jane, we have never relied upon the age of the student at issue to resolve the special relationship analysis. Rather, we have said that schools do not have a special relationship with students because "[p]arents remain the primary source for the basic needs of their children." *Hillsboro*, 113 F.3d at 1415. This is as much true

---

5. The Does (and our dissenting colleagues) contort a statement made by the Supreme Court in a wholly different context in *Ingraham v. Wright*, 430 U.S. 651, 97 S. Ct. 1401, 51 L. Ed. 2d 711 (1977), into a suggestion that the Court would find a special relationship in this case. Addressing claims brought by a group of students alleging that corporal punishment in public schools was prohibited by the Eighth Amendment, the Court stated that "[t]he schoolchild has little need for the protections of the Eighth Amendment" because "the public school remains an open institution," and "[e]xcept perhaps when very young, [a] child is not physically restrained from leaving school during school hours." *Id.* at 670. The Court then listed a number of reasons why schools are open institutions. Yet the Court did not suggest that a public school is no less an open institution if a student is restrained from freely leaving the school due to her young age or if a student is apart from teachers or other students, whether on campus or off. Indeed, in an opinion written far more recently than *Ingraham*, the Court explicitly stated in dicta that its opinions should not be read to "suggest that public schools as a general matter have such a degree of control over children as to give rise to a constitutional 'duty to protect.'" *Vernonia Sch. Dist. 47J v. Acton*, 515 U.S. 646, 655, 115 S. Ct. 2386, 132 L. Ed. 2d 564 (1995) (citing *DeShaney*, 489 U.S. at 200).

for elementary students as it is for high school students. No matter the age of the child, parents are the primary providers of food, clothing, shelter, medical care, and reasonable safety for their minor children. Thus, school children are returned to their parents' care at the end of each day, and are able to seek assistance from their families on a daily basis, unlike those who are incarcerated or involuntarily committed.

Jane's immaturity is insufficient to distinguish this case from our decisions in *Walton* and *Hillsboro*. The suggestion that we ought to examine an individual's characteristics to determine whether the state has assumed a duty to care for that person is wholly unsupported by precedent. The situations in which the state assumes a duty of care sufficient to create a special relationship are strictly enumerated and the restrictions of each situation are identical. In the circumstances of incarceration, involuntary institutionalization, and foster care, the state has, through an established set of laws and procedures, rendered the person in its care completely unable to provide for his or her basic needs and it assumes a duty to provide for these needs. Neither the Supreme Court nor this court has ever suggested that anything less than such a total restriction is sufficient to create a special relationship with the state, regardless of the age or competence of the individual. *See DeShaney*, 489 U.S. at 200 ("The affirmative duty to protect arises not from the State's knowledge of the individual's predicament or from its expressions of intent to help him, but from the limitation which it has imposed on his freedom to act on his own behalf.").

Moreover, the focus upon Jane's young age makes an essentially arbitrary distinction between the thirteen- and fourteen-year-old students in *Walton* and *Hillsboro* and nine-year-old students like Jane. If we were to accept this argument, schools [*860] would be required to evaluate the maturity of each student to determine whether the school has a special relationship with that student. Indeed, some students could "age out" of constitutional protection over the course of one academic year. A constitutional duty to protect a student from harm does not depend on the maturity of the student, a factor not in the control of the state. Through their public school systems, states take on the responsibility of educating students, but, no matter the age of the student, public schools simply do not take on the responsibility of providing "food, clothing, shelter, medical care, and reasonable safety" for the students they educate. *See DeShaney*, 489 U.S. at 200.

Particularly instructive on this question is the Ninth Circuit's recent decision in *Patel v. Kent School District*, 648 F.3d 965 (9th Cir. 2011). There, a developmentally disabled student had several sexual encounters with a classmate in a restroom adjacent to her classroom. *Id.* at 968. The student's parents had requested that she remain under adult supervision at all times because her disability prevented her from recognizing dangerous situations and caused her to act inappropriately with others. *Id.* at 968-70. Nevertheless, the student's teacher allowed her to use the restroom alone in order to foster her development. *Id.* at 969. The Ninth Circuit held that compulsory school attendance laws do not create a special relationship between public schools and students that would require schools to protect the students from harm. *Id.* at 973-74. Of particular import to this case, the Ninth Circuit also rejected the student's contention that the school was required to protect against her "special vulnerabilities." *Id.* at 974. The court reasoned that "[i]n the case of a minor child, custody does not exist until the state has so restrained the child's liberty that the parents cannot care for the child's basic needs," and the student's disability did not prevent her parents from caring for her basic needs. *Id.* (citing *DeShaney*, 489 U.S. at 199-201). Under the Ninth Circuit's reasoning, the existence of a special relationship does not depend on the characteristics of the individual. Consistent with *Patel*, we conclude that Jane's young age and immaturity do not provide a basis for finding a special relationship with her school.

Our conclusion that no special relationship exists between nine-year-old Jane and her school is consistent with the decisions of our sister circuits, four of which have addressed cases involving children who were approximately the same age or even younger than Jane. *See Allen v. Susquehanna Twp. Sch. Dist.*, 233 F. App'x 149, 151-53 (3d Cir. 2007) (finding no special relationship between school and developmentally disabled eleven-year-old student who left school grounds and was subsequently killed); *Worthington v. Elmore Cnty. Bd. of Educ.*, 160 F. App'x 877, 878, 881 (11th Cir. 2005) (finding no special relationship between school and developmentally disabled seven-year-old student who was sexually assaulted by another student on a school bus); *Stevenson*, 3 F. App'x at 30-31 (finding no special relationship between school and ten-year-old boy who had been beaten up repeatedly by bullies during the school day); *Maldonado*, 975 F.2d at 728, 731-33 (finding no special relationship between school and eleven-year-old boy who died of accidental strangulation in an unsupervised cloakroom adjacent to his classroom during the school day). While we should have every reason to expect that public schools can and will provide for the safety of public school students, no matter their age, our precedents, and the decisions of every other circuit to have considered this issue, **[*861]** dictate that schools are simply not *constitutionally* required to ensure students' safety from private actors. Despite her young age, Jane was not attending the school through the "affirmative exercise of [state] power," *DeShaney*, 489 U.S. at 200; she was attending the school because her parents voluntarily chose to send her there (as one of several ways to fulfill their compulsory education obligations), and they remained responsible for her basic needs.[6]

---

6. Although it is true that Jane's guardians were less able to protect Jane during the school day, this fact exists to some extent in every alleged special relationship case involving injuries that occurred at school. *See, e.g., Patel*, 648 F.3d at 969-70; *Hasenfus*, 175 F.3d at 70-71; *Middle Bucks*, 972 F.2d at 1366; *Maldonado*, 975 F.2d at 728, 732-33; *see also Stevenson*, 3 F. App'x at 27-28. This fact has never been found to create a special relationship, as the parents remain the primary caregivers, and the child can turn to his or her parents for help on a daily basis. *See Middle Bucks*, 972 F.2d at 1372 ("D.R.'s complaint alleges an ongoing series of assaults and abuse over a period of months. Although these acts allegedly took place during the school day, D.R. could, and did, leave the school building every day. The state did nothing to restrict her liberty after school hours and thus did not deny her meaningful access to sources of help.").

b. Compulsory School Attendance Laws

The Does also suggest that a special relationship exists because Jane's attendance at school was mandated by compulsory attendance laws. We have specifically held, however, that compulsory school attendance laws do not "alone create a special relationship." *Hillsboro Indep. Sch. Dist.*, 113 F.3d at 1415.

There is no indication that Jane's attendance at the school was somehow more compulsory as a nine-year-old than if she were a teenager. While it may be true that elementary school students are subject to more rules during the school day (a fact not pleaded), their attendance at school is no more or less mandatory than teenagers' attendance. In fact, Jane was subject to exactly the same Mississippi compulsory education laws as was the plaintiff in *Walton*, who voluntarily attended a residential school for the deaf. Mississippi requires parents to enroll their children in school until age seventeen, and parents may fulfill this requirement in several ways, only one of which is to send their child to public school. MISS. CODE ANN. § 37-13-91(3) (requiring that parent enroll compulsory school-age child in a public school, a "legitimate nonpublic school," or provide a "legitimate home instruction program"). It may well be true that, for the vast majority of parents in Mississippi, the only way for them to fulfill their obligation is to enroll their children in public school. But that practicality does not alter the fact that Jane's parents voluntarily sent her to the school as a means of fulfilling their obligation to educate her. Jane's parents were free at any time to remove Jane from the school if they felt that her safety was being compromised. This reality is a far cry from the situation of incarcerated prisoners, institutionalized mental health patients, or children placed in foster care. Mississippi's compulsory education law is therefore insufficient under our precedent to create a special relationship between the school and Jane, despite Jane's young age.

c. Release of Jane to Keyes

As a final effort to distinguish this case from the many others in this area, the Does contend that the "active, deliberately indifferent, conduct" of school officials in releasing Jane to Keyes formed a special relationship. The dissent similarly argues that a special relationship was created when the school separated Jane from her [*862] teachers and classmates and delivered her into Keyes' exclusive custody. This argument, however, has several flaws.

Even assuming that the school had custody over Jane to the exclusion of her legal guardians, which it did not, the school did not *knowingly* transfer that custody to an unauthorized individual. The complaint alleges that the school employee releasing Jane committed an affirmative act, but does not assert that the school employee actually knew that Keyes was unauthorized to take Jane from school. Implicit in the Supreme Court's holding that a state may create a special relationship through an "affirmative exercise of its power," *DeShaney*, 489 U.S. at 200, is the requirement that the state actor know that he or she is restricting an individual's liberty. When a state incarcerates a prisoner, institutionalizes a mental health patient, or places a child in foster care, the state knows that it has restricted the individual's liberty and rendered him unable to care for his basic human needs. When a school employee carelessly fails to ensure that an adult is authorized to take an elementary student from the school, no state actor has knowledge that the school has thereby restricted the student's liberty, because the adult taking the student from school may or may not be authorized.

The Does' (and the dissent's) theory also suggests that the same act that creates the special relationship can also violate the duty of care owed to the student. Under the special relationship exception, the state assumes a duty to care for and protect an individual. Once the special relationship is created, it is the failure to fulfill that duty that gives rise to a constitutional violation. An allegation of deliberate indifference may be sufficient to *violate* a constitutional duty, but it is not sufficient to *create* the constitutional duty. Furthermore, this theory suggests that the school's very act of *releasing* Jane into the custody of a private actor somehow created the state custody that is necessary for a *DeShaney* special relationship to exist in the first place. Such a theory is wholly inconsistent with *DeShaney* itself. 489 U.S. at 199-200 ("[W]hen the State takes a person *into its custody* and holds him there against his will, the Constitution imposes upon it a corresponding duty to assume some responsibility for his safety and general well-being.") (emphasis added).

The Tenth Circuit in *Graham v. Independent School District No. I-89*, 22 F.3d 991 (10th Cir. 1994), rejected an argument similar to the one the Does raise here. In that case, Graham brought suit under Section 1983 against a school district after certain students shot and killed her son on school property during the school day.[7] Graham alleged that the school knew that her child was in danger of being harmed, but failed to take appropriate protective measures. *Id.* at 993. The plaintiffs argued that the school's "knowledge of the violent propensities of one of its students . . . coupled with the quasi-custodial nature of school attendance, satisfies the standards articulated in *DeShaney*." *Id.* at 994. The court rejected this argument, holding that "foreseeability cannot create an affirmative duty to protect when plaintiff remains unable to allege a custodial relationship." *Id.* The court concluded:

> [i]naction by the state in the face of a known danger is not enough to trigger the obligation; according to *DeShaney* the state must have limited in some way **[*863]** the liberty of a citizen to act on his own behalf. In the absence of a custodial relationship, we believe plaintiffs cannot state a constitutional claim based upon the defendants' alleged knowledge of dangerous circumstances.

Id. at 995 (citation and internal quotation marks omitted). Thus, the state's failure to protect the student from private harm (even if foreseeable) did not give rise to a constitutional claim in the absence of a finding that a custodial relationship already existed.

---

7. The appeal was considered jointly with another suit, which was brought by the mother of a student who was stabbed on school premises. *Graham*, 22 F.3d at 993.

The Does point us to no distinguishing characteristics of this case that are sufficient to give rise to a *DeShaney* special relationship between Jane and her school. This case is ultimately no different than *Walton* and *Hillsboro*, and thus requires the same outcome.

4. Conclusion

The question posed to us is whether Jane's school, through its affirmative exercise of state power, assumed a *constitutional* duty to protect Jane from a private actor. We are compelled by our precedent, and by the Supreme Court's guidance in *DeShaney*, to conclude that the school did not assume that duty. The district court correctly held that the Does have failed to state a claim under § 1983 for a constitutional violation under the special relationship exception.

Because we find no special relationship, we do not address whether the school's alleged actions in releasing Jane to Keyes amounted to "deliberate indifference." As this en banc court previously explained in *McClendon v. City of Columbia*, 305 F.3d 314 (5th Cir. 2002), only where a state first creates a special relationship with an individual does the state then have "a constitutional duty to protect that individual from dangers, including, in certain circumstances, private violence." *Id.* at 324; *see also Walton*, 44 F.3d at 1300-01 (explaining that if a state creates a special relationship with an individual, it will then owe "some duty—arising under the Due Process Clause of the Fourteenth Amendment to the United States Constitution—to protect [the individual's] bodily integrity from third party non-state actors."). Without a special relationship, the school had no constitutional duty to protect Jane from private actors such as Keyes, and the question of its alleged deliberate indifference is simply immaterial.

Having concluded that the school had no special relationship with Jane that imposed on the school a constitutional duty to protect her from private harm, we now turn to the Does' remaining theories of liability.

B. State-Created Danger

The Does argue that they have stated a viable constitutional claim under the so-called "state-created" danger theory of liability. We find no such viable claim.

After *DeShaney*, many circuits[8] used the following language in the Court's opinion to provide an alternative basis for § 1983 liability for harm inflicted by private actors:

> While the State may have been aware of the dangers that Joshua faced in the free world, *it played no part in their creation, nor did it do anything to render*

---

8. *See, e.g., Lombardi v. Whitman*, 485 F.3d 73, 80 (2d Cir. 2007); *Kneipp v. Tedder*, 95 F.3d 1199, 1211 (3d Cir. 1996); *Kallstrom v. City of Columbus*, 136 F.3d 1055, 1066-67 (6th Cir. 1998); *Jackson v. Indian Prairie Sch. Dist. 204*, 653 F.3d 647, 654 (7th Cir. 2011); *Carlton v. Cleburne Cnty.*, 93 F.3d 505, 508 (8th Cir. 1996); *Wood v. Ostrander*, 879 F.2d 583, 589-90 (9th Cir. 1989); *Uhlrig v. Harder*, 64 F.3d 567, 572-73 (10th Cir. 1995).

him any more vulnerable to them. That the State once took temporary custody [*864] of Joshua does not alter the analysis, for when it returned him to his father's custody, *it placed him in no worse position than that in which he would have been had it not acted at all* . . . .

DeShaney, 489 U.S. at 201 (emphases added). Under the state-created danger theory, a state actor may be liable under § 1983 if the state actor created or knew of a dangerous situation and affirmatively placed the plaintiff in that situation. *See, e.g., Carlton v. Cleburne Cnty.*, 93 F.3d 505, 508 (8th Cir. 1996) ("In [the state-created danger] cases the courts have uniformly held that state actors may be liable if they affirmatively created the plaintiffs' peril or acted to render them more vulnerable to danger. In other words, the individuals would not have been in harm's way but for the government's affirmative actions.") (citation omitted). In *Wood v. Ostrander*, 879 F.2d 583, 586 (9th Cir. 1989), the Ninth Circuit adopted the state-created danger theory in the context of a § 1983 claim brought against police officers by the passenger of an impounded vehicle, who was raped after officers abandoned her on the side of a road in a high crime area in the early morning hours. *Id.* at 586, 588-90. Similarly, in *Kneipp v. Tedder*, 95 F.3d 1199 (3d Cir. 1996), the Third Circuit adopted the state-created danger theory in the context of a lawsuit brought against a city and several police officers on behalf of a woman who suffered extensive brain damage when the officers allegedly sent her home "unescorted in a seriously intoxicated state in cold weather." *Id.* at 1208-09.[9]

Unlike many of our sister circuits, we have never explicitly adopted the state-created danger theory. *See, e.g., McClendon*, 305 F.3d at 325. The district court in this case acknowledged our precedent, but held that even if the theory were recognized, the Does had failed to plead facts that would amount to a constitutional violation. The court held that the Does did not contend that the Education Defendants knew that their policy would allow Jane to be checked out of school by an unauthorized adult and sexually assaulted; therefore, the Does had not alleged that the Defendants were deliberately indifferent to a known danger.

---

9. Our sister circuits have since set out various multi-factor tests related to the state-created danger theory. The Seventh Circuit, for example, has developed a three-part test. *See Jackson*, 653 F.3d at 654 ("To establish a substantive due process claim under a state-created danger theory, [the plaintiff] must demonstrate that: (1) the district, by its affirmative acts, created or increased a danger that [the plaintiff] faced; (2) the district's failure to protect [the plaintiff] from danger was the proximate cause of her injuries; and (3) the district's failure to protect her 'shocks the conscience.'"). The Sixth Circuit has laid out a similar three-factor test. *See Estate of Smithers ex rel. Norris v. City of Flint*, 602 F.3d 758, 763 (6th Cir. 2010) ("A state-created danger claim has three elements: (1) an affirmative act by the state which either created or increased the risk that the plaintiff would be exposed to an act of violence by a third party; (2) a special danger to the plaintiff wherein the state's actions placed the plaintiff specifically at risk, as distinguished from a risk that affects the public at large; and (3) the state knew or should have known that its actions specifically endangered the plaintiff.").

The Does contend that this circuit has in fact adopted and applied the state-created danger theory in light of our decisions in *Scanlan v. Texas A&M University*, 343 F.3d 533 (5th Cir. 2003), and *Breen v. Texas A&M University*, 485 F.3d 325 (5th Cir. 2007), which arose out of the 1999 bonfire collapse at Texas A&M University. In *Scanlan*, the panel considered the allegations and stated that the "district court should have concluded that the plaintiffs stated a section 1983 claim under the [*865] state-created danger theory." 343 F.3d at 538. Despite this statement, subsequent panels have concluded that *Scanlan* did not in fact adopt the state-created danger theory. In *Rivera v. Houston Independent School District*, 349 F.3d 244 (5th Cir. 2003), for example, we explained that while *Scanlan* remanded the "case to the district court for further proceedings, [it] did not recognize the state created danger theory." *Id.* at 249 n.5; *see also Rios v. City of Del Rio, Tex.*, 444 F.3d 417, 422-23 (5th Cir. 2006) ("*[N]owhere* in the [*Scanlan*] opinion does the court expressly purport to adopt or approve th[e] [state-created danger] theory."). This understanding was complicated somewhat by our decision in *Breen*, where a panel of this court again interpreted *Scanlan*. 485 F.3d at 336. The *Breen* panel concluded that "[t]he *Scanlan* panel's clearly implied recognition of state-created danger as a valid legal theory applicable to the case is the law of the case with respect to these further appeals in these same cases now before this panel." *Id.* The panel, however, subsequently withdrew this portion of the opinion. *Breen v. Texas A&M Univ.*, 494 F.3d 516, 518 (5th Cir. 2007). Despite the potential confusion created by *Scanlan* and *Breen*, recent decisions have consistently confirmed that "[t]he Fifth Circuit has not adopted the 'state-created danger' theory of liability." *Kovacic v. Villarreal*, 628 F.3d 209, 214 (5th Cir. 2010); *see also Bustos v. Martini Club, Inc.*, 599 F.3d 458, 466 (5th Cir. 2010) ("[T]his circuit has not adopted the state-created danger theory.").

We decline to use this en banc opportunity to adopt the state-created danger theory in this case because the allegations would not support such a theory. Although we have not recognized the theory, we have stated the elements that such a cause of action would require. The *Scanlan* panel explained that the state-created danger theory requires "a plaintiff [to] show [1] the defendants used their authority to create a dangerous environment for the plaintiff and [2] that the defendants acted with deliberate indifference to the plight of the plaintiff." *Scanlan*, 343 F.3d at 537-38. To establish deliberate indifference for purposes of state-created danger, the plaintiff must show that "[t]he environment created by the state actors must be dangerous; they must know it is dangerous; and . . . they must have used their authority to create an opportunity that would not otherwise have existed for the third party's crime to occur." *Piotrowski v. City of Houston*, 237 F.3d 567, 585 (5th Cir. 2001) (citation and internal quotation marks omitted); *see also McClendon*, 305 F.3d at 326 n.8 ("To act with deliberate indifference, a state actor must know of and disregard an excessive risk to the victim's health or safety.") (internal quotation marks and alterations omitted). Critically, this court has explained that the "state-created danger theory is inapposite without a known victim." *Rios*, 444 F.3d at 424 (citation and internal quotation marks omitted); *see also Lester v. City of Coll. Station*, 103 F. App'x 814, 815-16 (5th Cir. 2004) ("[E]ven if it is assumed that the state-created-danger theory applies, liability exists only if the state actor is aware of an *immediate danger facing a known victim.*") (citing *Saenz v. Heldenfels Bros., Inc.*, 183 F.3d 389, 392 (5th Cir. 1999)) (emphasis added).

In support of their state-created danger claim, the Does allege that school officials "received complaints and inquiries and/or had internal discussions and safety meetings concerning checkout policies and procedures and access to students under their care and control by unauthorized individuals," and they therefore "had actual knowledge of the dangers created by their policies, customs and regulations, but they [*866] failed to take corrective action to reduce or prevent the danger." According to the Does, the school's failure to adopt a stricter policy amounted to "deliberate indifference." Nevertheless, the Does' allegations cannot make out a state-created danger claim, as they do not demonstrate the existence of "an immediate danger facing a known victim." *Saenz*, 183 F.3d at 392. At most, the Does allege that the school was aware of some general deficiencies in the check-out policy. They do *not* allege that the school knew about an immediate danger to Jane's safety, nor can the court infer such knowledge from the pleadings. Without such allegations, even if we were to embrace the state-created danger theory, the claim would necessarily fail.

We have consistently cautioned against finding liability under the state-created danger theory based upon an ineffective policy or practice in cases where the plaintiff's injury is inflicted by a private actor. In *Rivera v. Houston Independent School District*, for example, we rejected a state-created danger claim against a school after a student died as a result of gang-related violence, and explained:

> [T]o hold HISD responsible for the ultimate ineffectiveness of [its policies designed to combat gang violence] would turn the Due Process Clause's limited duty of care and protection into a guarantee of shelter from private violence. This result would be inimical to the Supreme Court's conclusion [in *DeShaney*] that the Due Process Clause does not require the State to protect individuals from private violence.

349 F.3d at 250; *see also Doe v. Hillsboro Indep. Sch. Dist.*, 113 F.3d 1412, 1415 (5th Cir. 1997) (finding no viable state-created danger claim in case where student was raped by a school custodian with no known criminal history, and explaining that a "post hoc attribution of known danger would turn inside out this limited exception to the principle of no duty"). We conclude that the Does' allegations do not support a claim under the state-created danger theory, even if that theory were viable in this circuit.

IV. CONCLUSION

In affirming the dismissal of the Does' complaint, we do not suggest that schools have no obligation to insure that their [*870] students remain safe from acts of private violence. State law provides the appropriate legal framework to address Jane's injury. The question we have addressed is simply whether the school's failure to check Keyes's identity and be certain that he was authorized to take Jane amounted to a *constitutional* violation. Supreme Court precedent, our precedent, and the decisions of every other circuit to address the special relationship exception compel this court to conclude that it does not. In addition, neither the state-created danger theory nor municipal liability provides a viable basis for recovery.

For these reasons, the judgment of the district court is AFFIRMED.

Concur by: E. Grady Jolly; Higginson

Concur

E. GRADY JOLLY, Circuit Judge, specially concurring:

I fully concur with the thorough and comprehensive opinion of Judge King. I specially concur, however, to underline the stubborn fact that the issue of whether a special relationship can be created between a school and its students has been before the en banc court three times and three times we have said the same thing. As this en banc court makes clear, the other two en banc cases, *Walton v. Alexander*, 44 F.3d 1297 (5th Cir. 1995) (en banc), and *Doe v. Hillsboro Independent School District*, 113 F.3d 1412 (5th Cir. 1997) (en banc), were not only fully consistent with one another—and their authority undiminished before this en banc court occurred—but now the combined authority of all three en banc cases affirms and makes unambiguous the rule of this court to be: We "strictly" construe *DeShaney v. Winnebago County Department of Social Services*, 489 U.S. 189, 199-200, 109 S. Ct. 998, 103 L. Ed. 2d 249 (1989), to hold that, "only when the state, by its affirmative exercise of power, has custody over an individual *involuntarily or against his will*, does a 'special relationship' exist between the individual and the state." *Walton*, 44 F.3d at 1303 (emphasis in original). *Walton* and *Hillsboro* are not just clear, they are emphatically clear that a special relationship under *DeShaney* "only arises" between the state and an individual when the individual "is involuntarily confined or otherwise restrained against his will pursuant to a governmental order or by the affirmative exercise of state power"; it "does not arise solely because the state exercises custodial control over an individual." *Id.* at 1299. When a person claiming the right of state protection is voluntarily within the care or custody of a state agency, such as a schoolchild who voluntarily subjects himself or herself "to the rules and supervision of [] School officials," any "willful relinquishment of a small fraction of liberty simply is *not comparable* to that measure of almost *total deprivation* experienced by a prisoner or involuntarily committed mental patient." *Id.* at 1305 (emphasis added). Expanding state liability for the acts of private persons can make constitutional sense only if the state has "effectively taken the plaintiff's liberty under terms that provide no realistic means of voluntarily terminating the state's custody *and* which thus deprives the plaintiff of the ability or opportunity to provide for his own care and safety." *Id.* (emphasis in original).

There is no room—not an inch—for confusion. The law yesterday and today is bare and bald: No *DeShaney* special relationship exists between a public school and its students. Absent a special relationship, any analysis of the defendant's conduct as deliberately indifferent to the rights of the student is, under *DeShaney*, irrelevant.

No further panel of this court should require us to iterate these clear statements of the law a fourth time.

[*871] HIGGINSON, Circuit Judge, concurring in the judgment:

Dicta in *DeShaney v. Winnebago Cnty. Dep't of Soc. Servs.*, 489 U.S. 189, 109 S. Ct. 998, 103 L. Ed. 2d 249 (1989), has contributed to twenty-three years of circuit (and intra-circuit) disharmony, and excited legions of law review articles, about whether the Constitution asserts positive or negative liberties, or regulates government action or inaction—all giving uncertain guidance to litigants and courts, as well as public officials, hence necessarily also giving uncertain relief to citizens whom government persons cause to be subjected to injury.

In this case, a plaintiff-father and his minor child Jane Doe ("Jane"), and others, complain that Jane was injured when unknown government actors (designated "EDUCATION DEFENDANTS A-Z"), among others, released her from public elementary school to an adult male ("Tommy Keyes"), who bore no relation to her and was not listed on her check-out form, who then raped her and returned her each time to school.

The district court dismissed this complaint as one that fails to state a legally cognizable claim. Our court today affirms that dismissal based on extensive, but nearly exclusive, discussion of the "special relationship" extra-statutory theory of liability adverted to by the Supreme Court in *DeShaney*. Although I agree that the enlargement of liability beyond Section 1983's literal requirements contemplated by the "special relationship" test is not a basis for liability in this case, I write separately to redirect inquiry back to Congress's exact language.

Section 1983 has a pedigree older than the harms it was found not to cover in *DeShaney*. Passed in 1871, Section 1983 reads:

> Every person who, under color of [law] . . . subjects, or causes to be subjected, any citizen of the United States or other person within the jurisdiction thereof to the deprivation of any rights, privileges, or immunities secured by the Constitution and laws, shall be liable to the party injured in an action at law, suit in equity, or other proper proceeding for redress . . . .

42 U.S.C. § 1983.

Set against this statutory language, the instant complaint makes a conclusory, and I ultimately conclude not facially cognizable, claim. Plaintiffs do not complain that government persons subjected Jane to rape, but they come close to complaining that government persons *caused her to be subjected* to rape. If the complaint had asserted that the affirmative act of releasing Jane to Keyes was a causal act of recklessness or deliberate indifference or intentionality that caused her to be subjected to injury, and specifically to the deprivation of her right to bodily integrity, the complaint properly would proceed through discovery to trial.

The Supreme Court considered similar challenged government action in *Martinez v. California*, 444 U.S. 277, 100 S. Ct. 553, 62 L. Ed. 2d 481 (1980), nine years before *DeShaney*. In *Martinez*, the Court assessed a complaint filed against parole officials who had released a parolee who, five months later, tortured and killed a child. The Court explained that, "[a]lthough the decision to release Thomas from prison was action by the State, the action of Thomas five months later cannot be fairly characterized as state action" depriving the decedent of her right to life protected by the Fourteenth Amendment. *Id.* at 284-85. The Court further elaborated that:

> We need not and do not decide that a parole officer could never be deemed to [*872] "deprive" someone of life by action taken in connection with the release of a prisoner on parole. But we do hold that at least under the particular circumstances of this parole decision, appellants' decedent's death is too remote a consequence of the parole officers' [release] action to hold them responsible under the federal civil rights law.

Id. at 285. Jane was raped on numerous school days, each time after she was released to her assailant, whereafter he returned her to complete her school day. On the day of Keyes' final rape, January 8, 2008, Jane was released despite the fact that to check her out of school Keyes allegedly "stated that *he* was the minor's *mother*" (emphasis added).

It may well be that a jury would conclude that an assault on the same day as a government release is too remote for causal attribution, if not in time then in location or circumstance. And a jury might always conclude that no more than negligent conduct was present, however tragic. *See Davidson v. Cannon*, 474 U.S. 344, 347, 106 S. Ct. 668, 88 L. Ed. 2d 677 (1986). But if a jury, not us, were to come to such conclusions, then we, as government persons, are not immunizing other government persons, here state public school officials, against accountability for their affirmative act of releasing Jane from school under whatever complicating, aggravating, or mitigating release circumstances might be developed through discovery and at trial. This assignment of decision-making responsibility to assess, check, or overlook government action as a cause-in-fact of an injury, and specifically a deprivation of a constitutionally protected right, is consistent with the choice made by electors who, through Congress in 1871, established that a cause of action exists when a government officer "causes to be subjected" a person to a "deprivation of any right[] . . . secured by the Constitution . . . ."

To the extent that our court contemplates this "causes to be subjected" statutory language before turning to *DeShaney*, it is in a footnote reference to our decision in *Doe v. Taylor Indep. Sch. Dist.*, 15 F.3d 443 (5th Cir. 1994) (en banc), which recognized a constitutional right to bodily integrity "vouchsafed by the Fourteenth Amendment" against state action. The court today infers from that important truism that "*Taylor* is inapplicable here because the *actual violation* of Jane's bodily integrity was caused by Keyes, a non-state actor" (emphasis added). But that conclusion substitutes this court for a jury in deciding one of three interrelated elements of Section 1983: (1) state action, as (2) the cause-in-fact of (3) a deprivation of right protected by the Constitution.[1] The conclusion also either constricts the statute—and government accountability for wrongdoing—from cases where a government person causes a victim "to be subjected" to a violation, just to cases where the government person "subjects" the victim to the actual violation, or constricts even more by rewriting the statute to [*873] make liable only government persons who actually "depriv[e]" others of rights secured by the Constitution.

Section 1983, as well as its historical moment and purpose, and as implied by the Supreme Court in *Martinez*, does not perceive only a divisible and binary world of government or non-government rights violations. Instead, these difficult cases arise often out of a grey zone where a government person's alleged recklessness or deliberate indifference or intentionality is inextricably intertwined with a not-remote injury allegedly inflicted by a third person, the first (government person) causing the citizen to be subjected to injury by the second (non-government) assailant. *See, e.g., Wood v. Ostrander*, 879 F.2d 583, 589-90 (9th Cir. 1989) (holding that a Section 1983 claim was triable when police arrested driver and impounded vehicle, leaving passenger alone in a high crime area at 2:30 a.m. who then was raped); *Reed v. Gardner*, 986 F.2d 1122, 1126-27 (7th Cir. 1993) (holding that a Section 1983 claim was triable when police arrested and removed driver but left drunk passenger with keys who then drove off and killed and injured individuals in another car in a head-on collision).

I do not think that this court would argue, for example, that an intentional and knowing release by a government person to a self-proclaimed rapist would immunize the releaser from liability simply because the violation physically was inflicted by another. Perhaps there even would be little disagreement about permitting a Section 1983 complaint to proceed to discovery and trial if the complaint alleged that Keyes had had a no-contact order excluding him from Jane's "check-out list," coupled with a school policy that mandated identity verification against that check-out list, yet a government person intentionally or

---

1. In any Section 1983 complaint, the challenged conduct must be conduct taken under color of state law because, as the Supreme Court held in *United States v. Cruikshank*, 92 U.S. 542, 544, 23 L. Ed. 588 (1885), when purely private conduct causes injury, the Fourteenth Amendment is not implicated. Here, therefore, what is challenged is the government's conduct releasing Jane. Whether that government conduct is too remote from the child's injury, in turn, is the statutory question of causation which, under *Martinez*, I contend can and should generally be resolved by a jury, *see Johnson v. Greer*, 477 F.2d 101, 105-08 (5th Cir. 1973), with the *DeShaney* proviso that government inaction—a failure to protect—may alone be actionable, hence causal pursuant to Section 1983, in the unique context of government-ordered custody.

recklessly or with deliberate indifference still released Jane to Keyes who immediately raped her.

I write separately, therefore, to affirm and clarify that citizens gain the protection that they have given themselves, through Congress, against government persons who cause them to be subjected to deprivations which the Constitution and laws disallow. Section 1983 was passed in a time when this was a real and specific threat. Today, these "silver platter" or grey zone cases thankfully are rare, yet government persons, intentionally or recklessly or through deliberate indifference, must know they will be held blameful if they cause a citizen to be subjected to a rights deprivation even if the "actual violation" is inflicted by a third person, as would be true if, for example, a sheriff released a prisoner to a vengeful lynch mob.

To the extent that this statutory validation has added constitutional importance, beyond checking government wrongdoing, it is that it assigns to jury resolution difficult grey zone questions about state action and causality when the challenged government conduct combines in time and circumstance with third party activity to cause a constitutional injury. See *Johnson v. Greer*, 477 F.2d at 105-08; *Anderson v. Nosser*, 456 F.2d 835, 841 (5th Cir. 1972) (en banc).

I do not mean to imply that *DeShaney*'s "special relationship" theory has no relevance. I ultimately conclude, concurring with the court, that the thrust of the plaintiffs' complaint alleges that the depriving act was the government's "failure to protect" Jane because of its discretionary identification check-out policy. To that extent, I agree that compulsory education laws did not force Jane into a custodial setting with Keyes so that her injury is attributable to school persons because of their policy failure to better protect children [*874] being released from school. The Supreme Court implied such extra-statutory, all-encompassing "special relationship" liability when the challenged government conduct is inactivity—so untethered by Section 1983's cause-in-fact element—only in the unique, double-confining setting of government-controlled custody which gives opportunity to aggressor-inmates and denies opportunities for self-defense to inmate-victims. Whereas post-*DeShaney* "special relationship" doctrine reads into the Fourteenth Amendment, at least for purposes of Section 1983 liability, a duty of protection when government-ordered custody makes self-help impractical or impossible, looking only at the victim and the victim's relationship to the government invites anguishing comparisons between whether a foster child is more or less helpless than a schoolchild, see *Griffith v. Johnston*, 899 F.2d 1427, 1439 (5th Cir. 1990) (extending "special relationship" theory of liability to placement of children in foster care), as well as unanswerable questions of moral duty and the perils of indifference. It may well be that nine-year-old Jane, like Joshua DeShaney, was no less helpless than an adult prison inmate, but for Section 1983 to make actionable government inaction, under the *DeShaney* "special relationship" theory, liability should attach only when the government has complete physical control of victims *and* their aggressors, as in prison, but unlike in schools or foster home circumstances.

The literal language approach, if persuasive to others, might also tighten *DeShaney* helpfully in a second sense. Every other court of appeals to have considered the issue, except us, has embraced the expanded claim of liability termed "state-created danger," which also derives from dicta in *DeShaney*. We have avoided this second judicial enlargement of liability presumably because its loose articulation (shielding persons from "perils" and "vulnerabilities" and "harm's way" said to be "created by" government action), like the "special relationship" theory, also was not the result of the lawmaking process. Moreover, the existence of this ill-defined notion of government liability has provided a leaky bucket for the grey zone cases that properly should go to a jury as to state action and causation without any extra-statutory gloss which courts conjure. *See* Maj. Op. at 22 n.9 (listing complexity of "various multi-factor tests related to the state created danger theory"). Indeed, our court in this case highlights, in part, the confusion, stating, alternatively, that, "[w]e decline to use this en banc opportunity to adopt the state-created danger theory in this case because the allegations would not support such a theory." The court goes on to write that, "we have stated the elements that such a cause of action would require," and then quotes a medley of non-statutory "factors," that include, but are not limited to, government creation of "'a dangerous environment,'" government "'deliberate indifference to the plight of the plaintiff,'" a "'third party's crime,'" a known and disregarded "'excessive risk to the victim's health or safety,'" and government "'*aware*[*ness*] of an immediate danger facing a known victim.'" The instant allegations then are said not to "support such a theory." It is unsurprising that no Section 1983 litigant in this circuit ever has been able to support such a theory.

To summarize, Section 1983 should be construed literally. Literal application of Section 1983 would narrow only to government custody the *DeShaney* "special relationship" theory of actionable inaction, as explicitly stated by the late Chief Justice Rehnquist, and literal application of Section 1983 would reduce only to statutory elements the amorphous "state-created [*875] danger" theory we have not endorsed. At the same time, literal application of Section 1983 would (1) acknowledge that the statute protects not just against government persons who subject citizens to a constitutional deprivation but also against government persons who cause citizens to be subjected to such deprivations; (2) avoid government persons (courts) from immunizing other government persons (state or local officials) from liability for wrongdoing which electors, through Congress, have made actionable and which non-government persons (jurors) should resolve; and (3) would apply Section 1983's syntax to comprehend the rare but tragic set of grey zone cases where government persons, intentionally or recklessly or through deliberate indifference, cause, consistent with *Martinez*, a victim to be subjected by a third person to a rights deprivation.

Having made the above statutory observation—urging narrowed liability on extra-statutory theories emanating from dicta in *DeShaney*, but recognizing liability for government persons who non-negligently cause in time and circumstance citizens to be subjected to constitutional injury actually inflicted by others—I nonetheless conclude that the instant complaint, put alongside the plain language of Section 1983, is not congruent enough to survive summary dismissal. Instead of setting forth a facially plausible charge of government recklessness or indifference or intentionality in the release of Jane that caused her to be subjected to her injury, the complaint's preliminary statement (paragraph 1), statement of facts (paragraphs 2-7), and above all its "[b]ut for" allegation in its "action for deprivation of civil rights" (paragraphs 20-25), focus exclusively on the opposite, namely the education defendants' alleged policy of inaction, giving school officials who check out children discretion to verify or not to verify the identification of receiving adults. That contention describes liability non-causally, which is the extra-statutory theory of liability recognized by the Supreme Court to apply only in custodial settings.

For the above reasons, I concur in the judgment of the court.

Dissent by: Wiener

Dissent

WIENER, Circuit Judge, joined by DENNIS, Circuit Judge, dissenting.

Like the law of nature, the law of man recognizes no more basic or extensive "special relationship" than that between parents and their "very young" children. Central to that relationship is the parents' exclusive right to the custody of their children and the concomitant duty to protect them. It must follow that when a state mandates that parents delegate the custody of their child to a state agency, subdivision, or municipality, such total delegation creates a special relationship between the delegatee and the child in its custody—at least when such child is "very young"—and imposes on such custodial state delegatee a duty to protect that child from violations of her constitutional rights. I am convinced that the parents' custodial delegatee here—the Covington County Elementary School ("the School")—cannot be permitted to evade its duty to protect its very young pupils while they are in its exclusive custody.

As is apparent from the Does' *Iqbal/Twombly*-compliant[1] complaint and the majority opinion, this case involves repeated decisions and acts by the School's officials to temporarily sub-delegate its exclusive custody of a nine-year-old fourth-grade girl, in the middle of six different school days, over a span of four months, to [*876] an unidentified adult, who was not authorized under the School's express policy to check her out, and whose identity it did not even attempt to verify. On each of those six occasions, that adult, Tommy Keyes, proceeded to brutally rape the little girl, Jane Doe, and then return her to the custody of the School—still during the course of the school day. This was no isolated or

---

1. *Ashcroft v. Iqbal*, 556 U.S. 662, 129 S. Ct. 1937, 173 L. Ed. 2d 868 (2009); *Bell Atl. Corp. v. Twombly*, 550 U.S. 544, 127 S. Ct. 1955, 167 L. Ed. 2d 929 (2007).

anecdotal incident, and the School's officials allegedly contributed to its recurrence by failing, each time, to verify Keyes's identity and his lack of authorization.

Despite our standard of review of dismissal of actions at their initial (Rule 12(b)(6)) stage, the majority raises the stakes of this appeal by not limiting its analysis to the Does' complaint, but instead asserting categorically that public schools have no *DeShaney* special relationship[2] with, and thus no constitutional duty to protect, any schoolchildren—not even the very young—from non-state actors. Thus, I address (1) whether a public school can *ever* have a constitutional duty to protect any subset of children in its care, (2) whether the Does adequately pleaded facts that would support such a duty, and (3) whether School officials violated that duty through their deliberate indifference to Jane's constitutional rights. Ultimately, I answer these questions in the affirmative. Assuming, as we must at this initial, pleadings stage of the proceedings, that the factual allegations of the Does' complaint are correct, I conclude that the School's actions constitute a serious derogation of the State's constitutional duty to protect a helpless individual while in its exclusive custody and care. Because I remain convinced that the majority's conclusion that the State had no such constitutional duty is contrary to both law and common sense, I respectfully but strenuously dissent.

I. SPECIAL RELATIONSHIP

The substantive component of the Due Process Clause of the Fourteenth Amendment protects individuals from state action that "shocks the conscience."[3] Although substantive Due Process does not generally protect individuals from private actors, the Supreme Court stated in *DeShaney* that there is an exception, and that the State does owe an individual a duty of protection when a special relationship exists between the State and the individual:

> [W]hen the State takes a person into its custody and holds him there against his will, the Constitution imposes upon it a corresponding duty to assume some responsibility for his safety and general well-being. . . . The rationale for this principle is simple enough: when the State by the affirmative exercise of its power so restrains an individual's liberty that it renders him unable to care for himself, and at the same time fails to provide for his basic human needs—e.g., food, clothing, shelter, medical care, and *reasonable safety*—it transgresses the substantive limits on state action set by the Eighth Amendment and the Due Process Clause.[4]

In this case, Jane attended a public elementary school in Mississippi, where attendance is compulsory[5] and where all the **[*877]** relevant events took place

---

2. *DeShaney v. Winnebago County Dept. of Social Services*, 489 U.S. 189, 199-200, 109 S. Ct. 998, 103 L. Ed. 2d 249 (1989).
3. *Rochin v. California*, 342 U.S. 165, 172, 72 S. Ct. 205, 96 L. Ed. 183 (1952).
4. *DeShaney*, 489 U.S. at 199-200 (citation omitted; emphasis added).
5. *See* Miss. Code Ann. § 37-13-91(3) (school attendance generally compulsory for children between the ages of six and seventeen).

during the school day, not at its end.[6] None disputes that more than compulsory public education is required to establish a special relationship between the State and a student, but this does not justify taking the leap of logic needed to reach the conclusion that a special relationship can *never* exist in the public school setting. When, in *Doe v. Hillsboro Independent School District*, we held that *alone* compulsory attendance does not create a special relationship between a state and a presumably pubescent, thirteen-year-old middle-school student, we quoted the following general explanation from the Supreme Court's decision in *Ingraham v. Wright* as to why public schools are distinguishable from, e.g., prisons and mental institutions:

> Though attendance may not always be voluntary, the public school remains an open institution. *Except perhaps when very young*, the child is not physically restrained from leaving school during school hours; and *at the end of the school day*, the child is invariably free to return home. Even while at school, the child brings with him the support of family and friends and is *rarely apart* from teachers and other pupils who may witness and protest any instances of mistreatment.[7]

Ingraham's latent exception for the "very young" public school attendee is finally before us, in the Does' complaint, for the first time.

The majority attempts to distinguish *Ingraham* based on that case's concern with the application of the Eighth Amendment to corporal punishment in public schools, but our decision in *Hillsboro* expressly recognized the obvious relevance of *Ingraham*'s analysis to the special relationship inquiry. Compounding the majority opinion's error in making this purported distinction, it strangely declares that the Supreme Court's reasoning does "not suggest that a public school is no less an open institution if a student is restrained from freely leaving the school due to her young age or if a student is apart from teachers or other students, whether on campus or off."[8] In fact, though, that is precisely what the Supreme Court's analysis suggests.

Specifically, the *Ingraham* exception can only mean that there may very well be a special relationship between a public school and a student who (1) is "very young," (2) is "physically restrained" by (and unable to leave freely) the school's custody, and (3) is isolated or kept "apart from teachers and other pupils who may witness and protest any instances of mistreatment"—as is precisely alleged here. Rather than superficially distinguishing what the Supreme Court has said—even in dicta—we should apply it, as I shall now attempt to do.

---

6. *Contra Doe v. Hillsboro Indep. School Dist.*, 113 F.3d 1412, 1414 (5th Cir. 1997) (no special relationship when student was raped after school hours).
7. 113 F.3d 1412, 1415 (5th Cir. 1997) (quoting *Ingraham v. Wright*, 430 U.S. 651, 670, 97 S. Ct. 1401, 51 L. Ed. 2d 711 (1977) (emphasis added)).
8. *See supra*, En Banc Majority Opinion at 13, note 5.

A. Jane Was of Such a Very Young Age That She Could Not Protect Herself

When Jane was repeatedly checked out of school and brutally raped, she was a very young, pre-pubescent, nine-year-old, fourth-grade girl. The majority refuses to acknowledge the obvious: that the degree of control exercised by a de jure and de facto custodian over very young children is [*878] necessarily much greater and more pervasive than over post-puberty teenagers or adults. The majority does not even acknowledge that the Does might be able to establish as much if given the opportunity to adduce evidence, especially expert reports and testimony. But expert testimony is not required to know that very young children like Jane are virtually never capable of protesting or challenging adult authority figures, particularly those whose authority is apparently endorsed by the very persons or institutions that such children trust.[9] Neither are such youngsters generally able to recognize and respond to subtle threats to their safety, which is the prime reason why they, unlike older students, are never permitted to leave school grounds by themselves. The defendants in this case do not assert that the School had a unique policy of allowing very young, fourth-grade students to come and go without restraint; indeed, the School's adoption of a formal check-out policy confirms that just the opposite is true. Add to this truism the two-step factual allegations of the Does' complaint that Jane was *first* taken from her class (and thus separated from the very teacher and classmates who, under *Ingraham*, were her support) and, *second*, turned over to Keyes outside the ken of these putative supporters, and the flaw in the majority's logic becomes all the more apparent. In such isolation, a very young child like Jane could hardly have stood up for herself in light of the actions taken by School officials.

Under the majority's analysis, the age of the schoolchild is categorically irrelevant to the special relationship inquiry: "No matter the age of the child, parents are the primary providers of food, clothing, shelter, medical care, and reasonable safety for their minor children"; and children return home at the end of each school day.[10] But neither the majority nor any decision it cites explains how or why parents' care of children *before and after* the school day can or should preclude the existence of a special relationship *during* school hours.[11] Although Jane's parents were presumably able to provide her with food, clothing, and protection before she left home in the morning and after she returned home at the end of each

---

9. *See A. v. Laredo Indep. School Dist.*, No. 5:05-cv-237, 2007 U.S. Dist. LEXIS 4445, 2007 WL 189458, at *4 (S.D. Tex. Jan. 22, 2007) ("The notion that a seven year-old child can be expected to assert his liberties in the face of institutional authority is questionable to say the least.... One may intuitively conclude that this reality gives rise to a commensurate supervisory duty to protect the child's basic physical safety.").

10. *See supra*, En Banc Majority Opinion at 13.

11. *See D.R. by L.R. v. Middle Bucks Area Vocational Technical School*, 972 F.2d 1364, 1379 (3d Cir. 1992) (Sloviter, C.J., dissenting) ("*DeShaney* contains no language to support the ... holding that the duty to protect can be triggered only by involuntary, round-the-clock, legal custody."); *see also id.* at 1381 ("prisoners are probably much more articulate about their complaints about mistreatment than are school children, particularly when the treatment consists, as in this case, of sexual abuse").

school day, this in no way enabled them to provide for her safety—reasonable or otherwise—throughout the course of the school day. Albeit in dicta, now-Chief Judge Jones exposed the fallacy of holding otherwise in *Johnson v. Dallas Independent School District*, which involved a shooting committed by a non-student, non-state actor on the school grounds:

> The argument against holding that public schools have "custody," at least for some purposes of protecting their physical well-being, appears to derive less from logic than from a pragmatic desire to limit their legal liability. As has been shown, students must attend school and may not leave without permission. To say that student attendance is voluntary because parents may elect to home-school their children or send them to a private school is lamentably, for most parents, a myth. *See D.R. v. Middle Bucks*, [972 F.2d 1364, 1380 (3d Cir. 1992) (Sloviter, C.J., dissenting)]. To intimate that parents retain effective responsibility for their children's well-being when the school alone makes critical decisions regarding student safety and discipline is inaccurate. To suggest that parents somehow are in a better position than the schools to protect their children from the ravages of weapons smuggled onto campus during the school day is cruelly irrational. To hope that students who are unarmed can protect themselves from the depredation of armed criminals in their midst is ridiculous. That parents yield so much of their children's care into the hands of public school officials may well be argued to place upon the officials an obligation to protect students at least from certain kinds of foreseeably dangerous harm during regular school hours.[12]

This reasoning is all the more powerful when, as here, the schoolchild who suffers injury to her bodily integrity is "very young." To contend that it is primarily up to parents to prevent public schools from handing off their nine-year-old girls to unknown men during the course of the school day would be outrageous. Yet the majority's emphasis on parents' responsibility for their children's needs, including safety from sexual predation, if not wholly irrelevant, can have no other meaning. At the same time, the majority never addresses just what it is that Jane's parents conceivably could have done, or should have done, to safeguard her in this situation. Even if it could somehow be imagined that the parents bear some responsibility, such a conclusion cannot be drawn from the Does' pleadings without the benefit of discovery.

The majority also suggests that the distinction between very young children and older children is "essentially arbitrary."[13] But, far from being arbitrary, distinguishing between pre-pubescent and pubescent or post-pubescent children is not just natural and intuitive—it is grounded in extensive science.[14] This distinction, which is based on biology and is reflected in the differentiation between

---

12. 38 F.3d 198, 203 n.7 (5th Cir. 1994).
13. *See supra*, En Banc Majority Opinion at 14.
14. *See* Theresa O'Lonergan & John J. Zodrow, *Pediatric Assent: Subject Protection Issues Among Adolescent Females Enrolled in Research*, 34 J.L. Med. & Ethics 451, 454 (2006) ("Sexual development

elementary school and junior high school, has historically been considered important by the medical profession and society at large.[15] In addressing numerous areas, Congress and state legislatures have treated pre-pubescent [*880] and post-pubescent children differently and have used age as a proxy for that distinction.[16] The particular *age* selected might appear to be arbitrary (though it could have been informed by expert analysis had this case been allowed to proceed), but not the distinction. A distinction with such deep biological and historical roots, and which remains vital in many legal realms, can hardly be considered "arbitrary."

The majority also contends that it would be impractical to assess every individual's characteristics to determine whether a special relationship exists. Not so: A schoolchild's age is an objective and easily-determined fact. I do not suggest—and we need not decide, in this case—that more subjective factors, such as a specific child's (Jane's) mental acuity or degree of social development, should be a part of the special relationship inquiry.[17] Line-drawing is inevitable in this area, but an approach guided by objective facts does not require line-drawing of unusual difficulty. By contrast, an approach that categorically ignores age—by, for example, ignoring the differences between a nine-year-old grammar school girl and a high

---

is the morphologically recognizable hallmark of adolescence. Of particular interest here is the bald fact that adolescent girls can conceive and bear children.").

15. *See id.* at 454-55 (footnotes omitted):

Adolescence is, by definition, a convergence of developmental factors. Historically, the law, religion and society have implicitly applied the "rule of sevens" to assign legal and moral responsibility to children and adolescents. Courts have treated seven-year-olds as capable of distinguishing right from wrong.... Likewise, religions and courts have treated fourteen-year-old adolescents as far more accountable than younger children for their actions and, in many cases, assign culpability.... [P]hysicians generally acknowledge that adolescents are differentially equipped to make medical decisions from thirteen years to adulthood.... In most states, adolescents may seek and obtain sexual and reproductive health information and services without the permission of or even notification of their parents.

16. *See, e.g.,* Fair Labor Standards Act, 29 U.S.C. §§ 201-19 (setting fourteen as the minimum age for most non-agricultural work); *see also* Charles A. Phipps, *Misdirected Reform: On Regulating Consensual Sexual Activity Between Teenagers*, 12 CORNELL J.L. & PUB. POL'Y 373, 429-31 (2003) (footnotes omitted):

Without exception, the law in all fifty states prohibits sexual activity between an adult and a pre-pubertal child.... [T]he criminal law treats post-pubescent victims differently from pre-pubescent victims. While post-pubertal minors are still deemed incapable of consenting to sexual activity with adults, the fact that they have reached puberty generally translates into lower criminal penalties for those who engage in sexual activity with victims in this category. Because the age of consent in the majority of states is sixteen, this means that [this type of post-pubertal] victim generally is one aged fourteen or fifteen.

17. It is worth noting, however, that the Supreme Court has considered such subjective factors in holding that a state's duty to protect an involuntarily committed psychiatric patient extends to "such training as may be reasonable in light of [the patient's] liberty interests in safety and freedom from unreasonable restraints[.]" *Youngberg v. Romeo,* 457 U.S. 307, 322, 102 S. Ct. 2452, 73 L. Ed. 2d 28 (1982). If individual characteristics were categorically irrelevant, then *Youngberg* would not have defined a state's constitutional duties to institutionalized psychiatric patients any more broadly than its duties to competent adult prisoners.

school senior twice her age—only heightens the arbitrariness of the line demarcating special relationships. Further, the majority's approach would presumably leave pre-schoolers and even infants in the State's care unprotected—a patently absurd result.

In short, nine-year-old, elementary-school students in general—not just Jane, subjectively—are significantly distinct from teenage, middle- and high-school students in their ability to provide for their own protection from sex offenders when they are mandatorily separated from their legal guardians during the school day. Jane's very young age is thus highly relevant to the existence of a special relationship between herself and the School. This factor need not be sufficient alone, however, because the School also affirmatively exercised its power to restrain Jane's liberty even more strictly, as detailed below.

B. The School Affirmatively Forced Jane into Keyes's Sole Custody at School and Allowed Keyes to Take Her Away from the School Where She Could Not Protect Herself

Under the well-pleaded allegations of the Does' complaint, the State had a special [*881] relationship with Jane, not just because of her very young age, but also because of the School's decision, while acting *in loco parentis* to the exclusion of all others, and pursuant to its express policies, (1) first, to separate Jane from her teachers and classmates, and (2) only then to deliver her into the exclusive custody of Keyes for the express purpose of his taking her away from the school grounds and later returning her there, all during the course of the school day. This affirmative exercise of state power is significant under the Supreme Court's analysis in *Ingraham*, quoted by this court in *Doe v. Hillsboro Independent School District*. By actively removing Jane from the classroom and then delivering her in isolation into Keyes's custody, the School rendered Jane (1) *entirely* "apart from teachers and other pupils who may witness and protest any instances of mistreatment,"[18] and (2) not "free to return home"[19]—except, exclusively, at Keyes's mercy. This was an affirmative exercise of state power, on six separate occasions, that further disabled Jane and further obliged the State to protect her.

We and other courts have held that a special relationship may exist when a state sub-delegates its delegated custody of an individual to a third party. For example, a state has a special relationship with a minor it places in foster care,[20] a burglary

---

18. *Doe v. Hillsboro Indep. School Dist.*, 113 F.3d at 1415 (quoting *Ingraham*, 430 U.S. at 670).
19. *Id.*
20. *Griffith v. Johnston*, 899 F.2d 1427, 1439 (5th Cir. 1990) (state agency "created a 'special relationship' . . . when it removed [children] from their natural homes and placed them under state supervision. At that time, [the state agency] assumed the responsibility to provide constitutionally adequate care for these children."); *see also DeShaney*, 489 U.S. at 201 n.9 ("Had the State by the affirmative exercise of its power removed [the child] from free society and placed him in a foster home operated by its agents, we might have a situation sufficiently analogous to incarceration or institutionalization to give rise to an affirmative duty to protect.").

suspect it temporarily places in the custody of a private club owner,[21] and a woman it threatens with arrest and physically places in her intoxicated boyfriend's truck.[22] In none of these or other such cases did a state actor physically hold the victim at the time of the injury (had no de facto "custody"), but the victim "was in the defendant officers' custody at the time she was forced into" the third party's control.[23] The State is therefore considered "a participant in the custody which led to the victim's death [or injury]."[24] The same reasoning has to apply here.

Moreover, these cases demonstrate that the special relationship doctrine is not inflexibly limited to "24/7" incarceration or institutionalization only. Rather than excluding broad areas of state action, such as public schools, from the reach of the special relationship doctrine, we must be sensitive to the factual context in which a case [*882] arises.[25] Here, the relevant context includes the School's affirmative decision to (1) isolate the "very young" Jane from her teachers and classmates and (2) deliver Jane into Keyes's exclusive custody, in those sequential steps rendering Jane and her parents utterly helpless.

In light of their decision to separate Jane from her teacher and classmates and then release her to Keyes, the school officials' role was not merely passive or simply negligent, as the majority asserts. The active nature of the School's role is underscored by the check-out policy in question. That policy admittedly—as the majority opinion states—"*permitted* school employees to release students to individuals,"[26] but, more importantly, *forced Jane, the student* to be released, giving her, as well as her teacher, her classmates, and her parents, no choice in the matter.[27] Only by examining the relationship between Jane and the State—not the

---

21. *Horton v. Flenory*, 889 F.2d 454, 458 (3d Cir. 1989) (state had duty to protect plaintiff when, pursuant to state policies, police officer left plaintiff in custody of club owner, who beat plaintiff to death).

22. *Stemler v. City of Florence*, 126 F.3d 856, 868-69 (6th Cir. 1997) (state had duty to protect woman who "was rendered unable to protect herself by virtue of both the threat of arrest and her physical placement in the truck by the officers"; woman was then killed when her boyfriend crashed the truck into a guardrail); *see also Davis v. Brady*, 143 F.3d 1021, 1024-26 (6th Cir. 1998) (state had special relationship with intoxicated police-car passenger abandoned on a highway).

23. *Stemler*, 126 F.3d at 869.

24. *Horton*, 889 F.2d at 458.

25. *See, e.g., Estate of Lance v. Lewisville Indep. School Dist.*, No. 4:11-CV-00032, 2011 U.S. Dist. LEXIS 103400, 2011 WL 4100960, at *7-8 (E.D. Tex. Aug. 23, 2011), *adopted*, 2011 U.S. Dist. LEXIS 103397, 2011 WL 4101164 (E.D. Tex. Sept. 13, 2011) (engaging in such an analysis and holding that the plaintiff adequately alleged a special relationship when a very young, disabled child was placed in in-school suspension); *Teague ex rel. C.R.T. v. Texas City Indep. School Dist.*, 348 F. Supp. 2d 785, 792-93 (S.D. Tex. 2004) (construing special relationship doctrine "in the context of this particular plaintiff" and holding that the plaintiff adequately alleged a special relationship between a public school and a child with Down's Syndrome), *vacated*, 386 F. Supp. 2d 893, 896 (S.D. Tex. 2005) (granting summary judgment to defendant when discovery revealed that the victim was in fact 18 years old at the time of the incident, was no longer subject to compulsory attendance, and had the mental capacity of a 13-year-old).

26. *See supra*, En Banc Majority Opinion at 3.

27. The complaint does not reveal Jane's reactions to being placed in Keyes's custody. Only discovery or trial evidence could resolve such an issue. In any event, a nine-year-old's possible failure

relationship (for these purposes irrelevant) between the State officials who set the School's policies and those who implemented them—does the question of a special relationship in this case come into proper focus.

The majority also reasons that the School's temporary delegation of its exclusive custody of Jane to Keyes does not support the existence of a special relationship because the School did not "*knowingly* transfer that custody to an unauthorized individual."[28] A state-knowledge requirement, the majority continues, is "implicit" in the principle that a special relationship may be created only through an "affirmative exercise" of state power.[29] But such a state-knowledge requirement—for which the majority cites no precedent—would not imply that, for there to be a special relationship, the state must know *all* the circumstances, i.e., each and every discrete fact, surrounding its custody of an individual.[30] As alleged here, the School clearly [*883] did affirmatively exercise its powers by separating Jane from her teachers and classmates and delivering her to Keyes, and it did so pursuant to its express policies. School personnel were perfectly aware that they were undertaking these actions-affirmatively, not passively.

It is technically true that the School did not "know" Keyes to be unauthorized, but all it had to do was (1) verify Keyes's identity, and (2) follow its own express policy by viewing Jane's check-out form. Although the School's self-inflicted lack of knowledge could arguably indicate that it was not deliberately indifferent to Jane's safety, that has nothing to do with the special relationship inquiry. For example, a state has a special relationship with and a concomitant duty to protect a prisoner even if the prisoner is injured because of an unknown or unexpected danger to which the official could not have shown deliberate indifference.[31] To conclude, however, that such a prisoner was never in a special relationship to begin with would be illogical. The same is true in this case. My point: the majority has conflated the special relationship and deliberate indifference inquiries.

Curiously, the majority goes on to assert that it is the Does who have conflated these questions, stating that, under the Does' theory, the "same act" both creates

---

affirmatively to protest being placed in the custody of a grown man, even one who repeatedly raped her, surely does not somehow convert that custody from involuntary to voluntary.

28. *See supra*, En Banc Majority Opinion at 17.

29. *DeShaney*, 489 U.S. at 200 ("when the State by the affirmative exercise of its power so restrains an individual's liberty that it renders him unable to care for himself, and at the same time fails to provide for his basic human needs—e.g., food, clothing, shelter, medical care, and reasonable safety—it transgresses the substantive limits on state action set by the Eighth Amendment and the Due Process Clause").

30. For example, if a state inadvertently imprisons the wrong person, it still owes a duty to protect the person it actually did imprison. The state's error in this regard does not immunize it from the constitutional consequences of its known, affirmative exercise of power—imprisoning the individual.

31. For example, in *Varnado v. Lynaugh*, 920 F.2d 320, 321 (5th Cir. 1991), we held that a state was not deliberately indifferent to a prisoner's serious medical needs when it allegedly failed to recognize the purported danger of forcing the prisoner to stand in line for meals. The state's lack of knowledge about this risk, however, did not imply that the state never had a duty to protect the prisoner at all.

the special relationship and demonstrates the State's deliberate indifference.[32] Although it is true, as the majority notes, that the creation of a special relationship does not itself demonstrate deliberate indifference, the Does have never made such a claim. Rather, they allege (1) the special relationship in this case was created when the School placed Jane, a nine-year-old student at a compulsory-attendance public school, in the exclusive custody of Keyes during school hours; and (2) the School officials' deliberate indifference consisted of their failure to verify Keyes's identity or his authority to check Jane out of school. *And, what could constitute indifference more deliberate than checking Jane out to a man who asserts that he is her mother?* It is only natural that the facts underlying the special relationship and those underlying the State's deliberate indifference are related, but those facts are nonetheless distinct.[33]

The majority also asserts that the School's act of releasing Jane into Keyes's custody cannot demonstrate the kind of state custody that is required for a special relationship to exist. This argument ignores the cases discussed above, however, which teach that a special relationship survives a state's delegation of its exclusive custody to a third party.[34]

[*884] Further, the majority's Wonderland-esque analysis of this point implies that, by removing Jane from her classroom and releasing her to Keyes for a portion of the school day, the School *secured* rather than *restrained* Jane's liberty. Really? In fact and in logic, just the opposite is true. By first isolating her and then delegating its exclusive custody of Jane to Keyes, the School (1) deprived Jane of any potential assistance of teachers and classmates, (2) left Jane helpless against Keyes's assault, and (3) eliminated any ability that Jane's parents had to protect her from danger by removing her from the School.[35] Even though Jane's parents presumably had the general ability to remove her from the School (at least for limited periods of time), neither they nor her teachers nor her fellow pupils had any ability to remove her or otherwise protect her once the School took her from their presence and delivered her into Keyes's custody. At this crucial juncture, the majority appears to reason that any special relationship there could ever have been between Jane and the School abruptly ceased. But what is the use of the special relationship doctrine and its protection of helpless individuals in the State's

---

32. *See supra*, En Banc Majority Opinion at 18.

33. Even if some of the same facts are relevant to both the special relationship and deliberate indifference inquiries, that does not mean that these prongs are somehow conflated under the Does' theory. *See Stemler*, 126 F.3d at 867 (describing these as "distinct, though interrelated inquiries"). For example, suppose that a state places a prisoner in an unreasonably unsafe prison—a clear 42 U.S.C. § 1983 claim under a special relationship theory. That placement, it could be argued, underlies both the special relationship and the state's putative deliberate indifference to the prisoner's reasonable safety. Yet none could deny that this scenario presents an actionable constitutional claim.

34. *See Stemler*, 126 F.3d at 869, *Griffith*, 899 F.2d at 1439; *Horton*, 889 F.2d at 458.

35. Even assuming *arguendo* that the School's duty to protect Jane would have been ceased had it released her to an authorized individual, that is not what happened in this case.

custody, "if it is in effect an umbrella which is taken away as soon as it begins to rain?"[36]

The majority concludes that it is "compelled" to rule that there is no special relationship in this case.[37] Although we have rejected the special relationship theory in most school situations, we have never foreclosed the application of that theory in "extreme circumstances."[38] Neither have we ever held that characteristics such as very young age are categorically irrelevant to the special relationship inquiry. Indeed, it is for the express reason of Jane's very young age that the School's acts in separating her from teachers and classmates during school hours and delivering her to Keyes caused Jane and her parents to have "no realistic means of voluntarily terminating the state's custody" and no "ability or opportunity to provide for [her] own care and safety."[39] I remain convinced that, under the Does' allegations, the State had a constitutional duty to protect Jane.

II. DELIBERATE INDIFFERENCE

A state does not violate its substantive due process duty to protect an individual pursuant to a special relationship when it merely acts negligently. Such a violation occurs when the state acts with "deliberate indifference" to that individual's health or safety.[40] Thus, in addition to alleging that a special relationship existed between Jane and the School, the Does needed to allege adequately that the School officials acted, at the very least, with deliberate indifference. "To act with deliberate indifference, a state actor must consciously disregard a [*885] known and excessive risk to the victim's health and safety."[41] Even though the majority does not reach this issue, any objective reading of the Does' complaint confirms that they have quite adequately pleaded that the State acted with deliberate indifference to Jane's safety.

The Does allege with specificity that the School adopted and implemented a flawed check-out policy despite its knowledge that the specific policy thus adopted posed excessive risks to students. In particular, the Does allege that the School's check-out policy included a "Permission to Check-Out" form for each student which listed by name the only adults authorized to check out that student during the school day. The Does also allege that (1) the policy did not direct School officials to verify the identity of an adult requesting to check out a student, and (2) the School failed adequately to train and supervise the cognizant officials

---

36. Abba Eban, Statement to the United Nations Security Council (June 6, 1967), *available at* http://www.mfa.gov.il/MFA/Foreign+Relations/Israels+Foreign+Relations+since+1947/1947-1974/19+Statement+to+the+Security+Council+by+Foreign+Mi.htm.

37. *See supra*, En Banc Majority Opinion at 19.

38. *Walton v. Alexander*, 44 F.3d 1297, 1305 (5th Cir. 1995) (finding no special relationship when student voluntarily attended state school for the deaf).

39. *Id.*

40. *Hernandez ex rel. Hernandez v. Texas Dept. of Protective and Regulatory Servs.*, 380 F.3d 872, 880 (5th Cir. 2004).

41. *Id.*

in the proper administration of the check-out policy. The Does further allege that these "customs and practices guaranteed that verification would not be checked which created an unreasonable danger to the minor child named herein." Thus, when Keyes checked Jane out on multiple occasions as her "father" (and, on at least one occasion, as her "mother"), School officials neither (1) verified Keyes's identity, nor (2) referred to Jane's check-out form, on which Keyes was not listed as an individual authorized to take custody of Jane.[42]

Importantly, the Does' pleadings expressly state that the School's officials were well aware of the risks that their flawed policies engendered, alleging that:

> Upon information and belief, the Education Defendants received complaints and inquiries and/or had internal discussions and safety meetings concerning checkout policies and procedures and access to students under their care and control by unauthorized individuals. The complaints, inquiries, discussions, and/or meetings show that the Education Defendants had actual knowledge of the dangers created by their policies, customs, and regulations, but they failed to take corrective action to reduce or prevent the danger.

These discrete allegations are sufficient to state a claim that School officials acted with deliberate indifference to a known risk to Jane's safety.

True, the Does do not allege that School officials knew that Keyes, in particular, was dangerous. But, "this court has never required state officials to be warned of a specific danger."[43] Indeed, state officials may be deliberately indifferent even if they do not know which particular individual poses the safety risk, or which potential victim will ultimately be injured.[44] An [*886] official is deliberately indifferent if he knows of and disregards "a substantial risk of serious harm."[45] And it is such awareness that the Does precisely allege.

The defendants' awareness of this risk to student safety is eminently plausible in light of (1) the alleged complaints, inquiries, discussions, and meetings among the defendants on the subject of unauthorized individuals' access to students; (2) the School's allowing Keyes to check out Jane on at least six occasions,

---

42. Had this case been allowed to proceed, the defendants would have remained free to raise any independent reasons that the School's officials might have had to believe that Keyes was authorized to check out Jane or did not pose a danger to her.

43. *Hernandez*, 380 F.3d at 881.

44. *Farmer v. Brennan*, 511 U.S. 825, 843, 114 S. Ct. 1970, 128 L. Ed. 2d 811 (1994) ("Nor may a prison official escape liability for deliberate indifference by showing that, while he was aware of an obvious, substantial risk to inmate safety, he did not know that the complainant was especially likely to be assaulted by the specific prisoner who eventually committed the assault."); *Curry v. Scott*, 249 F.3d 493, 507 (6th Cir. 2001) ("'actual knowledge' does not require that a prison official know a prisoner would, with certainty, be harmed, or that a particular prisoner would be harmed in a certain way"); *see also Rosa H. v. San Elizario Indep. Sch. Dist.*, 106 F.3d 648, 659 (5th Cir. 1997) (for "actual notice" purposes, "[s]tudents need not show that the district knew that a particular teacher would abuse a particular student").

45. *Farmer*, 511 U.S. at 837.

including one occasion when he signed her out as her *mother*, which these officials had to have known was bogus; and (3) the general awareness by schools and school boards—heightened in recent years—of the threat posed in the elementary school setting by deviant adults to young children.[46]

With regard to the last point, we learned in a recent appeal of a nationwide program employing an electronic tracking system to identify whether visitors to primary and secondary schools were registered sex offenders or otherwise presented threats to young students.[47] By 2006, the school year immediately preceding the one at issue here, this program had been endorsed by the U.S. Department of Justice, had received federal grant money, and had already been activated in at least 1,400 schools in some 100 school districts across ten states. In light of the ubiquitous awareness by schools of the threat posed by deviant adults preying on very young schoolchildren, it is certainly "plausible," and indeed highly likely, that the School knew that it was playing with fire. Of course, nothing more than plausibility is required at this stage of the proceedings.[48]

Despite their alleged awareness of the risk, School officials nevertheless checked Jane out to a man whose identity and authority they never bothered to verify. These allegations are sufficient, at least at this initial motion-to-dismiss stage, to state an actionable constitutional claim grounded in deliberate indifference.

III. CONCLUSION

Any case involving the rape of a child is, of course, a terrible one, so why is this case so shocking? Part of the special horror of this case is the appalling way in which Jane's parents' state-mandated trust in public school officials for the care and safety of their very young child was rewarded. In a case such as this, in which the alleged actions of state officials "shock the conscience,"[49] the proper remedy is not merely to compensate the victim in tort, but, additionally, to compensate all of us with a constitutional remedy under 42 U.S.C. § 1983, which is intended "to deter state actors from using the badge of their authority to deprive individuals of their federally guaranteed rights and to provide relief to victims if such deterrence fails."[50]

As one of our Tenth Circuit colleagues has aptly observed, "[w]e do not adequately discharge our duty to interpret the Constitution by merely describing the facts as **[*887]** 'tragic' and invoking state tort law[.]"[51] Neither do we adequately discharge our duty by interpreting the special relationship doctrine

---

46. This threat is arguably heightened in the middle of the school day, when—unlike at the end of the school day—an unauthorized adult seeking to take custody of a child will presumably not be confronted with the child's actual parent or guardian.
47. *Meadows v. Lake Travis Indep. Sch. Dist.*, 397 F. App'x 1 (5th Cir. 2010) (unpublished).
48. *Twombly*, 550 U.S. at 570.
49. *Rochin*, 342 U.S. at 172.
50. *Wyatt v. Cole*, 504 U.S. 158, 161, 112 S. Ct. 1827, 118 L. Ed. 2d 504 (1992).
51. *Maldonado v. Josey*, 975 F.2d 727, 735 (10th Cir. 1992) (Seymour, J., concurring).

so narrowly that a helpless nine-year-old girl, abruptly removed from her classroom by school personnel and wrongly delivered to an unauthorized grown man, falls through the mesh of the Constitution's safety net. The Does have more than adequately alleged discrete facts to show that the State had a constitutional duty to protect Jane and that it failed abysmally in that duty. These are the reasons why I dissent.

> **Questions Regarding *Doe v. Covington County School District***
>
> 1. In the majority opinion, Judge King says that compulsory attendance alone is insufficient to establish a special relationship, at least in part because in Mississippi, Jane Doe can fulfill her educational requirements through multiple means. Did this argument convince you?
> 2. The Fifth Circuit declined to adopt state-created danger theory in this case but still provided an analysis under the theory. Why do you think the Fifth Circuit bothered to do this?
> 3. What might the utility be of Judge Higginson's concurrence to future litigants arguing similar issues?

ASSIGNMENT 4: *ESTATE OF BROWN V. CYPRESS FAIRBANKS INDEPENDENT SCHOOL DISTRICT* CASE BRIEF

Read the case in its entirety first, highlighting and marking the pages as you go, then try to brief the case using the format you used for the *DeShaney* case brief.

Estate of Asher Brown v. Cypress Fairbanks Indep. Sch. Dist. is a case from the Southern District of Texas. What law is the Southern District of Texas bound to uphold?

ESTATE OF BROWN v. CYPRESS FAIRBANKS INDEPENDENT SCHOOL DISTRICT

United States District Court for the Southern District of Texas, Houston Division
May 23, 2012, Decided; May 23, 2012, Filed
Civil Action No. 11-cv-1491
Reporter: 863 F. Supp. 2d 632 *

Judges: Keith P. Ellison, United States District Judge.

Opinion by: Keith P. Ellison

Opinion

[*632] MEMORANDUM AND ORDER

Pending before the Court is Defendant's Motion for Reconsideration (Doc. No. 40). After considering the motion, the responses [*633] thereto, and the applicable law, the Court finds that Defendant's motion for reconsideration must be **GRANTED** and Plaintiff's due process claim brought pursuant to § 1983 dismissed.

I. BACKGROUND

Plaintiff Amy Truong, individually and in her representative capacity for the Estate of Asher Orrin Michael Brown ("Plaintiff" or "Truong"), brings this suit following the suicide of her son, Asher Orrin Michael Brown ("Asher"), a middle school student in the Cypress Fairbanks Independent School District. Plaintiff asserts that Asher committed suicide after suffering as a victim of constant bullying by other students. (Complaint ("Compl."), Doc. No. 12, at ¶ 98.) Plaintiff alleges that Cypress Fairbanks Independent School District ("CFISD" or "Defendant"), through its acts and omissions, failed to protect Asher from harm while he attended Hamilton Middle School.[1] (*Id.* ¶¶ 10-11.)

Plaintiff originally brought claims under the Rehabilitation Act and Title IX, as well as First Amendment, Equal Protection, and Due Process claims pursuant to 42 U.S.C. § 1983. Defendant filed a motion to dismiss all of Plaintiff's claims (Doc. No. 18). On February 21, 2012, this Court issued an order granting in part and denying in part Defendant's motion to dismiss.[2] ("February 21 Order," Doc. No. 36.) The Court ruled that Plaintiff had stated a due process claim pursuant to 42 U.S.C. § 1983 and a harassment claim under Title IX, 20 U.S.C. § 1681(a). (*Id.*) Defendant now asks this Court to reconsider its ruling on Plaintiff's due process claim in light of *Doe v. Covington County Sch. Dist.*, 675 F.3d 849, 2012 U.S. App. LEXIS 6080, 2012 WL 976349 (5th Cir. Mar. 23, 2012), an en banc Fifth Circuit decision issued after this Court's February 21 Order. Defendant contends that this recent decision clarifies that Plaintiff's due process claim fails as a matter of law and, therefore, asks this Court to dismiss Plaintiff's due process claim brought pursuant to § 1983. Plaintiff filed a response in opposition (Doc. No. 45) to Defendant's motion for reconsideration. Defendant filed a reply brief

---

1. A lengthy recounting of the factual allegations in this case is available in this Court's February 21, 2012 Order (Doc. No. 36).
2. This case was originally styled *Estate of Asher Brown v. Dr. John Ogletree, President of the School Board of the Cypress Fairbanks Independent School District, et al.* On April 27, 2012, Defendant filed an unopposed motion (Doc. No. 43) to dismiss John Ogletree and to substitute the Cypress Fairbanks Independent School District as the named defendant in this action. The Court granted Defendant's motion on April 30, 2012 (Order, Doc. No. 44).

(Doc. No. 46) and a supplemental authority in support of Defendant's argument (Doc. No. 47).

II. LEGAL STANDARD

A. Rule 59(e) motions

Rule 59(e) provides that a motion to alter or amend a judgment must be filed no later than twenty-eight days following the entry of judgment. FED. R. CIV. P. 59(e). Depending on the timing of the motion, the Fifth Circuit treats a motion for reconsideration as either a motion to alter or amend under Rule 59(e), or a motion for relief from judgment under Rule 60(b). *United States v. Turner*, No. CA 11-928, 2011 U.S. Dist. LEXIS 76735, 2011 WL 2836752, at *1 (E.D. La. July 15, 2011) (citing *Lavespere v. Niagara Mach. & Tool Works, Inc.*, 910 F.2d 167, 173 (5th Cir. 1990)). If the motion is filed within twenty-eight days of the judgment, then the motion constitutes a motion to alter or amend under Rule 59(e). *Id.*; FED. R. CIV. P. 59(e). A motion filed more than twenty-eight days after the judgment, but not more than one year **[*634]** after the entry of judgment, is governed by Rule 60(b). FED. R. CIV. P. 60(b).

Because Defendant's motion to dismiss was only partially granted, final judgment was never entered in this case. Therefore, the Court treats the instant motion as a Rule 59(e) motion for reconsideration. A district court has considerable discretion to grant or deny a motion under Rule 59(e). *Edward H. Bohlin Co. v. Banning Co.*, 6 F.3d 350, 355 (5th Cir. 1993). A court's reconsideration of an earlier order is an extraordinary remedy and should be granted sparingly. *Fields v. Pool Offshore, Inc.*, No. 97-3170, 1998 U.S. Dist. LEXIS 1122, 1998 WL 43217, at *2 (E.D. La. Feb. 3, 1998), *aff'd*, 182 F.3d 353 (5th Cir. 1999); *see also Rottmund v. Cont'l Assur. Co.*, 813 F. Supp. 1104, 1107 (E.D. Pa. 1992) (although federal district courts have inherent power over interlocutory orders and may modify, vacate, or set aside these orders when the interests of justice require, "[b]ecause of the interest in finality . . . courts should grant motions for reconsideration sparingly").

To succeed on a Rule 59(e) motion, a party must clearly establish at least one of the following factors: (1) an intervening change in the controlling law, (2) the availability of new evidence, or (3) a manifest error of law or fact. *Fields*, 1998 U.S. Dist. LEXIS 1122, 1998 WL 43217, at *2; *see also Schiller v. Physicians Res. Grp. Inc.*, 342 F.3d 563, 567 (5th Cir. 2003); *Ross v. Marshall*, 426 F.3d 745, 763 (5th Cir. 2005). As the Fifth Circuit has explained, "Rule 59(e) does not set forth any specific grounds for relief." *Lavespere v. Niagara Mach. & Tool Works, Inc.*, 910 F.2d 167, 174 (5th Cir. 1990), *abrogated on other grounds*, *Little v. Liquid Air Corp.*, 37 F.3d 1069 (5th Cir. 1994). Although a district court has "considerable discretion in deciding whether to reopen a case" under Rule 59(e), "[t]hat discretion, of course, is not limitless." *Id.* at 174. However, the Fifth Circuit has emphasized that a Rule 59(e) motion "is not the proper vehicle for rehashing evidence, legal theories, or arguments that could have been offered or raised before the entry of judgment." *Templet v. HydroChem Inc.*, 367 F.3d 473, 478-9 (5th Cir. 2004).

III. ANALYSIS

Relying on the recent Fifth Circuit decision in *Doe v. Covington County Sch. Dist.*, 675 F.3d 849, 2012 U.S. App. LEXIS 6080, 2012 WL 976349 (5th Cir. Mar. 23, 2012), Defendants argue that Plaintiff's § 1983 due process claim necessarily must fail as a matter of law. In *Covington*, the Fifth Circuit considered whether the plaintiff—a nine-year old elementary school student—adequately alleged a violation of a constitutional right where the plaintiff was checked-out and molested on six separate occasions by a man who was not authorized to take the plaintiff out of school. 2012 U.S. App. LEXIS 6080, 2012 WL 976349, at *3. As the Fifth Circuit explained, the plaintiff's constitutional claim was based not on the individual's molestation of the plaintiff, "but rather upon the school's allegedly deficient checkout policy, which allowed the molestation to occur" insofar as it did not require school officials to verify the identity of individuals before releasing children into their custody. *Id.* Finding that the school district defendants had no constitutional duty to protect the plaintiff from non-state actors, the Fifth Circuit determined that the plaintiff failed to allege a violation of any constitutional right. *Id.* Further, the Fifth Circuit clarified that a school district's duty to protect a student is contingent upon the existence of a special relationship, as defined in the Supreme Court's *DeShaney* opinion. *Id.*

"As a general matter . . . a state's failure to protect an individual against private violence simply does not constitute a violation of due process." *DeShaney v. Winnebago County Dep't of Soc. Servs.*, 489 U.S. 189, 197, 109 S. Ct. 998, 103 L. Ed. 2d 249 (1989). In *DeShaney*, the [*635] Supreme Court first mapped out the "special relationship" exception to that general rule. Under the special relationship exception, a state may be required to protect a citizen from harm, even private harm, "when the State takes a person into its custody and holds him there against his will." *Id.* at 199-200. The Fifth Circuit has subsequently extended the special relationship exception to the following three scenarios: (1) incarceration, (2) involuntary institutionalization, and (3) the placement of children in foster care. *Griffith v. Johnston*, 899 F.2d 1427, 1439 (5th Cir. 1990).

In the present case, Plaintiff argues that CFISD violated Asher's due process rights by failing to enforce anti-bullying policies at Hamilton Middle School. When this Court originally considered Defendant's motion to dismiss (Doc. No. 18), it contemplated three possible bases for Plaintiff's due process claim. First, the Court considered Plaintiff's argument that CFISD's inaction in failing to enforce the policies allowed the bullying—and harm to Asher's bodily integrity—to continue and, indeed, to escalate to the point that it became unbearable to Asher. Second, the "special relationship" exception could have been proposed to argue that the school district had duty to protect Asher.³ Third, the Court considered whether CFISD could be liable under a state-created danger theory of the case, as Plaintiff argued that CFISD's "culture that condoned bullying" increased the danger posed to Asher during the school day. The Court dismissed the latter bases for Plaintiff's claim, finding that Plaintiff had not advanced a special relationship theory and that Plaintiff's state-created danger theory failed as a matter of law.⁴ However, the Court allowed Plaintiff's due process claim to proceed under the first argument, reasoning that the existence of explicit CFISD policies mandating action on the part of Defendants in the face of student-on-student bullying gave rise to CFISD's duty to protect Asher from bodily harm and threats to his bodily integrity. Defendants now ask this Court to reconsider the viability of this first argument, arguing that, post-*Covington*, it can no longer serve as the foundation for Plaintiff's claim. The Court finds here that Defendants are correct.

The *Covington* opinion clarifies that the Fifth Circuit makes any public school student's right to bodily integrity contingent upon the existence of a special relationship between the student and the school. And the *Covington* decision further circumscribes the application of the special relationship exception, confining it to the three scenarios listed above. See *Covington*, 2012 U.S. App. LEXIS 6080, 2012 WL 976349, at *5 ("We have not extended the *DeShaney* special relationships exception beyond these three situations, and have **[*636]** explicitly held that the state does *not* create a special relationship with children attending public schools.").

Plaintiff argues that the facts of *Covington* are distinguishable from the instant case because here the policies in place would have been effective had they been enforced, in contrast to the defective policy at issue in *Covington*. Plaintiff's attempt at a distinction makes no difference. Regardless of whether the issue is existence of a policy or enforcement of a policy, CFISD policies promising school action to prevent student-on-student bullying cannot serve as a basis for Asher's constitutional due process rights. Because the policies at issue were intended to govern non-state actors—*i.e.*, the behavior between and among other school children—CFISD's failure to enforce the policies did not result in the violation of Asher's constitutional rights. CFISD had

---

3. At the time of the motion to dismiss, Plaintiff made clear that she did not offer a special relationship theory of liability in the case, and, therefore, the Court did not consider the special relationship exception in issuing its February 21 Order. (Doc No. 27, at 16.)

4. In her opposition to Defendant's motion for reconsideration, Plaintiff urges the Court to reinstate Plaintiff's state-created danger theory. As this Court explained in the February 21 Order, the status of the state-created danger theory in the Fifth Circuit remains unclear and recent Fifth Circuit decisions have declined to recognize the doctrine. (Doc. No. 36, at 18-19.) Contrary to Plaintiff's reading, nothing in *Covington* changes this. In fact, the *Covington* opinion reiterates that "recent decisions have consistently confirmed that '[t]he Fifth Circuit has not adopted the state-created danger theory of liability.'" 2012 U.S. App. LEXIS 6080, 2012 WL 976349, at *13 (quoting *Kovacic v. Villarreal*, 628 F.3d 209, 214 (5th Cir. 2010)). Further, the Fifth Circuit explicitly stated in *Covington*: "We decline to use this en banc opportunity to adopt the state-created danger theory." *Id.* Because the status of the state-created danger theory in the Fifth Circuit remains unchanged, Plaintiff's request to reinstate her state-created danger theory must be denied.

no constitutional duty to protect Asher from harm inflicted by a non-state actor and, therefore, could not have violated Asher's constitutional rights in failing to do so.

Plaintiff is correct in pointing out that this Court did not initially frame its decision allowing Plaintiff's § 1983 due process claim to proceed in terms of the special relationship exception. Instead, this Court focused on CFISD's inaction as evidence of deliberate indifference. This Court's focus was misplaced. *Covington* makes clear that any duty to protect must be moored to a special relationship. "Without a special relationship, a public school has no *constitutional* duty to ensure that its students are safe from private violence." *Covington*, 2012 U.S. App. LEXIS 6080, 2012 WL 976349, at *6 (emphasis in original). "An allegation of deliberate indifference may be sufficient to *violate* a constitutional duty, but it is not sufficient to *create* the constitutional duty." 2012 U.S. App. LEXIS 6080, [WL] at *10. Because there is no special relationship between CFISD and Asher, the Court's original basis for allowing Plaintiff's § 1983 claim to proceed was incorrect.[5]

Two prongs of Rule 59(e) are arguably satisfied here. To the extent that the *Covington* opinion holds that deliberate indifference alone, without the existence of a special relationship, is insufficient to give rise to a constitutional duty to protect a public school student from violence at the hands of other students, Defendants' motion for reconsideration must be granted on the grounds of an intervening change in the controlling law.[6] *Fields*, 1998 U.S. Dist. LEXIS 1122, 1998 WL [*637] 43217, at *2. As *Covington* makes clear, CFISD's "failure to protect the student [Asher] from

---

5. In the opposition to the motion for reconsideration, Plaintiff also urges this Court to allow Plaintiff's § 1983 claim to stand pursuant to what Plaintiff terms an "additional avenue for establishing a constitutional violation: the 'shocks the conscience' standard." (Doc. No. 45, at 10.) Plaintiff's characterization of the Fifth Circuit's discussion of the "shocks the conscience" standard as an additional avenue of relief is incorrect. As *Covington* makes clear, the shocks the conscience standard is *not* a separate exception to the *DeShaney* principle. 2012 U.S. App. LEXIS 6080, 2012 WL 976349, at *17. Where "[t]he actual harm inflicted upon [the student] ... was caused by [a] private actor, ... the state cannot be held constitutionally liable for its 'failure to protect an individual against private violence,' save for the special relationship theory and, in some circuits, the state-created danger theory." *Id.* (quoting *DeShaney*, 489 U.S. at 197). "To allow the [Plaintiff] to proceed on a shocks the conscience theory without first demonstrating a constitutional duty to protect would be wholly inconsistent with *DeShaney*." *Id.* Again, the absence of a special relationship precludes this Court's further consideration of Plaintiff's § 1983 claim.

6. The conclusion the Court is forced to reach here in no way diminishes the very real and disturbing allegations of deliberate indifference contained in Truong's Complaint. The Complaint pleads facts to demonstrate that CFISD had official policies in place—both a "Student Welfare" policy and a "District Improvement Plan" specific to the Hamilton Middle School campus—to address bullying among students. (Compl. ¶¶ 62-63.) The Complaint also pleads facts to show that, after learning of the bullying Asher suffered, Asher's parents made over a dozen attempts, through a variety of means, including phone calls, in-person visits, handwritten notes, and emails, to speak to school officials about Asher's bullying. (*Id.* ¶¶ 8, 99-100, 110-119.) Asher himself filed incident reports regarding the abuse he suffered, and several of Asher's classmates filed incident reports on his behalf. (*Id.* ¶¶ 103, 105-06, 125-26, 133.) All of these attempts to spur action by CFISD were continually rebuffed, as phone calls, notes, and emails were never returned or even acknowledged and incident reports were ignored. The Court thus reiterates that the Complaint adequately alleges that CFISD acted with deliberate indifference in "consciously disregard[ing] a known and excessive risk to [Asher]'s health and safety"; the Court laments the fact that these allegations of deliberate indifference are insufficient to allow Plaintiff's § 1983 claim to stand.

private harm (even if foreseeable) d[oes] not give rise to a constitutional claim in the absence of a finding that a custodial relationship already existed." 2012 U.S. App. LEXIS 6080, 2012 WL 976349, at *11; *see also* 2012 U.S. App. LEXIS 6080, 2012 WL 976349, at *12 ("Because we find no special relationship, we do not address whether the school's alleged actions . . . amounted to 'deliberate indifference.'"). To the extent that the *Covington* decision merely solidifies this position in the Fifth Circuit, as some of the language in the decision would suggest, this Court's prior ruling allowing Plaintiff's § 1983 claim to proceed on evidence of deliberate indifference alone constituted an error of law, also necessitating a grant of Defendant's motion here. *See, e.g., Covington*, 2012 U.S. App. LEXIS 6080, 2012 WL 976349, at *6 ("We reaffirm, then, decades of binding precedent: a public school does not have a *DeShaney* special relationship with its students requiring the school to ensure the students' safety from private actors.").

Plaintiff nonetheless argues that this Court may allow Truong's claim to proceed based solely on the plain language of 42 U.S.C. § 1983, even in the absence of any special relationship foundation.[7] Section 1983 states:

> Every person who under color of [law] . . . subjects, or *causes to be subjected*, any citizen of the United States or other person within the jurisdiction thereof to the deprivation of any rights, privileges, or immunities secured by the Constitution and laws, shall be liable to the party injured in an action of law . . . .

42 U.S.C. § 1983 (emphasis added). The language of § 1983, as further clarified under *Covington*, makes clear that Truong's claim cannot proceed. To state a claim under § 1983, "a plaintiff must (1) allege a violation of a right secured by the Constitution or laws of the United States and (2) demonstrate that the alleged deprivation was committed by a person acting under color of state law." *Covington*, 2012 U.S. App. LEXIS 6080, 2012 WL 976349, at *3 (citing *James v. Tex. Collin Cnty.*, 535 F.3d 365, 373 (5th Cir. 2008)). While the Fifth Circuit has previously recognized a student's right to bodily integrity, that right is only violated where a state actor deprives the student of that right. **[*638]** *Doe v. Taylor Indep. Sch. Dist.*, 15 F.3d 443, 451 (5th Cir. 1994).

Here, the alleged violations of Asher's bodily integrity were caused by other students at Hamilton Middle School who bullied Asher, and by Asher's own actions

---

7. Plaintiff's argument for stand-alone statutory liability under § 1983 is based entirely on Judge Higginson's concurring opinion in *Covington*. In his concurrence, Judge Higginson advocates for a literal reading of § 1983's "causes to be subjected" language and contemplates what he terms the "grey zone" cases "where a government person's alleged recklessness or deliberate indifference or intentionality is inextricably intertwined with a not-remote injury allegedly inflicted by a third person, the first (government person) causing the citizen to be subjected to injury by the second (non-government) assailant." 2012 U.S. App. LEXIS 6080, 2012 WL 976349, at *20. Plaintiff asserts that the facts of Asher's case fall into this "grey zone" category of cases and, therefore, that a jury should have the opportunity to decide whether Defendant's inaction was too causally remote for liability.

in taking his life. Plaintiff claims that CFISD caused Asher to be subjected to the deprivation of his right to bodily integrity by failing to investigate allegations of bullying or otherwise intervene in his defense. For CFISD to be liable under § 1983, CFISD must first have a constitutional duty to protect Asher from non-state actors. As the Fifth Circuit has underscored in *Covington*, CFISD had no such duty in the absence of a special relationship. Because Plaintiff has not—and cannot—allege such a special relationship, there is no foundation for stand-alone statutory liability under § 1983.[8]

The restraints placed on the Court by *Covington*—and, indeed, by *DeShaney* and its progeny in the Fifth Circuit—are nonetheless troubling. The holding in *Covington* has the undesirable effect here of allowing a school district to affirmatively enact anti-bullying policies which purport to assume responsibility to react to private violence, that is, violence inflicted by other students, yet absolve the same school district of responsibility for enforcement of such policies absent the existence of a special relationship. Sadly, this is not new. *See, e.g., Town of Castle Rock v. Gonzales*, 545 U.S. 748, 125 S. Ct. 2796, 162 L. Ed. 2d 658 (2005) (finding that plaintiff had failed to state a due process claim where police failure to enforce restraining order against plaintiff's estranged husband resulted in husband's killing of plaintiff's three daughters).

Further, the effect of *Covington* would seem to undermine state laws requiring schools to adopt—and, presumably, enforce—anti-bullying policies.[9] The Fifth Circuit is content to pass this concern on to the state courts, positing that schools "may have such a duty [to ensure that students are safe during the school day] by virtue of a state's tort or other laws." *Covington*, 2012 U.S. App. LEXIS 6080, 2012 WL 976349, at *7. This stance is especially unfortunate here given that the Texas Tort Claims Act forecloses Truong from pursuing a state law remedy

---

8. Plaintiff initially declined to plead a special relationship theory of the case. (Doc No. 27, at 16.) Plaintiff now requests leave to amend the Complaint should this Court dismiss Plaintiff's § 1983 claim. (Doc. No. 45, at 1.) Plaintiff's request to amend to include additional argument related to the special relationship deficiency must be denied. As *Covington* makes clear, a special relationship exists in only three circumstances: incarceration, involuntary commitment, and foster care. 2012 U.S. App. LEXIS 6080, 2012 WL 976349, at *5. Because none of these scenarios is applicable to the case at hand, any attempt by Plaintiff to plead the existence of a special relationship would be futile and, therefore, will not be permitted.

9. These laws include H.B. 283, passed in 2005, which was modeled after the federal Safe Schools Act and added sections to the Texas Education Code requiring state school boards to adopt "Student Codes of Conduct" to address bullying and to have methods in place to prevent and intervene in situations of harassment. (Compl. ¶ 58.) H.B. 283 further amended the Texas Education Code to require school districts to adopt "discipline management programs" to provide for prevention and education of unwanted verbal aggression and bullying. (*Id.* ¶ 59.) Finally, the Texas Association of School Boards ("TASB") distributed a memorandum to school boards statewide entitled "Harassment And Bullying Policies in Public Schools." (*Id.* ¶ 60.) The TASB memorandum explicitly warned school boards that "a school district could be liable when there is student-to-student harassment" where a district's "deliberate[] indifference cause [sic] students to undergo harassment or makes them vulnerable to it, and the harassment takes place in a context subject to the school district's control." (*Id.*)

in this case.[10] *See* TEX. CIV. PRAC. & REM. CODE § 101.001 *et seq.* **[*639]** Following *Covington*, in the absence of a special relationship between the school and the student, public school officials who enact anti-bullying policies do not violate a student's constitutional due process rights by failing to enforce such policies, no matter how pervasive the bullying, no matter how hateful, and no matter how many lives, in addition to Asher's, are lost.

IV. CONCLUSION

In light of the Fifth Circuit's ruling in *Doe v. Covington County Sch. Dist.*, 675 F.3d 849, 2012 U.S. App. LEXIS 6080, 2012 WL 976349 (5th Cir. Mar. 23, 2012), the Court has determined that Defendants' Motion for Reconsideration (Doc. No. 40) must be **GRANTED** and the Court hereby dismisses Plaintiff's due process claim under 42 U.S.C. § 1983 for failure to state a claim upon which relief can be granted.

IT IS SO ORDERED.

Questions Regarding *Estate of Asher Brown v. Cypress Fairbanks Independent School District*

1. How does the plaintiff in this case attempt to distinguish the ruling of *Covington County*?
2. The Southern District of Texas is ultimately forced to change its own ruling in light of the decision in *Covington County*. The court does not appear to be pleased by this, as evidenced by its lamentation toward the end of the opinion. If the court doesn't believe that adherence to *Covington County* is the most just course of action, why does it nevertheless adhere to it?

THE POWER OF STARE DECISIS

The *Deshaney-Covington-Asher Brown* case sequence is brutal, but it illuminates just how stare decisis operates. One decision announces a legal principle; that principle is in turn interpreted by a lower court; that interpretation then forces an even lower court to overturn its own decision and abide by the higher court's reasoning.

Having read *DeShaney*, you probably had an intuition about the likely result in *Covington*. Certainly by the time you read *Asher Brown*, you probably had a

---

10. Defendant argues that this is not entirely true, proposing that Plaintiff could sue the students who bullied Asher. (Doc. No. 46, at 4.)

(perhaps sinking) feeling about how that case would turn out as well. As frustrating as the law can be at times, American jurists' fidelity to precedent makes predicting court decisions a little bit easier. This is the last analytical skill to refine before diving into your first legal writing assignment: how well can you predict how a given court will interpret its binding precedent?

Imagine you were arguing today in the Southern District of Texas, the lowest court from the trio of cases you just read. Without doing any additional research and assuming the three cases you just read were the exclusive universe of applicable case law, can you answer the following questions?

> **Questions Regarding Anticipating How a Court Will Rule**
>
> 1. In *Doe v. Covington County School District,* the Fifth Circuit acknowledges three examples of special relationships: incarceration, institutionalization and foster care. Given your understanding of what triggers a special relationship and these examples, can you come up with a list of elements that would likely be necessary for the Fifth Circuit to recognize a special relationship outside of incarceration, institutionalization and foster care?
> 2. Of the elements you listed, which do you think would be the most difficult to meet? The easiest?
> 3. Can you come up with a hypothetical situation outside of incarceration, institutionalization and foster care that would almost certainly meet the standard for special relationship?
> 4. The Fifth Circuit has yet to adopt or reject the state-created danger theory for substantive due process. Given the precedent cases you've read, how likely do you think it is that the Fifth Circuit will one day adopt it? Explain your answer.
> 5. Of all the elements and sub-elements of the Fifth Circuit's articulation of state-created danger, which do you think is the hardest to prove? The easiest?

chapter 6

Legal Writing Fundamentals

EFFICIENCY, FOCUS AND FORMALITY

Now that you have some grounding in U.S. law and some experience summarizing and analyzing cases, it's time to discuss the fundamental principles of legal writing. Let's start with the three hallmarks of legal writing mentioned in the preface: **efficiency, focus** and **formality**. A personal essay and even some academic essays can effectively utilize a circuitous, even sprawling approach to argument. The author finds their way toward a thesis (assuming there is one). For many genres of writing, this can be a real pleasure. It's as if you and the author were embarking on a journey of discovery together. Legal writing does not invite this kind of loose organization. Whether you're writing a memorandum, an advice letter, a motion or an appellate brief, you're writing with a specific purpose and to a specific audience. You're answering some question or series of questions, and your reader expects the answers to those questions right away, preferably on the first page of your document.

The goals of efficiency and focus are related: you want to focus on the questions you've been tasked with answering, and you want to avoid tangents. Tangents provide little added value, as they represent analysis that isn't relevant to the questions you're supposed to answer. If anything, they risk diminishing your work, both diluting the salient parts of the analysis and risking unnecessary mistakes that could hurt your credibility. As you answer the relevant issues presented, you want to do so as efficiently as possible, avoiding repetition and crafting prose that is as clear and to the point as possible.

Your audience for the legal document in question should help you gauge the appropriate formality, but all legal writing should have a baseline level of discourse somewhere above casual conversation. Whether you're writing to a fellow attorney or to a Supreme Court justice, you're doing so as a professional in a field of professionals. Attention to formality, however, is not synonymous with fancy writing. I once had a student change the names of the "Issues

Presented," "Answers" and "Discussion" sections of their memorandum to the following:

- Issues Presented → Matters of Contention
- Answers → Acknowledgment of Contentions
- Discussion → Symposium

"Matters of Contention" says less efficiently what "Issues Presented" already says. Why use three words when two will do? But at least those two phrases are synonymous. An "acknowledgment" of a contention *could* be an answer to the contention, but it could also just be an expression of awareness. Discussion can happen at a "Symposium," but a written discussion in a legal memorandum is never a symposium. In the student's attempt to appear smart and sophisticated, they ended up over-complicating the prose and produced headings that read more like nonsense than a useful designation of content.

WRITING EFFECTIVELY

Your last mobile phone contract notwithstanding, legal writing, at its best, is reader-friendly. When I was a junior associate at my old law firm, I was asked to write a memorandum of law for one of the most respected partners at the firm. I was terrified when I walked into her office to get my assignment, a research memorandum. I remember poring over every detail before submitting it to her. One day, she called me into her office to discuss my findings. I took the elevator downstairs, checked in with her secretary and braced myself for the worst. During the meeting, she thanked me for my memo, which she said was very thorough, but she had a few questions. I no longer recall the topic of the document, but I do remember that I'd written it in the high legalese style that I noticed many mid-level associates had adopted. I remember how she read one of my sentences out loud: a long and Latin-speckled excursus into the assigned subject. Finally, she looked up from the document and asked, "But what does that mean?"

To be clear, the partner wasn't angry with me (at least I don't think she was). I'd done what she'd asked, and she trusted that I had the answers she was looking for. But she couldn't quite glean them from what I'd written, or if she could, she didn't want to go through the effort if it was easier just to ask a simple question in the hopes of getting a simple answer. I'd made an error in my approach. Instead of trying to answer her questions clearly and simply, I was trying to show off, trying to approximate a voice I thought would impress her. The language, rather than serving my purpose, rather than being the bridge between my understanding and hers, became an impediment. She didn't want me to wow her; she was a busy woman with a lot on her plate. She just wanted me to answer her questions clearly and concisely. Keep that in mind as you tackle your first legal writing assignments. And heed the advice in the following sections as well.

Build Your Argument

Structure your prose logically. For example, when detailing a sequence of events in a statement of facts, do so in chronological order. Consider a timeline with dates aligned on one side of the document and events on the other:

October 2021: Plaintiff, Adrika Y., released a book of poetry loosely based on her life.
November 2021: Defendant, Vibhav L., wrote a parody of Y.'s poetry and posted it on social media.
December 2021: Y. sent L. a cease-and-desist letter, threatening to sue him for copyright infringement.

When presenting arguments, consider placing your strongest arguments first. The start of your argument is when your reader's attention will be sharpest, and these first pages will shape the reader's impression of what's to follow. When building toward a conclusion, especially when dealing with a complicated set of law, move from familiar to new information. Establish a baseline understanding first, then build on that foundation, like building a house.

If it feels as if you're sometimes writing more like a teacher than a lawyer, remember that an important part of an advocate's job is educating their readers. Take your reader step by step through the necessary steps to reach your legal conclusions. Understand that conclusions have no weight unless they follow from a logical and support-driven argument.

Craft Your Sentences

In terms of syntax or sentence structure, make the agents of the action (or subjects) explicit, and put them at the start of the sentence.

> **Instead of:** "The contract was drafted by the sister of the defendant, Anna H.,"
> **consider:** "Anna H., the defendant's sister, drafted the contract."

Move from shorter to longer bundles of information and keep the longest bundles after the verb.

> **Instead of:** "The alleged plagiarizing of the plaintiff's instructor's manual for toy cars was committed by Susan L.,"
> **consider:** "Susan L. allegedly plagiarized Plaintiff's instructor's manual on toy cars."

Try to avoid gaps between subjects and verbs and between verbs and objects.

> **Instead of:** "Luke A., a real estate tycoon known for his business savvy but without knowledge of Defendant's alleged prior misconduct, invested in the project a grand sum of $4.2 million,"
> **consider:** "Luke A. is a real estate tycoon known for his business savvy. Before he knew about Defendant's alleged misconduct, he invested $4.2 million in the project."

Write short sentences: try to keep the average sentence under 20-25 words. It helps to avoid putting too many messages in a single sentence. It's better if your prose is a little choppy than if the reader is confused by multiple messages at once.

> **Instead of:** "Using Congress's Commerce Clause power as justification, the government claims the statute should be subject to rational basis review and that the law passes rational basis as it is reasonably related to a legitimate state interest,"
>
> **consider:** "The government claims the statute is justified under Congress's Commerce Clause power. The statute is accordingly subject to rational basis review. The statute meets rational basis because the law is reasonably related to a legitimate state interest."

Use parallel construction when possible. For example, "hiking, biking and took a boat ride" should be "hiking, biking and boating." Finally, cut down on nominalizations, which are verbs in noun form. For example: "He translated" is better than "He performed a translation."

Be Concise

Clarity and economy are virtues in this genre of writing. Don't use two or more words when one will do. For example, "give, devise and bequeath" can just be "give." Avoid legal jargon and words derived from Latin or French. Students new to legal writing often try to emulate the language from the cases they read. This is generally not a good idea for two reasons: (1) not all judicial decisions are written well, and (2) there's a high risk that you'll say something you don't mean to say. Sometimes, to avoid incorrectly paraphrasing or summarizing law, novice legal writers will simply quote huge swaths of text from the precedent. This is not a good idea, either. It's fine to quote from cases, but only quote the necessary parts. When you include both relevant and irrelevant material in a quote, you're putting the onus on the reader to figure out what's important and what's not. The best legal writers take their understanding of the law and translate it into their own prose, which is ideally even more accessible than the case law's.

Be Concrete

Use as many concrete words (things you can see, hear, touch and feel) as possible to illustrate your arguments. Legal analysis necessarily deals in a number of abstractions (e.g., "reasonable doubt" and "due process"), so when your analysis touches on something that can actually be observed by the senses (e.g., a sulfurous odor leading to a nuisance lawsuit), latch on to that imagery.

Avoid negative expressions when possible.

> **Instead of:** "This is not to say that the argument is not without merit,"
> **consider:** "The argument lacks merit."

Remember also that legal writing is functional above all else; it's unusual for an academic paper to make frequent use of bullet points or numbered lists, but you should feel free to utilize any device that makes your argument easier to understand. This includes visual illustrations, bullets and graphs.

Cite Everything

When you are writing specifically about legal authority, remember to always identify through citation the sources of the law you use, even when what you're citing is common knowledge among laypeople and lawyers alike (e.g., U.S. Const. amend. I). When citing legal authority, follow the sequence of the hierarchy of law: the Constitution if it applies, then any applicable statute, then cases from the highest court in the relevant jurisdiction down to the lowest court. When you're discussing a court's holdings in a case, feel free to use the verbs "held" or "found." But avoid those verbs if you're citing dicta. Instead, use verbs like "said," "stated" or "explained."

Avoid string cites. A string cite is a list of cases cited to support the same legal proposition. For example: "Courts, in general, have resisted expanding the scope of substantive due process. See, e.g., *Deshaney v. Winnebago Cnty. Dep't of Soc. Servs.*, 489 U.S. 189 (1989); *Doe v. Covington Cnty. Sch. Dist.*, 675 F.3d 849 (5th Cir. 2012); *Estate of Asher Brown v. Cypress Fairbanks Indep. Sch. Dist.*, 863 F. Supp. 2d 632 (S.D. Tex. 2012)." On the one hand, it's good to know that multiple cases support the general proposition. The cases are also listed in the appropriate order, with higher authority coming before lower authority. But there's not much that's added to the analysis by this bare list, and that's a missed opportunity. Consider utilizing the same cases but with parentheticals summarizing the relevant holdings instead. For example: "Courts, in general, have resisted expanding the scope of substantive due process. See, e.g., *Deshaney v. Winnebago Cnty. Dep't of Soc. Servs.*, 489 U.S. 189 (1989) (rejecting a domestic violence victim's substantive due process claim when a social worker failed to remove a child from an abusive father's home); *Doe v. Covington Cnty. Sch. Dist.*, 675 F.3d 849 (5th Cir. 2012) (rejecting a sexual molestation victim's substantive due process claim when a school continually released a student to a stranger without consulting its own check-out sheet); *Estate of Asher Brown v. Cypress Fairbanks Indep. Sch. Dist.*, 863 F. Supp. 2d 632 (S.D. Tex. 2012) (rejecting a suicide victim's substantive due process claim when a school failed to enforce its own bullying policy and the repeated victim took his own life)." The additional context that the parentheticals offer adds more weight and substance to the case support.

Adhere to Accepted Formats

When writing to certain courts in the United States, there are very specific rules about how to format your document. Sometimes these rules can be as granular as prescribing the allowed margins on each piece of paper. Courts may also have particular demands on the spacing of the document and on where page numbers should appear.

In terms of substance, almost all legal analysis follows some variation on the **IRAC structure**: Issue → Rule → Application → Conclusion. The **issue** is the legal question you'll be addressing. The **rule** is where you unpack the applicable law that you're using to answer that question. The **application** is where you apply the facts of your case to that law. And the **conclusion** is where you offer your final answer on the issue you presented based on your analysis of the rule and the material facts. For almost all legal tasks, this method of argument-building will be the optimal approach, not to mention the expected one from your reader. There's a logic to it: you start with a question and end with an answer. In between, you identify the law that governs the question and then you apply that law to the facts of the case. Straying from this structure without a good reason risks confusion.

As you tackle various genres of legal writing, start with any prescribed rhetorical rules or conventions (such as the formatting rules a court might have about documents submitted to it), follow guides and templates (such as the ones offered in this text) and seek exemplars (law firms often keep databases of every internal memorandum written by their attorneys). It's fine to be creative in the substance of your arguments, but it's risky to reinvent the wheel when it comes to the structures of legal writing. Even within the limitations of Issue → Rule → Application → Conclusion, there is room for rhetorical variation. Innovate within conventions as opposed to trying to change the genre.

Stay Close to the Law

For the IRAC structure above, which will be explained in more detail in the next chapter, students understand the general order well enough. They start with their issue. They cite the relevant law. Then they apply the case's facts to that law. But too often in the application, students stray from the law they've just established. Imagine if the issue you were tackling was whether Client X was guilty of fraud. In the rule, you'd unpack and cite the applicable law of fraud. Then, in the application, you'd obviously apply the facts of the case to establish whether the elements of fraud were met or not. Too often, though, students will use the application to identify every potential issue of law they see. They'll make arguments relevant to fraud, but they'll also make arguments relevant to conspiracy, for example. These additional arguments muddle the analysis. Think of the rule discussion as equivalent to setting the boundaries of a game. The application is where you play the game—setting forth the best arguments for your side (the main argument) and the opposing side (the counterargument). But you still must stay within the boundaries of the game you've set up. If you do that correctly, then your conclusion (which declares the game's winner) will be that much clearer.

Avoid Repetition

Generally speaking, in the interest of efficiency, you don't want to repeat the same legal proposition multiple times in the same document. An exception to this might be if a rule discussion enumerates a multi-prong test; the application section might then repeat the substance of each prong, perhaps as subheadings, before applying facts to each prong. You may also end up repeating certain conclusions of law. For example, in a memorandum, you'll put the answers to the main questions you've been asked upfront. But those conclusions will likely recur both in the discussion section of the memorandum (which will include all your analysis) and the memorandum's final conclusion.

Write. Rewrite. Repeat.

Absent extreme circumstances, I don't grant extensions on writing assignments. The reason isn't just because legal writers need to learn how to meet deadlines (though they do!); it's also because part of learning how to be a good writer is learning how to manage one's time. Writing isn't just putting words onto a page. It's a process. Whenever I was given an assignment as a lawyer, I always took the time given to me and cut it in half. That halfway point was when I aimed to have a first full draft completed. If I was successful in that, I had the opportunity to:

- Go back to the assigner to ask any follow-up questions.
- Seek feedback from a colleague or mentor.
- Give myself time away from the work, allowing me the distance necessary to revise the assignment with fresh eyes (as tired eyes often see what one meant to write as opposed to what's actually on the document).

Writing is revising. No one's first draft is their best draft. On the rare occasion when I grant an extension, I know I'm not going to get the student's best work because I know the work will not be properly revised. Use your time strategically, and give yourself the best opportunity for success.

Introduction to Legal Memoranda

chapter 7

A legal memorandum is a formal legal analysis focused on answering specific questions regarding a case or set of cases. Much of the research lawyers perform culminates in memoranda. On rare occasions, for particularly important matters, an attorney may receive an assignment memorandum detailing what is being asked of them. More often, however, one is given the request informally, via e-mail, phone or in-person conference.

GETTING THE ASSIGNMENT

The first step in writing an effective memorandum is making sure you understand what the assigner wants in your finished work product. There are few things worse than turning in a three-paragraph e-mail when your supervisor was expecting an in-depth 12-page memo. Make sure you understand the scope of what you're being asked to do. You don't want to omit something the assigner wants, but at the same time, especially in a law firm where your time is billed to a client, you don't want to do unnecessary work. Make sure you understand the format the assigner expects your finished product to take; if you're unsure, err on the side of formality.

Know when the final deadline of your memorandum is and if the assigner wants progress reports leading up to the final submission. If you're given a significant amount of time (say, for example, four weeks) to write a memorandum, aim to complete your research and have a first draft written halfway to your deadline (in the above scenario, at the two-week mark). The more time you give yourself to edit, the more likely it is that the finished result will be thoughtful and well crafted.

One more piece of advice: be honest with an assigner about what you know and don't know about whatever subject matter you're about to tackle. A supervising attorney can often save you (and your client!) precious billed time by explaining basic information you don't have to research later.

KNOWING YOUR AUDIENCE

Typically, the primary audience for a memorandum is the assigner. Most memoranda you'll write will likely be of the interoffice variety: meant for your colleagues at your place of work. Memoranda are often stored in large databases so that future attorneys can reference previous work product. If you're given a specific research assignment regarding a doctrine in copyright law, for example, you might start by searching your own workplace's database to see if any other attorney has written about that same doctrine. The case facts will obviously be different, but the basic law might still apply (though you should do follow-up research to make sure). What this means for you as the writer is that even if you're addressing your memo to an assigning partner who understands the facts of the case, you shouldn't assume that that partner will be the only person utilizing your memo. Accordingly, you should provide enough information in the document so that someone completely unfamiliar with the matter can be brought up to speed with your memo alone.

If you're writing a memorandum to a client, especially a non-lawyer client, you should make sure your explanations are tailored so that a layperson can understand them. It's especially important to err on the side of formality in client memos as the client will know just how many hours were billed for whatever you submit.

FORMATTING THE MEMORANDUM

The following description of the memorandum writing process assumes you're being tasked with a typical litigation-based query, where you're asked to opine on a client's chances measured against an opponent's. But memos should always be dictated by the assigner's specific questions, so if you're being asked for a simple summary of case law in a particular jurisdiction, you'll use a different structure than what's presented below. For most predictive memoranda of moderate complexity or more, however, the elements below should be sufficient:

1. Heading
2. Issue(s) Presented
3. Brief Answer(s)
4. Statement of Facts
5. Discussion
6. Conclusion

Check to see if your workplace has a standard template (including designs and font preferences) for memoranda. If not, you can use already-developed templates from trusted applications or you can design your own—preferably something sleek and easy to read that looks professional. No matter what format you choose, remember to insert page numbers so that if there are any questions or follow-ups, the assigner can direct you to specific places within your document. Consider strategies throughout the presentation that might aid in your reader's understanding of your analysis, including:

- Lists or bullets where appropriate.
- Headings and section breaks to organize the argument and to make it easier for the reader to navigate the parts of your memorandum.
- Visual aids (e.g., charts and graphs) that show trends amidst voluminous data points.

CRAFTING THE HEADING

If you have been given an assignment memo with a proper heading, you should replicate the same format for the heading of your responsive memo. Generally, a heading should have the following information:

1. The recipient of the memo, including any carbon copy (cc) recipients
2. The author of the memo
3. The date you are submitting the memo
4. The subject of the memo

Unless your assigner tells you otherwise, the recipient of the memo should be the person who assigned you the memo. If someone was carbon copied in the assignment memo itself, carbon copy them in your responsive memo. The date of the memo is especially important if it's ever used as a reference in the future. For example, if you were writing the aforementioned copyright memorandum in 2020, you'd likely be more interested in a memo on the same issue from 2019 as opposed to 2001. For the subject of the memorandum, be as detailed as you can be. A subject line that just reads "Copyright Infringement" is less helpful than something more specific, such as "Third Circuit Copyright Infringement: Likelihood of Successful Fair Use Defense." Below is an example of a heading:

Mann & McMahon, LLP

Memorandum

To: Kasia Rudnicki

Cc: Ben Rosenthal

From: Trenton Stone

Date: August 3, 2021

Subject: Third Circuit Copyright Infringement: Likelihood of Successful Fair Use Defense

CRAFTING THE ISSUE(S) PRESENTED

Issues presented should start with some brief context so that the reader can understand what you've been tasked with doing. Again, since you're assuming an audience wider than just the person who gave you the memo assignment, explain the basic situation of your task (e.g., "Our firm represents Client X, who is currently trying to decide whether it makes sense to continue her copyright infringement lawsuit against Defendant Y."), then pose whatever questions you were asked to address in your memorandum. If an assigner has asked you to opine on the likelihood of success for a client, then the first issue presented could be:

1. What is the likelihood that Client X will succeed in her copyright infringement suit against Defendant Y?
Pursuant to answering that primary question, however, other issues or sub-issues may arise, such as:
2. What is Defendant Y's best argument for a fair use defense?
3. How likely is it that Defendant's fair use argument will succeed against Client X?

Just as with Issues in a case brief, it's useful to number the issues presented and to align those issues with the answers in parallel lists. If an issue is complicated, don't feel pressured to articulate it in a single sentence. It's essential that this part of the memo be as clear as possible, so take as many sentences as you need.

It might seem odd to start a memorandum with a list of pointed questions. You might be tempted to start with the statement of facts (as a case often does), offering the narrative of the underlying matter as context. But remember that a memorandum exists because the assigner had specific and focused concerns. That same assigner wants to know the answers to those concerns as soon as possible, without having to wade through a statement of facts.

In ordering your questions, start with the broadest and most important queries first (often whether one's client will succeed in their lawsuit or not), then handle any sub-questions necessary to address the larger query. Use the assigner's framing of the questions as a guide: begin with the assigner's questions first and make sure to answer all their queries, at the very least.

CRAFTING THE BRIEF ANSWER(S)

Your Issues Presented posed one or more questions that the memorandum will address. Here you should provide direct answers to those questions with very brief explanations. There's no need for cited law (unless an Issue asks specifically for it); just give the short responses, knowing that your reader will understand that the longer explanation with full citations will follow.

Below are examples of Answers to the Issues Presented above:

1. Client X is likely to succeed in their copyright infringement suit against Defendant Y despite Defendant Y's likely fair use defense.

2. Defendant Y's strongest defense under the fair use factors is that Defendant Y only sampled a small portion (approximately 25%) of Client X's work in their allegedly infringing song.
3. Fair use, however, is decided based on the balance of four factors, and arguably all four factors cut in favor of Client X. Accordingly, Client X should be able to withstand Defendant Y's fair use defense:
    a. *The purpose of the work:* Defendant Y's work is a commercial song, in the same market as Client X's.
    b. *The nature of the work:* Client X's work, as a purely creative work, is afforded the highest degree of copyright protection.
    c. *The amount of the original work used:* Even though Defendant Y only used 25 percent of the original work, it was the chorus of the song, the most well-known part of the work.
    d. *The effect on the original's market:* There is at least some evidence that consumers believed Defendant Y was the originator of the copied portion in question, leading to a risk of market substitution.

Brief answers are the main conclusions of your memorandum. They represent the document's entire reason for being. That's why they show up right away in the memorandum. The structure of your Answers depends on the structure of your Issues Presented, as the two sections should work in concert. Make sure to answer the questions presented directly with at least a hint of the substantive reasoning behind your conclusion (think of it as a sneak preview of a movie but with spoilers encouraged).

CRAFTING THE STATEMENT OF FACTS

Similar to the Facts section of a case brief, the Statement of Facts is where you provide an account of what happened between the litigants leading to the lawsuit. Introduce the people involved. Explain the cause of action and the context of your representation. Tell the narrative of the case in chronological order, with an emphasis on facts relevant to the issues you'll be discussing in your memorandum. Again, as in a case brief, make sure the Statement of Facts includes every fact you refer to later in your Discussion.

Here is an example of a Statement of Facts:

- In 2020, Client X wrote and released Song Z through Cloud Records; at the apex of its popularity, the song reached number four on the Billboard Pop Chart.
- In June 2021, Defendant Y released Song W through Phantom Records; in only its third week after release, the song reached number two on the Billboard Pop Chart.
- Defendant Y admits that they "sampled" part of Client X's work in their song; they also admit that they never asked permission for use of any part of Song Z.

Every material fact, or every fact relevant to the underlying legal issues, must be represented in this Statement. Think of this section as the human story of the case or the leadup to the lawsuit. If you can present that story as a linear timeline, do so. If the facts are particularly involved, consider dividing the timeline into sections, covering various time periods or events.

CRAFTING THE DISCUSSION

If the Discussion is particularly long or involved, consider starting with a roadmap that alerts the reader to the issues to be discussed and the order in which you plan to discuss them. As mentioned above in the Formatting section of the chapter, subject headings within the Discussion will help guide your reader through each discrete issue and sub-issue.

Remember to organize your analysis around issues, not precedent cases (unless your task is to actually provide a survey of cases). Imagine you're answering two major questions throughout your memo and in answering those questions, you end up citing 12 cases. Your discussion shouldn't begin with 12 mini case briefs. Your job is to extract exactly what's necessary from those cases and to use that law to answer those major questions. The best way to ensure that is to use the aforementioned IRAC structure (Issue → Rule → Application → Conclusion) to address each legal issue.

Issue

This could either be a repetition of an issue presented or a sub-issue developed pursuant to answering an issue presented. Again, there's no need to fit the issue in one sentence if it's particularly complex, but if you feel as if you're answering multiple questions in one sentence, considering breaking it up into two or more. Issues should be framed as questions to be answered, not as general subject matter areas.

> **Instead of:** "Copyright Infringement,"
> **consider:** "Whether Client X can successfully prove the elements of copyright infringement against Defendant Y."

Just as memoranda are documents designed to answer specific questions with specific answers, the arguments leading to those answers should be similarly focused and framed in a way that leads to a clear and efficient explanation of your Conclusions/Brief Answers. You don't have to unpack the history of intellectual property law in the United States to show whether a particular copyright claim is valid or not.

Rule

Present the applicable rule in order of its force within the hierarchy of law (e.g., the Constitution comes before federal statutes, which come before Supreme

Court precedent, which comes before Circuit Court precedent, etc.). Try to keep rule discussions brief and isolated to the part of the Constitution, statute or case law that articulates most clearly the law you need to apply. Be especially discriminating about facts from precedent cases and whether they're actually necessary for understanding the general rule. For example, if you were applying the multi-pronged state-created danger standard from *Doe v. Covington Cnty. Sch. Dist.* to a given set of facts, is it necessary to know that *Covington County* is about a school that continually released a young girl to a child molester? Make sure to cite everything properly; the rule provides the underlying authority for your analysis, and if you get this wrong, everything that flows from it — including your ultimate conclusions — will be compromised.

A rule discussion on the copyright infringement issue discussed above could read like this:

> A copyright infringement action requires a plaintiff to prove:
> 1. Ownership of a valid copyright, and
> 2. Copying of constituent elements of the work that are original.
>
> *Feist Publ'ns, Inc. v. Rural Tel. Serv. Co.*, 499 U.S. 340, 361 (1991).

While rule discussions can be as simple as the enumeration of elements above, sometimes the law is more complicated. Think back to the standard for special relationship from *DeShaney v. Winnebago County*. For special relationship, there isn't a clear articulation of necessary elements. Instead there's a discussion you'd likely paraphrase about what triggers the duty to protect (e.g., the state restraining a person's liberty to protect or care for themselves). You might also offer examples of special relationships that courts have upheld in the past (such as incarceration, institutionalization and foster care). When the legal test is straightforward and easy to understand, you'll likely need less explanation in this section. When the standard is more nuanced or opaque, you'll need to provide more elaboration and examples. No matter what, make sure that by the end of the rule section, you've captured the entire legal framework you intend to apply to your facts.

Application

Here is where the real analysis starts. In this section, you'll cover both your argument and the counterargument against you.

First, apply the facts of the case to the rule you've established. What are the best arguments for your side under the precedent law? For clarity's sake, you may need to repeat the relevant language of the Rule above (especially if you're applying a multi-prong test). Again, you want to make clear that you're covering all necessary parts of the law. You also never want your reader to be confused about why you're bringing up a particular fact or argument. The elegance of a properly executed IRAC is that the reader should be able to follow the logic of every sentence in sequence as you unpack your argument.

You may also cite additional precedent law, including prior case facts, to draw comparisons between your side's facts and the facts from favorable case law. If a similar case was decided in a way that's good for your side, it only makes sense to draw as many comparisons to that case as possible. For example, if you were representing the state in a substantive due process matter involving a social worker who failed to intervene in a domestic abuse case, you'd want to draw comparisons to the facts of *DeShaney v. Winnebago County*.

But your application shouldn't end with just an analysis of your client's best arguments. After you've completed the application for your side, you should apply the facts to the law from your opponent's perspective. What are the best arguments for opposing counsel under the precedent law? Again, you may cite additional precedent, this time drawing from the facts of unfavorable case law. Present the strongest case for your opponent just as you presented the strongest case for your side. Avoid *straw man arguments*: presenting a deliberately weak counterargument to try to bolster your argument only weakens the credibility of your analysis and conclusions.

The application argument for the copyright infringement elements could read like this:

With regard to element (1) of copyright infringement, there is no question that Client X and Cloud Records own a valid copyright to Song Z. It was acquired in 2020 well before the release of Song W. Defendant Y does not dispute Client X's or Cloud Records' ownership of a valid copyright.

With regard to element (2) of copyright infringement, almost the entire chorus of Song Z is replicated in Song W. This accounts for approximately 25 percent of Song Z. Defendant Y may try to argue that while the melody and lyrics are identical between the two choruses, Defendant Y's changes in music style and tempo qualitatively change the constituent elements of Client X's work.

Conclusion

After you've presented the best arguments under the law for both your side and your opponent's, you can answer the question of which side you think is more likely to prevail in the relevant jurisdiction. If you're writing an interoffice or client memo, remember that your job is to be objective. Unlike a piece of advocacy for a court, like a motion or appellate brief, your job isn't to zealously defend your client and then allow an arbiter to make the final judgment. You're being asked to opine on the most likely outcome under the law. Present that outcome, whether it's in your favor or not.

The Conclusion of the copyright infringement issue above could read like this:

Despite Defendant Y's claims, which are more relevant to its fair use defense than to rebutting element (2) of copyright infringement, Client X has the superior claim under both elements of copyright infringement.

CRAFTING THE MEMO'S CONCLUSION

It's possible that at the end of your Discussion, you will have reached a number of seemingly contradictory conclusions. Let's say that your ultimate objective in the memo was to determine whether a defendant had a valid fair use defense in a copyright infringement action. As mentioned above, fair use is determined by a balance of four factors. Imagine a Discussion in which you divided your analysis by those four factors and ultimately concluded that the plaintiff has the stronger argument for two of the four factors and the defendant has the stronger argument for the other two. Your memo's conclusion can be where you finish the work of balancing that four-factor analysis and opine on which side you think will ultimately prevail and why.

If you don't have to resolve a split in your analysis, then the Conclusion can just be a summary of your analysis above. Think of it as a longer version of your brief answer with more context.

CASE CITATIONS

It's important to cite all sources of law in any legal document, and the memorandum is no exception. The first time you cite a case, use the full citation, the elements of which were detailed in Chapter 4. Here is an example of a full citation with the pincite left blank:

DeShaney v. Winnebago Cnty. Dep't of Soc. Servs., 489 U.S. 189, ___ (1989). (Full Citation)

If you cite the same case again immediately afterward, you can use *Id.* (Latin for *idem*, meaning the same) and the pincite: *Id.* at ___. If the pincite is the exact same as the previous citation, you can just write *Id.* If you cite some other source of law—a statute or another case—in between, you should use the case's short citation form, which will include one party's name, a comma, the volume of the reporter, the reporter, the word "at" and the pincite:

DeShaney, 489 U.S. at ___. (Short Citation)

Accordingly, the full citation for any case should only appear once in a legal document, the first time the case is cited.

Below is a rubric for evaluating legal memoranda. Again, because the structure of legal memoranda shifts with different objectives, the criteria below might not always apply, but for most legal memos, you should consider the following:

LEGAL MEMORANDUM RUBRIC

Category	Accomplished	Competent	Beginning
Presentation and Professionalism			
· Writes in clear and accessible prose			
· Employs logical organization, including adherence to IRAC			
· Shows command of grammar, syntax and citation			
Substantive Argument			
· Introduction explains memorandum's purpose			
· Parallel issues and answers provide all requested legal conclusions			
· Statement of facts is logically presented and properly curated			
· Rule discussions are complete and accurate			
· Application analysis focuses on relevant law			
· Application objectively covers both argument and counterargument			
· Conclusions are clear and supported by argument			
General Comments and Suggestions for Improvement:			

Grade: _____

Below is a sample of a student-written legal memorandum. The memo is partially responsive to a past version of Assignment 9: First Amendment Rights at Kinnear High, found in Chapter 10. But at the time of this student's memorandum, the U.S. Supreme Court had yet to hear the *Mahanoy* case. The student accordingly used the Third Circuit's prior decision in *Mahanoy*, which has since been supplanted by the Supreme Court's decision. This is why it's imperative in the real world for lawyers to check the currency of the law they cite; one decision can render an entire analysis obsolete. It would therefore not be a good idea to adopt all the legal reasoning or conclusions from this memorandum in crafting your Assignment 9, but the memo remains a fine example of the legal memorandum form.

Learned Foot, LLP

Memorandum

To: Antonio Elefano

From: Student H—

Subject: First Amendment Rights at Kinnear High

The firm represents both Giorgio Bankard and Elise Condon in their 42 U.S.C. § 1983 claims against the Jeevers Independent School District (JISD) in the U.S. District Court of Delaware, accusing the school district of violating their First Amendment rights. Each student has a separate team within the firm representing them. This memorandum specifically analyzes Mr. Bankard's pieces of speech to determine his likelihood of success against JISD.

Issues Presented

Under the interpretation of the First Amendment by the Supreme Court and the Third Circuit Court of Appeals, did JISD have the right to punish Mr. Bankard for:

1. His Twitter messages?
2. His placement of a sock in his trousers?

Brief Answer

1. Since Mr. Bankard's Twitter messages occurred off-campus, JISD had no right to punish him for his speech on Twitter.
2. Since Mr. Bankard's stuffing of a sock in his crotch occurred on-campus, JISD had the right to punish the speech if it was foreseeably disruptive or impermissibly lewd.
   a. Given the lack of documented disruption, JISD has a low chance of proving that the sock incident was "foreseeably disruptive."
   b. JISD, however, has a moderate chance of proving the sock was "impermissibly lewd" and that the punishment for this piece of speech was justified.

Statement of Facts

Both Giorgio Bankard and Elise Condon attend Kinnear High School (KHS) in the Jeevers Independent School District (JISD) of Jeevers, Delaware. In September 2020, Mr. Bankard discovered that his current "Introduction to Cinema" teacher, Roderick Davidson, had previously starred in several pornographic films during his early twenties under the stage name "Scout Mercer." As Scout Mercer, Mr. Davidson appeared in three films, entitled *The Ass Menagerie, Saving Ryan's Privates,* and

Peeing on John Malkovich. Surprised by Mr. Davidson's past career, Mr. Bankard went on Twitter during school hours (as confirmed by the tweet's metadata) and tweeted:

> **Mr. Davidson = Scout Mercer. Seriously, look it up! 💧→ 📦 ☺**

While Mr. Bankard tweeted the message above from a private account, the account was followed by over three hundred students at KHS. On the same day of these posts, Mr. Bankard's classmate, Elise Condon, sent a reply to Bankard's tweet (also during school hours.) The message read:

> **😲 🔫 to Mr. Davidson! I hope he gets 💧ed!**

After reading Ms. Condon's reply, Mr. Bankard responded to her tweet with:

> **Lighten up. Davidson's a good guy. I just thought it was funny**

In response, Ms. Condon replied back:

> **Nothing funny about lust, Whore-gio. It's one of the seven deadly sins and any man who could do what he did shouldn't be teaching in a school.**

Two dozen other classmates commented on the above Twitter exchange that same evening. About half of the classmates supported Mr. Bankard's defense of Mr. Davidson, while the other half supported Ms. Condon's efforts to have Mr. Davidson removed from teaching at KHS. The next morning, to demonstrate their support of Mr. Davidson and their interest in promoting "open discussions of sexuality in school," Mr. Bankard and three of his friends arrived at school with socks stuffed inside the crotches of their trousers. On the same school day, Ms. Condon walked to the whiteboard outside Mr. Davidson's classroom which advertised the films Mr. Davidson was watching at the time. Ms. Condon erased the prior contents of the whiteboard ("What I'm Watching: *Howard's End*") and replaced it with the titles of Mr. Davidson's adult films: "*The Ass Menagerie, Saving Ryan's Privates, Peeing on John Malkovich.*"

Immediately after these events, the school principal, Cory Zare, became aware of the tweets and sock incident of Mr. Bankard and the tweets and whiteboard post of Ms. Condon. As a punishment for these acts of speech, Ms. Zare suspended both students for three days, even though Mr. Davidson did not want either student suspended. In fact, Mr. Davidson claims that he suffered no injury from his outing as a former pornographic actor. He is still employed by the school. His hallway whiteboard, however, has been removed.

Discussion

Mr. Bankard contends that JISD violated his free speech by suspending him for two acts of speech which discussed Mr. Davidson's former pornographic career. Free speech claims are rooted in the First Amendment when it states "Congress shall make no law respecting an establishment of religion, or prohibiting the free exercise thereof; or abridging the freedom of speech." The Supreme Court, in *Tinker v. Des*

Moines Indep. Cmty. Sch. Dist., 393 U.S. 503 (1969), explicitly guarantees students the presumption of free speech in public schools, determining that students and teachers do not "shed their constitutional rights to freedom of speech or expression at the schoolhouse gate." *Id.* at 506. The Court does acknowledge, however, that school officials have some authority to regulate speech given "the special characteristics of the school environment." *Id.* at 507. Within *Tinker* itself, the Court gives schools the right to censor speech which "materially disrupts classwork or involves substantial disorder or invasion of the rights of others." *Id.* at 513. In addition to the substantial disruption and invasion of rights standards provided by *Tinker*, the Supreme Court has since introduced "lewdness" as an exception to free speech in public schools. *Bethel Sch. Dist. No. 403 v. Fraser*, 478 U.S. 675 (1986). Interpreting these rulings, the Third Circuit Court of Appeals has provided further guidance on the topic of free speech in public schools with *B.H. ex rel. Hawk v. Easton Area Sch. Dist.*, 725 F.3d 293 (3d Cir. 2013), and *B.L. v. Mahanoy Area Sch. Dist.*, 2020 U.S. App. LEXIS 20365 (3d Cir. 2020). Therefore, to see if Mr. Bankard's speech was protected by the First Amendment, we must examine each piece of Mr. Bankard's speech in relation to the relevant free speech standards provided by these cases.

Twitter Posts

To determine if Mr. Bankard's posts on Twitter merit the broader protection of free speech in the public environment or the limited protection of free speech in the school environment, we must conclude whether these posts occurred "on-campus" or "off-campus" according to the definitions provided by the Third Circuit in *B.L.*, 2020 U.S. App. LEXIS 20365, at *16. In *B.L.*, the Third Circuit rejects the "reasonable foreseeability" to make its way onto campus standard established by the Second Circuit in *Wisniewski ex rel. Wisniewski v. Bd. of Educ. of the Weedsport Cent. Sch. Dist.*, 494 F.3d 34 (2d Cir. 2007), and states that "a student's online speech is not rendered 'on campus' simply because it involves the school, mentions teachers or administrators, is shared with or accessible to students, or reaches the school environment." *B.L.*, 2020 U.S. App. LEXIS 20365, at *16. Instead, the Third Circuit holds that speech is "on-campus" if it took place in a school-sponsored forum, in a "context that bear[s] the imprimatur of the school," or on an online platform that the school owns or operates. *Id.*

Held to this definition, Mr. Bankard's Twitter posts likely constitute "off-campus speech." Since JISD does not own or operate Twitter, these messages were not in a school-sponsored forum or a school-operated website. Beyond that, since Mr. Bankard posted his messages on a personal account, not a school-sponsored account, his messages did not "bear the imprimatur of the school." The school district may contend that the tweets were on-campus since they were posted while Mr. Bankard was on school grounds. In *B.L.*, while the Third Circuit does cite the fact that B.L. posted her message away from campus when ruling in her favor, they do not explicitly hold that on-campus online speech should not receive the same protection if it otherwise still occurs on a non-school-sponsored platform. *Id.* If speech occurs off-campus, then it is not subject to the restrictions of *Tinker* or *Fraser*. *Id.* at

*33-38. Therefore, since a clear standard for online speech on school grounds does not exist, the U.S. District Court of Delaware should defer to the protection of free speech by considering Mr. Bankard's tweets "off-campus" and not subject to school regulation.

If, however, the District of Delaware considered Mr. Bankard's tweets "on-campus" speech, the Court would need to decide whether the *Tinker* or *Fraser* exception to First Amendment rights applies. As mentioned above, *Tinker* gave schools the right to prohibit speech which "foreseeably" or "materially and substantially disrupt[s] the work and discipline of the school." *Tinker*, 393 U.S. at 513. When applying *Tinker* to Mr. Bankard's tweets, there are strong arguments both in favor of and against substantial disruption. The defendants could argue that Mr. Bankard's tweet informed students about Mr. Davidson's former profession, thus inspiring Mr. Bankard's friends to wear socks in their trousers and Ms. Condon to write the adult film titles on the class whiteboard. This argument only works, however, if the acts which Mr. Bankard inspired were indeed disruptive. Given the facts currently available to the firm, there is little indication that the actions of Mr. Bankard, his friends, or Ms. Condon directly prevented a student from learning. Mr. Davidson himself has expressed support for both Bankard and Condon, saying that he has not suffered as a result of their actions. Mr. Davidson's positive comments support the notion that no disruption occurred.

The defendants may also contend that even if the tweet did not cause actual substantial disruption, it could have caused foreseeable disruption by causing students to gossip and disrespect Mr. Davidson. While *Tinker* does allow schools to prohibit speech which could foreseeably disrupt the school environment, that foreseeable disruption must be "more than a mere desire to avoid the discomfort and unpleasantness that always accompany an unpopular viewpoint." *Id.* at 509. Given the scandalous nature of Mr. Davidson's profession, our client could argue that he was punished not for causing foreseeable disruption, but for simply disseminating truths which made the administration uncomfortable.

JISD has a much higher chance of justifying their response to Mr. Bankard's tweets through the legal pathway provided by *Bethel v. Fraser*. In *Fraser*, the Supreme Court holds that public schools have the right "to prohibit the use of vulgar and offensive terms in public discourse" in order to promote "fundamental values necessary to the maintenance of a democratic political system." *Fraser*, 478 U.S. at 682-683. This holding provides JISD the ability to restrict speech which can be considered impermissibly lewd. In *B.H. v. Easton*, 725 F.3d, at 308-316, the Third Circuit extends and clarifies the free speech restrictions of *Fraser*, creating a three-tiered system of designation for lewd speech, ruling that:

1. Plainly lewd speech, which offends for the same reasons obscenity offends, can be categorically restricted regardless of whether it comments on political or social issues.

2. Speech that does not rise to the level of plainly lewd but that a reasonable observer can interpret as lewd can be categorically restricted as long as it can not plausibly be interpreted as commenting on political or social issues.
3. Speech that does not rise to the level of plainly lewd and that can plausibly be interpreted as commenting on political or social issues can not be categorically restricted.

Given these three classifications ("lewd," "ambiguously lewd but apolitical," and "ambiguously lewd but political"), we must first determine whether the tweets were either "plainly lewd" or "ambiguously lewd." *B.H.* defines "ambiguously lewd" as "speech that a reasonable observer could interpret as either lewd or non-lewd." *Id.* at 306. "Plainly lewd," therefore, refers to speech which can only be interpreted as lewd. Since a reasonable person who is unfamiliar with emoji slang could interpret the message "🍆 → ☐ 😍" as a random selection of symbols meaning "eggplant, right arrow, hole, heart eyes," Mr. Bankard's emoji message does not reach the severity of "plainly lewd." However, since the message does suggest penetrative sex to those more aware of emojis' meanings, it could likely be considered "ambiguously lewd."

Since the message could likely be "ambiguously lewd," we must now determine whether it can plausibly be interpreted as commenting on political or social issues. Based on the combination of these answers, we can determine how JISD should treat the website message under *Fraser* and *B.H.* The defense will certainly contend that when compared to the overt anti-Vietnam War sentiments of *Tinker* or the breast cancer awareness sentiments of *B.H.*, Mr. Bankard's message clearly lacks a political or social message. This argument has a high chance of success, but we still must present an argument in favor of Mr. Bankard. Our client may argue that he posted his emoji message for the same reasons he wore a sock in his trousers: "to open discussions of sexuality in school." According to this logic, if students learned through playful emoji language that their teacher was a former adult film star, they would feel more comfortable openly talking about safe and healthy sex. To succeed, this counterargument depends on whether students perceived this social message when they saw him walking down the halls. If student testimony shows recognition of this social purpose, the tweets could merit First Amendment protection under *B.H.* If the testimony fails to recognize such a purpose, JISD would maintain the right to punish him. Given the maturity of high school students, the latter seems more likely, but again, only if the tweets are considered on-campus speech.

Sock Incident

When analyzing Mr. Bankard's second piece of contested speech, the act of stuffing a sock in the crotch of his trousers at school, we do not need to debate whether the act occurred on-campus or off-campus per *B.L.* Mr. Bankard wore the sock on school grounds and during school hours; the act was clearly on-campus. Therefore, the "sock incident" falls under the restrictions of both *Tinker* and *Fraser.*

Like the tweets, there is no evidence that the boys' sock wearing disrupted anyone's educational experience. Therefore, the Court will likely conclude there was no substantial disruption. The defendants could contend that the school reasonably foresaw students being distracted or made uncomfortable by the visual innuendo. Again, however, the foreseeable disruption must rise above mere "discomfort and unpleasantness." *Tinker,* 393 U.S. at 509. One could assume that the misguided fashion decisions of high school students often make teachers feel uncomfortable. That discomfort, however, does not give teachers the right to suspend students for their apparel.

Similar to the tweets, the defendants have a better chance of justifying their punishment by framing the "sock incident" as impermissibly lewd under *Fraser* and *B.H.* According to *B.H.*'s tiers of lewdness, Mr. Bankard's sock incident probably does not constitute "plain lewdness." Even though someone could see the stuffed sock as a sexually-charged suggestion of a large phallus referencing Mr. Davidson's films, a reasonable person could also perceive the large bulge as the result of Mr. Bankard being naturally prominent in that area or having an awkward fold in his pants. Since this bulge could be perceived both ways, it fits better within the classification "ambiguously lewd."

If the sock is perceived as ambiguously lewd, Mr. Bankard can resort to the same political message as his tweets: that the act sought to encourage open discussions of sexuality within the school. Given the discussion on social media and Mr. Davidson's relief that his secret is out, it appears Mr. Bankard's efforts have somewhat succeeded. Overall, however, the school has a better chance of proving the sock as ambiguously lewd with no discernible political or social message. This would make the school's punishment for this piece of speech constitutional.

Conclusion

Mr. Bankard's Twitter message has the highest chance of receiving First Amendment protection because it occurred "off-campus" in accord with *B.L. v. Mahanoy,* 2020 U.S. App. LEXIS 20365. Since Mr. Bankard's sock stuffing occurred "on-campus," it is subject to the free speech restrictions of *Tinker v. Des Moines* and *Bethel v. Fraser.* JISD has a much higher chance of justifying their punishment for the sock stuffing through the "impermissible lewdness" standard of *Fraser/B.H.* Although the sock stunt would not likely be considered "plainly lewd," as long as Mr. Bankard fails to imbue his "ambiguously lewd" sock stuffing with a political message, JISD has a high chance of proving the acts of speech were "impermissibly lewd" and properly regulated by the school.

> **Tips for Legal Memoranda**
>
> 1. When you start writing the memorandum, it might make sense to draft in the following order:
>   a. Issues Presented
>   b. Statement of Facts
>   c. Discussion
>   d. Conclusion
>   e. Brief Answers
> 2. Avoid accurate but irrelevant arguments. Make sure that every part of your memo answers the questions you have been asked to answer.
> 3. As with all types of legal writing, clarity is key. Legal arguments are almost always complex, so keep the prose as simple and efficient as possible.
> 4. When you've gotten the language just as you like it in the memo, the last step is a cite check. Go through every legal citation in your document and cross-reference it to the underlying cases or statutes (this will be much faster if you've printed or downloaded all cited authority and highlighted the relevant sections).

In Chapters 8 through 10 you will be given five memorandum assignments (Assignments 5-9) using increasingly large case universes. The first two assignments in Chapter 8 only use one case as precedent. The third assignment in Chapter 9 uses three cases, but they're three cases you've already read and briefed (the trio of substantive due process cases from Chapters 4 and 5). The final two assignments in Chapter 10, which center on First Amendment rights in schools, use the same five-case universe.

chapter 8

One-Case Memorandum Assignments

For this first memo assignment, an interoffice memo intended for fellow attorneys, it will be useful to know the following terms:

- *Pro bono:* work undertaken without charge
- *Writ of habeas corpus:* petition to a court by a prisoner to determine the legality of their current detention, including the conditions of confinement
- *Prima facie:* sufficient to establish a fact or raise a presumption unless that fact or presumption can be disproved or rebutted
- *Order to show cause:* demand from a judge for a party to prove why the court should not grant a particular motion
- *Traverse:* denial of a matter of fact alleged in an opposing party's pleadings
- *Facial challenge:* contention that a law is unconstitutional as written, or on its face. This differs from an *as applied challenge,* which merely asserts that a law is unconstitutional as applied to the particular litigant challenging it. The result of a successful facial challenge to a law is invalidation of that law for everyone. A successful applied challenge allows the law to stand, except as it applies to the challenging party.

ASSIGNMENT 5: RELIGIOUS LIBERTY MEMORANDUM

Learned Foot, LLP

Memorandum

To: Associates

From: [Your Professor/Supervising Partner]

Subject: Religious Liberty Memorandum for California Prisoner Rusty Doucet

Background:

As part of Learned Foot, LLP's ongoing commitment to pro bono work, we have taken on the habeas corpus case of Rusty Doucet, a prisoner in the California State Prison of Los Angeles. Last month, Mr. Doucet filed a petition for writ of habeas corpus on his own behalf challenging the denial of his request to be transferred from his current windowless cell to any cell within the facility with a window. Doucet claims that his religion, called the Ark of Light, requires that he has access to natural light every day of his life.

Mr. Doucet is serving the first of a three-year sentence for second-degree robbery. The conviction stemmed from an incident last fall when Mr. Doucet robbed the Loomis, CA Dairy Hut. Brandishing a pistol, he entered the Dairy Hut five minutes before its closing and demanded that the manager give him all the money in the cash register as well as "all the burgers in the place, including the fixins." The manager complied, and approximately fifteen minutes later, Doucet left the Dairy Hut with two trash bags filled with approximately $1400, over twenty pounds of ground beef, five dozen hamburger buns, and a crisper's worth of lettuce, tomatoes, American cheese and onions. The manager called the police once Doucet's car fled the parking lot, and Doucet was arrested within the hour. He was convicted in Loomis Superior Court at the beginning of this year.

In denying Doucet's request for transfer, the prison's warden, Yance Boudreaux, claimed that cell transfer requests are difficult to accommodate because of the high population in California state prisons. Only a quarter of the cells in his particular prison have windows, and those cells' current occupants are all prisoners who've been incarcerated for over five years; additionally, almost all of those prisoners have had zero or minimal incident reports. While Mr. Doucet has yet to have a reported incident himself, he has also been in the California State Prison for a relatively short amount of time. Boudreaux claims that granting Doucet's request could lead to similar requests and throw off the meritocracy/longevity standard that has worked well at keeping order. He also claims that Mr. Doucet and almost all prisoners outside of solitary confinement are given at least one hour of outside time every day, through which Doucet could fulfill his religious needs. Mr. Boudreaux did concede, however, that on occasion, outside privileges are suspended prison-wide for various administrative reasons, though typically for no longer than a day or two at a time.

Applicable Law:

The relevant statute is the Religious Land Use and Institutionalized Persons Act of 2000 (RLUIPA), 42 U.S.C. § 2000cc et seq. The two relevant sections of RLUIPA are: 42 U.S.C. § 2000cc-1—Protection of religious exercise of institutionalized persons, and 42 U.S.C. § 2000cc-2—Judicial relief. The relevant parts of each statute are excerpted below:

42 U.S.C. § 2000cc-1(a).

(a) General rule.

No government shall impose a substantial burden on the religious exercise of a person residing in or confined to an institution . . . even if the burden results from a rule of general applicability, unless the government demonstrates that imposition of the burden on that person—
    (1) is in furtherance of a compelling governmental interest; and
    (2) is the least restrictive means of furthering that compelling governmental interest.

42 U.S.C. § 2000cc-2(b).

(b) Burden of persuasion.

If a plaintiff produces prima facie evidence to support a claim alleging a violation of the Free Exercise Clause or a violation of section 2 [42 U.S.C.S. § 2000cc], the government shall bear the burden of persuasion on any element of the claim, except that the plaintiff shall bear the burden of persuasion on whether the law (including a regulation) or government practice that is challenged by the claim substantially burdens the plaintiff's exercise of religion.

Additionally, there is a relevant California Court of Appeal case from our Appellate District (the Third): *In re Margarito Jesus Garcia,* 202 Cal. App. 4th 892 (Ct. App. 2012). For the time being, you should isolate your analysis to the excerpted statutory sections and *Garcia*.

Issues Presented:

Upon receiving Mr. Doucet's near-incomprehensible petition for writ of habeas corpus, the Loomis Superior Court contacted our offices to see if we were willing to take on the case pro bono. There is little documentation on Mr. Doucet's religion, the Ark of Light. We do know that the religion has its roots in east Texas and that one of the original members moved to California and began an offshoot in Loomis approximately two years ago. There are five aphorisms that the Ark of Light abide by: Light, Intuition, Refraction, Opposites and Music. Beyond that, the only fact we know is that the majority of its members, including Mr. Doucet at the time, live in one large compound in downtown Loomis.

Your job is to review the RLUIPA sections above and the *Garcia* case. For now, only focus on RLUIPA and *Garcia*'s holdings on RLUIPA; another set of associates will deal with the constitutional/First Amendment issues. Lay out the relevant burdens of proof on both sides. Then apply the law above to the current facts to determine how strong a claim you think Mr. Doucet has against the California Department of Corrections and Rehabilitation (CDCR).

IN RE GARCIA

Court of Appeal of California, Third Appellate District
January 11, 2012, Filed
C066452

Reporter: 202 Cal. App. 4th 892 *

Judges: Opinion by Hull, J., with Blease, Acting P.J., and Mauro, J., concurring.

Opinion by: Hull

Opinion (Edited for Content)

Hull, J.—Petitioner Margarito Jesus Garcia, a prison inmate subject to the custody and control of California's Department of Corrections and Rehabilitation (CDCR), filed a petition for writ of habeas corpus challenging the denial of his request to participate in an existing kosher meals program. Petitioner contends his religion, Messianic Judaism, requires that he maintain a kosher diet, and the denial of his request violates his First and Fourteenth Amendment rights as well as the Religious Land Use and Institutionalized Persons Act of 2000 (RLUIPA). (42 U.S.C. § 2000cc et seq.)

(1) We conclude that, under the circumstances presented, prison officials are in violation of petitioner's statutory rights under RLUIPA. Prison officials [*896] have not disputed either the sincerity of petitioner's religious beliefs or the requirement that he maintain a kosher diet. Nor have they demonstrated the burden imposed on petitioner's religious beliefs by virtue of his exclusion from the kosher meals program furthers a compelling governmental interest and is the least restrictive means of furthering that interest, as required by RLUIPA. In light of the foregoing conclusion, it is unnecessary to address petitioner's constitutional claims.

FACTS AND PROCEEDINGS

Petitioner is an inmate of the CDCR who, at the time of the petition herein, was housed at Mule Creek State Prison in Ione, California (Mule Creek). On July 27, 2009, petitioner submitted a CDCR form requesting to participate in Mule Creek's Jewish kosher diet program (JKDP). On the form, petitioner identified his religion as Messianic Judaism and indicated he had been practicing the religion for the prior two years. He also identified the following dietary law to which he must adhere: "According to the Torah, I am not allowed to eat meat with blood in it, and I am not allowed to eat foods that are mixed with unclean food."

Petitioner's request was denied by Mule Creek's Jewish chaplain, Rabbi Korik. As the basis for the denial, Korik explained: "Inmate Garcia has confirmed during the interview that he does not practice Judaism, rather the messianic belief. Per JKDP regulations only inmates practicing Judaism as their sincerely held belief may be approved for the JKDP."

Petitioner filed an administrative appeal, which was denied. He thereafter exhausted his administrative remedies and, at each step, the denial was upheld. At no time during this process did prison officials question the sincerity of petitioner's beliefs or the requirement that he adhere to a kosher diet.

Petitioner filed a petition for writ of habeas corpus in the superior court, which was denied. He then filed a petition for writ of habeas corpus in this court. We issued an order to show cause returnable in the superior court. (*In re Garcia* (May 3, 2010, C064186) [order to show cause issued].)

Petitioner presented a declaration in the superior court affirming his commitment to Messianic Judaism. Petitioner stated: "One tenet of the Messianic Jewish faith pertains to diet, and while not all Messianic Jews keep kosher, I have embraced this tenet and sincerely wish to follow a kosher diet." Petitioner explained Mule Creek does not currently have a Messianic rabbi, but he averred that he met weekly with other Messianic inmates to study and pray. Petitioner also noted: "I do wish to convert formally to the Messianic Jewish faith, but I currently consider myself to be a Messianic Jew, and this belief is sincere."

[*897]

Petitioner also submitted correspondence concerning the Messianic Jewish faith and other documentation, including a publication from the State of Washington, Department of Corrections. (State of Wn., Dept. of Corrections, Handbook of Religious Beliefs and Practices (rev. 2d ed. 2004) (Washington Handbook).) The Washington Handbook explains: "Messianic Judaism (MJ) is the religion of the followers of Yeshua (Jesus) who desire to recover the Hebrew roots of their faith, worshipping and living in accordance with the Torah (Law) of Moses as taught by Yeshua and His disciples. In the 1st Century CE (AD), MJ was one of the many sects of Judaism. As such, it adheres to many of the tenants [*sic*] and practices of ancient Judaism." (*Id.* at p. 35.)

With regard to diet, the handbook explains: "MJ groups observe various degrees of kosher eating. The more strict groups follow a traditional rabbinic kosher diet. . . . Where strict kosher diet is being observed, the highest kosher symbols (those of the Orthodox) should be used since these are the most consistent and reliable." (Washington Handbook, *supra*, at p. 44.) The Washington Handbook describes some of the specific kosher rules in more detail, noting: "The kosher food laws are given in Leviticus and Deuteronomy. Only meat from kosher animals is permitted. These are those that chew the cud and have divided hooves (e.g., cows, goats, sheep, etc.). Kosher fowl are primarily those which are not birds of prey (e.g., chickens, ducks, geese, turkeys). Kosher meat must be slaughtered in such a way as to allow the blood to be entirely drained off. Meat which contains blood is not kosher. Kosher seafood are from fish that have scales and fins. All other seafood is non-kosher (e.g., lobster, crab, and all shellfish). All vegetables and fruit are kosher." (*Ibid.*)

The superior court denied the petition.

Petitioner then filed the current petition in this court. On January 28, 2011, we issued an order to show cause returnable before this court to respondent Michael Martel, Warden of Mule Creek. Respondent filed a return on February 28, 2011, and petitioner filed a traverse on March 30, 2011.

After respondent filed its return, petitioner was transferred to Ironwood State Prison in Blythe, California. Petitioner advised this court of the transfer. Respondent filed a motion to dismiss the petition as moot in light of the transfer. We denied the motion. Petitioner provided this court with documentation, of which we took judicial notice, indicating the rabbi at his current institution denied a request by petitioner to participate in the JKDP there because petitioner "is not compliant with traditional Judaism for which the Kosher Program was established."

Respondent submitted three declarations with its return. The first is from L. Maurino, the departmental food administrator of the CDCR. Maurino is [*898] familiar with the dietary programs at the adult institutions of the CDCR, has personal knowledge of the construction, development, and administration of the meal programs and policies, and is a registered dietician. Maurino identifies the following CDCR food programs: (1) a pork-free meal program, (2) a vegetarian meal program, (3) a religious meat alternate program, and (4) the JKDP. The JKDP requires certification by a rabbi, separate utensils, dishes, and storage to ensure no contact between meat and dairy foods, and assembly in a separate kitchen area by trained staff.

According to Maurino, 684 inmates participate in the JKDP throughout the 33 California prisons. Maurino states: "The current budgeted food cost per inmate is $2.90 a day for the regular meals, $2.62 for the Vegetarian Meal Program, and $3.20 for the Religious Meat Alternate Program. The cost of the [JKDP] is approximately $7.97 per inmate per day. Because of the smaller number of participants in the [JKDP], the higher cost of this food program can be absorbed in the food budget." Maurino opines: "A prospective increase in the numbers of inmates participating in the kosher meal program would require more preparation space, more storage areas, increased training and supervision of cooks, and more equipment, labor, and time devoted for food preparation. As such, the department's food budget would be significantly burdened if even a small percentage of other non-Jewish religious groups were allowed to receive kosher meals." Maurino also asserts there are approximately 5,000 inmates who self-identify as Muslim in state prison and 1,200 inmates who self-identify as Pagans or other nontraditional, non-Jewish groups, including (but not limited to) Odinists and the House of Yahweh. Maurino indicates he is "aware that inmates representing these religious groups" have asked to participate in the JKDP.

A similar declaration was submitted by J. Yates, the assistant correctional food manager at Mule Creek. Yates asserts that 43 of approximately 3,600 inmates at Mule Creek receive kosher meals. Kosher meals are purchased from a vendor "as either prepackaged shelf-stable entrees or frozen entrees." At Mule Creek, kosher meals are prepared in a separate kitchen used solely for that purpose. Breakfast and lunch kosher meals are delivered the previous evening, served cold, and distributed at breakfast. Dinner meals are heated in separately designated microwave ovens and delivered hot. Inmates who receive kosher meals use kosher meal cards, go through the general population feeding lines, present their cards at the serving window, and are given their kosher meals.

Yates indicates items such as vegetables, fruit, and salad are provided with kosher meals. When a salad is prepared in the kitchen, it too must be kosher certified using procedures specified by a rabbi, including separate pans, utensils, and a specially designated area. Yates explains: "This remains [*899] feasible because of the relatively small number of inmates participating in the [JKDP]." According to Yates: "If the number of inmates who receive kosher meals increase[s], the situation would create staffing, training, and supervision problems. The necessary procedures and precautions that are involved in preparing kosher food compel[] prison authorities to require more supervision of staff and inmate workers to prevent ritual contamination and sabotage. Further, unlike Mule Creek, most prisons do not have a separate kosher kitchen, but have at best, a designated microwave and separate food preparation area for kosher food. Even a modest increase in the number of participants, would require increased storage, more staffing, increased training of new workers, and strain already limited resources allotted for the program."

Yates notes that kosher food is much desired by non-Jewish inmates because it is perceived as better tasting and of higher quality. He explains: "The kosher program offers items that are not offered in the other inmate meal programs such as honey, and whole, uncut fruits and vegetables. Thus, Jewish kosher meal items are frequently stolen to be consumed, bartered, or sold as contraband. Even with the relatively small number of participants in the kosher meal program, theft prevention, inventory control, and associated custody problems with contraband are ongoing problems. This problem would be greatly exacerbated if the kosher meal program was expanded to include other non-Jewish inmates."

Finally, respondent submitted a declaration by Rabbi Grossbaum, the current rabbi at Mule Creek. Rabbi Grossbaum states: "Though Messianic Judaism claims to be a part of Judaism, the belief of Messianic Jews that a messiah has already arrived is contrary to the beliefs and practices of Judaism. However, it is my understanding that Messianic Jews study the Torah, and attempt to adhere, in whole or in part, to the tenets and practices of ancient Judaism." He further states: "An inmate who wants to participate in the [JKDP] must be a Jew and/or demonstrate a commitment to Judaism through religious study, attendance at services and an attempt to live and apply Jewish practices into his daily life as an inmate. Conversion is not necessarily required to receive a kosher meal. To the best of my knowledge, [petitioner] has not availed himself of those opportunities or otherwise attempted to qualify to participate in the [JKDP]. And to the extent that [petitioner] proclaims [himself] to be a Jew, albeit a messianic Jew, requiring him to commit to a study of Jewish religious texts, attendance at services, and integrating Jewish practices into his life to qualify to participate in the kosher meal program, would not appear to violate or repudiate his beliefs."

DISCUSSION

I [omitted]

II [omitted]

[*902]III

Petitioner's RLUIPA Claim

In his petition for writ of habeas corpus in this court, petitioner asserts the denial of his request to participate in the JKDP violates his rights under RLUIPA. Petitioner also asserts such denial violates his First Amendment right to practice his religion and his Fourteenth Amendment right to equal protection.

(6) "A fundamental principle of constitutional adjudication is that a court will not decide constitutional questions unless absolutely required to do so to dispose of the matter before the court, which means we will not reach constitutional questions where other grounds are available and dispositive of the issues of the case. (*Lyng v. Northwest Indian Cemetery Prot. Assn.* (1988) 485 U.S. 439, 445 [99 L. Ed. 2d 534, 544, 108 S. Ct. 1319]; *Santa Clara County Local Transportation Authority v. Guardino* (1995) 11 Cal. 4th 220, 230-231 [45 Cal. Rptr. 2d 207, 902 P.2d 225]; *Matrixx Initiatives, Inc. v. Doe* (2006) 138 Cal. App. 4th 872, 881 [42 Cal. Rptr. 3d 79].)" (*Teachers' Retirement Bd. v. Genest* (2007) 154 Cal. App. 4th 1012, 1043 [65 Cal. Rptr. 3d 326].) "[T]he appropriate exercise of judicial power requires that important constitutional issues not be decided unnecessarily where narrower grounds exist for according relief." (*Communist Party of Indiana v. Whitcomb* (1974) 414 U.S. 441, 451, fn. 1 [38 L. Ed. 2d 635, 644, 94 S. Ct. 656] (conc. opn. of Powell, J.).) At oral argument, the parties agreed this matter should be resolved, if possible, on statutory rather than constitutional grounds.

In support of his RLUIPA claim, petitioner relies on the traverse he filed in support of his petition in the superior court. On page 3 of that traverse, petitioner asserted "CDCR has failed to show how refusing to provide Petitioner with a kosher diet serves a compelling state interest . . . ." He further asserted the denial of his participation in the JKDP "has substantially burdened the exercise of his religion." The traverse contains 11 pages of argument as to why petitioner's exclusion from the JKDP violates RLUIPA.

[*903]

In his return to the petition, respondent asserts: "[Petitioner] cannot raise his RLUIPA claim in habeas corpus; rather he must raise the claim in a separate civil proceeding as provided by statute. Even so, respondent denies that [petitioner]'s rights under RLUIPA have been violated because prison officials have not substantially burdened his exercise of religion." However, except for arguing the unavailability of habeas corpus relief because of an adequate remedy in federal court, as discussed above, respondent included no argument in his return as to why petitioner has not stated a valid claim under RLUIPA. The bulk of the return addresses petitioner's First Amendment claim, with approximately one page dedicated to the equal protection challenge.

At oral argument, respondent asserted the refusal to allow petitioner to participate in the JKDP did not interfere with the practice of his religion because he is not a Jew and because a vegetarian diet is available to petitioner that would satisfy his religious requirements. As we shall explain, these arguments are not persuasive.

"RLUIPA is the latest of long-running congressional efforts to accord religious exercise heightened protection from government-imposed burdens, consistent with [United States Supreme Court] precedents. Ten years before RLUIPA's enactment, the Court held, in *Employment Div., Dept. of Human Resources of Oregon v. Smith*, 494 U.S. 872, 878-882 [108 L. Ed. 2d 876, 110 S. Ct. 1595] (1990), that the First Amendment's Free Exercise Clause does not inhibit enforcement of otherwise valid laws of general application that incidentally burden religious conduct. . . .

"Responding to *Smith*, Congress enacted the Religious Freedom Restoration Act of 1993 (RFRA), 107 Stat. 1488, 42 U.S.C. § 2000bb *et seq.* RFRA 'prohibits "[g]overnment" from "substantially burden[ing]" a person's exercise of religion even if the burden results from a rule of general applicability unless the government can demonstrate the burden "(1) is in furtherance of a compelling governmental interest; and (2) is the least restrictive means of furthering that compelling governmental interest."' . . . In *City of Boerne* [*v. Flores* (1997) 521 U.S. 507 [138 L. Ed. 2d 624, 117 S. Ct. 2157]], [the United States Supreme Court] invalidated RFRA as applied to States and their subdivisions, holding that the Act exceeded Congress' remedial powers under the Fourteenth Amendment. *Id.*, at 532-536 [138 L. Ed. 2d 624, 117 S. Ct. 2157].

"Congress again responded, this time by enacting RLUIPA. Less sweeping than RFRA, and invoking federal authority under the Spending and Commerce Clauses, RLUIPA targets two areas: Section 2 of the Act concerns land-use regulation, 42 U.S.C. § 2000cc; § 3 relates to religious exercise by [*904] institutionalized persons, § 2000cc-1." (*Cutter v. Wilkinson* (2005) 544 U.S. 709, 714-715 [161 L. Ed. 2d 1020, 1030, 125 S. Ct. 2113], citation omitted, fns. omitted (*Cutter*).)

(7) Title 42 United States Code section 2000cc-1, part of RLUIPA, provides in part: "No government shall impose a substantial burden on the religious exercise of a person residing in or confined to an institution, . . . even if the burden results from a rule of general applicability, unless the government demonstrates that imposition of the burden on that person—[¶] (1) is in furtherance of a compelling governmental interest; and [¶] (2) is the least restrictive means of furthering that compelling governmental interest." (42 U.S.C. § 2000cc-1(a).) Unlike cases arising under the First Amendment, the foregoing prohibition applies even where the burden placed on a prisoner's religious freedom results from a rule of general applicability. (*Koger v. Bryan* (7th Cir. 2008) 523 F.3d 789, 796.)

(8) In pursuing a claim under RLUIPA, "the plaintiff bears the initial burden of showing (1) that he seeks to engage in an exercise of religion, and (2) that the challenged practice substantially burdens that exercise of religion. 42 U.S.C. § 2000cc-2(b). Once the plaintiff establishes this prima facie case, the defendants 'bear the burden of persuasion on any [other] element of the claim,' *id.*, namely whether their practice 'is the least restrictive means of furthering a compelling governmental interest.' [Citation.]" (*Koger v. Bryan, supra*, 523 F.3d at p. 796.)

In *Cutter*, the United States Supreme Court rejected a facial challenge to RLUIPA. However, in doing so, the court cautioned: "We have no cause to believe that RLUIPA would not be applied in an appropriately balanced way, with particular sensitivity to security concerns. While the Act adopts a 'compelling governmental interest' standard, [citation], '[c]ontext matters' in the application of that standard. [Citation.] Lawmakers supporting RLUIPA were mindful of the urgency of discipline, order, safety, and security in penal institutions. [Citation.] They anticipated that courts would apply the Act's standard with 'due deference to the experience and expertise of prison and jail administrators in establishing necessary regulations and procedures to maintain good order, security and discipline, consistent with consideration of costs and limited resources.' [Citation.]" (*Cutter, supra*, 544 U.S. at pp. 722-723 [161 L. Ed. 2d at p. 1035], fns. omitted.)

In the present matter, respondent does not argue the rejection of petitioner's request to participate in the JKDP furthers a compelling governmental interest and is the least restrictive means of doing so, as required by RLUIPA. We are not surprised. On this record, we fail to see any legitimate governmental interest, let alone a compelling interest, in allowing traditional Jews to **[*905]** receive kosher meals but denying the same accommodation to Messianic Jews who sincerely hold similar beliefs concerning diet. Respondent points to evidence they have offered concerning the resources devoted to the kosher meal program, the difficulty in setting aside space and ensuring proper training and administration of the program, and security and custodial concerns. However, CDCR has determined that kosher meals can be provided in a cost-effective manner to Jewish inmates. Implicit in that determination is the judgment that providing kosher meals is not currently cost prohibitive.

As for whether expanding the program to include petitioner would harm prison administration, respondent fails to make any showing of how many inmates, like petitioner, practice Messianic Judaism and wish to participate in the JKDP. The reference to a broad group of others in prison, in Maurino's declaration, is entirely inapposite, considering that respondent does not identify particular groups whose religious beliefs are tied to kosher rules. In the absence of such evidence, we cannot conclude either that the JKDP will be overwhelmed or that a limited extension to include petitioner would place a significant strain on prison resources.

Because respondent does not attempt to establish that excluding petitioner from participation in the JKDP furthers a compelling governmental interest in the least restrictive way, any concerns expressed in *Cutter* regarding prison security and limited resources have no bearing on this dispute.

At oral argument, respondent asserted the denial of petitioner's request to participate in the JKDP did not interfere with the exercise of his religion because he is not a Jew, as defined by the rabbi at Mule Creek, i.e., is not a traditional Jew, and petitioner's dietary requirements can be met through a vegetarian diet.

(9) The fact that petitioner is not a traditional Jew as determined by the local Jewish rabbi is an artificial construct that has no bearing on the issue presented. CDCR regulations for the JKDP limit participation to traditional Jewish inmates "as determined by a Jewish Chaplain." (Cal. Code Regs., tit. 15, § 3054.2, subd. (a).) However, those regulations might just as readily have opened participation to all Jews or to all non-Christians or limited participation to Jews with red hair. RLUIPA prohibits imposition of a substantial burden on an inmate's religious exercise. (42 U.S.C. § 2000cc-1(a).) "Religious exercise" includes "any exercise of religion, whether or not compelled by, or central to, a system of religious belief." (42 U.S.C. § 2000cc-5(7).) The issue here is not whether petitioner is a Jew but whether his system of religious beliefs includes maintaining a kosher diet.

In a declaration attached to the traverse submitted to the superior court, which is attached to the petition in this matter, petitioner asserted he **[*906]** considers Messianic Judaism to be his religion and "[o]ne tenet of the Messianic Jewish faith pertains to diet, and while not all Messianic Jews keep kosher, I have embraced this tenet and sincerely wish to follow a kosher diet."

As noted earlier, respondent has never challenged this assertion by petitioner or the sincerity of his claim that maintaining a kosher diet is a part of his system of religious beliefs. Respondent instead insists petitioner's religious needs can be met by a vegetarian diet. But petitioner has consistently stated that he wants to follow a kosher diet consistent with the Torah and his religious beliefs. Respondent's own evidence reflects the differences in preparation of kosher meals from nonkosher meals, indicating that neither the pork-free nor the vegetarian option is consistent with a traditional kosher diet. Kosher food must be prepared in a separate area with separate pans, utensils, dishes, and storage.

In any event, the availability of an alternate diet was not the basis for petitioner's exclusion from the JKDP. Throughout the administrative process, respondent rejected petitioner's request and various administrative appeals solely because he is not a traditional Jew. Thus, the issue of whether petitioner's religious requirements can be met with a vegetarian diet was not litigated. On the record before us, there is no basis whatsoever to conclude petitioner's system of religious beliefs does not include maintaining a kosher diet and this can be satisfied with a vegetarian diet.

We conclude respondent's denial of petitioner's request to participate in the JKDP violates petitioner's rights under RLUIPA. To the extent prison policy and regulations permit such action, they cannot stand. We emphasize, however, that our decision in this regard is based on the procedural and factual posture of this matter. Respondent has made no attempt to challenge petitioner's assertions regarding his religious beliefs or his claim that maintaining a kosher diet is an integral part thereof. Respondent already has in place a kosher diet program and has not established a compelling interest in restricting that program to traditional Jews. Under these circumstances, petitioner's exclusion from the JKDP violates his rights under RLUIPA.

Having so concluded, we need not and do not consider petitioner's constitutional challenges.

DISPOSITION

The petition for writ of habeas corpus is granted. The Department of Corrections and Rehabilitation is directed to permit petitioner to participate in its existing kosher meals program, as described in title 15, section 3054.2 of **[*907]** the California Code of Regulations. In the event such program is not available at the institution in which petitioner is currently being held, and petitioner's CDCR classification otherwise permits it, the Department of Corrections and Rehabilitation is directed to transfer petitioner to an appropriate institution where a kosher meals program is available.

Blease, Acting P.J., and Mauro, J., concurred.

Questions Regarding *In re Garcia*

1. A plaintiff bringing a RLUIPA claim has the initial burden of proof. What must the plaintiff prove for the suit to proceed?
2. If the plaintiff establishes their initial prima facie case, the burden then shifts to the defendant. What must the defendant prove to rebut the plaintiff's case?

Tips for Religious Liberty Memorandum for California Prisoner Rusty Doucet

1. Be clear about the burdens of proof on both sides and in what order they're triggered.
2. Both the plaintiff's and defendant's cases involve multiple elements that have to be proven. Make sure your analysis stays focused on those elements.
3. If you decide to make factual comparisons between our case and *Garcia*, make sure to provide enough context about *Garcia* so that a reader who has never read that case can appreciate the comparison.

ASSIGNMENT 6: COPYRIGHT INFRINGEMENT ADVICE MEMORANDUM

The next memo assignment also functions as an advice letter; it is the only assignment in this textbook (other than perhaps the personal statement in Chapter 14) that is written for a lay audience. When writing to a fellow lawyer, you can make certain assumptions about their baseline knowledge (though again, you should still always cite sources of law). When writing to a layperson, however, especially a client, you must make sure to educate your reader while taking care not to overwhelm them with too much detail. Efficiency and clarity are especially important here. As with the other memorandum assignments, you must be objective in your conclusions (even if it's bad news for the client). You must also be mindful of what the reader is most interested in knowing (whether he will win his case or not) and make that your first issue and answer.

You can retain the same basic memorandum format, starting with the specific issues and answers that have led you to your conclusion about the case's likelihood of success. A statement of facts is also a good idea because even though you're describing events the client already knows about, you should confirm your understanding of the underlying events. The discussion should then unpack your legal analysis, using the IRAC structure. The only difference with this memorandum is that you should be especially vigilant in explaining legal terms of art that a layperson wouldn't know (such as "summary judgment") and consider using more examples to illustrate difficult or unfamiliar concepts. You might also consider including a pleasantry or two in your introduction and conclusion, something you wouldn't include in a memo to a fellow lawyer.

For this memo assignment, it will be useful to know the following terms:

- *Defamation:* a statement that injures another's reputation.
- *Preliminary injunction:* order from a judge, typically granted before or during trial, with the goal of preserving the status quo before a final judgment

---

Learned Foot, LLP

Memorandum

To: Associates
From: [Your Professor/Supervising Partner]
Subject: Copyright Infringement of Poet Igor Krichevsky

Background:

We represent renowned Russian-American poet Igor Krichevsky. Krichevsky is an award-winning writer and a professor in the creative writing department at Los

Angeles University. His 2012 collection of sonnets and poems, entitled *Memories of Myself,* was the third best-selling collection of poetry that year. One of his most famous works from that collection is entitled "Crisp Like Carrots." It is reproduced below:

Crisp Like Carrots

Age tightened the skin
over their bones
and made this once soft, fleshy couple
crisp like carrots

They sit on the swing
in parallel affection
and reminisce
about curvier times

In January of this year, poet Sophie Blum, a former student of Krichevsky's, posted the following on her poetry blog, *Musings*:

He Likes Carrots

Vanity tightened the skin
over his bones
making this once soft, agreeable giant
cross like conductors

I sit in my chair
wanting to offer him a sandwich
dreaming, wondering
about cookier times

In her post, Ms. Blum makes no reference to Krichevsky's work. Upon being made aware of Ms. Blum's poem, Mr. Krichevsky contacted Ms. Blum via e-mail. The text of that message is reproduced below:

Sophie,
    A graduate student currently in our program brought your recent blog post, entitled "He Likes Carrots," to my attention. I am not amused. I can only assume you wrote this in revenge for some perceived slight during your time at LAU. I won't pretend to remember what that could possibly be. I only write to demand that you take down your "poem" as soon as possible. I have a team of lawyers at my disposal. I am not afraid to dispatch them.

Sincerely,
Igor Krichevsky

A day later, Ms. Blum replied to Krichevsky's e-mail:

> Dear Igor,
>   Didn't you teach us imitation is the sincerest form of flattery? Be flattered. Don't be a dick. And have a Cinnabun, for God's sake. You were nicer when you were fat.
>
> Sincerely,
> Sophie

As soon as Mr. Krichevsky received the e-mail above, he contacted our firm. Following our advice, he ceased all contact with Ms. Blum. Before we file a copyright infringement action against his former student, however, he wants to know the likelihood of a quick adjudication of the case.

Mr. Krichevsky's employer and the Los Angeles University creative writing department head, Amy Mesle, does not want the publicity that would come with a trial between her most renowned professor and a former student. Mr. Krichevsky and Ms. Mesle would like to know the chances that this action could be adjudicated by the court as a matter of law—via summary judgment—such that neither he nor Ms. Blum would ever have to step foot in a courtroom.

Applicable Law:

Mr. Krichevsky knows little about the law, but as a Don Henley fan, he is familiar with the case *Henley v. Devore*, 2010 U.S. Dist. LEXIS 67987 (C.D. Cal. 2010), which happens to have been decided in our district. This was an unpublished case, and it accordingly shouldn't be cited in anything we write to the court. The case's explanations of infringement and fair use are still accurate, however, so for the time being, you can use this opinion's explanation of infringement and fair use as the primary source for your memorandum. In addition, you should also consider the following holding from the Ninth Circuit in 2015. According to the court in *Lenz v. Universal Music Publ'g, Inc.*, 815 F.3d 1145, 1157 (9th Cir. 2016), "Copyright holders cannot shirk their duty to consider—in good faith and prior to sending a takedown notification—whether allegedly infringing material constitutes fair use, a use which the DMCA plainly contemplates as authorized by the law." No need to read the text of *Lenz* as of now; just make note of the holding above if you think it's relevant.

Issues Presented:

Last fall, during the time in which Mr. Krichevsky had Ms. Blum in class, he suffered a mild heart attack and was told by his doctors that he needed to change his lifestyle. Over the course of that year, he lost over 50 pounds. He believes that Ms. Blum's poem is a direct—if crude—comment on her perception of his changed demeanor, pre- and post-weight loss.

138 | Chapter 8

> Your job is to review the *Henley* case and to apply its holdings and the excerpted holding of *Lenz* to the current facts. Write a memorandum to Mr. Krichevsky explaining our best arguments, Ms. Blum's best counterarguments, and our likelihood of succeeding in a copyright infringement claim against Ms. Blum.

HENLEY v. DEVORE

United States District Court for the Central District of California
June 10, 2010, Decided; June 10, 2010, Filed
Case No: SACV 09-481 JVS (RNBx)
Reporter: 733 F. Supp. 2d 1144 *

Judges: James V. Selna, United States District Judge.

Opinion by: James V. Selna

Opinion (Edited for Content)

[*1147] ORDER RE MOTIONS FOR SUMMARY JUDGMENT

Musician Don Henley ("Henley") claims that politician Charles DeVore ("DeVore") infringed the copyrighted songs "The Boys of Summer" and "All She Wants to Do Is Dance" with two political advertisements featuring the songs "The Hope of November" and "All She Wants to Do Is Tax." DeVore claims fair use. The Court also considers whether DeVore's songs falsely suggest endorsement by Henley.

I. BACKGROUND

Plaintiff Henley is a world-famous, Grammy-winning, multi-platinum-album-selling songwriter and recording artist.[1] He is a founding member of the Eagles, credited with one of the best-selling albums of all time. He has also enjoyed a successful solo career, releasing the multi-platinum album *Building the Perfect Beast* in 1984. Two of the songs on the album, "The Boys of Summer" ("Summer") and "All She Wants to Do Is Dance" ("Dance"), were top-ten hits at the time.

"Summer" was written by Henley and Plaintiff Mike Campbell ("Campbell"), a founding member of Tom Petty and the Heartbreakers, and the two jointly own the copyright to the song. The main theme of the song is the singer's nostalgia for a past summer romance, though the [*1148] Defendants contend that the song

---

1. Unless otherwise noted, the recited facts are undisputed.

has a political theme, noting the line where the singer "saw a DEADHEAD[2] sticker on a Cadillac," which they argue demonstrates nostalgia for the liberal politics of the 1960's. The lyrics to "Summer" are attached in Appendix A.

"Dance" was written by Plaintiff Danny Kortchmar ("Kortchmar"), a respected songwriter, producer, and recording artist. Kortchmar is the beneficial owner of the copyright to "Dance." The song depicts an American couple on a trip to an unspecified foreign country in the midst of violence and unrest. The woman is either oblivious to or ignores the tumult and simply wants to dance, party, and "get down." The Defendants interpret the song as being a comment on American foreign policy in Latin America and the American public's apathy towards the situation. The lyrics to "Dance" are attached in Appendix B.

DeVore is a California assemblyman currently seeking the Republican nomination for one of California's U.S. Senate seats. Justin Hart ("Hart") is the DeVore campaign's Director of Internet Strategies and New Media. His primary duty is to conduct online-based fundraising activities and otherwise get publicity for the DeVore campaign. He does this through various means, such as creating videos to be posted on DeVore's website and on YouTube.[3] Hart's compensation is directly tied to the amount of funds he brings in.

This case arises from two online videos produced by DeVore and Hart for DeVore's campaign. The first contains the song "The Hope of November" ("November"), a play on "Summer." DeVore was inspired to create the song in March 2009 after seeing a Barack Obama ("Obama") sticker on a Toyota Prius, which reminded him of the "DEADHEAD sticker" lyric from "Summer." DeVore proceeded to revise the lyrics of "Summer" to create a song that pokes fun at Obama, House Speaker Nancy Pelosi ("Pelosi"), and Obama's supporters. The lyrics to "November" are attached in Appendix A.

Hart and DeVore decided to produce a campaign video using "November." Hart downloaded a karaoke version of "Summer" which simulates the song's instrumental track. Hart supplied the vocals for "November," attempting to emulate Henley's style. He then produced the video by compiling images of Obama, Pelosi, and a few others, and synchronized the "November" track with the video. This video was posted to YouTube and other online sites sometime in late March 2009.

Once Henley got wind of the Defendants' online video in early April 2009, he sent a notice to YouTube under the Digital Millennium Copyright Act ("DMCA"), 17 U.S.C. § 512, requesting that the video be removed, and YouTube promptly complied.[4] A few days later, DeVore sent a DMCA counter notification to YouTube

---

2. "Deadhead" refers to a fan of the Grateful Dead, a rock band popular during the 1960's and 70's. *See United States v. Washington*, 106 F.3d 983, 1017, 323 U.S. App. D.C. 175 (D.C. Cir. 1997).

3. YouTube is a website which hosts videos posted by third parties like the DeVore campaign.

4. Under the DMCA, a "service provider," such as YouTube, is not liable for copyright infringement for material posted on its website by others so long as it promptly removes the material upon receiving a notification of infringement from the copyright holder. *See* 17 U.S.C. § 512(c). However, to avoid liability to the person who originally posted the allegedly infringing material, the service provider must replace the material upon receiving a counter notification from the original poster. *Id.* § 512(g).

requesting that the video be reposted on the grounds that it constituted parody. Meanwhile, [*1149] DeVore decided to use a second Henley song for his campaign. This time, DeVore and Hart created a campaign video featuring the song "All She Wants to Do is Tax" ("Tax"), their take on "Dance."

"Tax" was written by DeVore, who modified the lyrics of "Dance" to lampoon Barbara Boxer ("Boxer"), one of California's U.S. Senators and Democratic Senatorial Candidate, and to criticize cap-and-trade and global-warming polices. The lyrics to "Tax" are attached in Appendix B. Just as with "November," Hart used an instrumental-only track of "Dance," supplied his own vocals using DeVore's lyrics, and paired the song with a video he created using a variety of online images and videos of, among others, Boxer, Al Gore, and Disney character Scrooge McDuck. The Defendants posted the video to YouTube on or about April 14, 2009. On April 17, 2009, this action was filed by Henley, Campbell, and Kortchmar, alleging copyright infringement . . . .

II. LEGAL STANDARD

Summary judgment is appropriate only where the record, read in the light most favorable to the nonmoving party, indicates that "there is no genuine issue as to any material fact and . . . the moving party is entitled to a judgment as a matter of law." Fed. R. Civ. P. 56(c); *see also Celotex Corp. v. Catrett*, 477 U.S. 317, 323-24, 106 S. Ct. 2548, 91 L. Ed. 2d 265 (1986). Summary adjudication, or partial summary judgment "upon all or any part of a claim," is appropriate where there is no genuine issue of material fact as to that portion of the claim. Fed. R. Civ. P. 56(a), (b); *see also Lies v. Farrell Lines, Inc.*, 641 F.2d 765, 769 n.3 (9th Cir. 1981) ("Rule 56 authorizes a summary adjudication that will often fall short of a final determination, even of a single claim . . . .") (internal quotation marks omitted).

Material facts are those necessary to the proof or defense of a claim, and are determined by reference to substantive law. *Anderson v. Liberty Lobby, Inc.*, 477 U.S. 242, 248, 106 S. Ct. 2505, 91 L. Ed. 2d 202 (1986). "[A] complete failure of proof concerning an essential element of the nonmoving party's case necessarily renders all other facts immaterial." *Celotex*, 477 U.S. at 323. A fact issue is genuine "if the evidence is such that a reasonable jury could return a verdict for the nonmoving party." *Anderson*, 477 U.S. at 248. To demonstrate a genuine issue, the opposing party "must do more than simply show that there is some metaphysical doubt as to the material facts. . . . [T]he nonmoving party must come forward with specific facts showing that there is a genuine issue for trial." *Matsushita Elec. Indus. Co., Ltd. v. Zenith Radio Corp.*, 475 U.S. 574, 586-87, 106 S. Ct. 1348, 89 L. Ed. 2d 538 (1986) (internal quotation marks and citations omitted). In deciding a motion for summary judgment, "[t]he evidence of the nonmovant is to be believed, and all justifiable inferences are to be drawn in his favor." *Anderson*, 477 U.S. at 255. Nevertheless, inferences are not drawn out of the air, and it is the opposing party's obligation to produce a factual predicate [*1150] from which the inference may be drawn. *See Richards v. Nielsen Freight Lines*, 602 F. Supp. 1224, 1244-45 (E.D. Cal. 1985), *aff'd*, 810 F.2d 898, 902 (9th Cir. 1987).

The burden initially is on the moving party to demonstrate an absence of a genuine issue of material fact. *Celotex*, 477 U.S. at 323. If the moving party meets its burden, then the nonmoving party must produce enough evidence to rebut the moving party's claim and create a genuine issue of material fact. *See id.* at 322-23. If the nonmoving party meets this burden, then the motion will be denied. *Nissan Fire & Marine Ins. Co. v. Fritz Co., Inc.*, 210 F.3d 1099, 1103 (9th Cir. 2000). Where the parties have made cross-motions for summary judgment, the Court must consider each motion on its own merits. *Fair Hous. Council of Riverside County, Inc. v. Riverside Two*, 249 F.3d 1132, 1136 (9th Cir. 2001). The Court will consider each party's evidentiary showing, regardless of which motion the evidence was tendered under. *See id.* at 1137.

III. DISCUSSION

A. Copyright Infringement

To prevail on a claim of copyright infringement, Plaintiffs must show "(1) ownership of a valid copyright, and (2) copying of constituent elements of the work that are original." *Feist Publ'ns, Inc. v. Rural Tel. Serv. Co.*, 499 U.S. 340, 361, 111 S. Ct. 1282, 113 L. Ed. 2d 358 (1991). The parties do not dispute that the Plaintiffs own valid copyrights to "Summer" and "Dance," nor that "November" and "Tax" copy substantial portions of the originals. The parties only dispute whether the Defendants' use of the originals constitutes fair use.

1. Fair Use

Fair use is an exception to a copyright holder's right to exclusive use of the original work and its derivatives. It has been described as "a privilege in others than the owner of the copyright to use the copyrighted material in a reasonable manner without his consent." *Harper & Row, Publishers, Inc. v. Nation Enters.*, 471 U.S. 539, 549, 105 S. Ct. 2218, 85 L. Ed. 2d 588 (1985) (quoting H. Ball, *Law of Copyright & Literary Property* 260 (1944)). The privilege reflects a recognition that some limited use of copyrighted material is necessary to allow artists and authors to improve upon, comment on, or criticize prior works. *See id.*; *Campbell v. Acuff-Rose Music, Inc.*, 510 U.S. 569, 575, 114 S. Ct. 1164, 127 L. Ed. 2d 500 (1994).

Section 107 of the Copyright Act codified the common law framework for identifying fair use:

> In determining whether the use made of a work in any particular case is a fair use the factors to be considered shall include
> (1) the purpose and character of the use, including whether such use is of a commercial nature or is for nonprofit educational purposes;
> (2) the nature of the copyrighted work;
> (3) the amount and substantiality of the portion used in relation to the copyrighted work as a whole; and
> (4) the effect of the use upon the potential market for or value of the copyrighted work.

17 U.S.C. § 107. The analysis "permits and requires courts to avoid rigid application of the copyright statute when, on occasion, it would stifle the very creativity which that law is designed to foster." *Campbell*, 510 U.S. at 577 (quoting *Stewart v. Abend*, 495 U.S. 207, 236, 110 S. Ct. 1750, 109 L. Ed. 2d 184 (1990)) (internal brackets omitted). The factors are not winner-take-all categories [*1151] to be tallied at the end to determine the prevailing party; they are intended to be carefully weighed case by case with an eye towards the policies underlying copyright protection. *See id.* "Nor may the four statutory factors be treated in isolation one from another. All are to be explored, and the results weighed together, in light of the purposes of copyright." *Id.* at 578; accord *Dr. Seuss Enters., L.P. v. Penguin Books USA, Inc.* ("*Dr. Seuss II*"), 109 F.3d 1394, 1399 (9th Cir. 1997).

Application of the fair use doctrine is a mixed question of law and fact. *Harper & Row*, 471 U.S. at 560. Thus, where the material facts are not subject to dispute, summary judgment on the fair use question is appropriate. *Fisher v. Dees*, 794 F.2d 432, 436 (9th Cir. 1986). Because fair use is an affirmative defense to copyright infringement, the defendant bears the burden of proving fair use. *Campbell*, 510 U.S. at 590; *Perfect 10, Inc. v. Amazon.com, Inc.*, 508 F.3d 1146, 1158 (9th Cir. 2007).

Under the first factor, the "purpose and character of the use," the Court considers the extent to which the new work is "transformative." *Mattel, Inc. v. Walking Mountain Prods.*, 353 F.3d 792, 800 (9th Cir. 2003). The new work must add "something new, with a further purpose or different character, altering the first with new expression, meaning, or message." *Id.* (quoting *Campbell*, 510 U.S. at 579). The Court also considers whether the purpose of the new work was for- or not-for-profit. *Id.*

The second factor, the "nature of the copyrighted work," reflects a recognition "that creative works are 'closer to the core of intended copyright protection' than informational and functional works." *Id.* at 803 (quoting *Dr. Seuss II*, 109 F.3d at 1402).

The third factor "asks whether the amount and substantiality of the portion used in relation to the copyrighted work as a whole, are reasonable in relation to the purpose of copying." *Id.* (quoting *Dr. Seuss II*, 109 F.3d at 1402) (internal quotation marks omitted).

Under the fourth and final factor, the question is "whether actual market harm resulted from the defendant's use . . . and whether 'unrestricted and widespread conduct of the sort engaged by the defendant . . . would result in a substantially adverse impact on the potential market' for the original or its derivatives." *Id.* at 804 (quoting *Campbell*, 510 U.S. at 590). The relevant inquiry is whether the new work tends to supplant or substitute for the potential market for the original or its derivatives. *Campbell*, 510 U.S. at 592. Harm caused by effective criticism or disparagement is not cognizable injury under the Copyright Act. *Id.* at 591-92.

The Defendants' primary fair use argument is that their works constitute parody. Parody is the use of some portion of a work in order to "hold[] it up to ridicule," or otherwise comment or shed light on it. *Dr. Seuss II*, 109 F.3d at 1400-01 (citation omitted). Courts have deemed parody worthy of protection within the fair use framework. First, parody has been considered transformative because it provides socially-valuable criticism or commentary of the subject work. *Campbell*, 510 U.S. at 579. Second, parodies are permitted to draw from the most creative expressions because they "almost invariably copy publicly known, expressive works." *Id.* at 586. Third, the parodist needs to use at least some portion of the original because the effectiveness of parody depends on its ability to mimic or "conjure up" the original. *Id.* at 580-81, 588. Finally, because the author is unlikely to permit the use of his or her work to criticize [*1152] or ridicule that work, a parody is unlikely to supplant the market for the original or its derivatives. *Id.* at 592.

In the seminal case of *Campbell v. Acuff-Rose Music, Inc.*, the Supreme Court distinguished "between parody (in which the copyrighted work is the target) and satire (in which the copyrighted work is merely a vehicle to poke fun at another target)." *Dr. Seuss II*, 109 F.3d at 1400 (citing *Campbell*, 510 U.S. at 580). The parodist is justified in using the original work because a parody's effectiveness "necessarily springs from recognizable allusion to its object through distorted imitation. Its art lies in the tension between a known original and its parodic twin." *Campbell*, 510 U.S. at 588. The parodist has no alternative but to use the work. *See id.* In contrast, the satirist who ridicules subjects unrelated to the work lacks the same claim to use of the work, which the satirist "merely uses to get attention or to avoid the drudgery in working up something fresh." *Id.* at 580. As the Court put it:

> Parody needs to mimic an original to make its point, and so has some claim to use the creation of its victim's (or collective victims') imagination, whereas satire can stand on its own two feet and so requires justification for the very act of borrowing.

Id. at 580-81.

"The threshold question when fair use is raised in defense of a parody is whether a parodic character may reasonably be perceived." *Id.* at 582. This is not, however, the end of the inquiry: "parody, like any other use, has to work its way through the relevant factors and be judged case by case, in light of the ends of copyright law." *Id.* at 581. Indeed, the Supreme Court recognizes that parody is not a binary question, but rather a matter of degree. *See id.* at 580 n.14. The parodist that directly targets the original work has a greater justification for appropriation than the parodist whose aim at the original is looser. *See id.* The "loose" parodist has a greater burden of proving the necessity of the use and that the parody does not risk superseding potential markets for the original. *Id.* at 580 n.14, 582 n.16.

Justice Kennedy, concurring in *Campbell*, cautioned courts to be wary of post hoc rationalizations of parody. *Id.* at 600 (Kennedy, J., concurring). He held the view that the defendant must demonstrate "[m]ore than arguable parodic content," and that "doubts about whether a given use is fair should not be resolved in favor of the self-proclaimed parodist." *Id.* at 599.

This case raises the somewhat novel issue of whether, under *Campbell*'s parody/satire distinction, criticism of the *author* of an original work falls on either the parody or satire side of the line. In other words, is a work which appropriates from the original to criticize the original's author—but does not directly criticize the content of the original—validly classified as "parody"? The appellate courts have yet to squarely address the issue,[6] and the district courts that have are split.

In a recent case in the Southern District of New York, the district court flatly rejected the argument that use of a work to criticize the work's author constitutes parody under *Campbell*. See *Salinger v. Colting* ("*Salinger I*"), 641 F. Supp. 2d 250, 257 [*1153] (S.D.N.Y. 2009), *rev'd on other grounds*, 607 F.3d 68, 2010 WL 1729126 (2d Cir. 2010). In *Salinger I*, the defendant had written a novel imagining the adventures of the character Holden Caufield from J.D. Salinger's *Catcher in the Rye* as a septuagenarian. *Id.* at 253-54, 258. The defendant had included Salinger himself as a character in the novel, and in the ensuing litigation argued that the novel was, in part, a parody of Salinger's persona. *Id.* at 261. The court, at the preliminary injunction stage, held that a work that only criticizes the author, and not the content, of the original does not qualify as parody. *Id.* at 257, 261.

However, in another recent Southern District of New York case, the same court seemingly accepted the "parody-of-the-author" fair use defense. See *Bourne Co. v. Twentieth Century Fox Film Corp.*, 602 F. Supp. 2d 499, 507 (S.D.N.Y. 2009). In *Bourne*, the defendants had written the song "I Need a Jew" with a tune and lyrics similar to "When You Wish Upon a Star." *Id.* at 501, 502. The defendants argued that their song was intended in part to poke fun at Walt Disney's purported anti-Semitism. *Id.* at 507. Although Disney had not actually written the song and did not own the copyright, but was merely associated with it, the court accepted this argument as supporting a parodic character and granted summary judgment for the defendant.[7] *Id.* at 507-08, 511.

This split extends to southern California as well. In a case in the Central District of California, the court found parody where the allegedly infringing work targeted the artist rather than the art. See *Burnett v. Twentieth Century Fox Film Corp.*, 491 F. Supp. 2d 962, 968-69 (C.D. Cal. 2007). The defendants in *Burnett* used an animated character in their television show resembling a character, the Charwoman,

---

6. The Second Circuit in *Salinger v. Colting* ("*Salinger II*"), 607 F.3d 68, 2010 WL 1729126 (2d Cir. 2010), did note the lower court's rejection of a "parody-of-the-author" fair use defense, but did not explicitly reject or endorse the lower court's holding on that issue. See 607 F.3d 68, [WL] at *3, *12.

7. In *Salinger I*, the court distinguished its prior decision in *Bourne* on the grounds that the targeting of Walt Disney in *Bourne* "reinforced and reiterated" the parodic purpose of targeting the song itself because of the intimate association between Disney and the song. 641 F. Supp. 2d at 261 n.4. Thus, under *Salinger I*'s reasoning, "parody-of-the-author" is not sufficiently transformative on its own, but may serve to supplement or highlight a legitimate parody targeting the original work.

played by Carol Burnett in a different show. *Id.* at 966. The defendants argued that the use of Burnett's character was intended to poke fun at Burnett herself. *Id.* at 968. Upon the plaintiff's objection that targeting Burnett was not valid parody, the court found that "it is immaterial whether the target of [the defendants'] 'crude joke' was Burnett, the Carol Burnett show, the Charwoman, Carol's Theme Music or all four." *Id.* The court held that the defendants' use constituted parody because it put "Carol Burnett/the Charwoman in an awkward, ridiculous, crude, and absurd situation in order to lampoon and parody her as a public figure." *Id.* at 969.

However, a court in the Southern District of California appears to have reached the opposite conclusion. *See Dr. Seuss Enters., L.P. v. Penguin Books USA, Inc.* ("*Dr. Seuss I*"), 924 F. Supp. 1559, 1568 (S.D. Cal. 1996). The defendants in *Dr. Seuss I* mimicked the rhymes, illustrations, and packaging of books by Theodor S. Geisel, better known as Dr. Seuss, to recount the O.J. Simpson murder trial. *Id.* at 1561. The court, in its exposition on the parody/satire distinction, made the following statement:

> [T]he potential satirist has many alternatives to pilfering the protected expression of a copyrighted work . . . . The satirist (*or one intending to parody an author but not any particular work*) may freely evoke another artist by using the artist's general style. . . . Only when the satirist wishes to parody *the copyrighted* [*1154] *work itself* does the taking . . . become permissible.

Id. at 1567-68 (emphasis added). This statement, however, appears to be dictum as it relates to the "parody-of-the-author" issue because the defendants in the case did not argue that they were targeting Geisel himself. *See id.* at 1569 (defendants argued their book "suggest[ed] limits to the Seussian imagination," i.e., "comment[ing] on the naivete of the original").

The act of ridiculing and lampooning public figures is a rich part of our First Amendment tradition and has been accorded special constitutional protections. *See, e.g., Hustler Magazine v. Falwell,* 485 U.S. 46, 108 S. Ct. 876, 99 L. Ed. 2d 41 (1988); *N.Y. Times Co. v. Sullivan,* 376 U.S. 254, 84 S. Ct. 710, 11 L. Ed. 2d 686 (1964). In the defamation context, for example, critics of public figures have extra leeway to make charges against their targets. *N.Y. Times,* 376 U.S. at 279-80 (public officials in a defamation action must prove that defendants acted with "actual malice"). In granting this protection, the Court recognized the social value of criticism of public figures and the dangers of suppressing it. *See id.* at 269-70.

In many cases, the most effective tool of ridiculing a public figure — a time-honored, First Amendment activity — is through that person's own creations. This is particularly true where a person's fame derives from that person's expressive works, as the case often is with artists, musicians, authors, and the like. The First Amendment demands that these public figures be open to ridicule, just as their works should be. Yet without the ability to evoke their works — the very reason these figures live in the public eye — a would-be parodist may lack an adequate tool with which to lampoon. *Cf. Smith v. Wal-Mart Stores, Inc.,* 537 F. Supp. 2d

1302, 1316 (N.D. Ga. 2008) (in trademark case, finding parody where the "Wal-Mart" mark was used to evoke the company rather than the mark itself). In this case, for example, the Defendants argue that they sought to poke fun at Henley, a famous musician. The best, and perhaps only, way to conjure up Henley in a manner recognizable to the public is through his music.

The courts in *Salinger I* and *Dr. Seuss* relied primarily on the phrasing of the parody distinction in *Campbell* and its progeny in rejecting the "parody-of-the-author" argument. *Salinger I* emphasized the *Campbell* definition of parody as "the use of some elements of a prior author's *composition* to create a new one that, at least in part, comments on that author's *works.*" 641 F. Supp. 2d at 257 (quoting *Campbell*, 510 U.S. at 580) (emphasis added in *Salinger I*). However, *Campbell*'s language does not necessarily preclude parodies targeting the author. In fact, the Court recognized that parody resists a strict definition. *See Campbell*, 510 U.S. at 580 n.14. Under *Campbell*'s reasoning, rather than its precise phrasing, criticism of the author via the author's works may fit within the structure of protectable parody.

First, such use may qualify as "transformative" under the "purpose" factor. The purpose of an author-parodying work is to evoke the author in order to provide socially-valuable criticism of the author, a public figure necessarily open to ridicule.[8] *See id.* at 580-81. Second, under the "nature of the copyrighted work" factor, criticism of public figures through their work may require the use of well-known creative expressions as a **[*1155]** means to conjure up the figures in the public eye, especially where a person's fame arises from the work. *See id.* at 586. Third, under the "amount used" factor, the necessity of referencing public figures through their work may require the use of a least some portion of those works. *See id.* at 588. Finally, under the "effect on the market" factor, a parody lampooning the author may be unlikely to supplant any potential market for the original or derivatives thereof because of the unlikelihood that authors would license parodies ridiculing themselves. *See id.* at 592 ("People ask . . . for criticism, but they only want praise." (citation omitted)); *Fisher*, 794 F.2d at 437 ("Self-esteem is seldom strong enough to permit the granting of permission [for a parody] even in exchange for a reasonable fee.").

However, it is important to distinguish between a use which directly targets the author for holding a particular view and a use which merely targets a view that happens to be held by the author. *See Bourne*, 602 F. Supp. 2d at 507-08 (finding parody where new work ridiculed Walt Disney for holding anti-Semitic views); *Burnett*, 491 F. Supp. 2d at 968-69 (finding parody where use ridiculed Carol Burnett's wholesome image). The parodist targeting the author may be justified in using the original work to conjure up the author, whereas the would-be parodist who targets the author's viewpoints generally is essentially creating satire

---

8. The Court has no occasion to consider whether the same reasoning would apply if the author was not a public figure.

and therefore lacks the need to reference the author. *Cf. Campbell*, 510 U.S. at 580-81. Under this analysis, parody of the author would not be achieved merely by the ironic use of the author's works to criticize the author's views (unless, or course, those views are reflected in the work parodied). The would-be parodist that merely criticizes the author's views (and not the author directly) simply lacks adequate justification for using the author's work.

Ultimately, the Court need not determine on the facts of this case whether *any* altered work that parodies the original's author would qualify as a transformative parody under *Campbell*. Even assuming that "parody-of-the-author" is a legitimate transformative purpose, the Defendants' songs do not satisfy the fair use analysis, as discussed below. "Tax" does not target Henley at all, and "November," which only implicitly targets Henley, appropriates too much from "Summer" in relation to its slight jab at Henley and risks market substitution for "Summer" or its derivatives.

On a related note, assuming that "parody-of-the-author" is legitimate fair use, the parties debate whether it is necessary that the author actually hold that attribute for which the author is being ridiculed. In this case, the Defendants assert that they are poking fun at Henley because of his status as a member of the liberal "Hollywood and entertainment elite." (Defs.' Mot. Br. 5; DeVore Decl. ¶ 5.) Henley disputes that he is liberal and notes that he has donated to and supported Republican candidates such as John McCain. (Pls.' Statement of Uncontroverted Facts ("Pls.' SS") 31; Henley Decl. ¶¶ 22-23; Henley Supp. Decl. ¶ 9; Henley Depo. at 59:15-24.) However, because the relevant question is whether "a parodic character can reasonably be perceived," it does not matter whether Henley is liberal or not. *See Bourne*, 602 F. Supp. 2d at 507-08 (finding that it did not matter whether Walt Disney was actually anti-Semitic). The only inquiry under the "parody-of-the-author" theory is whether an audience could reasonably perceive the Defendants' songs as poking fun at Henley for his supposed liberal views. Of course, where a parodist's charge is clearly false, this may demonstrate the lack of actual parodic character **[*1156]** and expose the parodist's argument as a post hoc rationalization.

With this framework in mind, and assuming that "parody-of-the-author" is a legitimate transformative purpose, the Court now considers the four primary elements of the fair use inquiry for each of the allegedly infringing songs.

I. Purpose and Character of the Use

It is under this factor where the Court considers whether "a parodic character may reasonably be perceived." *Campbell*, 510 U.S. at 582. The Court first tackles "November," the Defendants' take on "Summer."

"Summer" is, at least on the surface, a song about nostalgia for a lost summer romance. The narrator laments the fact that summer is over and that his love interest has gone. *See* Appendix A ("Nobody on the road / Nobody on the beach / I feel it in the air / The summer's out of reach"; "I never will forget those nights /

I wonder if it was a dream / . . . / Now I don't understand / What happened to our love."). Yet the narrator can still picture his love interest and longs to rekindle the romance. *See id.* ("But I can see you — / Your brown skin shinin' in the sun / . . . / And I can tell you my love for you will still be strong / After the boys of summer have gone.").

The Defendants acknowledge this general theme of nostalgia but argue that the final verse contains a subtle political theme. The narrator states: "Out on the road today, / I saw a DEADHEAD sticker on a Cadillac / A little voice inside my head said, / 'Don't look back. You can never look back.' / . . . / Those days are gone forever /I should just them go." *Id.* As the Defendants interpret the verse, the narrator is bemoaning the failure of 1960's liberal politics (symbolized by the Deadhead sticker) to change the status quo (symbolized by the Cadillac). (Defs.' Mot. Br. 6.) This interpretation finds support in an interview Henley gave to Rolling Stone, explaining the last verse of "Summer": "We raised all that hell in the Sixties, and then what did we come up with in the Seventies? . . . After all our marching and shouting and screaming didn't work, we withdrew and became yuppies and got into the Me Decade." (Arledge Decl., Ex. 3.)[9]

The Defendants argue that "November" parodies the original by using its themes of nostalgia and disillusionment to mock Henley and other Obama supporters who, in "November," look back wistfully at Obama's campaign and bemoan his failure to deliver on the promised "hope." (Defs.' Mot. Br. 6.) This, however, does not comment on or criticize the content of "Summer" — the themes of nostalgia and disillusionment in general, or on summer romances, Deadheads, or Cadillacs in particular. Rather, "November" uses those themes and devices to mock a separate subject entirely, namely Obama and his supporters. Even the "Summer" narrator's supposed disappointment with 1960's politics is merely echoed, rather than critiqued or ridiculed, by the "November" narrator's disappointment with Obama's post-election performance. *See* Appendix A.

In *Salinger I*, the court found that the defendant, who wrote an "unofficial sequel" to *Catcher in the Rye,* had failed to demonstrate a probability of success on his parody defense because the sequel, rather than commenting on the character of Holden **[*1157]** Caufield, merely repeated the elements of the character in a new setting. *See* 641 F. Supp. 2d at 258-260 ("It is hardly parodic to repeat that same exercise in contrast, just because society and the characters have aged."). The defendant had simply taken the Caufield character, aged him sixty years, and placed him in a modern environment, without giving legitimate commentary on the character. *Id.*

---

9. The Plaintiffs object to the Rolling Stone article as hearsay. *See Larez v. City of Los Angeles,* 946 F.2d 630, 642 (9th Cir. 1991) (a reporter's transcriptions of a party's statement is hearsay). However, the Court declines to exclude this evidence for summary judgment purposes in recognition that the Defendants may be able to make the reporter available for cross-examination at trial.

Similarly here, the Defendants' song simply takes the narrator of "Summer," who is (supposedly) disappointed by the result of 1960's politics and places him in the current political environment, where he is disappointed by the result of Obama's election. (*Compare* "Out on the road today, / I saw a DEADHEAD sticker on a Cadillac / A little voice inside my head said, / 'Don't look back. You can never look back.' / I thought I knew what love was / What did I know? / Those days are gone forever / I should just let them go," *with* "Out on the road today, / I saw a [sic] OBAMA sticker on a Cadillac / A little voice inside my head said, / 'Don't look back. You can never look back.' / We thought we knew what love was / What did we know? / Those days are gone forever / We should just let them go"). "November" simply does not comment on or critique the disappointment expressed in "Summer."

The Defendants also argue that "November" pokes fun at Henley himself as a supporter of Obama. According to the Defendants, Henley can be seen as the narrator of "November"—given that he was the singer of "Summer"—who is disappointed and disillusioned with Obama and nostalgic for the hopeful days of Obama's campaign. As discussed above, assuming that criticism of the author can qualify as parody, it must target the author directly, as opposed to targeting the author's views generally. Here, "November" pokes fun at Obama and the naivete and subsequent disappointment of his supporters, which includes Henley, the song's narrator. Thus, assuming the validity of "parody-of-the-author," the Court finds that the parodic theme—the lampooning of Henley himself—is reasonably perceptible. It is, however, a relatively minor element of the main satirical purpose of the song—targeting Obama and his supporters.

"Dance" contains more explicit social commentary than "Summer." The song appears to recount an American couple's trip to a foreign country in the midst of revolutionary unrest. *See* Appendix B ("They're pickin' up prisoners and puttin' 'em in a pen / . . . / Rebels been rebels since I don't know when / . . . / Well, we barely made the airport for the last plane out / As we taxied down the runway I could hear the people shout / They said, 'Don't come back here Yankee!' "). The woman, however, ignores the unrest and simply wants to enjoy herself and dance. *See id.* ("She can't feel the heat comin' off the street / She wants to party / She wants to get down / All she wants to do is . . . dance.")

The Defendants argue that the song can be interpreted as a criticism of American foreign policy in Latin America in the 1980's, when the song was released, and the American public's indifference toward the situation.[10] (Defs.' Mot. Br. 6-7.) Even taking the Defendants' interpretation as true,[11] their song does not comment

---

10. The Defendants rely in part on an online music video alleged to be Henley's. (*See* Supp. Arledge Decl. ¶ 3.) Because this evidence was not produced during discovery pursuant to the Plaintiffs' request, the Court declines to consider it. Fed. R. Civ. P. 37(c)(1); *Yeti by Molly, Ltd. v. Deckers Outdoor Corp.*, 259 F.3d 1101, 1106-07 (9th Cir. 2001).

11. Both Kotchmar, who wrote the song, and Henley, who performed it, dispute this interpretation. (Kortchmar Decl. ¶ 7; Supp. Henley Decl. ¶ 7.)

[*1158] on "Dance," but instead uses the same themes to comment on entirely different subjects, namely Boxer, taxation, global warming, and the proposed cap-and-trade program. In "Tax," American taxpayers are upset with "back-breaking" taxes and the cap-and-trade program, *see* Appendix B ("They're pickin' up the taxpayers and puttin' 'em in a jam / . . . / Cap and trade program — from D.C. Inc. / . . . / They push and pull us right over the brink / . . . / And we finished up the campaign she could hear the people shout / They said, 'Don't come back here Boxer!'"), but Boxer either ignores or is oblivious to the taxpayers' unhappiness and insists on more taxation, *see id.* ("She can't feel the heat comin' off the street / She wants to party / She wants to get down / All she wants to do is . . . tax."). "Tax" makes no mention of American foreign policy, Latin America, or the apathy of the American public. Instead, as with "November," the Defendants evoked the same themes of the original in order to attack an entirely separate subject. This is satire, not parody.

Nor does "Tax" directly target either Henley or Kortchmar, the author of "Dance." Unlike "November," which at least implicitly references Henley as the song's narrator, "Tax" makes no implicit or explicit reference to Henley or Kortchmar, much less ridicule them. The song may mock political views that Henley allegedly supports, but that is insufficient justification for appropriating Henley's works, as discussed above. The Defendants have innumerable alternatives with which to mock Boxer and her policies.

The Defendants also argue that, even if their works are more satirical than parodic, they may still constitute fair use, citing *Blanch v. Koons*, 467 F.3d 244, 247 (2d Cir. 2006). This is undoubtedly true; parody is not the only form of fair use. However, as noted in *Campbell*, satire faces a higher bar for fair use because it requires greater justification for appropriating the original work.

In *Blanch*, a painting by artist Jeff Koons incorporated part of the plaintiff's photograph. *Id.* at 247-48. Koons had scanned the photograph into a computer, removed all but the legs and feet of a woman in the photograph, adjusted the orientation of the legs, modified the coloring, and set it in a landscape painting among three other sets of women's legs hovered above images of confections. *Id.* The court found that the use was fair, despite being mostly satire rather than parody. *Id.* at 254-55, 259. The court noted the transformative nature of the work, *id.* at 253, the fact that it copied only the most uncreative portions of the original, *id.* at 257-58, and the plaintiff's admissions that Koons's work did not harm the market for her work, *id.* at 258.

The Defendants' songs are manifestly distinguishable from the work in *Blanch*. *Blanch* involved an intense transformation of a fashion photograph to create a museum piece. Here, the Defendants made minimal changes to the lyrics of the Plaintiffs' songs to make new songs about different subjects. This is hardly transformative in the manner of *Blanch*. Moreover, as discussed below, the Defendants have borrowed heavily from the creative aspects of "Summer" and "Dance," unlike Koons's minor appropriation in *Blanch*.

The "purpose" factor also requires the Court to consider whether the defendant's use is commercial or noncommercial. See 17 U.S.C. § 107; Harper & Row, 471 U.S. at 562. "The crux of the profit/nonprofit distinction is not whether the sole motive of the use is monetary gain but whether the user stands to profit from exploitation of the copyrighted material without paying the customary price." Id.

[*1159] The Plaintiffs argue that use of the songs in campaign advertisements qualifies as commercial use under the Harper & Row standard because DeVore stands to get publicity for his campaign and openly hoped that his use of Henley's music would spur campaign donations. They note that each of the videos produced by the Defendants contained a link to DeVore's campaign website, where one could make online donations to the campaign, and that emails sent out by the campaign to publicize the videos contained a link directly to DeVore's donation webpage. (Pls.' SS 40-41, 120-124.)

District courts that have actually considered whether campaign advertisements are commercial in the fair use context come down on the side of noncommercial. See MasterCard Int'l Inc. v. Nader 2000 Primary Comm., Inc., No. 00 Civ.6068(GBD), 2004 U.S. Dist. LEXIS 3644, 2004 WL 434404, at *12 (S.D.N.Y. Mar. 8, 2004); Keep Thomson Governor Committee v. Citizens for Gallen Committee, 457 F. Supp. 957, 961 (D.N.H. 1978). However, in the Ninth Circuit, "monetary gain is not the sole criterion[,] particularly in a setting where profit is ill-measured in dollars." Worldwide Church of God v. Phila. Church of God, Inc., 227 F.3d 1110, 1117 (9th Cir. 2000) (quoting Weissmann v. Freeman, 868 F.2d 1313, 1324 (2d Cir. 1989)) (internal alterations omitted).

In Worldwide Church, a church made verbatim copies of a religious text for distribution among its members. Id. at 1113. The copyright owner sued for infringement and the defendant church asserted fair use. Id. at 1114-15. On the "profit/nonprofit" factor, the court noted that it did not matter whether the defendant actually received monetary benefit:

> [H]aving in mind that like academia, religion is generally regarded as "not dollar dominated," [the] use unquestionably profits [the defendant] by providing it at no cost with the core text essential to its members' religious observance, by attracting through distribution of [the text] new members who tithe ten percent of their income to [the defendant], and by enabling the ministry's growth. . . . It is beyond dispute that [the defendant] "profited" from copying [the text] — it gained an "advantage" or "benefit" from its distribution and use of [the text] without having to account to the copyright holder.

Id. at 1118.

Like the church in Worldwide Church, which stood to gain parishioners through the unlicensed use of the plaintiff's copyrighted work, DeVore and Hart stood to gain publicity and campaign donations from their use of Henley's music. In fact, the videos contained links directing viewers to the DeVore campaign website, encouraging them to donate. Thus, under the reasoning of Worldwide Church, the Defendants "profited" from their use by gaining an advantage without having to pay customary licensing fees to the Plaintiffs.[12] *Id.* In fact, Hart himself directly profited, as his compensation was tied to the amount of funds he raised. (Pls.' SS 38.)

Accordingly, both songs are used for commercial purposes under the fair use analysis, which weighs against the Defendants. The fact that "Tax" does not constitute parody also weighs against the Defendants. Assuming that "parody-of-the-author" is legitimate transformation under *Campbell*, "November's" implicit targeting of Henley weighs slightly in the Defendants' favor.

[*1160]

II. Nature of the Copyrighted Work

There is no dispute that the Plaintiffs' works are expressive and at the core of copyright protection. However, with respect to "November," which may have some parodic character, this factor does not weigh heavily in the overall analysis in recognition that parodies "invariably copy publicly known, expressive works." *Campbell*, 510 U.S. at 586.

"Tax," on the other hand, has little claim to parody, as discussed above. Thus, the fact that "Tax" borrows from a musical composition, a highly expressive work that is at the core of copyright, weighs against the Defendants in the fair use balancing.

III. Amount and Substantiality of the Portion Used

In the parody context, the third factor turns on "the persuasiveness of a parodist's justification for the particular copying done, . . . [;] the extent of permissible copying varies with the purpose and character of the use." *Campbell*, 510 U.S. at 586-87. The analysis of this factor will "also tend to address the fourth, by revealing the degree to which the parody may serve as a market substitute for the original or potentially licensed derivatives." *Id.* at 587.

Because a parody must be able to conjure up the work commented on (or possibly the work's author), at least some copying of a work is permitted. *Id.* at 588. "[U]sing some characteristic features cannot be avoided." *Id.* However, as the Supreme Court stated:

> Once enough has been taken to assure identification, how much more is reasonable will depend, say, on the extent to which the song's overriding purpose and character is to parody the original or, in contrast, the likelihood that the parody may serve as a market substitute for the original.

Id.; accord Dr. Seuss II, 109 F.3d at 1400 ("[T]he parodist is permitted a fair use of a copyrighted work if it takes no more than is necessary to 'recall' or 'conjure up'

---

12. Significantly, the Defendants paid licensing fees for video footage used in the "Tax" video (Pls.' SS 115), but paid no fee for the use of the Plaintiffs' music.

the object of his parody."); but *see Burnett*, 491 F. Supp. 2d at 970 ("[T]here is no requirement that 'parodists take the *bare minimum* amount of copyright material necessary to conjure up the original work.'" (citation omitted, emphasis in original)). A parodist is generally permitted greater license to borrow when parodying music: "Like a speech, a song is difficult to parody effectively without exact or near-exact copying. . . . This 'special need for accuracy,' provides some license for 'closer' parody." *Fisher*, 794 F.2d at 439.

It is undisputed that both "November" and "Tax" borrow heavily from the respective originals. The Defendants used karaoke tracks of each song as background and Hart supplied vocals. (Pls.' SS 58-59, 111.) The melodies remain identical, as do the rhyme scheme and syntax. (Pls.' SS 53-54, 104.) While the Defendants changed some of the lyrics, 65% of the "Summer" lyrics and 74.7% of the "Dance" lyrics were copied verbatim. (Pls.' SS 152.) This factor turns on whether such extensive copying was justified.

As discussed above with respect to the first factor, "Tax" is almost entirely satirical in nature and contains little or no parodic character. It therefore lacks the parody justification for appropriation. Otherwise, the transformation of the work is minimal—while their alterations somewhat change the meaning, the Defendants copied the music, rhyme scheme, and syntax almost entirely. The amount borrowed is excessive in relation to the transformation.

With "November," the question is much closer, assuming legitimate parodic character. As discussed above, "November" may have some parodic element—it implicitly pokes fun of Henley as a disillusioned Obama supporter. It may therefore be justified [*1161] in using at least some of "Summer" in order to evoke Henley's image. However, this does not necessarily justify the extent to which "November" copies. In *Campbell*, the Court found that the defendant's song commented on the naivete of the original work. 510 U.S. at 583. The defendants' song borrowed the opening riff and first line of the original, but substantially changed the lyrics, added new musical elements, and altered the beat of the original. *Id.* at 589. Nevertheless, the Court remanded the case for determination of whether the amount taken—just the opening riff and the opening line—was excessive in relation to the parodic element. *Id.*

The Defendants' copying in "November" exceeds that in *Campbell*, where the Court declined to decide the fair use question despite finding legitimate parodic purpose. *See id.* at 589. Indeed, the amount of the Defendants' copying goes far beyond anything that has been found to be fair use in the parody context. *See, e.g., Fisher*, 794 F.2d at 438-39 (29-second recording); *Bourne*, 602 F. Supp. 2d at 509-10 (new melody meant to evoke rather than copy original, with parodic lyrics); *Burnett*, 491 F. Supp. 2d at 970 (18-second scene of Carol Burnett); *Mastercard*, 2004 U.S. Dist. LEXIS 3644, 2004 WL 434404, at *14 (majority of parody involved original work by parodist); *Abilene Music*, 320 F. Supp. 2d at 93 (only three lines from original, which were altered in word, melody, and style); *Elsmere Music*, 482 F. Supp. at 744 (only four notes and two words taken from 100-measure and

45-word song). Indeed, the Defendants' appropriation approaches or exceeds the amounts borrowed in many cases where courts rejected the fair use defense. *See, e.g., Dr. Seuss II*, 109 F.3d at 1402-03 (defendants copied visual elements of main character and rhyme scheme but substantially changed language); *MCA*, 677 F.2d at 185 (defendants merely substituted dirty lyrics into song); *Walt Disney Prods. v. Air Pirates*, 581 F.2d 751, 757-58 (9th Cir. 1978) (defendants copied visual elements of animated characters rather than evoking them); *Columbia Pictures*, 11 F. Supp. 2d at 1185-86 (defendants copied the "total 'look and feel'" of plaintiff's poster and merely substituted character).

The Defendants' only (potentially) legitimate justification for the extensive copying of "Summer" is the necessity of evoking Henley. While this may allow for some appropriation, the Court finds that the amount borrowed goes far beyond that reasonably necessary to conjure up Henley. The Defendants did not take a portion of the song or alter the melody—they took virtually everything. Many of the "November" lyrics do not serve the purpose of ridiculing Henley and drift into pure satire, targeting Obama and Nancy Pelosi. *See* Appendix A ("Obama overload / Obama overreach / We feel it everywhere / Trillions in the breach / Empty bank, empty Street / Dollar goes down alone / Pelosi's in the House / So we now all must atone."). The Defendants argue that a lesser amount, a 30-second snippet perhaps, would have diluted the parody's impact and they would have been unable to "convey all of the political and parodic points they wished to make." (Defs.' Mot. Br. 12.) However, the parodic element, if any, of "November" is its lampooning of Henley, not of Obama, Pelosi, or their supporters generally. Using Henley's music to make those political points is not justified under *Campbell*.

IV. Effect of the Use on the Potential Market

Under the "market effect" factor, the Court focuses on the extent to which the Defendants' works usurp the potential market for the originals or their derivatives. *Campbell*, 510 U.S. at 592. It is not relevant that a use may damage the original's value through criticism. **[*1162]** *Id.* at 591-92. "[T]he role of the courts is to distinguish between 'biting criticism that merely suppresses demand and copyright infringement, which usurps it.'" *Id.* at 592 (quoting *Fisher*, 794 F.2d at 438) (internal brackets omitted).

This analysis requires consideration of more than just the market effect of the particular infringement at issue. Courts are to consider "'whether unrestricted and widespread conduct of the sort engaged in by the defendant . . . would result in a substantially adverse impact on the potential market' for the original." *Id.* at 590 (citation omitted). The burden is on the defendant to "bring forward favorable evidence" that potential markets will not be harmed. *Dr. Seuss II*, 109 F.3d at 1403. "[U]ncontroverted submissions that there was no likely effect on the market" do not suffice. *See id.* (quoting *Campbell*, 510 U.S. at 590).

With respect to market impact on the originals, the Defendants point out that their songs were part of freely-available internet videos and were not sold in any format. Moreover, they note Hart's apparent lack of talent as a vocalist in suggesting that their songs are unlikely to supplant the market for the original. The Plaintiffs seem to agree that Hart's musical stylings are unlikely to threaten Henley's. (Henley Depo. at 9:4-13, 103:20-104:14; Campbell Depo. at 14:15-16:4; Kortchmar Depo. at 103:9-24.)

However, the Court does not find that the Defendants have made an adequate showing on this factor. The question is not whether "November" and "Tax" specifically threaten the market for the original; the question is whether widespread dissemination of similar satirical spins on the Plaintiffs' music will harm the market for the originals. *See Campbell*, 510 U.S. at 590. Relevant to this inquiry is the fact that the Defendants have taken the entire musical composition and have changed a minimal amount of lyrics. The Court cannot say as a matter of law that widespread use in a similar manner would not harm the market for the originals.

The parties also dispute the effect on the market for derivative works. The Defendants' primary argument is that there is no market for licensed use of the works because the Plaintiffs refuse to license their works. (Pls.' SS 13; Henley Depo. at 90:25-91:9.) This is disputed, as the Plaintiffs have licensed their works for satirical or other commercial uses in the past and intend to consider licensing their works in the future.[13] (Pls.' SS 10, 13, 14; Henley Depo. at 91:10-14.) Moreover, whether the Plaintiffs have actually permitted licensing is irrelevant because the copyright laws protect the "potential market" for derivatives. *Castle Rock Entm't, Inc. v. Carol Publ'g Group, Inc.*, 150 F.3d 132, 145-46 (2d Cir. 1998) ("Although [plaintiff] has evidenced little if any interest in exploiting this market for derivative works . . . , the copyright law must respect that creative and economic choice."). "Even an author who had disavowed any intention to publish his work during his lifetime was entitled to protection of his copyright, first, because the relevant consideration was the 'potential market' and, second, because he has the right to change his mind." *Worldwide Church*, 227 F.3d at 1119 (citing *Salinger v. Random House, Inc.*, 811 F.2d 90, 99 (2d Cir. 1987)); *accord Salinger I*, 641 F. Supp. 2d at 268. The Defendants offer no evidence demonstrating **[*1163]** that their songs would not usurp the potential licensing market for remakes or remixes of the Plaintiffs' songs, should they choose to license them.

Indeed, the Plaintiffs have shown evidence that the Defendants' use does supplant the market for derivatives of "Summer" and "Dance." The Plaintiffs' expert testifies that licensees and advertisers do not like to use songs that are already associated with a particular product or cause. (Pls.' SS 155-58.) The Defendants argue that this sort of harm is not market-substitution. The Court disagrees. The advertisers would be deterred from using the Plaintiffs' music *because it has been used before*, not because of the particular association with DeVore's message

---

13. Campbell once licensed the song "Stop Draggin' My Heart Around," performed by Stevie Nicks, to Weird Al Yankovic for his satirical remake, "Stop Draggin' My Car Around." (Pls.' SS 14.)

(though that may impact the valuation as well). (Pls.' SS 155-58.) This injury is the very essence of market substitution.

Therefore, with respect to "Tax," which does not have significant parodic character, the Defendants fail to meet their burden of demonstrating the absence of harm to the potential market for "Dance" or its derivatives.

However, with respect to "November," the analysis is a bit different because "November" does target Henley in part, which, as discussed above, may be a legitimate parodic purpose. Because Henley would be unlikely to license use of his song to ridicule himself, such a song serves a different market than the original or its derivatives. *See Fisher*, 794 F.2d at 438. On the other hand, the alleged parodic element of "November" is slight in comparison to its main satirical thrust at Obama and his supporters generally. It may thus have some effect on the market for satirical versions of "Summer." Indeed, the substantial amount of material borrowed from "Summer" heightens the likelihood of market substitution even if there is some parodic element. *See Campbell*, 510 U.S. at 593 n.24. Because "Summer" and "November" are so similar in style and form, the Court cannot presume that there would be no derivative market usurpation, and the Defendants present no affirmative evidence of its absence.

Though it is a closer question than with regard to "Tax"—assuming legitimate parody—the Court finds that the Defendants have not demonstrated a lack of potential market harm by "November."

v. Aggregate Assessment

The fair use analysis involves a delicate balancing of the four factors with an eye towards the purposes of copyright. "The doctrine has been said to be 'so flexible as virtually to defy definition.'" *Princeton Univ. Press v. Mich. Document Servs., Inc.*, 99 F.3d 1381, 1392 (6th Cir. 1996) (quoting *Time Inc. v. Bernard Geis Assocs.*, 293 F. Supp. 130, 144 (S.D.N.Y. 1968)). The case-by-case analysis resists bright-line determinations and the resulting decisions inevitably represent a sort of rough justice.

That said, the Defendants' song "Tax" does not present a difficult question. The song is pure satire which fails to take aim at the original or its author. It therefore lacks justification to borrow from "Dance," which, as a musical composition, lies at the core of copyright protection. And it does far more than borrow from "Dance"—it appropriates the entire melody, rhyme scheme, syntax, and a majority of the lyrics. The Defendants have also failed to show that widespread use of this and similar satirical songs would not affect either the market for the original or potential derivatives. "Tax" is clearly not fair use.

"November," on the other hand, presents a closer question, assuming that targeting the author is a legitimate parodic purpose. Although it primarily targets Obama, it does, in part, lampoon Henley as an Obama supporter. It may thus contain [*1164] some parodic element and would be justified in appropriating some of "Summer." However, "November" goes far beyond what is necessary to conjure up Henley to hold him up to ridicule. As with "Tax," "November" copies the melody, rhyme, syntax, and most of the lyrics, and the lyrics are mostly satirical in nature. Given the extent of the copying, the Defendants have not met their burden of demonstrating the absence of market impact. Although the Court finds this to be a closer question than "Tax," the Defendants have not met their burden of demonstrating that "November" constitutes fair use.

As noted above, the parties do not dispute that the Plaintiffs own a copyright to "Summer" and "Dance," or that the Defendants' songs "November" and "Tax" copy substantial portions of those songs. Because the Defendants have failed to meet their burden of establishing a fair use defense, the Plaintiffs are entitled to summary judgment on their direct copyright infringement claim.

IV. CONCLUSION

For the foregoing reasons, the Court GRANTS summary judgment in favor of the Plaintiffs and against the Defendants on the issue of copyright infringement of both "Summer" and "Dance."

IT IS SO ORDERED.

APPENDIX A

The Boys of Summer	**The Hope of November**
Nobody on the road	Obama overload
Nobody on the beach	Obama overreach
I feel it in the air	We feel it everywhere
The summer's out of reach	Trillions in the breach
Empty lake, empty streets	Empty bank, empty Street
The sun goes down alone	Dollar goes down alone
I'm drivin' by your house	Pelosi's in the House
Though I know you're not home	So we now all must atone
But I can see you—	But we can see through—
Your brown skin shinin' in the sun	Your broken promises oh One
You got your hair combed back and your sunglasses on, baby	*You got your head cocked back and your teleprompter on, maybe*
And I can tell you my love for you will still be strong	And can we tell you our love for you will still be strong
After the boys of summer have gone	After the hope of November's gone?
I never will forget those nights	We never will forget those nights
I wonder if it was a dream	We wonder if it was a dream
Remember how you made me crazy?	Remember how you made us crazy?

Remember how I made you scream	Remember how I made you beam
Now I don't understand	Now we do understand
What happened to our love.	What happened to our love.
But babe, I'm gonna get you back	Barack, we're gonna cut no slack
I'm gonna show you what I'm	We're gonna show you what we're
made of	made of
I can see you—	We can see through—
Your brown skin shinin' in the sun	Your broken promises oh One
I see you walkin' real slow and	*We see you talkin' real slow and*
you're smilin' at everyone	*you're smilin' at everyone*
I can tell you my love for you will	Can we tell you our love for you will
still be strong	still be strong
After the boys of summer have gone	After the hope of November's gone?
Out on the road today,	Out on the road today,
I saw a DEADHEAD sticker on a Cadillac	I saw a OBAMA sticker on a Cadillac
A little voice inside my head said,	A little voice inside my head said,
Don't look back. You can never look	Don't look back. You can never look
back."	back."
I thought I knew what love was	We thought we knew what love was
What did I know?	What did we know?
Those days are gone forever	Those days are gone forever
I should just let them go but—	We should just let them go but—
I can see you—	We can see through—
Your brown skin shinin' in the sun	Your broken promises oh One
You got that top pulled down and	*You got that Rush pulled down and*
that radio on, baby	*talk radio gone, maybe*
And I can tell you my love for you	And can we tell you our love for you
will still be strong	will still be strong
After the boys of summer have gone	After the hope of November's gone?
I can see you—	We can see through—
Your brown skin shinin' in the sun	Your broken promises oh One
You got that hair slicked back and	*You got your head cocked back and*
those Wayfarers on, baby	*your teleprompter on, maybe*
I can tell you my love for you will	Can we tell you our love for you will

still be strong
After the boys of summer have gone

(Charlesworth Decl., Ex. 6; DeVore Decl., Ex. C.)

still be strong
After the hope of November's gone?

(Charlesworth Decl., Ex. 7; DeVore Decl., Ex. E.)

[*1170]

APPENDIX B

All She Wants to Do Is Dance

They're pickin' up the prisoners and
puttin' 'em in a pen
And all she wants to do is dance, dance
Rebels been rebels since I don't know when
And all she wants to do is dance
Molotov cocktail—the local

drink
And all she wants to do is dance, dance
They mix 'em up right in the kitchen sink
And all she wants to do is dance
Crazy people walkin' around with blood in their eyes
And all she wants to do is dance, dance
Wild-eyed pistol wavers who ain't

afraid to die
And all she wants to do is—
All she wants to do is dance and make romance

She can't feel the heat comin' off the street
She wants to party
She wants to get down
All she wants to do is—
All she wants to do is dance

All She Wants to Do Is Tax

They're pickin' up the taxpayers and
puttin' 'em in a jam
And all she wants to do is tax, tax
Liberals been liberals since I don't know when
And all she wants to do is tax
Cap and trade program—from D.C.

Inc.
And all she wants to do is tax, tax
They pull and push us right over the brink
And all she wants to do is tax
Barbara Boxer talkin' round—control in her sight
And all she wants to do is tax, tax
Wild-eyed global warmers who ain't

afraid to lie
And all she wants to do is—
All she wants to do is tax and break our backs

She can't feel the heat comin' off the street
She wants to party
She wants to get down
All she wants to do is—
All she wants to do is tax

All She Wants to Do Is Dance	**All She Wants to Do Is Tax**
Well, the government bugged the men's room in the local disco lounge	Well, the government rigged the market in the carbon trading scam
And all she wants to do is dance, dance	*And all she wants to do is tax, tax*
To keep the boys from sellin' all the weapons they could scrounge	To keep the boys a sellin' all the credits they could, ma'am
And all she wants to do is dance	*And all she wants to do is tax*
But that don't keep the boys from makin' a buck or two	But that don't keep the boys from makin' a buck or two
And all she wants to do is dance, dance	*And all she wants to do is tax, tax*
They still can sell the army all the drugs they can do	They still can sell the public on the good that they can do
And all she wants to do is —	*And all she wants to do is —*
All she wants to do is dance and make romance	All she wants to do is tax and break our backs
Well, we barely made the airport for the last plane out	Well, we barely made twenty ten, the vote was in doubt
As we taxied down the runway could hear the people shout	And we finished up the campaign she could hear the people shout
They said, "Don't come back here Yankee!"	They said, "Don't come back here Boxer!"
But if I ever do — I'll bring more money	But if she ever does — we'll bring more money
'Cause all she wants to do is dance and make romance	*'Cause all she wants to do is tax and break our backs*
Never mind the heat comin' off the street	Never mind the heat comin' off the street
She wants to party	She wants to party
She wants to get down	She wants to get down
All she wants to do is —	*All she wants to do is —*
All she wants to do is dance	*All she wants to do is tax*
All she wants to do is dance and make romance	*All she wants to do is tax and break our backs*
All she wants to do is dance	*All she wants to do is tax*
(Charlesworth Decl., Ex. 8; DeVore Decl., Ex. G.)	(Charlesworth Decl., Ex. 9; DeVore Decl., Ex. I.)

Questions Regarding *Henley v. DeVore*

1. A plaintiff bringing a copyright infringement claim has the initial burden of proof. What must the plaintiff prove for the suit to proceed?
2. For a defendant's fair use defense, there are four factors to be balanced together. Which of the four factors appears the most straightforward? The most complicated?
3. Do the definitions the court adopts for "parody" and "satire" align with your understanding of these terms prior to reading the case? If they differ, how so?
4. What is the difference between a parody of the work and a parody of the author? Are both parodies treated the same under the relevant law?
5. According to the U.S. District Court of the Central District of California, if a derivative work is parodic in nature, then two fair use factors (nature of the copyrighted work and amount/substantiality used) are essentially neutralized. Why?

Tips for Copyright Infringement Memorandum for Poet Igor Krichevsky

1. Since you are writing to a client and not a lawyer, make sure your language is as accessible as possible.
2. When you introduce a concept that might be foreign to Mr. Krichevsky, explain it right away.
3. Be mindful of a court's order of operations and mimic that order in your work: start with copyright infringement and then move to fair use, not the other way around.
4. Explain what fair use is generally before laying out the factors. List out the four factors and explain how they're weighed before positing specific arguments under each factor.

chapter 9

Three-Case Memorandum Assignment

For Assignment 7, you will use multiple cases as precedent: the substantive due process cases from Chapters 4 and 5. One unusual wrinkle in this assignment is that on top of deciding whether we will win our case or not, you will also be asked to opine on which of two simultaneously represented clients has the stronger case. As you'll see below, there is a potential *conflict of interest* in our representation of both clients. A conflict of interest is when the interests of an attorney and of their client or clients conflict. Attorneys are obligated to represent all their clients zealously, and if zealous representation of one client compromises the same attorney's zealous representation of another, then the attorney should withdraw from one or both cases.

Most aspiring law students know that to practice law in a given state, they'll have to pass a bar exam covering the substantive law of that jurisdiction. But did you know that every single state also requires members of the bar to pass some kind of character and fitness test? Lawyers are both representatives of their clients and officers of the court; they have an obligation to do their work competently and scrupulously. Attorneys are also expected to be prompt and diligent—they have to meet court deadlines (as missing deadlines can often have grave consequences for one's clients); they are expected to maintain consistent communication with their clients and to keep those communications confidential.

Lawyers are entrusted with a great deal of responsibility in our legal system, and lawyers who go beyond the boundaries of ethical behavior can be censured or even disbarred. Knowing the rules of ethics is just as important as knowing any area of substantive law. Effective attorneys must be ethical attorneys, too.

ASSIGNMENT 7: SUBSTANTIVE DUE PROCESS MEMORANDUM

Learned Foot, LLP

Memorandum

To: Associates

From: [Your Professor/Supervising Partner]

Subject: Substantive Due Process in the Bubman Independent School District

Background:

In 2015, pursuant to Tex. Educ. Code § 37.082: Bullying Prevention Policies and Procedures, the Bubman Independent School District (BISD) enacted an extensive bullying policy for all its schools. Included in that policy was a "Detention Counseling" provision, reproduced below:

Detention Counseling

The BISD recognizes that punishment alone is often insufficient to deter future acts of bullying. Bullying prevention often requires delving into the roots of bully-victim dynamics. Accordingly, in instances of repeated bullying [according to another section of the policy, bullying is "repeated" upon a "third incident involving the same parties"] the BISD mandates three hours of Detention Counseling to occur afterschool, supervised by the school's counselor, and divided into sessions lasting no longer than one hour apiece. The Counseling must commence and end within one month of this provision being triggered. Failure by a student—either bully or victim—to attend a scheduled counseling session can result in suspension or expulsion, at the discretion of the school's principal.

By the admission of the drafters of this provision, Detention Counseling was contemplated primarily for elementary and middle school students. The provision, however, was not placed in a section of the policy specific to particular grade levels and was accordingly effective in all BISD schools.

In fall of last year, Cody Simmons was a second-year senior at Bubman High School. He was infamous at Bubman High, having had the dubious distinction of being suspended at least once every year of his schooling starting in the fifth grade. The offenses that triggered the suspensions varied from theft to assault against a fellow student to assault against a teacher, which resulted in a full-semester suspension. (With regard to the final incident, the teacher at issue was trying to break up a fight between Mr. Simmons and another student, and Mr. Simmons inadvertently threw an elbow in the teacher's face.)

At the same time, Eli Manning—no relation to the two-time Super Bowl champion quarterback—was a freshman at Bubman High. He was a member of the tennis team and competed in numerous academic events, including number sense (mental math) and debate (Lincoln-Douglas).

In September, Mr. Simmons, apparently annoyed by the style of Mr. Manning's dress, locked Mr. Manning in a janitor's closet, using a mop handle to keep the door shut. Mr. Manning was released 30 minutes later when his cries were heard by a teacher. This was the first reported incident of bullying between Mr. Simmons and Mr. Manning. Mr. Simmons was given a week of detention for the act.

Upon his return to school, Mr. Simmons, still angry that Mr. Manning had "ratted [him] out," cornered Mr. Manning beside a dumpster during Mr. Manning's lunch break. He punched Mr. Manning three times in the stomach and once in the face, resulting in a fractured nose and multiple bruises. For this second reported incident of bullying, both Mr. Simmons's mother and Mr. Manning's parents were called into the school and an informal meeting was held with Principal JJ Walker. Principal Walker suspended Mr. Simmons for two weeks and warned Mr. Simmons that one more incident of bullying would result in his permanent expulsion from the school.

In October of last year, after Mr. Manning had recovered from his injuries, he spotted Mr. Simmons in the cafeteria. Mr. Manning was angry that his tennis season had been cut short because of his injuries and approached Mr. Simmons. Mr. Simmons sat alone at a corner table and by all accounts did his best to ignore Mr. Manning. Mr. Manning, surrounded by three of his friends, began shouting at Mr. Simmons, calling him "white trash" and "a fatherless piece of human garbage." Mr. Simmons did not react, but a teacher overheard the exchange and sent both Mr. Manning and Mr. Simmons to Principal Walker's office.

Though Principal Walker determined that Mr. Manning was the perpetrator of the bullying this time, he decided that under the "Detention Counseling" provision, this occurrence still counted as the "third incident [of bullying] involving the same parties." He accordingly assigned them to Guidance Counselor Nat Guilford for Detention Counseling.

In mid-October, during Mr. Simmons's and Mr. Manning's first Detention Counseling session, Mr. Guilford received a call from his estranged wife ten minutes into a reportedly unproductive counseling session. He told both students to stay in the classroom where the detention was being held while he stepped into the hallway to take the call. Cell reception was spotty, however, and Mr. Guilford had to walk several yards away into an adjacent hallway before he could return his wife's call. Accounts of how long he was gone vary. Mr. Guilford claims he was only gone for ten minutes. Mr. Simmons and Mr. Manning claim it was closer to thirty.

In the time while Mr. Guilford was away, a brawl broke out between Mr. Simmons and Mr. Manning. Mr. Manning verbally taunted Mr. Simmons. Mr. Simmons responded by punching Mr. Manning in the face. Mr. Manning then scrambled to his teacher's desk where he grabbed a pair of scissors. He then stabbed Mr. Simmons in the chest. By the time Mr. Guilford returned to the classroom, Mr. Simmons was on the floor, bleeding heavily. Mr. Manning was on top of him, using a balled-up American flag to try and slow the bleeding. Mr. Guilford immediately called 911. Both students were taken to the hospital. Mr. Manning was treated for a re-fracturing of his nose. Mr. Simmons required two thoracic surgeries as a result of his injuries, but according to his doctors, is expected to make a full recovery.

Applicable Law:

The BISD adopted the relevant language of Tex. Educ. Code § 37.082: Bullying Prevention Policies and Procedures for its definition of bullying. That language is below:

Sec. 37.0832. Bullying Prevention Policies and Procedures.

(a) In this section:

(1) "Bullying":

(A) means a single significant act or a pattern of acts by one or more students directed at another student that exploits an imbalance of power and involves engaging in written or verbal expression, expression through electronic means, or physical conduct that satisfies the applicability requirements provided by Subsection (a-1), and that:

(i) has the effect or will have the effect of physically harming a student, damaging a student's property, or placing a student in reasonable fear of harm to the student's person or of damage to the student's property;

(ii) is sufficiently severe, persistent, or pervasive enough that the action or threat creates an intimidating, threatening, or abusive educational environment for a student;

(iii) materially and substantially disrupts the educational process or the orderly operation of a classroom or school; or

(iv) infringes on the rights of the victim at school; and

(B) includes cyberbullying.

(2) "Cyberbullying" means bullying that is done through the use of any electronic communication device, including through the use of a cellular or other type of telephone, a computer, a camera, electronic mail, instant messaging, text messaging, a social media application, an Internet website, or any other Internet-based communication tool.

(a-1) This section applies to:

(1) bullying that occurs on or is delivered to school property or to the site of a school-sponsored or school-related activity on or off school property;

(2) bullying that occurs on a publicly or privately owned school bus or vehicle being used for transportation of students to or from school or a school-sponsored or school-related activity; and

(3) cyberbullying that occurs off school property or outside of a school-sponsored or school-related activity if the cyberbullying:

(A) interferes with a student's educational opportunities; or

(B) substantially disrupts the orderly operation of a classroom, school, or school-sponsored or school-related activity.

Substantive due process claims against schools typically invoke the following statutory and constitutional provisions:

42 U.S.C. § 1983: Civil action for deprivation of rights

Every person who, under color of any statute, ordinance, regulation, custom, or usage, of any State or Territory or the District of Columbia, subjects, or causes to be subjected, any citizen of the United States or other person within the jurisdiction thereof to the deprivation of any rights, privileges, or immunities secured by the Constitution and laws, shall be liable to the party injured in an action at law, suit in equity, or other proper proceeding for redress, except that in any action brought against a judicial officer for an act or omission taken in such officer's judicial capacity, injunctive relief shall not be granted unless a declaratory decree was violated or declaratory relief was unavailable. For the purposes of this section, any Act of Congress applicable exclusively to the District of Columbia shall be considered to be a statute of the District of Columbia.

U.S. Const. amend. XIV, § 1

All persons born or naturalized in the United States, and subject to the jurisdiction thereof, are citizens of the United States and of the state wherein they reside. No state shall make or enforce any law which shall abridge the privileges or immunities of citizens of the United States; nor shall any state deprive any person of life, liberty, or property, without due process of law; nor deny to any person within its jurisdiction the equal protection of the laws.

In terms of case law, you can isolate your analysis to three cases: *DeShaney v. Winnebago Cnty. Dep't of Soc. Servs.*, 489 U.S. 189 (1989), *Doe v. Covington Cnty. Sch. Dist.*, 675 F.3d 849 (5th Cir. 2012), and *Estate of Asher Brown v. Cypress Fairbanks Indep. Sch. Dist.*, 863 F. Supp. 2d 632 (S.D. Tex. 2012).

Issues Presented:

We currently represent both Mr. Simmons and Mr. Manning in their substantive due process claims against BISD with two different partners acting as lead attorney for each boy's case. The senior partnership is growing concerned, however, about the possibility of Simmons and his mother suing Manning for Simmons's injuries in addition to suing the school. From the start of these cases we have erected an ethical wall between the Simmons and Manning teams at Learned Foot LLP, but given that we are still at an early stage of litigation, the senior partnership would like you to opine on which of the two clients has the superior case if we were forced to choose one over the other to avoid a conflict of interest.

Mr. Simmons has suffered the most serious injury. His mother also claims that the counselor at issue, Mr. Guilford, never liked her son, and she suspects that

Mr. Guilford left him alone hoping that Mr. Simmons would bully Mr. Manning again, thus triggering his expulsion from Bubman High. Mr. Guilford denies the accusation.

Mr. Manning, upon reviewing the school's definition of bullying, believes that his taunting of Mr. Simmons should not have been considering bullying at all. Accordingly, he believes that his taunting in the cafeteria should not have triggered the "third incident" rule that led to Detention Counseling. He also claims that he stabbed Mr. Simmons in self-defense.

Please review the relative merits of both Mr. Simmons's and Mr. Manning's substantive due process claims under the applicable law above. Was either party in a "special relationship" with the school, giving rise to BISD's duty to protect? Did the counselor's actions give rise to a "state-created danger"? What is the likelihood of success for both parties in the relevant court, which is the U.S. District Court for the Southern District of Texas?

Case Citations

For your reference, below are the proper citations for the three cases you'll be analyzing in this memo. Make sure you use the same reporter used below for your pincites (the place for these is indicated by a blank (___)). The only time you don't need a pincite is if you're referring to the case as a whole as opposed to a specific page or page range. Remember that the first time you cite a case, you use the full citation. If you cite it again immediately afterward, you can use *Id.* and the pincite: *Id.* at ___. If you cite something else in between, you should use the short citation.

- *DeShaney v. Winnebago Cnty. Dep't of Soc. Servs.*, 489 U.S. 189, ___ (1989). (Full Citation)
- *DeShaney*, 489 U.S. at ___. (Short Citation)
- *Doe v. Covington Cnty. Sch. Dist.*, 675 F.3d 849, ___ (5th Cir. 2012). (Full Citation)
- *Covington County*, 675 F.3d at ___. (Short Citation)
- *Estate of Asher Brown v. Cypress Fairbanks Indep. Sch. Dist.*, 863 F. Supp. 2d 632, ___ (S.D. Tex. 2012). (Full Citation)
- *Asher Brown*, 863 F. Supp. 2d at ___. (Short Citation)

> **Tips for Substantive Due Process Memorandum in the Bubman Independent School District**
>
> 1. Concluding that one of the two clients has a greater likelihood of success is not the same as saying what that likelihood of success is. Make sure you do both. In other words, it's entirely possible that Manning has a stronger claim than Simmons under state-created danger but that that stronger claim would still lose against BISD.
> 2. Remember that while this case stemmed from incidents of bullying, the only law you're being asked to apply in the memorandum relates to substantive due process.
> 3. You're being asked to compare two clients' cases, not just provide a conclusion on which of the two is stronger. For the reader to fully understand your conclusion, you must provide the best arguments for both sides and then explain why you chose one over the other.
> 4. For the Application arguments under special relationship and state-created danger, it might be helpful to think of this as a three-part analysis:
>   a. Best argument for Simmons
>   b. Best argument for Manning
>   c. Best counterarguments against both by BISD
>   Then follow with your Conclusion regarding:
>   a. Which of the two boys has the stronger claim, and
>   b. Whether that stronger claim would ultimately prevail against BISD.
> 5. Make clear that state-created danger has not yet been adopted (or rejected) in our jurisdiction. It would be wise to consider not only whether the elements of the proposed standard are met but whether it would make sense as a policy matter for the court to adopt the standard moving forward.

chapter 10

Five-Case Memorandum Assignments

The two assignments in this chapter use the same five-case sequence as their legal universe. The larger case universe is necessary as the problems identified in these assignments are more complicated than in the previous scenarios; that said, the expansion of available precedent should also allow you to add more nuance to your analysis: more fact comparisons, more opportunities for novel lines of argument. With the expanded array of cases, it's especially important to keep in mind that your memo's organization should be focused on issues, not cases. Cases provide the legal framework and support for your arguments, but a memo should never read like a survey of precedent with relevant analysis attached. As always, stay focused on the assigned tasks, be objective, adhere to IRAC (including fair consideration of counterargument), and you should be just fine.

ASSIGNMENT 8: FIRST AMENDMENT RIGHTS AT MORNING GLORY HIGH

Learned Foot, LLP

Memorandum

To: Associates

From: [Your Professor/Supervising Partner]

Subject: First Amendment Rights at Morning Glory High

Background:

We represent Maya Smoot, a high school student at Morning Glory High School (MGHS) in the Jeevers Independent School District (JISD), located in Jeevers, Delaware. Over the past few years, MGHS has had two sex scandals involving two

171

different teachers. In January of last year, chemistry teacher Gloria Jenkins was revealed to have engaged in sexual intercourse with an 18-year-old senior, T.G. When the principal and school board learned of the tryst, they immediately fired Ms. Jenkins for violating § 42 of the JISD Faculty Handbook, enacted in September 2020 and reproduced below:

§ 42: Teacher-Student Fraternization

(1) GENERAL

The relationship between faculty and students must be, at all times, professional and respectful. Faculty must set strict boundaries with students and conduct themselves professionally, both on campus and off.

(2) PROHIBITED CONDUCT

Faculty are prohibited from engaging in any of the following types of conduct, regardless of whether the conduct occurs on or outside of school property or whether the conduct occurs during or outside of school hours:

(a) Engage in a romantic or sexual relationship with a student, including dating, sexual contact, inappropriate touching, or sexually suggestive comments.

(b) Foster or encourage an inappropriate emotional relationship with a student, outside the bounds of a reasonable, professional teacher-student dynamic.

(c) Communicate with a student for reasons unrelated to any school-related purpose, including telephone calls; electronic communication; webcams; or photographs.

(d) Socialize with students outside of class time for reasons unrelated to school.

(e) Provide alcohol or drugs—either prescription or illegal.

(3) SANCTIONS

The district will take appropriate disciplinary action, up to and including dismissal, against any faculty member found to have violated this non-fraternization policy.

Ms. Jenkins was a popular teacher on campus and many students bemoaned her dismissal, especially given the age of T.G. at the time. Certain administrators expressed reluctance in doling out the maximum penalty to Ms. Jenkins, but fearing a lawsuit from T.G.'s parents and with pressure from other parents demanding an example be made of Ms. Jenkins, the school board dismissed her under the rule above.

At the same time, for many years, rumors had circulated about librarian Kristopher Chapman's inappropriate relationships with students. No formal complaint, however, had ever been filed. Then in June of last year, at a local college's frat party, an MGHS graduate, Patty Watt, admitted to sleeping with Mr. Chapman numerous times during her junior and senior years of high school.

In September, upon learning of Ms. Watt's admission, Maya Smoot, a current senior at MGHS, informed her school principal, Leonard Heath, of what Ms. Watt had said. Mr. Heath expressed dismay at the news and informed Ms. Smoot that he would investigate the matter. Ms. Smoot waited two weeks before confronting

Principal Heath again. She had expected that Mr. Chapman would be dismissed in the same way that Ms. Jenkins had been. However, Principal Heath explained to her that Mr. Chapman had denied the accusation and (1) since Mr. Chapman wasn't technically faculty and not subject to the fraternization policy above and (2) since Ms. Watt was no longer a student at MGHS and hadn't filed the complaint herself, he could do no more in the matter.

Last month, outside of school hours and at her personal computer at home, Ms. Smoot, unsatisfied by Principal Heath's response, created a webpage entitled "Library Cad." The site did not reveal its author nor did it use Mr. Chapman's full name or the name of his school, but the site did include numerous references to the predator's "Chap-Stick." It also included a picture of him, taken from the MGHS staff website. The site began with the account of Ms. Watt, using her name, but only referring to her paramour as "Library Cad." Ms. Smoot opened a "Comments" section, inviting other victims of the Library Cad to share their stories. Ms. Smoot posted a link to the Library Cad site on her personal Facebook page and within a week, she had gotten over 50 responses, mostly anonymous.

The vast majority of the comments appear to be jokes. One student, for example, claimed that the Library Cad used the janitor's closet as a sex dungeon and that the cafeteria ladies were all his slaves. A few of the comments, however, appeared to be genuine. For example:

> 5—He did the same thing to me and another girl five years ago. He was cute and I totally had a crush on him but looking back, it was a big mistake.
>
> 15—This is not a joke! I know for a fact he's been pulling this crap for over a decade. I can't believe he's still working there!
>
> 27—I go to school with this guy now, and I can confirm that he's a total perv. He leers at any girl with a B-cup or higher and most of them are taken in by him even though he's old and gross. Just say no to the Chap-Stick!
>
> 32—I don't understand what the big deal is. It's not like the guy is forcing himself on anyone. From what I hear, it's the other way around. Grow up already. Whoever created this site is probably some jealous uggo, angry that he wouldn't give her the time of day.
>
> 45—So let me get this straight: Gloria Jenkins sleeps with an 18-year-old one time a few months before his graduation and gets fired, and this asshole pokes his crooked Chap-Stick into anything with a pulse for YEARS and gets nothing??? Our new school motto should be "Bros before Hos"!

Though by all accounts, Ms. Smoot did not access or contribute to the "Library Cad" site during school hours, news about the website soon spread across campus. At least eight teachers reported students talking about the site during class. One day, all the computers in the library had their homepage reset to the "Library Cad" webpage. Subsequently, three parents and five students demanded that Principal Heath conduct a thorough investigation of Mr. Chapman.

Principal Heath called Ms. Smoot to his office and confronted her about the website. Ms. Smoot admitted to creating it. Principal Heath then asked her if she would consider taking down the site, and Ms. Smoot replied that she would take it down as soon as Mr. Chapman was fired. Principal Heath said this was not a negotiation and that Ms. Smoot was violating school rules, though at the time he did not specify which rule it was. He told Ms. Smoot that he understood her concerns but that she needed to trust him to take care of it. Ms. Smoot then became silent. When Principal Heath pressed her, she said she understood and left his office.

The next day at school, Ms. Smoot came to school an hour early and distributed by the flagpole opposite the school entrance the following two items: (1) Chapstick and (2) a pinned badge reading "Bros Before Hos—JISD." Inside the school, in front of the library entrance, Ms. Smoot mounted a poster reading "Stay out unless you want to get JISD on."

The poster was only up for ten minutes before a teacher saw it and pulled it down, but by then, dozens of students had taken pictures of the image and posted them online. Additionally, about a quarter of the school population, mostly young women, donned the "Bros Before Hos—JISD" badge before a loud speaker announcement demanded that everyone remove them or risk suspension. Everyone did as was told, and while there was still much chatter about Ms. Smoot's actions that day, no one resisted the order. Ms. Smoot was then summoned from her first period class and taken to the principal's office.

Ms. Smoot did not deny that she had created the library poster and had created and distributed the "Bros before Hos" badges. She also admitted that she had distributed several Chapsticks, a giant pile of which had been growing steadily just outside the front office. Principal Heath, without consulting anyone else in the JISD administration, suspended Ms. Smoot for two days for two violations of the JISD Disciplinary Code: (1) falsely accusing a staff member of the school and (2) using foul language on school property; additionally, he made her reinstatement contingent upon Ms. Smoot taking down the "Library Cad" website. The two applicable Disciplinary Code sections are reproduced below:

> § 51, False Accusation. No student shall knowingly or recklessly accuse a member of the school staff of misconduct, including but not limited to commissions of crimes and violations of the Faculty Handbook. If a student suspects misconduct, he or she should first report the offense to the principal.
>
> § 89, Obscenity and Profanity. Students are forbidden from using foul language—vulgar and profane words or phrases—including but not limited to sexually explicit or suggestive language.

As soon as Ms. Smoot was suspended, her mother retained our services. We contacted the JISD Superintendent and told her of our intention to file a § 1983 claim on First Amendment grounds along with a request for a preliminary injunction to stay Principal Heath's reinstatement condition pending a decision on the § 1983 claim. The Superintendent agreed to lift the condition, but not the two-day suspension and will allow Ms. Smoot back to school after the two days even if she does not take down the "Library Cad" site.

Ms. Smoot's suspension has ended, and she has not taken down the "Library Cad" site, which now has over 300 comments, mostly in support of Ms. Smoot, but with a sizeable portion defending Mr. Chapman. Some even note that the original accuser, Ms. Watt, has since gone back on her original accusation and has asked Ms. Smoot to take down her story from the "Library Cad" site. According to Ms. Smoot, she has received the above request from Ms. Watt; Ms. Smoot, however, refused to delete Ms. Watt's account, but did replace her actual name on the website with the moniker "Violated Violet."

Applicable Law:
The relevant statutory and constitutional provisions are below:

42 U.S.C. § 1983: Civil action for deprivation of rights

Every person who, under color of any statute, ordinance, regulation, custom, or usage, of any State or Territory or the District of Columbia, subjects, or causes to be subjected, any citizen of the United States or other person within the jurisdiction thereof to the deprivation of any rights, privileges, or immunities secured by the Constitution and laws, shall be liable to the party injured in an action at law, suit in equity, or other proper proceeding for redress, except that in any action brought against a judicial officer for an act or omission taken in such officer's judicial capacity, injunctive relief shall not be granted unless a declaratory decree was violated or declaratory relief was unavailable. For the purposes of this section, any Act of Congress applicable exclusively to the District of Columbia shall be considered to be a statute of the District of Columbia.

U.S. Const. amend. I

Congress shall make no law respecting an establishment of religion, or prohibiting the free exercise thereof; or abridging the freedom of speech, or of the press; or the right of the people peaceably to assemble, and to petition the government for a redress of grievances.

In terms of case law, you can isolate your analysis to five cases: *Tinker v. Des Moines Indep. Cmty. Sch. Dist.*, 393 U.S. 503 (1969), *Bethel Sch. Dist. No. 403 v. Fraser*, 478 U.S. 675 (1986), *Wisniewski ex rel. Wisniewski v. Bd. of Educ. of the Weedsport Cent. Sch. Dist.*, 494 F.3d 34 (2d Cir. 2007), *Mahanoy Area Sch. Dist. v. B.L.*, 2021 U.S. LEXIS 3395 (2021), *B.H. ex rel. Hawk v. Easton Area Sch. Dist.*, 725 F.3d 293 (3d Cir. 2013).

Issues Presented:
Given the recent media attention on this matter, this case is high priority. Accordingly, the senior partnership would like a memorandum of law laying out arguments for both Ms. Smoot and the JISD in the District of Delaware and your opinion on the likelihood of success for Ms. Smoot for each piece of speech.

TINKER v. DES MOINES INDEPENDENT COMMUNITY SCHOOL DISTRICT

Supreme Court of the United States
November 12, 1968, Argued; February 24, 1969, Decided
No. 21
Reporter: 393 U.S. 503 *

Judges: Warren, Black, Douglas, Harlan, Brennan, Stewart, White, Fortas, Marshall

Opinion by: Fortas

Opinion (Edited for Content)

[*504] Mr. Justice FORTAS delivered the opinion of the Court.

Petitioner John F. Tinker, 15 years old, and petitioner Christopher Eckhardt, 16 years old, attended high schools in Des Moines, Iowa. Petitioner Mary Beth Tinker, John's sister, was a 13-year-old student in junior high school.

In December 1965, a group of adults and students in Des Moines held a meeting at the Eckhardt home. The group determined to publicize their objections to the hostilities in Vietnam and their support for a truce by wearing black armbands during the holiday season and by fasting on December 16 and New Year's Eve. Petitioners and their parents had previously engaged in similar activities, and they decided to participate in the program.

The principals of the Des Moines schools became aware of the plan to wear armbands. On December 14, 1965, they met and adopted a policy that any student wearing an armband to school would be asked to remove it, and if he refused he would be suspended until he returned without the armband. Petitioners were aware of the regulation that the school authorities adopted.

On December 16, Mary Beth and Christopher wore black armbands to their schools. John Tinker wore his armband the next day. They were all sent home and suspended from school until they would come back without their armbands. They did not return to school until after the planned period for wearing armbands had expired—that is, until after New Year's Day.

This complaint was filed in the United States District Court by petitioners, through their fathers, under § 1983 of Title 42 of the United States Code. It prayed for an injunction restraining the respondent school officials and the respondent members of the board of directors of the school district from disciplining the petitioners, and it sought nominal damages. After an evidentiary hearing the District Court dismissed the complaint. It upheld [*505] the constitutionality of the school authorities' action on the ground that it was reasonable in order to prevent disturbance of school discipline. 258 F. Supp. 971 (1966). The court referred to but expressly declined to follow the Fifth Circuit's holding in a similar case that the wearing of symbols like the armbands cannot be prohibited unless it "materially and substantially interfere[s] with the requirements of appropriate discipline in the operation of the school." *Burnside v. Byars*, 363 F.2d 744, 749 (1966).[1]

On appeal, the Court of Appeals for the Eighth Circuit considered the case *en banc*. The court was equally divided, and the District Court's decision was accordingly affirmed, without opinion. 383 F.2d 988 (1967). We granted certiorari. 390 U.S. 942 (1968).

I.

The District Court recognized that the wearing of an armband for the purpose of expressing certain views is the type of symbolic act that is within the Free Speech Clause of the First Amendment. See *West Virginia v. Barnette*, 319 U.S. 624 (1943); *Stromberg v. California*, 283 U.S. 359 (1931). Cf. *Thornhill v. Alabama*, 310 U.S. 88 (1940); *Edwards v. South Carolina*, 372 U.S. 229 (1963); *Brown v. Louisiana*, 383 U.S. 131 (1966). As we shall discuss, the wearing of armbands in the circumstances of this case was entirely divorced from actually or potentially disruptive conduct by those participating in it. It was closely akin to "pure speech" **[*506]** which, we have repeatedly held, is entitled to comprehensive protection under the First Amendment. Cf. *Cox v. Louisiana*, 379 U.S. 536, 555 (1965); *Adderley v. Florida*, 385 U.S. 39 (1966).

First Amendment rights, applied in light of the special characteristics of the school environment, are available to teachers and students. It can hardly be argued that either students or teachers shed their constitutional rights to freedom of speech or expression at the schoolhouse gate. This has been the unmistakable holding of this Court for almost 50 years. In *Meyer v. Nebraska*, 262 U.S. 390 (1923), and *Bartels v. Iowa*, 262 U.S. 404 (1923), this Court, in opinions by Mr. Justice McReynolds, held that the Due Process Clause of the Fourteenth Amendment prevents States from forbidding the teaching of a foreign language to young students. Statutes to this effect, the Court held, unconstitutionally interfere with the liberty of teacher, student, and parent.[2] . . .

---

1. In *Burnside*, the Fifth Circuit ordered that high school authorities be enjoined from enforcing a regulation forbidding students to wear "freedom buttons." It is instructive that in *Blackwell v. Issaquena County Board of Education*, 363 F.2d 749 (1966), the same panel on the same day reached the opposite result on different facts. It declined to enjoin enforcement of such a regulation in another high school where the students wearing freedom buttons harassed students who did not wear them and created much disturbance.

2. *Hamilton v. Regents of Univ. of Cal.*, 293 U.S. 245 (1934), is sometimes cited for the broad proposition that the State may attach conditions to attendance at a state university that require individuals to violate their religious convictions. The case involved dismissal of members of a religious denomination from a land grant college for refusal to participate in military training. Narrowly viewed, the case turns upon the Court's conclusion that merely requiring a student to participate in school training in military "science" could not conflict with his constitutionally protected freedom of conscience. The decision cannot be taken as establishing that the State may impose and enforce any conditions that it chooses upon attendance at public institutions of learning, however violative they may be of fundamental constitutional guarantees. See, *e.g., West Virginia v. Barnette*, 319

[*507] In *West Virginia v. Barnette*, [319 U.S. 624 (1943)], this Court held that under the First Amendment, the student in public school may not be compelled to salute the flag. Speaking through Mr. Justice Jackson, the Court said:

"The Fourteenth Amendment, as now applied to the States, protects the citizen against the State itself and all of its creatures—Boards of Education not excepted. These have, of course, important, delicate, and highly discretionary functions, but none that they may not perform within the limits of the Bill of Rights. That they are educating the young for citizenship is reason for scrupulous protection of Constitutional freedoms of the individual, if we are not to strangle the free mind at its source and teach youth to discount important principles of our government as mere platitudes." 319 U.S., at 637.

On the other hand, the Court has repeatedly emphasized the need for affirming the comprehensive authority of the States and of school officials, consistent with fundamental constitutional safeguards, to prescribe and control conduct in the schools. See *Epperson v. Arkansas, supra,* at 104; *Meyer v. Nebraska, supra,* at 402. Our problem lies in the area where students in the exercise of First Amendment rights collide with the rules of the school authorities.

II.

The problem posed by the present case does not relate to regulation of the length of skirts or the type of clothing, [*508] to hair style, or deportment. Cf. *Ferrell v. Dallas Independent School District*, 392 F.2d 697 (1968); *Pugsley v. Sellmeyer*, 158 Ark. 247, 250 S.W. 538 (1923). It does not concern aggressive, disruptive action or even group demonstrations. Our problem involves direct, primary First Amendment rights akin to "pure speech."

The school officials banned and sought to punish petitioners for a silent, passive expression of opinion, unaccompanied by any disorder or disturbance on the part of petitioners. There is here no evidence whatever of petitioners' interference, actual or nascent, with the schools' work or of collision with the rights of other students to be secure and to be let alone. Accordingly, this case does not concern speech or action that intrudes upon the work of the schools or the rights of other students.

Only a few of the 18,000 students in the school system wore the black armbands. Only five students were suspended for wearing them. There is no indication that the work of the schools or any class was disrupted. Outside the classrooms, a few students made hostile remarks to the children wearing armbands, but there were no threats or acts of violence on school premises.

U.S. 624 (1943); *Dixon v. Alabama State Board of Education*, 294 F.2d 150 (C.A. 5th Cir. 1961); *Knight v. State Board of Education*, 200 F. Supp. 174 (D.C. M.D. Tenn. 1961); *Dickey v. Alabama State Board of Education*, 273 F. Supp. 613 (D.C. M.D. Ala. 1967). See also Note, Unconstitutional Conditions, 73 Harv. L. Rev. 1595 (1960); Note, Academic Freedom, 81 Harv. L. Rev. 1045 (1968).

The District Court concluded that the action of the school authorities was reasonable because it was based upon their fear of a disturbance from the wearing of the armbands. But, in our system, undifferentiated fear or apprehension of disturbance is not enough to overcome the right to freedom of expression. Any departure from absolute regimentation may cause trouble. Any variation from the majority's opinion may inspire fear. Any word spoken, in class, in the lunchroom, or on the campus, that deviates from the views of another person may start an argument or cause a disturbance. But our Constitution says we must take this risk, *Terminiello v. Chicago*, 337 U.S. 1 (1949); and our history says that it is this sort of hazardous freedom—this kind of openness—that is [*509] the basis of our national strength and of the independence and vigor of Americans who grow up and live in this relatively permissive, often disputatious, society.

In order for the State in the person of school officials to justify prohibition of a particular expression of opinion, it must be able to show that its action was caused by something more than a mere desire to avoid the discomfort and unpleasantness that always accompany an unpopular viewpoint. Certainly where there is no finding and no showing that engaging in the forbidden conduct would "materially and substantially interfere with the requirements of appropriate discipline in the operation of the school," the prohibition cannot be sustained. *Burnside v. Byars, supra*, at 749.

In the present case, the District Court made no such finding, and our independent examination of the record fails to yield evidence that the school authorities had reason to anticipate that the wearing of the armbands would substantially interfere with the work of the school or impinge upon the rights of other students. Even an official memorandum prepared after the suspension that listed the reasons for the ban on wearing the armbands made no reference to the anticipation of such disruption.[3]

[*510] On the contrary, the action of the school authorities appears to have been based upon an urgent wish to avoid the controversy which might result from the expression, even by the silent symbol of armbands, of opposition to this

---

3. The only suggestions of fear of disorder in the report are these:

"A former student of one of our high schools was killed in Viet Nam. Some of his friends are still in school and it was felt that if any kind of a demonstration existed, it might evolve into something which would be difficult to control."

"Students at one of the high schools were heard to say they would wear arm bands of other colors if the black bands prevailed."

Moreover, the testimony of school authorities at trial indicates that it was not fear of disruption that motivated the regulation prohibiting the armbands; the regulation was directed against "the principle of the demonstration" itself. School authorities simply felt that "the schools are no place for demonstrations," and if the students "didn't like the way our elected officials were handling things, it should be handled with the ballot box and not in the halls of our public schools."

Nation's part in the conflagration in Vietnam.[4] It is revealing, in this respect, that the meeting at which the school principals decided to issue the contested regulation was called in response to a student's statement to the journalism teacher in one of the schools that he wanted to write an article on Vietnam and have it published in the school paper. (The student was dissuaded.[5])

It is also relevant that the school authorities did not purport to prohibit the wearing of all symbols of political or controversial significance. The record shows that students in some of the schools wore buttons relating to national political campaigns, and some even wore the Iron Cross, traditionally a symbol of Nazism. The order prohibiting the wearing of armbands did not extend to these. Instead, a particular symbol—black armbands worn to exhibit opposition to this Nation's involvement [*511] in Vietnam—was singled out for prohibition. Clearly, the prohibition of expression of one particular opinion, at least without evidence that it is necessary to avoid material and substantial interference with schoolwork or discipline, is not constitutionally permissible.

In our system, state-operated schools may not be enclaves of totalitarianism. School officials do not possess absolute authority over their students. Students in school as well as out of school are "persons" under our Constitution. They are possessed of fundamental rights which the State must respect, just as they themselves must respect their obligations to the State. In our system, students may not be regarded as closed-circuit recipients of only that which the State chooses to communicate. They may not be confined to the expression of those sentiments that are officially approved. In the absence of a specific showing of constitutionally valid reasons to regulate their speech, students are entitled to freedom of expression of their views. As Judge Gewin, speaking for the Fifth Circuit, said, school officials cannot suppress "expressions of feelings with which they do not wish to contend." *Burnside v. Byars, supra*, at 749.

In *Meyer v. Nebraska, supra*, at 402, Mr. Justice McReynolds expressed this Nation's repudiation of the principle that a State might so conduct its schools as to "foster a homogeneous people." He said:

---

4. The District Court found that the school authorities, in prohibiting black armbands, were influenced by the fact that "the Viet Nam war and the involvement of the United States therein has been the subject of a major controversy for some time. When the arm band regulation involved herein was promulgated, debate over the Viet Nam war had become vehement in many localities. A protest march against the war had been recently held in Washington, D.C. A wave of draft card burning incidents protesting the war had swept the country. At that time two highly publicized draft card burning cases were pending in this Court. Both individuals supporting the war and those opposing it were quite vocal in expressing their views." 258 F. Supp., at 972-973.

5. After the principals' meeting, the director of secondary education and the principal of the high school informed the student that the principals were opposed to publication of his article. They reported that "we felt that it was a very friendly conversation, although we did not feel that we had convinced the student that our decision was a just one."

"In order to submerge the individual and develop ideal citizens, Sparta assembled the males at seven into barracks and intrusted their subsequent education and training to official guardians. Although such measures have been deliberately approved by men of great genius, their ideas touching the relation between individual and State were wholly different from those upon which our institutions rest; and it hardly will be affirmed that any legislature could impose such restrictions upon the people of a [*512] State without doing violence to both letter and spirit of the Constitution."

This principle has been repeated by this Court on numerous occasions during the intervening years. In *Keyishian v. Board of Regents*, 385 U.S. 589, 603, Mr. Justice Brennan, speaking for the Court, said:

" 'The vigilant protection of constitutional freedoms is nowhere more vital than in the community of American schools.' *Shelton v. Tucker*, [364 U.S. 479,] at 487. The classroom is peculiarly the 'marketplace of ideas.' The Nation's future depends upon leaders trained through wide exposure to that robust exchange of ideas which discovers truth 'out of a multitude of tongues, [rather] than through any kind of authoritative selection.' "

The principle of these cases is not confined to the supervised and ordained discussion which takes place in the classroom. The principal use to which the schools are dedicated is to accommodate students during prescribed hours for the purpose of certain types of activities. Among those activities is personal intercommunication among the students.[6] This is not only an inevitable part of the process of attending school; it is also an important part of the educational process. A student's rights, therefore, do not embrace merely the classroom hours. When he is in the cafeteria, or on the playing field, or on [*513] the campus during the authorized hours, he may express his opinions, even on controversial subjects like the conflict in Vietnam, if he does so without "materially and substantially interfer[ing] with the requirements of appropriate discipline in the operation of the school" and without colliding with the rights of others. *Burnside v. Byars, supra*, at 749. But conduct by the student, in class or out of it, which for any reason—whether it stems from time, place, or type of behavior—materially disrupts classwork or involves substantial disorder or invasion of the rights of others is, of course, not immunized by the constitutional guarantee of freedom of speech. Cf. *Blackwell v. Issaquena County Board of Education*, 363 F.2d 749 (C.A. 5th Cir. 1966).

---

6. In *Hammond v. South Carolina State College*, 272 F. Supp. 947 (D.C. S.C. 1967), District Judge Hemphill had before him a case involving a meeting on campus of 300 students to express their views on school practices. He pointed out that a school is not like a hospital or a jail enclosure. Cf. *Cox v. Louisiana*, 379 U.S. 536 (1965); *Adderley v. Florida*, 385 U.S. 39 (1966). It is a public place, and its dedication to specific uses does not imply that the constitutional rights of persons entitled to be there are to be gauged as if the premises were purely private property. Cf. *Edwards v. South Carolina*, 372 U.S. 229 (1963); *Brown v. Louisiana*, 383 U.S. 131 (1966).

Under our Constitution, free speech is not a right that is given only to be so circumscribed that it exists in principle but not in fact. Freedom of expression would not truly exist if the right could be exercised only in an area that a benevolent government has provided as a safe haven for crackpots. The Constitution says that Congress (and the States) may not abridge the right to free speech. This provision means what it says. We properly read it to permit reasonable regulation of speech-connected activities in carefully restricted circumstances. But we do not confine the permissible exercise of First Amendment rights to a telephone booth or the four corners of a pamphlet, or to supervised and ordained discussion in a school classroom.

If a regulation were adopted by school officials forbidding discussion of the Vietnam conflict, or the expression by any student of opposition to it anywhere on school property except as part of a prescribed classroom exercise, it would be obvious that the regulation would violate the constitutional rights of students, at least if it could not be justified by a showing that the students' activities would materially and substantially disrupt the work and discipline of the school. Cf. *Hammond* [*514] *v. South Carolina State College*, 272 F. Supp. 947 (D.C. S.C. 1967) (orderly protest meeting on state college campus); *Dickey v. Alabama State Board of Education*, 273 F. Supp. 613 (D.C. M.D. Ala. 1967) (expulsion of student editor of college newspaper). In the circumstances of the present case, the prohibition of the silent, passive "witness of the armbands," as one of the children called it, is no less offensive to the Constitution's guarantees.

As we have discussed, the record does not demonstrate any facts which might reasonably have led school authorities to forecast substantial disruption of or material interference with school activities, and no disturbances or disorders on the school premises in fact occurred. These petitioners merely went about their ordained rounds in school. Their deviation consisted only in wearing on their sleeve a band of black cloth, not more than two inches wide. They wore it to exhibit their disapproval of the Vietnam hostilities and their advocacy of a truce, to make their views known, and, by their example, to influence others to adopt them. They neither interrupted school activities nor sought to intrude in the school affairs or the lives of others. They caused discussion outside of the classrooms, but no interference with work and no disorder. In the circumstances, our Constitution does not permit officials of the State to deny their form of expression.

We express no opinion as to the form of relief which should be granted, this being a matter for the lower courts to determine. We reverse and remand for further proceedings consistent with this opinion.

Reversed and remanded.

Concur by: Stewart; White

Concur

Mr. Justice STEWART, concurring.

Although I agree with much of what is said in the Court's opinion, and with its judgment in this case, I [*515] cannot share the Court's uncritical assumption that, school discipline aside, the First Amendment rights of children are co-extensive with those of adults. Indeed, I had thought the Court decided otherwise just last Term in *Ginsberg v. New York*, 390 U.S. 629. I continue to hold the view I expressed in that case: "[A] State may permissibly determine that, at least in some precisely delineated areas, a child—like someone in a captive audience—is not possessed of that full capacity for individual choice which is the presupposition of First Amendment guarantees." *Id.*, at 649-650 (concurring in result). Cf. *Prince v. Massachusetts*, 321 U.S. 158.

Mr. Justice WHITE, concurring.

While I join the Court's opinion, I deem it appropriate to note, first, that the Court continues to recognize a distinction between communicating by words and communicating by acts or conduct which sufficiently impinges on some valid state interest; and, second, that I do not subscribe to everything the Court of Appeals said about free speech in its opinion in *Burnside v. Byars*, 363 F.2d 744, 748 (C.A. 5th Cir. 1966), a case relied upon by the Court in the matter now before us.

Dissent by: Black; Harlan

Dissent

Mr. Justice BLACK, dissenting.

The Court's holding in this case ushers in what I deem to be an entirely new era in which the power to control pupils by the elected "officials of state supported public schools . . ." in the United States is in ultimate effect transferred to the Supreme Court.[1] The Court brought [*516] this particular case here on a petition for certiorari urging that the First and Fourteenth Amendments protect the right of school pupils to express their political views all the way "from kindergarten through high school." Here the constitutional right to "political expression" asserted was a right to wear black armbands during school hours and at classes in order to demonstrate to the other students that the petitioners were mourning

---

1. The petition for certiorari here presented this single question:

"Whether the First and Fourteenth Amendments permit officials of state supported public schools to prohibit students from wearing symbols of political views within school premises where the symbols are not disruptive of school discipline or decorum."

because of the death of United States soldiers in Vietnam and to protest that war which they were against. Ordered to refrain from wearing the armbands in school by the elected school officials and the teachers vested with state authority to do so, apparently only seven out of the school system's 18,000 pupils deliberately refused to obey the order. One defying pupil was Paul Tinker, 8 years old, who was in the second grade; another, Hope Tinker, was 11 years old and in the fifth grade; a third member of the Tinker family was 13, in the eighth grade; and a fourth member of the same family was John Tinker, 15 years old, an 11th grade high school pupil. Their father, a Methodist minister without a church, is paid a salary by the American Friends Service Committee. Another student who defied the school order and insisted on wearing an armband in school was Christopher Eckhardt, an 11th grade pupil and a petitioner in this case. His mother is an official in the Women's International League for Peace and Freedom.

As I read the Court's opinion it relies upon the following grounds for holding unconstitutional the judgment of the Des Moines school officials and the two courts below. First, the Court concludes that the wearing of armbands is "symbolic speech" which is "akin to 'pure speech'" and therefore protected by the First and Fourteenth Amendments. Secondly, the Court decides that the public schools are an appropriate place to exercise "symbolic speech" as long as normal school functions [*517] are not "unreasonably" disrupted. Finally, the Court arrogates to itself, rather than to the State's elected officials charged with running the schools, the decision as to which school disciplinary regulations are "reasonable."

Assuming that the Court is correct in holding that the conduct of wearing armbands for the purpose of conveying political ideas is protected by the First Amendment, cf., e.g., *Giboney v. Empire Storage & Ice Co.*, 336 U.S. 490 (1949), the crucial remaining questions are whether students and teachers may use the schools at their whim as a platform for the exercise of free speech — "symbolic" or "pure" — and whether the courts will allocate to themselves the function of deciding how the pupils' school day will be spent. While I have always believed that under the First and Fourteenth Amendments neither the State nor the Federal Government has any authority to regulate or censor the content of speech, I have never believed that any person has a right to give speeches or engage in demonstrations where he pleases and when he pleases. This Court has already rejected such a notion. In *Cox v. Louisiana*, 379 U.S. 536, 554 (1965), for example, the Court clearly stated that the rights of free speech and assembly "do not mean that everyone with opinions or beliefs to express may address a group at any public place and at any time."

While the record does not show that any of these armband students shouted, used profane language, or were violent in any manner, detailed testimony by some of them shows their armbands caused comments, warnings by other students, the poking of fun at them, and a warning by an older football player that other, non-protesting students had better let them alone. There is also evidence that a teacher of mathematics had his lesson period practically "wrecked" chiefly by disputes with Mary Beth Tinker, who wore her armband for her "demonstration." [*518] Even a casual reading of the record shows that this armband did divert students' minds from their regular lessons, and that talk, comments, etc., made John Tinker "self-conscious" in attending school with his armband. While the absence of obscene remarks or boisterous and loud disorder perhaps justifies the Court's statement that the few armband students did not actually "disrupt" the classwork, I think the record overwhelmingly shows that the armbands did exactly what the elected school officials and principals foresaw they would, that is, took the students' minds off their classwork and diverted them to thoughts about the highly emotional subject of the Vietnam war. And I repeat that if the time has come when pupils of state-supported schools, kindergartens, grammar schools, or high schools, can defy and flout orders of school officials to keep their minds on their own schoolwork, it is the beginning of a new revolutionary era of permissiveness in this country fostered by the judiciary. The next logical step, it appears to me, would be to hold unconstitutional laws that bar pupils under 21 or 18 from voting, or from being elected members of the boards of education.[2]

The United States District Court refused to hold that the state school order violated the First and Fourteenth Amendments. 258 F. Supp. 971. Holding that the protest was akin to speech, which is protected by the First [*519] and Fourteenth Amendments, that court held that the school order was "reasonable" and hence constitutional. There was at one time a line of cases holding "reasonableness" as the court saw it to be the test of a "due process" violation. Two cases upon which the Court today heavily relies for striking down this school order used this test of reasonableness, *Meyer v. Nebraska*, 262 U.S. 390 (1923), and *Bartels v. Iowa*, 262 U.S. 404 (1923). The opinions in both cases were written by Mr. Justice McReynolds; Mr. Justice Holmes, who opposed this reasonableness test, dissented from the holdings as did Mr. Justice Sutherland. This constitutional test of reasonableness prevailed in this Court for a season. It was this test that brought on President Franklin Roosevelt's well-known Court fight. His proposed legislation did not pass, but the fight left the "reasonableness" constitutional test dead on the battlefield, so much so that this Court in *Ferguson v. Skrupa*, 372 U.S. 726, 729, 730, after a thorough review of the old cases, was able to conclude in 1963:

"There was a time when the Due Process Clause was used by this Court to strike down laws which were thought unreasonable, that is, unwise or incompatible with some particular economic or social philosophy.

. . .

---

2. The following Associated Press article appeared in the Washington Evening Star, January 11, 1969, p. A-2, col. 1:

"BELLINGHAM, Mass. (AP)—Todd R. Hennessy, 16, has filed nominating papers to run for town park commissioner in the March election.

"'I can see nothing illegal in the youth's seeking the elective office,' said Lee Ambler, the town counsel. 'But I can't overlook the possibility that if he is elected any legal contract entered into by the park commissioner would be void because he is a juvenile.'

"Todd is a junior in Mount St. Charles Academy, where he has a top scholastic record."

"The doctrine that prevailed in *Lochner, Coppage, Adkins, Burns*, and like cases—that due process authorizes courts to hold laws unconstitutional when they believe the legislature has acted unwisely—has long since been discarded."

The *Ferguson* case totally repudiated the old reasonableness-due process test, the doctrine that judges have the power to hold laws unconstitutional upon the belief of judges that they "shock the conscience" or that they are [*520] "unreasonable," "arbitrary," "irrational," "contrary to fundamental 'decency,'" or some other such flexible term without precise boundaries. I have many times expressed my opposition to that concept on the ground that it gives judges power to strike down any law they do not like. If the majority of the Court today, by agreeing to the opinion of my Brother Fortas, is resurrecting that old reasonableness-due process test, I think the constitutional change should be plainly, unequivocally, and forthrightly stated for the benefit of the bench and bar. It will be a sad day for the country, I believe, when the present-day Court returns to the McReynolds due process concept. Other cases cited by the Court do not, as implied, follow the McReynolds reasonableness doctrine. *West Virginia v. Barnette*, 319 U.S. 624, clearly rejecting the "reasonableness" test, held that the Fourteenth Amendment made the First applicable to the States, and that the two forbade a State to *compel* little schoolchildren to salute the United States flag when they had religious scruples against doing so.[3] Neither *Thornhill v. Alabama*, 310 U.S. 88; *Stromberg v. California*, 283 U.S. 359; *Edwards* [*521] *v. South Carolina*, 372 U.S. 229; nor *Brown v. Louisiana*, 383 U.S. 131, related to schoolchildren at all, and none of these cases embraced Mr. Justice McReynolds' reasonableness test; and *Thornhill*, *Edwards*, and *Brown* relied on the vagueness of state statutes under scrutiny to hold them unconstitutional. *Cox v. Louisiana*, 379 U.S. 536, 555, and *Adderley v. Florida*, 385 U.S. 39, cited by the Court as a "compare," indicating, I suppose, that these two cases are no longer the law, were not rested to the slightest extent on the *Meyer* and *Bartels* "reasonableness-due process-McReynolds" constitutional test.

I deny, therefore, that it has been the "unmistakable holding of this Court for almost 50 years" that "students" and "teachers" take with them into the "schoolhouse gate" constitutional rights to "freedom of speech or expression." Even *Meyer* did not hold that. It makes no reference to "symbolic speech" at all; what it did was to strike down as "unreasonable" and therefore unconstitutional a Nebraska

---

3. In *Cantwell v. Connecticut*, 310 U.S. 296, 303-304 (1940), this Court said:

"The First Amendment declares that Congress shall make no law respecting an establishment of religion or prohibiting the free exercise thereof. The Fourteenth Amendment has rendered the legislatures of the states as incompetent as Congress to enact such laws. The constitutional inhibition of legislation on the subject of religion has a double aspect. On the one hand, it forestalls compulsion by law of the acceptance of any creed or the practice of any form of worship. Freedom of conscience and freedom to adhere to such religious organization or form of worship as the individual may choose cannot be restricted by law. On the other hand, it safeguards the free exercise of the chosen form of religion. Thus the Amendment embraces two concepts,—freedom to believe and freedom to act. The first is absolute but, in the nature of things, the second cannot be. Conduct remains subject to regulation for the protection of society."

law barring the teaching of the German language before the children reached the eighth grade. One can well agree with Mr. Justice Holmes and Mr. Justice Sutherland, as I do, that such a law was no more unreasonable than it would be to bar the teaching of Latin and Greek to pupils who have not reached the eighth grade. In fact, I think the majority's reason for invalidating the Nebraska law was that it did not like it or in legal jargon that it "shocked the Court's conscience," "offended its sense of justice," or was "contrary to fundamental concepts of the English-speaking world," as the Court has sometimes said. See, e.g., *Rochin v. California*, 342 U.S. 165, and *Irvine v. California*, 347 U.S. 128. The truth is that a teacher of kindergarten, grammar school, or high school pupils no more carries into a school with him a complete right to freedom of speech and expression than an anti-Catholic or anti-Semite carries with him a complete freedom of [*522] speech and religion into a Catholic church or Jewish synagogue. Nor does a person carry with him into the United States Senate or House, or into the Supreme Court, or any other court, a complete constitutional right to go into those places contrary to their rules and speak his mind on any subject he pleases. It is a myth to say that any person has a constitutional right to say what he pleases, where he pleases, and when he pleases. Our Court has decided precisely the opposite. See, e.g., *Cox v. Louisiana*, 379 U.S. 536, 555; *Adderley v. Florida*, 385 U.S. 39.

In my view, teachers in state-controlled public schools are hired to teach there. Although Mr. Justice McReynolds may have intimated to the contrary in *Meyer v. Nebraska, supra*, certainly a teacher is not paid to go into school and teach subjects the State does not hire him to teach as a part of its selected curriculum. Nor are public school students sent to the schools at public expense to broadcast political or any other views to educate and inform the public. The original idea of schools, which I do not believe is yet abandoned as worthless or out of date, was that children had not yet reached the point of experience and wisdom which enabled them to teach all of their elders. It may be that the Nation has outworn the old-fashioned slogan that "children are to be seen not heard," but one may, I hope, be permitted to harbor the thought that taxpayers send children to school on the premise that at their age they need to learn, not teach.

The true principles on this whole subject were in my judgment spoken by Mr. Justice McKenna for the Court in *Waugh v. Mississippi University* in 237 U.S. 589, 596-597. The State had there passed a law barring students from peaceably assembling in Greek letter fraternities and providing that students who joined them could be expelled from school. This law would appear on the surface to run afoul of the First Amendment's [*523] freedom of assembly clause. The law was attacked as violative of due process and of the privileges and immunities clause and as a deprivation of property and of liberty, under the Fourteenth Amendment. It was argued that the fraternity made its members more moral, taught discipline, and inspired its members to study harder and to obey better the rules of discipline and order. This Court rejected all the "fervid" pleas of the fraternities' advocates and decided unanimously against these Fourteenth Amendment arguments. The

Court in its next to the last paragraph made this statement which has complete relevance for us today:

"It is said that the fraternity to which complainant belongs is a moral and of itself a disciplinary force. This need not be denied. But whether such membership makes against discipline was for the State of Mississippi to determine. It is to be remembered that the University was established by the State and is under the control of the State, and the enactment of the statute may have been induced by the opinion that *membership in the prohibited societies divided the attention of the students and distracted from that singleness of purpose which the State desired to exist in its public educational institutions.* It is not for us to entertain conjectures in opposition to the views of the State and annul its regulations upon disputable considerations of their wisdom or necessity." (Emphasis supplied.)

It was on the foregoing argument that this Court sustained the power of Mississippi to curtail the First Amendment's right of peaceable assembly. And the same reasons are equally applicable to curtailing in the States' public schools the right to complete freedom of expression. Iowa's public schools, like Mississippi's university, are operated to give students an opportunity to learn, not to talk politics by actual speech, or by "symbolic" [*524] speech. And, as I have pointed out before, the record amply shows that public protest in the school classes against the Vietnam war "distracted from that singleness of purpose which the State [here Iowa] desired to exist in its public educational institutions." Here the Court should accord Iowa educational institutions the same right to determine for themselves to what extent free expression should be allowed in its schools as it accorded Mississippi with reference to freedom of assembly. But even if the record were silent as to protests against the Vietnam war distracting students from their assigned class work, members of this Court, like all other citizens, know, without being told, that the disputes over the wisdom of the Vietnam war have disrupted and divided this country as few other issues ever have. Of course students, like other people, cannot concentrate on lesser issues when black armbands are being ostentatiously displayed in their presence to call attention to the wounded and dead of the war, some of the wounded and the dead being their friends and neighbors. It was, of course, to distract the attention of other students that some students insisted up to the very point of their own suspension from school that they were determined to sit in school with their symbolic armbands.

Change has been said to be truly the law of life but sometimes the old and the tried and true are worth holding. The schools of this Nation have undoubtedly contributed to giving us tranquility and to making us a more law-abiding people. Uncontrolled and uncontrollable liberty is an enemy to domestic peace. We cannot close our eyes to the fact that some of the country's greatest problems are crimes committed by the youth, too many of school age. School discipline, like parental discipline, is an integral and important part of training our children to be good citizens — to be better citizens. Here a very small number of students have crisply and summarily [*525] refused to obey a school order designed to give pupils who want to learn the opportunity to do so. One does not need to be a prophet or the son of a prophet to know that after the Court's holding today some students in Iowa schools and indeed in all schools will be ready, able, and willing to defy their teachers on practically all orders. This is the more unfortunate for the schools since groups of students all over the land are already running loose, conducting break-ins, sit-ins, lie-ins, and smash-ins. Many of these student groups, as is all too familiar to all who read the newspapers and watch the television news programs, have already engaged in rioting, property seizures, and destruction. They have picketed schools to force students not to cross their picket lines and have too often violently attacked earnest but frightened students who wanted an education that the pickets did not want them to get. Students engaged in such activities are apparently confident that they know far more about how to operate public school systems than do their parents, teachers, and elected school officials. It is no answer to say that the particular students here have not yet reached such high points in their demands to attend classes in order to exercise their political pressures. Turned loose with lawsuits for damages and injunctions against their teachers as they are here, it is nothing but wishful thinking to imagine that young, immature students will not soon believe it is their right to control the schools rather than the right of the States that collect the taxes to hire the teachers for the benefit of the pupils. This case, therefore, wholly without constitutional reasons in my judgment, subjects all the public schools in the country to the whims and caprices of their loudest-mouthed, but maybe not their brightest, students. I, for one, am not fully persuaded that school pupils are wise enough, even with this Court's expert help from Washington, to run the 23,390 public school [*526] systems[4] in our 50 States. I wish, therefore, wholly to disclaim any purpose on my part to hold that the Federal Constitution compels the teachers, parents, and elected school officials to surrender control of the American public school system to public school students. I dissent.

Mr. Justice HARLAN, dissenting.

I certainly agree that state public school authorities in the discharge of their responsibilities are not wholly exempt from the requirements of the Fourteenth Amendment respecting the freedoms of expression and association. At the same time I am reluctant to believe that there is any disagreement between the majority and myself on the proposition that school officials should be accorded the widest authority in maintaining discipline and good order in their institutions. To translate that proposition into a workable constitutional rule, I would, in cases like this, cast upon those complaining the burden of showing that a particular school measure was motivated by other than legitimate school concerns—for example, a desire to prohibit the expression of an unpopular point of view, while permitting expression of the dominant opinion.

Finding nothing in this record which impugns the good faith of respondents in promulgating the armband regulation, I would affirm the judgment below.

---

4. Statistical Abstract of the United States (1968), Table No. 578, p. 406.

> **Questions Regarding *Tinker v. Des Moines Independent Community School District***
>
> 1. According to the majority in *Tinker*, are students' First Amendment rights the same at school as they are outside of school?
> 2. According to the majority in *Tinker*, when prohibiting speech on the basis of substantial disruption, does a school have to wait for the disruption to actually occur before acting to stop or punish the speech?
> 3. Can you posit some circumstances that would clearly fit the definition of substantial disruption to the operation of a school?

BETHEL SCHOOL DISTRICT NO. 403 v. FRASER

Supreme Court of the United States
March 3, 1986, Argued; July 7, 1986, Decided
No. 84-1667

Reporter: 478 U.S. 675 *

Judges: Burger, C.J., delivered the opinion of the Court, in which White, Powell, Rehnquist, and O'Connor, JJ., joined. Brennan, J., filed an opinion concurring in the judgment, post, p. 687. Blackmun, J., concurred in the result. Marshall, J., post, p. 690, and Stevens, J., post, p. 691, filed dissenting opinions.

Opinion by: Burger

Opinion

[*677] Chief Justice BURGER delivered the opinion of the Court.

We granted certiorari to decide whether the First Amendment prevents a school district from disciplining a high school student for giving a lewd speech at a school assembly.

I

A

On April 26, 1983, respondent Matthew N. Fraser, a student at Bethel High School in Pierce County, Washington, delivered a speech nominating a fellow student for student elective office. Approximately 600 high school students, many of whom were 14-year-olds, attended the assembly. Students were required to attend the assembly or to report to the study hall. The assembly was part of a school-sponsored educational program in self-government. Students who elected not to attend the assembly were required to report to study hall. During the entire speech, Fraser referred [*678] to his candidate in terms of an elaborate, graphic, and explicit sexual metaphor.

Two of Fraser's teachers, with whom he discussed the contents of his speech in advance, informed him that the speech was "inappropriate and that he probably should not deliver it," App. 30, and that his delivery of the speech might have "severe consequences." *Id.*, at 61.

During Fraser's delivery of the speech, a school counselor observed the reaction of students to the speech. Some students hooted and yelled; some by gestures graphically simulated the sexual activities pointedly alluded to in respondent's speech. Other students appeared to be bewildered and embarrassed by the speech. One teacher reported that on the day following the speech, she found it necessary to forgo a portion of the scheduled class lesson in order to discuss the speech with the class. *Id.*, at 41-44.

A Bethel High School disciplinary rule prohibiting the use of obscene language in the school provides:

"Conduct which materially and substantially interferes with the educational process is prohibited, including the use of obscene, profane language or gestures."

The morning after the assembly, the Assistant Principal called Fraser into her office and notified him that the school considered his speech to have been a violation of this rule. Fraser was presented with copies of five letters submitted by teachers, describing his conduct at the assembly; he was given a chance to explain his conduct, and he admitted to having given the speech described and that he deliberately used sexual innuendo in the speech. Fraser was then informed that he would be suspended for three days, and that his name would be removed from the list of candidates for graduation speaker at the school's commencement exercises.

Fraser sought review of this disciplinary action through the School District's grievance procedures. The hearing officer determined that the speech given by respondent was "indecent, lewd, and offensive to the modesty and decency of [*679] many of the students and faculty in attendance at the assembly." The examiner determined that the speech fell within the ordinary meaning of "obscene," as used in the disruptive-conduct rule, and affirmed the discipline in its entirety. Fraser served two days of his suspension, and was allowed to return to school on the third day.

B

Respondent, by his father as guardian ad litem, then brought this action in the United States District Court for the Western District of Washington. Respondent alleged a violation of his First Amendment right to freedom of speech and sought both injunctive relief and monetary damages under 42 U.S.C. § 1983. The District Court held that the school's sanctions violated respondent's right to freedom of speech under the First Amendment to the United States Constitution, that the school's disruptive-conduct rule is unconstitutionally vague and overbroad, and that the removal of respondent's name from the graduation speaker's list violated the Due Process Clause of the Fourteenth Amendment because the disciplinary rule makes no mention of such removal as a possible sanction. The District Court awarded respondent $278 in damages, $12,750 in litigation costs and attorney's fees, and enjoined the School District from preventing respondent from speaking at the commencement ceremonies. Respondent, who had been elected graduation speaker by a write-in vote of his classmates, delivered a speech at the commencement ceremonies on June 8, 1983.

The Court of Appeals for the Ninth Circuit affirmed the judgment of the District Court, 755 F.2d 1356 (1985), holding that respondent's speech was indistinguishable from the protest armband in *Tinker v. Des Moines Independent Community School Dist.*, 393 U.S. 503 (1969). The court explicitly rejected the School District's argument that the speech, unlike the passive conduct of wearing a black armband, had a disruptive effect on the educational process. The Court of [*680] Appeals also rejected the School District's argument that it had an interest in protecting an essentially captive audience of minors from lewd and indecent language in a setting sponsored by the school, reasoning that the School District's "unbridled discretion" to determine what discourse is "decent" would "increase the risk of cementing white, middle-class standards for determining what is acceptable and proper speech and behavior in our public schools." 755 F.2d, at 1363. Finally, the Court of Appeals rejected the School District's argument that, incident to its responsibility for the school curriculum, it had the power to control the language used to express ideas during a school-sponsored activity.

We granted certiorari, 474 U.S. 814 (1985). We reverse.

II

This Court acknowledged in *Tinker v. Des Moines Independent Community School Dist.*, *supra*, that students do not "shed their constitutional rights to freedom of speech or expression at the schoolhouse gate." *Id.*, at 506. The Court of Appeals read that case as precluding any discipline of Fraser for indecent speech and lewd conduct in the school assembly. That court appears to have proceeded on the theory that the use of lewd and obscene speech in order to make what the speaker considered to be a point in a nominating speech for a fellow student was essentially the same as the wearing of an armband in *Tinker* as a form of protest or the expression of a political position.

The marked distinction between the political "message" of the armbands in *Tinker* and the sexual content of respondent's speech in this case seems to have been given little weight by the Court of Appeals. In upholding the students' right to engage in a nondisruptive, passive expression of a political viewpoint in *Tinker*, this Court was careful to note that the case did "not concern speech or action that intrudes upon the work of the schools or the rights of other students." *Id.*, at 508.

[*681] It is against this background that we turn to consider the level of First Amendment protection accorded to Fraser's utterances and actions before an official high school assembly attended by 600 students.

III

The role and purpose of the American public school system were well described by two historians, who stated: "[Public] education must prepare pupils for citizenship in the Republic. . . . It must inculcate the habits and manners of civility as values in themselves conducive to happiness and as indispensable to the practice of self-government in the community and the nation." C. Beard & M. Beard, New Basic History of the United States 228 (1968). In *Ambach v. Norwick*, 441 U.S. 68, 76-77 (1979), we echoed the essence of this statement of the objectives of public education as the "[inculcation of] fundamental values necessary to the maintenance of a democratic political system."

These fundamental values of "habits and manners of civility" essential to a democratic society must, of course, include tolerance of divergent political and religious views, even when the views expressed may be unpopular. But these "fundamental values" must also take into account consideration of the sensibilities of others, and, in the case of a school, the sensibilities of fellow students. The undoubted freedom to advocate unpopular and controversial views in schools and classrooms must be balanced against the society's countervailing interest in teaching students the boundaries of socially appropriate behavior. Even the most heated political discourse in a democratic society requires consideration for the personal sensibilities of the other participants and audiences.

In our Nation's legislative halls, where some of the most vigorous political debates in our society are carried on, there are rules prohibiting the use of expressions offensive to other participants in the debate. The Manual of Parliamentary [*682] Practice, drafted by Thomas Jefferson and adopted by the House of Representatives to govern the proceedings in that body, prohibits the use of "impertinent" speech during debate and likewise provides that "[no] person is to use indecent language against the proceedings of the House." Jefferson's Manual of Parliamentary Practice §§ 359, 360, reprinted in Manual and Rules of House of Representatives, H.R. Doc. No. 97-271, pp. 158-159 (1982); see *id.*, at 111, n. *a* (Jefferson's Manual governs the House in all cases to which it applies). The Rules of Debate applicable in the Senate likewise provide that a Senator may be called to order for imputing improper motives to another Senator or for referring offensively to any state. See Senate Procedure, S. Doc. No. 97-2, Rule XIX, pp. 568-569, 588-591 (1981). Senators have been censured for abusive language directed at other Senators. See Senate Election, Expulsion and Censure Cases from 1793 to 1972, S. Doc. No. 92-7, pp. 95-98 (1972) (Sens. McLaurin and Tillman); *id*., at 152-153 (Sen. McCarthy). Can it be that what is proscribed in the halls of Congress is beyond the reach of school officials to regulate?

The First Amendment guarantees wide freedom in matters of adult public discourse. A sharply divided Court upheld the right to express an antidraft viewpoint in a public place, albeit in terms highly offensive to most citizens. See *Cohen v. California*, 403 U.S. 15 (1971). It does not follow, however, that simply because the use of an offensive form of expression may not be prohibited to adults making what the speaker considers a political point, the same latitude must be permitted to children in a public school. In *New Jersey v. T. L. O.*, 469 U.S. 325, 340-342 (1985), we reaffirmed that the constitutional rights of students in public school are not automatically coextensive with the rights of adults in other settings. As cogently expressed by Judge Newman, "the First Amendment gives a high school student the classroom right to wear Tinker's armband, but not Cohen's jacket." *Thomas v. Board of Education, Granville Central School* [*683] *Dist.*, 607 F.2d 1043, 1057 (CA2 1979) (opinion concurring in result).

Surely it is a highly appropriate function of public school education to prohibit the use of vulgar and offensive terms in public discourse. Indeed, the "fundamental values necessary to the maintenance of a democratic political system" disfavor the use of terms of debate highly offensive or highly threatening to others. Nothing in the Constitution prohibits the states from insisting that certain modes of expression are inappropriate and subject to sanctions. The inculcation of these values is truly the "work of the schools." *Tinker*, 393 U.S., at 508; see *Ambach v. Norwick, supra*. The determination of what manner of speech in the classroom or in school assembly is inappropriate properly rests with the school board.

The process of educating our youth for citizenship in public schools is not confined to books, the curriculum, and the civics class; schools must teach by example the shared values of a civilized social order. Consciously or otherwise, teachers—and indeed the older students—demonstrate the appropriate form of civil discourse and political expression by their conduct and deportment in and out of class. Inescapably, like parents, they are role models. The schools, as instruments of the state, may determine that the essential lessons of civil, mature conduct cannot be conveyed in a school that tolerates lewd, indecent, or offensive speech and conduct such as that indulged in by this confused boy.

The pervasive sexual innuendo in Fraser's speech was plainly offensive to both teachers and students—indeed to any mature person. By glorifying male sexuality, and in its verbal content, the speech was acutely insulting to teenage girl students. See App. 77-81. The speech could well be seriously damaging to its less mature audience, many of whom were only 14 years old and on the threshold of awareness of human sexuality. Some students were reported as [*684] bewildered by the speech and the reaction of mimicry it provoked.

This Court's First Amendment jurisprudence has acknowledged limitations on the otherwise absolute interest of the speaker in reaching an unlimited audience where the speech is sexually explicit and the audience may include children. In *Ginsberg v. New York*, 390 U.S. 629 (1968), this Court upheld a New York statute banning the sale of sexually oriented material to minors, even though the material in question was entitled to First Amendment protection with respect to adults. And in addressing the question whether the First Amendment places any limit on the authority of public schools to remove books from a public school library, all Members of the Court, otherwise sharply divided, acknowledged that the school board has the authority to remove books that are vulgar. *Board of Education v. Pico*, 457 U.S. 853, 871-872 (1982) (plurality opinion); *id.*, at 879-881 (Blackmun, J., concurring in part and in judgment); *id.*, at 918-920 (Rehnquist, J., dissenting). These cases recognize the obvious concern on the part of parents, and school authorities acting *in loco parentis*, to protect children — especially in a captive audience — from exposure to sexually explicit, indecent, or lewd speech.

We have also recognized an interest in protecting minors from exposure to vulgar and offensive spoken language. In *FCC v. Pacifica Foundation*, 438 U.S. 726 (1978), we dealt with the power of the Federal Communications Commission to regulate a radio broadcast described as "indecent but not obscene." There the Court reviewed an administrative condemnation of the radio broadcast of a self-styled "humorist" who described his own performance as being in "the words you couldn't say on the public, ah, airwaves, um, the ones you definitely wouldn't say ever." *Id.*, at 729; see also *id.*, at 751-755 (Appendix to opinion of the Court). The Commission concluded that "certain words depicted sexual and excretory activities in a patently offensive manner, [and] noted **[*685]** that they 'were broadcast at a time when children were undoubtedly in the audience.'" The Commission issued an order declaring that the radio station was guilty of broadcasting indecent language in violation of 18 U.S.C. § 1464. 438 U.S., at 732. The Court of Appeals set aside the Commission's determination, and we reversed, reinstating the Commission's citation of the station. We concluded that the broadcast was properly considered "obscene, indecent, or profane" within the meaning of the statute. The plurality opinion went on to reject the radio station's assertion of a First Amendment right to broadcast vulgarity:

> "These words offend for the same reasons that obscenity offends. Their place in the hierarchy of First Amendment values was aptly sketched by Mr. Justice Murphy when he said: '[Such] utterances are no essential part of any exposition of ideas, and are of such slight social value as a step to truth that any benefit that may be derived from them is clearly outweighed by the social interest in order and morality.' *Chaplinsky v. New Hampshire*, 315 U.S., at 572." *Id.*, at 746.

We hold that petitioner School District acted entirely within its permissible authority in imposing sanctions upon Fraser in response to his offensively lewd and indecent speech. Unlike the sanctions imposed on the students wearing armbands in *Tinker*, the penalties imposed in this case were unrelated to any political viewpoint. The First Amendment does not prevent the school officials from determining that to permit a vulgar and lewd speech such as respondent's would undermine the school's basic educational mission. A high school assembly or classroom is no place for a sexually explicit monologue directed towards an unsuspecting audience of teenage students. Accordingly, it was perfectly appropriate for the school to disassociate itself to make the point to the pupils that vulgar speech and lewd conduct is wholly inconsistent with the "fundamental values" of public [*686] school education. Justice Black, dissenting in *Tinker*, made a point that is especially relevant in this case:

> "I wish therefore, . . . to disclaim any purpose . . . to hold that the Federal Constitution compels the teachers, parents, and elected school officials to surrender control of the American public school system to public school students." 393 U.S., at 526.

IV

Respondent contends that the circumstances of his suspension violated due process because he had no way of knowing that the delivery of the speech in question would subject him to disciplinary sanctions. This argument is wholly without merit. We have recognized that "maintaining security and order in the schools requires a certain degree of flexibility in school disciplinary procedures, and we have respected the value of preserving the informality of the student-teacher relationship." *New Jersey v. T. L. O.*, 469 U.S., at 340. Given the school's need to be able to impose disciplinary sanctions for a wide range of unanticipated conduct disruptive of the educational process, the school disciplinary rules need not be as detailed as a criminal code which imposes criminal sanctions. Cf. *Arnett v. Kennedy*, 416 U.S. 134, 161 (1974) (Rehnquist, J., concurring). Two days' suspension from school does not rise to the level of a penal sanction calling for the full panoply of procedural due process protections applicable to a criminal prosecution. Cf. *Goss v. Lopez*, 419 U.S. 565 (1975). The school disciplinary rule proscribing "obscene" language and the prespeech admonitions of teachers gave adequate warning to Fraser that his lewd speech could subject him to sanctions.*

[*687] The judgment of the Court of Appeals for the Ninth Circuit is

Reversed.

---

* Petitioners also challenge the ruling of the District Court that the removal of Fraser's name from the ballot for graduation speaker violated his due process rights because that sanction was not indicated as a potential punishment in the school's disciplinary rules. We agree with the Court of Appeals that this issue has become moot, since the graduation ceremony has long since passed and Fraser was permitted to speak in accordance with the District Court's injunction. No part of the damages award was based upon the removal of Fraser's name from the list, since damages were based upon the loss of two days' schooling.

Justice BLACKMUN concurs in the result.

Concur by: Brennan

Concur

[Editor's Note: The page numbers of this document may appear to be out of sequence; however, this pagination accurately reflects the pagination of the original published document.]

Justice BRENNAN, concurring in the judgment.

Respondent gave the following speech at a high school assembly in support of a candidate for student government office:

"'I know a man who is firm—he's firm in his pants, he's firm in his shirt, his character is firm—but most . . . of all, his belief in you, the students of Bethel, is firm.

"'Jeff Kuhlman is a man who takes his point and pounds it in. If necessary, he'll take an issue and nail it to the wall. He doesn't attack things in spurts—he drives hard, pushing and pushing until finally—he succeeds.

"'Jeff is a man who will go to the very end—even the climax, for each and every one of you.

"'So vote for Jeff for A.S.B. vice-president—he'll never come between you and the best our high school can be.'" App. 47.

The Court, referring to these remarks as "obscene," "vulgar," "lewd," and "offensively lewd," concludes that school officials properly punished respondent for uttering the speech. Having read the full text of respondent's remarks, I find it difficult to believe that it is the same speech the Court describes. To my mind, the most that can be said about respondent's speech—and all that need be said—is that in light of the discretion school officials have to teach high school students how to conduct civil and effective public discourse, and to prevent disruption of school educational activities, it was [*688] not unconstitutional for school officials to conclude, under the circumstances of this case, that respondent's remarks exceeded permissible limits. Thus, while I concur in the Court's judgment, I write separately to express my understanding of the breadth of the Court's holding.

The Court today reaffirms the unimpeachable proposition that students do not "'shed their constitutional rights to freedom of speech or expression at the schoolhouse gate.'" *Ante*, at 680 (quoting *Tinker v. Des Moines Independent Community School Dist.*, 393 U.S. 503, 506 (1969)). If respondent had given the same speech outside of the school environment, he could not have been penalized simply because government officials considered his language to be inappropriate, see *Cohen v. California*, 403 U.S. 15 (1971); the Court's opinion does not suggest otherwise.[1] Moreover, despite the Court's characterizations, the language respondent used is far removed from the very narrow class of "obscene" speech which the Court has held is not protected by the First Amendment. *Ginsberg v. New York*, 390 U.S. 629, 635 (1968); *Roth v. United States*, 354 U.S. 476, 485 (1957). It is true, however, that the State has interests in teaching high school students how to conduct civil and effective public discourse and in avoiding disruption of educational school activities. Thus, the Court holds that under certain circumstances, high school students may properly be reprimanded for giving a speech at a high school assembly which school officials conclude disrupted the school's educational **[*689]** mission.[2] Respondent's speech may well have been protected had he given it in school but under different circumstances, where the school's legitimate interests in teaching and maintaining civil public discourse were less weighty.

In the present case, school officials sought only to ensure that a high school assembly proceed in an orderly manner. There is no suggestion that school officials attempted to regulate respondent's speech because they disagreed with the views he sought to express. Cf. *Tinker, supra*. Nor does this case involve an attempt by school officials to ban written materials they consider "inappropriate" for high school students, cf. *Board of Education v. Pico*, 457 U.S. 853 (1982), or to limit what students should hear, read, or learn about. Thus, the Court's holding concerns only the authority that school officials have to restrict a high school student's use of disruptive language in a speech given to a high school assembly.

The authority school officials have to regulate such speech by high school students is not limitless. See *Thomas v. Board of Education, Granville Central School Distr.*, 607 F.2d 1043, 1057 (CA2 1979) (Newman, J., concurring in result) ("[School] officials . . . do [not] have limitless discretion to apply their own notions of indecency. Courts have a First **[*690]** Amendment responsibility to insure that robust rhetoric . . . is not suppressed by prudish failures to distinguish the vigorous from

---

1. In the course of its opinion, the Court makes certain remarks concerning the authority of school officials to regulate student language in public schools. For example, the Court notes that "[nothing] in the Constitution prohibits the states from insisting that certain modes of expression are inappropriate and subject to sanctions." *Ante*, at 683. These statements obviously do not, and indeed given our prior precedents could not, refer to the government's authority generally to regulate the language used in public debate outside of the school environment.

2. The Court speculates that the speech was "insulting" to female students, and "seriously damaging" to 14-year-olds, so that school officials could legitimately suppress such expression in order to protect these groups. *Ante*, at 683. There is no evidence in the record that any students, male or female, found the speech "insulting." And while it was not unreasonable for school officials to conclude that respondent's remarks were inappropriate for a school-sponsored assembly, the language respondent used does not even approach the sexually explicit speech regulated in *Ginsberg v. New York*, 390 U.S. 629 (1968), or the indecent speech banned in *FCC v. Pacifica Foundation*, 438 U.S. 726 (1978). Indeed, to my mind, respondent's speech was no more "obscene," "lewd," or "sexually explicit" than the bulk of programs currently appearing on prime time television or in the local cinema. Thus, I disagree with the Court's suggestion that school officials could punish respondent's speech out of a need to protect younger students.

the vulgar"). Under the circumstances of this case, however, I believe that school officials did not violate the First Amendment in determining that respondent should be disciplined for the disruptive language he used while addressing a high school assembly.[3] Thus, I concur in the judgment reversing the decision of the Court of Appeals.

Dissent by: Marshall; Stevens

Dissent

Justice MARSHALL, dissenting.

I agree with the principles that Justice Brennan sets out in his opinion concurring in the judgment. I dissent from the Court's decision, however, because in my view the School District failed to demonstrate that respondent's remarks were indeed disruptive. The District Court and Court of Appeals conscientiously applied *Tinker v. Des Moines Independent Community School Dist.*, 393 U.S. 503 (1969), and concluded that the School District had not demonstrated any disruption of the educational process. I recognize that the school administration must be given wide latitude to determine what forms of conduct are inconsistent with the school's educational mission; nevertheless, where speech is involved, we may not unquestioningly accept a teacher's or administrator's assertion that certain pure speech interfered with education. Here the School District, despite a clear opportunity to do so, failed to bring in evidence sufficient to convince either of the two lower courts that education at Bethel School was disrupted by respondent's speech. I therefore see no reason to disturb the Court of Appeals' judgment.

[*691] Justice STEVENS, dissenting.

"Frankly, my dear, I don't give a damn."

When I was a high school student, the use of those words in a public forum shocked the Nation. Today Clark Gable's four-letter expletive is less offensive than it was then. Nevertheless, I assume that high school administrators may prohibit the use of that word in classroom discussion and even in extracurricular activities that are sponsored by the school and held on school premises. For I believe a school faculty must regulate the content as well as the style of student speech in carrying out its educational mission.[1] It does seem to me, however, that if a

---

3. Respondent served two days' suspension and had his name removed from the list of candidates for graduation speaker at the school's commencement exercises, although he was eventually permitted to speak at the graduation. While I find this punishment somewhat severe in light of the nature of respondent's transgression, I cannot conclude that school officials exceeded the bounds of their disciplinary authority.

1. "Because every university's resources are limited, an educational institution must routinely make decisions concerning the use of the time and space that is available for extracurricular

student is to be punished for using offensive speech, he is entitled to fair notice of the scope of the prohibition and the consequences of its violation. [*692] The interest in free speech protected by the First Amendment and the interest in fair procedure protected by the Due Process Clause of the Fourteenth Amendment combine to require this conclusion.

This respondent was an outstanding young man with a fine academic record. The fact that he was chosen by the student body to speak at the school's commencement exercises demonstrates that he was respected by his peers. This fact is relevant for two reasons. It confirms the conclusion that the discipline imposed on him — a 3-day suspension and ineligibility to speak at the school's graduation exercises — was sufficiently serious to justify invocation of the School District's grievance procedures. See *Goss v. Lopez*, 419 U.S. 565, 574-575 (1975). More importantly, it indicates that he was probably in a better position to determine whether an audience composed of 600 of his contemporaries would be offended by the use of a four-letter word — or a sexual metaphor — than is a group of judges who are at least two generations and 3,000 miles away from the scene of the crime.[2]

The fact that the speech may not have been offensive to his audience — or that he honestly believed that it would be inoffensive — does not mean that he had a constitutional right to deliver it. For the school — not the student — must prescribe the

---

activities. In my judgment, it is both necessary and appropriate for those decisions to evaluate the content of a proposed student activity. I should think it obvious, for example, that if two groups of 25 students requested the use of a room at a particular time — one to view Mickey Mouse cartoons and the other to rehearse an amateur performance of Hamlet — the First Amendment would not require that the room be reserved for the group that submitted its application first. Nor do I see why a university should have to establish a 'compelling state interest' to defend its decision to permit one group to use the facility and not the other. In my opinion, a university should be allowed to decide for itself whether a program that illuminates the genius of Walt Disney should be given precedence over one that may duplicate material adequately covered in the classroom. Judgments of this kind should be made by academicians, not by federal judges, and their standards for decision should not be encumbered with ambiguous phrases like 'compelling state interest.'" *Widmar v. Vincent*, 454 U.S. 263, 278-279 (1981) (Stevens, J., concurring in judgment) (footnotes omitted).

"Any student of history who has been reprimanded for talking about the World Series during a class discussion of the First Amendment knows that it is incorrect to state that a 'time, place, or manner restriction may not be based upon either the content or subject matter of speech.'" *Consolidated Edison Co. v. Public Service Comm'n of N.Y.*, 447 U.S. 530, 544-545 (1980) (Stevens, J., concurring in judgment).

2. As the Court of Appeals noted, there "is no evidence in the record indicating that any students found the speech to be offensive." 755 F.2d 1356, 1361, n. 4 (CA9 1985).

In its opinion today, the Court describes respondent as a "confused boy," *ante*, at 683, and repeatedly characterizes his audience of high school students as "children," *ante*, at 682, 684. When a more orthodox message is being conveyed to a similar audience, four Members of today's majority would treat high school students like college students rather than like children. See *Bender v. Williamsport Area School Dist.*, 475 U.S. 534 (1986) (dissenting opinions).

rules of conduct in an educational institution.³ But it [*693] does mean that he should not be disciplined for speaking frankly in a school assembly if he had no reason to anticipate punitive consequences.

One might conclude that respondent should have known that he would be punished for giving this speech on three quite different theories: (1) It violated the "Disruptive Conduct" rule published in the student handbook; (2) he was specifically warned by his teachers; or (3) the impropriety is so obvious that no specific notice was required. I discuss each theory in turn.

The Disciplinary Rule

At the time the discipline was imposed, as well as in its defense of this lawsuit, the school took the position that respondent violated the following published rule:

"'In addition to the criminal acts defined above, the commission of, or participation in certain noncriminal activities or acts may lead to disciplinary action. Generally, these are acts which disrupt and interfere with the educational process.

. . .

"'*Disruptive Conduct*. Conduct which materially and substantially interferes with the educational process is prohibited, including the use of obscene, profane language or gestures.'" 755 F.2d 1356, 1357, n. 1 (CA9 1985).

Based on the findings of fact made by the District Court, the Court of Appeals concluded that the evidence did not show "that the speech had a materially disruptive effect on the educational process." *Id.*, at 1361. The Court of Appeals explained the basis for this conclusion:

"[The] record now before us yields no evidence that Fraser's use of a sexual innuendo in his speech materially interfered with activities at Bethel High School. While the students' reaction to Fraser's speech may fairly be characterized as boisterous, it was hardly disruptive [*694] of the educational process. In the words of Mr. McCutcheon, the school counselor whose testimony the District relies upon, the reaction of the student body 'was not atypical to a high school auditorium assembly.' In our view, a noisy response to the speech and sexually suggestive movements by three students in a crowd of 600 fail to rise to the level of a material interference with the educational process that justifies impinging upon Fraser's First Amendment right to express himself freely.

"We find it significant that although four teachers delivered written statements to an assistant principal commenting on Fraser's speech, none of them suggested

---

3. See *Arnold v. Carpenter*, 459 F.2d 939, 944 (CA7 1972) (Stevens, J., dissenting).

that the speech disrupted the assembly or otherwise interfered with school activities. *See* Finding of Fact No. 8. Nor can a finding of material disruption be based upon the evidence that the speech proved to be a lively topic of conversation among students the following day." *Id.*, at 1360-1361.

Thus, the evidence in the record, as interpreted by the District Court and the Court of Appeals, makes it perfectly clear that respondent's speech was not "conduct" prohibited by the disciplinary rule.[4] Indeed, even if the language of the rule could be stretched to encompass the nondisruptive use of obscene or profane language, there is no such language in respondent's speech. What the speech does contain is a sexual metaphor that may unquestionably be offensive to some listeners in some settings. But if an impartial judge puts his [*695] or her own views about the metaphor to one side, I simply cannot understand how he or she could conclude that it is embraced by the above-quoted rule. At best, the rule is sufficiently ambiguous that without a further explanation or construction it could not advise the reader of the student handbook that the speech would be forbidden.[5]

The Specific Warning by the Teachers

Respondent read his speech to three different teachers before he gave it. Mrs. Irene Hicks told him that she thought the speech "was inappropriate and that he probably should not deliver it." App. 30. Steven DeHart told respondent "that this would indeed cause problems in that it would raise eyebrows." *Id.*, at 61. The third teacher, Shawn Madden, did not testify. None of the three suggested that the speech might violate a school rule. *Id.*, at 49-50.

The fact that respondent reviewed the text of his speech with three different teachers before he gave it does indicate that he must have been aware of the possibility that it would provoke an adverse reaction, but the teachers' responses certainly did not give him any better notice of the likelihood of discipline than did the student handbook itself. In my opinion, therefore, the most difficult

---

4. The Court's reliance on the school's authority to prohibit "unanticipated conduct disruptive of the educational process," *ante*, at 686, is misplaced. The findings of the District Court, which were upheld by the Court of Appeals, established that the speech was not "disruptive." Departing from our normal practice concerning factual findings, the Court's decision rests on "utterly unproven, subjective impressions of some hypothetical students." *Bender v. Williamsport Area School Dist.*, 475 U.S., at 553 (Burger, C.J., dissenting).

5. The school's disruptive conduct rule is entirely concerned with "the educational process." It does not expressly refer to extracurricular activities in general, or to student political campaigns or student debates. In contrast, "[in] our Nation's legislative halls, where some of the most vigorous political debates in our society are carried on, there are rules prohibiting the use of expressions offensive to other participants in the debate." See *ante*, at 681. If a written rule is needed to forewarn a United States Senator that the use of offensive speech may give rise to discipline, a high school student should be entitled to an equally unambiguous warning. Unlike the Manual of Parliamentary Practice drafted by Thomas Jefferson, this School District's rules of conduct contain no unequivocal prohibition against the use of "impertinent" speech or "indecent language."

question is whether the speech was so obviously offensive that an intelligent high school student must be presumed to have realized that he would be punished for giving it.

[*696] *Obvious Impropriety*

Justice Sutherland taught us that a "nuisance may be merely a right thing in the wrong place, — like a pig in the parlor instead of the barnyard." *Euclid v. Ambler Realty Co.*, 272 U.S. 365, 388 (1926). Vulgar language, like vulgar animals, may be acceptable in some contexts and intolerable in others. See *FCC v. Pacifica Foundation*, 438 U.S. 726, 750 (1978). Indeed, even ordinary, inoffensive speech may be wholly unacceptable in some settings. See *Schenck v. United States*, 249 U.S. 47, 52 (1919); *Pacifica, supra*, at 744-745.

It seems fairly obvious that respondent's speech would be inappropriate in certain classroom and formal social settings. On the other hand, in a locker room or perhaps in a school corridor the metaphor in the speech might be regarded as rather routine comment. If this be true, and if respondent's audience consisted almost entirely of young people with whom he conversed on a daily basis, can we—at this distance—confidently assert that he must have known that the school administration would punish him for delivering it?

For three reasons, I think not. First, it seems highly unlikely that he would have decided to deliver the speech if he had known that it would result in his suspension and disqualification from delivering the school commencement address. Second, I believe a strong presumption in favor of free expression should apply whenever an issue of this kind is arguable. Third, because the Court has adopted the policy of applying contemporary community standards in evaluating expression with sexual connotations, this Court should defer to the views of the district and circuit judges who are in a much better position to evaluate this speech than we are.

I would affirm the judgment of the Court of Appeals.

Questions Regarding *Bethel School District No. 403 v. Fraser*

1. Was *Bethel* decided on *Tinker* substantial disruption grounds? In other words, did the Supreme Court hold that the Bethel School District was justified in punishing Fraser because his speech could have led to a substantial disruption on campus?
2. Do you believe Fraser's speech, reproduced in Brennan's concurrence, would still be considered impermissibly lewd by today's standards?

WISNIEWSKI EX REL. WISNIEWSKI v. BOARD OF EDUCATION OF THE WEEDSPORT CENTRAL SCHOOL DISTRICT

United States Court of Appeals for the Second Circuit
April 17, 2007, Heard; July 5, 2007, Decided
Docket No. 06-3394-cv

Reporter: 494 F.3d 34 *

Judges: Before: Newman, Walker, and Straub, Circuit Judges.

Opinion by: Jon O. Newman

Opinion (Edited for Content)

[*35] JON O. NEWMAN, Circuit Judge.

This appeal concerns a First Amendment challenge to an eighth-grade student's suspension for sharing with friends via the Internet a small drawing crudely, but clearly, suggesting that a named teacher should be shot and killed. Plaintiffs-Appellants Martin and Annette Wisniewski, the parents of Aaron Wisniewski, appeal from the June 30, 2006, amended judgment of the District Court for the Northern District of New York (Norman A. Mordue, Chief Judge), dismissing their federal civil rights claims against the Defendants-Appellees Weedsport Central School District Board of Education and School Superintendent Richard Mabbett.... We conclude that the federal claims were properly dismissed because it was reasonably foreseeable that Wisniewski's communication would cause a disruption within the school environment.... We therefore affirm.

BACKGROUND

Facts of the episode. This case arose out of an Internet transmission by an eighth-grader at Weedsport Middle School, in the Weedsport Central School District in upstate New York. In April 2001, the pupil, Aaron Wisniewski ("Aaron"), was using AOL Instant Messaging ("IM") software on his parents' home computer. Instant messaging enables a person using a computer with Internet access to exchange messages in real time with members of a group (usually called "buddies" in IM lingo) who have the same IM software on their computers. Instant messaging permits rapid exchanges of text between any two members of a "buddy list" who happen to be on-line at the same time. Different IM programs use different notations for indicating which members of a user's "buddy list" are on-line at any one time. Text sent to and from a "buddy" remains on the computer screen during the entire exchange of messages between any two users of the IM program.

The AOL IM program, like many others, permits the sender of IM messages to display on the computer screen an icon, created by the sender, which serves as an identifier of the sender, in addition to the sender's name. The IM icon of the sender and that of the person replying remain on the screen during the exchange of text messages between the two "buddies," and each can copy the icon of the other and [*36] transmit it to any other "buddy" during an IM exchange.

Aaron's IM icon was a small drawing of a pistol firing a bullet at a person's head, above which were dots representing splattered blood.[1] Beneath the drawing appeared the words "Kill Mr. VanderMolen." Philip VanderMolen was Aaron's English teacher at the time. Aaron created the icon a couple of weeks after his class was instructed that threats would not be tolerated by the school, and would be treated as acts of violence. Aaron sent IM messages, displaying the icon to some 15 members of his IM "buddy list." The icon was not sent to VanderMolen or any other school official.

The icon was available for viewing by Aaron's "buddies" for three weeks, at least some of whom were Aaron's classmates at Weedsport Middle School. During that period it came to the attention of another classmate, who informed VanderMolen of Aaron's icon and later supplied him with a copy of the icon. VanderMolen, distressed by this information, forwarded it to the high school and middle school principals, who brought the matter to the attention of the local police, the Superintendent Mabbett, and Aaron's parents. In response to questioning by the school principals, Aaron acknowledged that he had created and sent the icon and expressed regret. He was then suspended for five days, after which he was allowed back in school, pending a superintendent's hearing. VanderMolen asked and was allowed to stop teaching Aaron's class.

At the same time, a police investigator who interviewed Aaron concluded that the icon was meant as a joke, that Aaron fully understood the severity of what he had done, and that Aaron posed no real threat to VanderMolen or to any other school official. A pending criminal case was then closed. Aaron was also evaluated by a psychologist, who also found that Aaron had no violent intent, posed no actual threat, and made the icon as a joke.

The superintendent's hearing. In May 2001 a superintendent's hearing, regarding a proposed long-term suspension of Aaron, was held before a designated hearing officer, attorney Lynda M. VanCoske. Aaron was charged under New York Education Law § 3214(3) with endangering the health and welfare of other students and staff at the school.

In her decision of June 2001, VanCoske found that the icon was threatening and should not have been understood as a joke. Although the threatening act took place outside of school, she concluded that it was in violation of school rules and disrupted school operations by requiring special attention from school officials, replacement of the threatened teacher, and interviewing pupils during class time. The hearing officer acknowledged the opinions of the police investigator and the psychologist that Aaron did not intend to harm VanderMolen and that he did not

---

1. The Appellants, in something of an understatement, describe Aaron's icon as "distasteful." *See* Brief for Appellants at 3 n.1.

pose any real threat, but stated that "intent [is] irrelevant." Citing the evidentiary standard followed in New York suspension hearings, the decision concluded:

> Substantial and competent evidence exists that Aaron engaged in the act of sending a threatening message to his buddies, the subject of which was a teacher. He admitted it. Competent and substantial evidence exists that this message disrupted the educational environment....
>
> [*37] As a result of the foregoing, I conclude that Aaron did commit the act of threatening a teacher, in violation of page 11 of the student handbook, creating an environment threatening the health, safety and welfare of others, and his actions created a disruption in the school environment.

The hearing officer recommended suspension of Aaron for one semester. The recommendation was presented to the district's Board of Education ("Board"),[2] which approved the one semester suspension in late September 2001. Aaron was suspended for the first semester of the 2001-2002 school year. During the period of suspension the school district afforded Aaron alternative education. He returned to school for the spring term. At oral argument, we were advised that because of school and community hostility, the family moved from Weedsport.

The District Court litigation. In November 2002 Aaron's parents filed on his behalf the current suit against the Board and Superintendent Mabbett, seeking damages under 42 U.S.C. § 1983. The complaint included five counts: the first count claimed that Aaron's icon was not a "true threat," but was protected speech under the First Amendment. It therefore alleged that in suspending Aaron the Board acted in a retaliatory manner in violation of his First Amendment rights. The second and third counts alleged that the Board and Mabbett, respectively, had failed to train school staff in threat assessment, thereby leading to the violation of Aaron's First Amendment rights. The fourth and fifth counts claimed the Board had violated New York State Education Law.

In June 2006, Chief Judge Mordue granted the Defendants' motion for summary judgment. The District Court first found that the hearing officer had made a factual determination, entitled to preclusive effect, that the icon was a threat and, as such, not protected by the First Amendment. Alternatively, the Court made its own determination that the icon was reasonably to be understood as a "true threat" lacking First Amendment protection. The Court also found that, in any event, Mabbett would be entitled to qualified immunity....

DISCUSSION

... [W]e turn directly to the merits of the Plaintiffs' claim that Aaron's icon was protected speech under the First Amendment.

---

2. Although Superintendent Mabbett was authorized under the statute to decide Aaron's discipline, the issue was brought before the Board due to his prior involvement in the case.

In assessing that claim, we do not pause to resolve the parties' dispute as to whether transmission of the icon constituted a "true 'threat' " within the meaning of the Supreme Court's decision in *Watts v. United States*, 394 U.S. 705, 708, 89 S. Ct. 1399, 22 L. Ed. 2d 664 (1969). *Watts* concerned a criminal prosecution for violating 18 U.S.C. § 871(a), which provides punishment for "knowingly and willfully . . . mak[ing] [a] threat against the President." The defendant had said at a public rally on the grounds of the Washington Monument, "If they ever make me carry a rifle the first man I want to get in my sights is L.B.J." **[*38]** *Id.* at 706. The Court noted that "a statute such as this one, which makes *criminal* a form of pure speech, must be interpreted with the commands of the First Amendment clearly in mind," and added, "What is a threat must be distinguished from what is constitutionally protected speech." *Id.* at 707(emphasis added). Ruling that "the statute initially requires the Government to prove a true 'threat,' " the Court concluded, "We do not believe that the kind of political hyperbole indulged in by [the defendant] fits within that statutory term." *Id.* at 708.

Although some courts have assessed a student's statements concerning the killing of a school official or a fellow student against the "true 'threat' " standard of *Watts, see, e.g., Doe v. Pulaski County Special School District*, 306 F.3d 616, 621-27, 627-32 (8th Cir. 2002) (en banc); *Lovell v. Poway Unified School District*, 90 F.3d 367, 371-73 (9th Cir. 1996), we think that school officials have significantly broader authority to sanction student speech than the *Watts* standard allows. With respect to school officials' authority to discipline a student's expression reasonably understood as urging violent conduct, we think the appropriate First Amendment standard is the one set forth by the Supreme Court in *Tinker v. Des Moines Independent Community School District*, 393 U.S. 503, 89 S. Ct. 733, 21 L. Ed. 2d 731 (1969).

Tinker, it will be recalled, concerned students (two at a high school and one at a junior high school) suspended by school authorities for coming to school wearing black armbands signifying their opposition to the Vietnam War. *See id.* at 504. Noting that the students' conduct was "a silent, passive expression of opinion," *id.* at 508, the Court stated, "In order for the State in the person of school officials to justify prohibition of a particular expression of opinion, it must be able to show that its action was caused by something more than a mere desire to avoid the discomfort and unpleasantness that always accompany an unpopular viewpoint." *Id.* at 509. The Court used several formulations to describe student conduct that would merit school discipline: conduct that (1) "would substantially interfere with the work of the school," *id.*, or (2) would cause "material and substantial interference with schoolwork or discipline," *id.* at 511, or (3) "would materially and substantially disrupt the work and discipline of the school," *id.* at 513, or (4) "might reasonably have led school authorities to forecast substantial disruption of or material interference with school activities," *id.* at 514. Seeing no evidence of any of such risks, the Court ruled that the students' wearing of the armbands was speech protected against school discipline by the First Amendment. *See id.* at 511-14. In its most recent consideration of a First Amendment challenge to school discipline in response to a student's allegedly protected speech, the Supreme Court viewed the third formulation as *Tinker*'s holding: "*Tinker* held that student expression may not be suppressed unless school officials reasonably conclude that it will 'materially and substantially disrupt the work and discipline of the school.'" *Morse v. Frederick*, 551 U.S. 393, 127 S. Ct. 2618, 168 L. Ed. 2d 290, 2007 U.S. LEXIS 8514, 2007 WL 1804317, at *7 (Sup. Ct. 2007) (quoting *Tinker*, 393 U.S. at 513).

Even if Aaron's transmission of an icon depicting and calling for the killing of his teacher could be viewed as an expression of opinion within the meaning of *Tinker*, we conclude that it crosses the boundary of protected speech and constitutes student conduct that poses a reasonably foreseeable risk that the icon would come to the attention of school authorities and that [*39] it would "materially and substantially disrupt the work and discipline of the school." *Id.* (internal quotation marks omitted). For such conduct, *Tinker* affords no protection against school discipline. *See LaVine v. Blaine School District*, 257 F.3d 981, 989-92 (9th Cir. 2001) (upholding, under *Tinker*, suspension of high school student based in part on poem describing shooting of students); *Boucher v. School Board*, 134 F.3d 821, 827-28 (7th Cir. 1998) (upholding, under *Tinker*, one-year expulsion of high school student for writing article in underground newspaper outlining techniques for hacking into school computers); *J.S., a Minor v. Bethlehem Area School District*, 757 A.2d 412, 422 (Pa. Cmwlth. 2000) (upholding, under *Tinker*, permanent expulsion of student for placing on web-site picture of severed head of teacher and soliciting funds for her execution).

The fact that Aaron's creation and transmission of the IM icon occurred away from school property does not necessarily insulate him from school discipline.[3] We have recognized that off-campus conduct can create a foreseeable risk of substantial disruption within a school, *see Thomas v. Board of Education*, 607 F.2d 1043, 1052 n.17 (2d Cir. 1979) ("We can, of course, envision a case in which a group of students incites substantial disruption within the school from some remote locale."), as have other courts, *see Pulaski*, 306 F.3d at 625-27 (letter, written and kept at home, that threatened killing of fellow student); *Sullivan v. Houston Independent School District*, 475 F.2d 1071, 1075-77 (5th Cir. 1973) (underground newspaper distributed off-campus but near school grounds); *J.S.*, 757 A.2d at 418-22 (material created on home computer).

In this case, the panel is divided as to whether it must be shown that it was reasonably foreseeable that Aaron's IM icon would reach the school property or whether the undisputed fact that it did reach the school pretermits any inquiry as to this aspect of reasonable foreseeability. We are in agreement, however, that, on

---

3. Since the Supreme Court in *Morse* rejected the claim that the student's location, standing across the street from the school at a school approved event with a banner visible to most students, was not "at school," *Morse*, 2007 U.S. LEXIS 8514, 2007 WL 1804317, at *5, it had no occasion to consider the circumstances under which school authorities may discipline students for off-campus activities.

the undisputed facts, it was reasonably foreseeable that the IM icon would come to the attention of school authorities and the teacher whom the icon depicted being shot.[4] The potentially threatening content of the icon and the extensive distribution of it, which encompassed 15 recipients, [*40] including some of Aaron's classmates, during a three-week circulation period, made this risk at least foreseeable to a reasonable person, if not inevitable. And there can be no doubt that the icon, once made known to the teacher and other school officials, would foreseeably create a risk of substantial disruption within the school environment.

Whether these aspects of reasonable foreseeability are considered issues of law or issues of fact as to which, on this record, no reasonable jury could disagree, foreseeability of both communication to school authorities, including the teacher, and the risk of substantial disruption is not only reasonable, but clear. These consequences permit school discipline, whether or not Aaron intended his IM icon to be communicated to school authorities or, if communicated, to cause a substantial disruption. As in *Morse*, the student in the pending case was not disciplined for conduct that was merely "offensive," *Morse*, 2007 U.S. LEXIS 8514, 2007 WL 1804317, at *10, or merely in conflict with some view of the school's "educational mission," *id.* 2007 U.S. LEXIS 8514, [WL] at *18 (Alito, J., with whom Kennedy, J., joins, concurring).

Although the Appellants contend that the First Amendment barred the imposition of any discipline, they make no distinct challenge to the extent of the discipline. Thus, we need not determine whether such a challenge would have to be grounded on the First Amendment itself or the substantive component of the Due Process Clause of the Fourteenth Amendment. *Cf. Graham v. Connor*, 490 U.S. 386, 395, 109 S. Ct. 1865, 104 L. Ed. 2d 443 (1989) ("Because the Fourth Amendment provides an explicit textual source of constitutional protection against this sort of physically intrusive governmental conduct, that Amendment, not the more generalized notion of 'substantive due process,' must be the guide for analyzing these claims."). And we are mindful that "[i]t is not the role of the federal courts to set aside decisions of school administrators which the court may view as lacking a basis in wisdom or compassion."

---

4. Judge Walker, who otherwise fully concurs in this opinion and in the judgment, would hold that a school may discipline a student for off-campus expression that is likely to cause a disruption on campus only if it was foreseeable to a reasonable adult, cognizant of the perspective of a student, that the expression might reach campus. *Cf. Skoros v. City of New York*, 437 F.3d 1, 23 (2d Cir. 2006) (discussing perspective of reasonable adult who assesses religious display aware that it will be seen primarily by children). He believes that to hold otherwise would run afoul of *Thomas*, 607 F.2d at 1045 (holding that "the arm of [school] authority does not [generally] reach beyond the schoolhouse gate"), and would raise substantial First Amendment concerns, as it might permit a school to punish a student for the content of speech the student could never have anticipated reaching the school, such as a draft letter concealed in his night-stand, stolen by another student, and delivered to school authorities, *cf. Porter v. Ascension Parish School Board*, 393 F.3d 608, 615 n.22 (5th Cir. 2004) ("[T]he fact that Adam's drawing was composed off-campus and remained off-campus for two years until it was unintentionally taken to school by his younger brother takes the present case outside the scope of [*Tinker*].").

Wood v. Strickland, 420 U.S. 308, 326, 95 S. Ct. 992, 43 L. Ed. 2d 214 (1975). However, in the absence of a properly presented challenge, we do not decide whether the length of the one semester suspension exceeded whatever constitutional limitation might exist. We rule only that the First Amendment claims against the School Board and the Superintendent were properly dismissed, and that the state law claims were properly left for whatever state court adjudication might be available . . . .

CONCLUSION

The judgment of the District Court is affirmed.

Questions Regarding *Wisniewski ex rel. Wisniewski v. Board of Education of the Weedsport Central School District*

1. Is *Wisniewski* binding or persuasive authority for either Assignment in this chapter, both of which are to be heard in the District of Delaware?
2. Did the majority in *Wisniewski* decide the case under a "true threat" analysis?
3. The panel in *Wisniewski* agreed that it was reasonably foreseeable that the icon at issue would come to the attention of the school. Under this standard, who do you think constitutes "the school"? The principal? A teacher? A student? How many teachers or students have to be made aware of the speech?

MAHANOY AREA SCHOOL DISTRICT v. B. L.

Supreme Court of the United States
April 28, 2021, Argued; June 23, 2021, Decided
No. 20-255.

Reporter: 2021 U.S. LEXIS 3395 *

Notice: This preliminary Lexis version is unedited and subject to revision. The LEXIS pagination of this document is subject to change pending release of the final published version.

Judges: Roberts, Thomas, Breyer, Alito, Sotomayor, Kagan, Gorsuch, Kavanaugh, Barrett.

Opinion by: Breyer

Opinion (Edited for Content)

Justice BREYER delivered the opinion of the Court.

A public high school student used, and transmitted to her Snapchat friends, vulgar language and gestures criticizing both the school and the school's cheerleading team. The student's speech took place outside of school hours and away from the school's campus. In response, the school suspended the student for a year from the cheerleading team. We must decide whether the Court of Appeals for the Third [*6] Circuit correctly held that the school's decision violated the First Amendment. Although we do not agree with the reasoning of the Third Circuit panel's majority, we do agree with its conclusion that the school's disciplinary action violated the First Amendment.

I

A

B. L. (who, together with her parents, is a respondent in this case) was a student at Mahanoy Area High School, a public school in Mahanoy City, Pennsylvania. At the end of her freshman year, B. L. tried out for a position on the school's varsity cheerleading squad and for right fielder on a private softball team. She did not make the varsity cheerleading team or get her preferred softball position, but she was offered a spot on the cheerleading squad's junior varsity team. B. L. did not accept the coach's decision with good grace, particularly because the squad coaches had placed an entering freshman on the varsity team.

That weekend, B. L. and a friend visited the Cocoa Hut, a local convenience store. There, B. L. used her smartphone to post two photos on Snapchat, a social media application that allows users to post photos and videos that disappear after a set period of time. B. L. posted the images to her Snapchat "story," a feature of the application [*7] that allows any person in the user's "friend" group (B. L. had about 250 "friends") to view the images for a 24 hour period.

The first image B. L. posted showed B. L. and a friend with middle fingers raised; it bore the caption: "Fuck school fuck softball fuck cheer fuck everything." App. 20. The second image was blank but for a caption, which read: "Love how me and [another student] get told we need a year of jv before we make varsity but tha[t] doesn't matter to anyone else?" The caption also contained an upside-down smiley-face emoji. *Id.*, at 21.

B. L.'s Snapchat "friends" included other Mahanoy Area High School students, some of whom also belonged to the cheerleading squad. At least one of them, using a separate cellphone, took pictures of B. L.'s posts and shared them with other members of the cheerleading squad. One of the students who received these photos showed them to her mother (who was a cheerleading squad coach), and the images spread. That week, several cheerleaders and other students approached the cheerleading coaches "visibly upset" about B. L.'s posts. *Id.*, at 83-84. Questions about the posts persisted during an Algebra class taught by one of the two coaches. *Id.*, at [*8] 83.

After discussing the matter with the school principal, the coaches decided that because the posts used profanity in connection with a school extracurricular activity, they violated team and school rules. As a result, the coaches suspended B. L. from the junior varsity cheerleading squad for the upcoming year. B. L.'s subsequent apologies did not move school officials. The school's athletic director, principal, superintendent, and school board, all affirmed B. L.'s suspension from the team. In response, B. L., together with her parents, filed this lawsuit in Federal District Court.

B

The District Court found in B. L.'s favor. It first granted a temporary restraining order and a preliminary injunction ordering the school to reinstate B. L. to the cheerleading team. In granting B. L.'s subsequent motion for summary judgment, the District Court found that B. L.'s Snapchats had not caused substantial disruption at the school. Cf. *Tinker v. Des Moines Independent Community School Dist.*, 393 U.S. 503 (1969). Consequently, the District Court declared that B. L.'s punishment violated the First Amendment, and it awarded B. L. nominal damages and attorneys' fees and ordered the school to expunge her disciplinary record.

On appeal, a panel of the Third Circuit affirmed the District [*9] Court's conclusion. See 964 F.3d 170, 194 (2020). In so doing, the majority noted that this Court had previously held in *Tinker* that a public high school could not constitutionally prohibit a peaceful student political demonstration consisting of "'pure speech'" on school property during the school day. 393 U.S., at 505-506, 514. In reaching its conclusion in *Tinker*, this Court emphasized that there was no evidence the student protest would "substantially interfere with the work of the school or impinge upon the rights of other students." *Id.*, at 509. But the Court also said that: "[C]onduct by [a] student, in class or out of it, which for any reason—whether it stems from time, place, or type of behavior—materially disrupts classwork or involves substantial disorder or invasion of the rights of others is . . . not immunized by the constitutional guarantee of freedom of speech." *Id.*, at 513.

Many courts have taken this statement as setting a standard—a standard that allows schools considerable freedom on campus to discipline students for conduct that the First Amendment might otherwise protect. But here, the panel majority held that this additional freedom did "not apply to off-campus speech," which it defined as "speech that is outside school-owned, -operated, or -supervised [*10] channels and that is not reasonably interpreted as bearing the school's imprimatur." 964 F.3d, at 189. Because B. L.'s speech took place off campus, the panel concluded that the *Tinker* standard did not apply and the school consequently could not discipline B. L. for engaging in a form of pure speech.

A concurring member of the panel agreed with the majority's result but wrote that the school had not sufficiently justified disciplining B. L. because, whether the *Tinker* standard did or did not apply, B. L.'s speech was not substantially disruptive.

C

The school district filed a petition for certiorari in this Court, asking us to decide "[w]hether [*Tinker*], which holds that public school officials may regulate speech that would materially and substantially disrupt the work and discipline of the school, applies to student speech that occurs off campus." Pet. for Cert. I. We granted the petition.

II

We have made clear that students do not "shed their constitutional rights to freedom of speech or expression," even "at the school house gate." *Tinker*, 393 U.S., at 506; see also *Brown v. Entertainment Merchants Assn.*, 564 U.S. 786, 794 (2011) ("[M]inors are entitled to a significant measure of First Amendment protection" (alteration in original; internal quotation marks omitted)). But we have also made clear that [*11] courts must apply the First Amendment "in light of the special characteristics of the school environment." *Hazelwood School Dist. v. Kuhlmeier*, 484 U.S. 260, 266 (1988) (internal quotation marks omitted). One such characteristic, which we have stressed, is the fact that schools at times stand *in loco parentis*, i.e., in the place of parents. See *Bethel School Dist. No. 403 v. Fraser*, 478 U.S. 675, 684 (1986).

This Court has previously outlined three specific categories of student speech that schools may regulate in certain circumstances: (1) "indecent," "lewd," or "vulgar" speech uttered during a school assembly on school grounds, see *id.*, at 685; (2) speech, uttered during a class trip, that promotes "illegal drug use," see *Morse v. Frederick*, 551 U.S. 393, 409 (2007); and (3) speech that others may reasonably perceive as "bear[ing] the imprimatur of the school," such as that appearing in a school-sponsored newspaper, see *Kuhlmeier*, 484 U.S., at 271.

Finally, in *Tinker*, we said schools have a special interest in regulating speech that "materially disrupts classwork or involves substantial disorder or invasion of the rights of others." 393 U.S., at 513. These special characteristics call for special leeway when schools regulate speech that occurs under its supervision.

Unlike the Third Circuit, we do not believe the special characteristics that give schools additional license to regulate student speech always disappear [*12] when a school regulates speech that takes place off campus. The school's regulatory interests remain significant in some off-campus circumstances. The parties' briefs, and those of *amici*, list several types of off-campus behavior that may call for school regulation. These include serious or severe bullying or harassment targeting particular individuals; threats aimed at teachers or other students; the failure to follow rules concerning lessons, the writing of papers, the use of computers, or participation in other online school activities; and breaches of school security devices, including material maintained within school computers.

Even B. L. herself and the *amici* supporting her would redefine the Third Circuit's off-campus/on-campus distinction, treating as on campus: all times when the school is responsible for the student; the school's immediate surroundings; travel en route to and from the school; all speech taking place over school laptops or on a school's website; speech taking place during remote learning; activities taken for school credit; and communications to school e-mail accounts or phones. Brief for Respondents 36-37. And it may be that speech related to extracurricular [*13] activities, such as team sports, would also receive special treatment under B. L.'s proposed rule. See Tr. of Oral Arg. 71, 85.

We are uncertain as to the length or content of any such list of appropriate exceptions or carveouts to the Third Circuit majority's rule. That rule, basically, if not entirely, would deny the off-campus applicability of *Tinker*'s highly general statement about the nature of a school's special interests. Particularly given the advent of computer-based learning, we hesitate to determine precisely which of many school-related off-campus activities belong on such a list. Neither do we now know how such a list might vary, depending upon a student's age, the nature of the school's off-campus activity, or the impact upon the school itself. Thus, we do not now set forth a broad, highly general First Amendment rule stating just what counts as "off campus" speech and whether or how ordinary First Amendment standards must give way off campus to a school's special need to prevent, *e.g.*, substantial disruption of learning-related activities or the protection of those who make up a school community.

We can, however, mention three features of off-campus speech that often, even if not always, distinguish [*14] schools' efforts to regulate that speech from their efforts to regulate on-campus speech. Those features diminish the strength of the unique educational characteristics that might call for special First Amendment leeway.

First, a school, in relation to off-campus speech, will rarely stand *in loco parentis*. The doctrine of *in loco parentis* treats school administrators as standing in the place of students' parents under circumstances where the children's actual parents cannot protect, guide, and discipline them. Geographically speaking, off-campus speech will normally fall within the zone of parental, rather than school-related, responsibility.

Second, from the student speaker's perspective, regulations of off-campus speech, when coupled with regulations of on-campus speech, include all the speech a student utters during the full 24-hour day. That means courts must be more skeptical of a school's efforts to regulate off-campus speech, for doing so may mean the student cannot engage in that kind of speech at all. When it comes to political or religious speech that occurs outside school or a school program or activity, the school will have a heavy burden to justify intervention.

Third, the school itself [*15] has an interest in protecting a student's unpopular expression, especially when the expression takes place off campus. America's public schools are the nurseries of democracy. Our representative democracy only works if we protect the "marketplace of ideas." This free exchange facilitates an informed public opinion, which, when transmitted to lawmakers, helps produce laws that reflect the People's will. That protection must include the protection of unpopular ideas, for popular ideas have less need for protection. Thus, schools have a strong interest in ensuring that future generations understand the workings in practice of the well-known aphorism, "I disapprove of what you say, but I will defend to the death your right to say it." (Although this quote is often attributed to Voltaire, it was likely coined by an English writer, Evelyn Beatrice Hall.)

Given the many different kinds of off-campus speech, the different potential school-related and circumstance-specific justifications, and the differing extent to which those justifications may call for First Amendment leeway, we can, as a general matter, say little more than this: Taken together, these three features of much off-campus speech mean that [*16] the leeway the First Amendment grants to schools in light of their special characteristics is diminished. We leave for future cases to decide where, when, and how these features mean the speaker's off-campus location will make the critical difference. This case can, however, provide one example.

III

Consider B. L.'s speech. Putting aside the vulgar language, the listener would hear criticism, of the team, the team's coaches, and the school—in a word or two, criticism of the rules of a community of which B. L. forms a part. This criticism did not involve features that would place it outside the First Amendment's ordinary protection. B. L.'s posts, while crude, did not amount to fighting words. See *Chaplinsky v. New Hampshire*, 315 U.S. 568 (1942). And while B. L. used vulgarity, her speech was not obscene as this Court has understood that term. See *Cohen v. California*, 403 U.S. 15, 19-20 (1971). To the contrary, B. L. uttered the kind of pure speech to which, were she an adult, the First Amendment would provide strong protection. See *id.*, at 24; cf. *Snyder v. Phelps*, 562 U.S. 443, 461 (2011) (First Amendment protects "even hurtful speech on public issues to ensure that we do not stifle public debate"); *Rankin v. McPherson*, 483 U.S. 378, 387 (1987) ("The inappropriate . . . character of a statement is irrelevant to the question whether it deals with a matter of public concern").

Consider too when, where, and how B. L. spoke. Her posts [*17] appeared outside of school hours from a location outside the school. She did not identify the school in her posts or target any member of the school community with vulgar or abusive language. B. L. also transmitted her speech through a personal cellphone, to an audience consisting of her private circle of Snapchat friends. These features of her speech, while risking transmission to the school itself, nonetheless (for reasons we have just explained, *supra*, at 7-8) diminish the school's interest in punishing B. L.'s utterance.

But what about the school's interest, here primarily an interest in prohibiting students from using vulgar language to criticize a school team or its coaches—at least when that criticism might well be transmitted to other students, team members, coaches, and faculty? We can break that general interest into three parts.

First, we consider the school's interest in teaching good manners and consequently in punishing the use of vulgar language aimed at part of the school community. See App. 35 (indicating that coaches removed B. L. from the cheer team because "there was profanity in [her] Snap and it was directed towards cheerleading"); see also *id.*, at 27, 47, and n. [*18] 9, 78, 82. The strength of this anti-vulgarity interest is weakened considerably by the fact that B. L. spoke outside the school on her own time. See *Morse*, 551 U.S., at 405 (clarifying that although a school can regulate a student's use of sexual innuendo in a speech given within the school, if the student "delivered the same speech in a public forum outside the school context, it would have been protected"); see also *Fraser*, 478 U.S., at 688 (Brennan, J., concurring in judgment) (noting that if the student in *Fraser* "had given the same speech outside of the school environment, he could not have been penalized simply because government officials considered his language to be inappropriate").

B. L. spoke under circumstances where the school did not stand *in loco parentis*. And there is no reason to believe B. L.'s parents had delegated to school officials their own control of B. L.'s behavior at the Cocoa Hut. Moreover, the vulgarity in B. L.'s posts encompassed a message, an expression of B. L.'s irritation with, and criticism of, the school and cheerleading communities. Further, the school has presented no evidence of any general effort to prevent students from using vulgarity outside the classroom. Together, these facts convince [*19] us that the school's interest in teaching good manners is not sufficient, in this case, to overcome B. L.'s interest in free expression.

Second, the school argues that it was trying to prevent disruption, if not within the classroom, then within the bounds of a school-sponsored extracurricular activity. But we can find no evidence in the record of the sort of "substantial disruption" of a school activity or a threatened harm to the rights of others that might justify the school's action. *Tinker*, 393 U.S., at 514. Rather, the record shows that discussion of the matter took, at most, 5 to 10 minutes of an Algebra class "for just a couple of days" and that some members of the cheerleading team were "upset" about the content of B. L.'s Snapchats. App. 82-83. But when one of B. L.'s coaches was asked directly if she had "any reason to think that this particular incident would disrupt class or school activities other than the fact that kids kept asking . . . about it," she responded simply, "No." *Id.*, at 84. As we said in *Tinker*, "for the State in the person of school officials to justify prohibition of a particular expression of opinion, it must be able to show that its action was caused by something more than a mere desire [*20] to avoid the discomfort and unpleasantness that always accompany an unpopular viewpoint." 393 U.S., at 509. The alleged disturbance here does not meet *Tinker*'s demanding standard.

Third, the school presented some evidence that expresses (at least indirectly) a concern for team morale. One of the coaches testified that the school decided to suspend B. L., not because of any specific negative impact upon a particular member of the school community, but "based on the fact that there was negativity put out there that could impact students in the school." App. 81. There is little else, however, that suggests any serious decline in team morale—to the point where it could create a substantial interference in, or disruption of, the school's efforts to maintain team cohesion. As we have previously said, simple "undifferentiated fear or apprehension . . . is not enough to overcome the right to freedom of expression." *Tinker,* 393 U.S., at 508.

It might be tempting to dismiss B. L.'s words as unworthy of the robust First Amendment protections discussed herein. But sometimes it is necessary to protect the superfluous in order to preserve the necessary. See *Tyson & Brother v. Banton,* 273 U.S. 418, 447 (1927) (Holmes, J., dissenting). "We cannot lose sight of the fact that, in what otherwise might seem **[*21]** a trifling and annoying instance of individual distasteful abuse of a privilege, these fundamental societal values are truly implicated." *Cohen,* 403 U.S., at 25.

* * *

Although we do not agree with the reasoning of the Third Circuit's panel majority, for the reasons expressed above, resembling those of the panel's concurring opinion, we nonetheless agree that the school violated B. L.'s First Amendment rights. The judgment of the Third Circuit is therefore affirmed.

It is so ordered.

A concurrence by Justice Alito and a dissent by Justice Thomas have been omitted.

> **Questions Regarding** *Mahanoy Area School District v. B. L.*
>
> 1. The Supreme Court affirmed the Third Circuit's decision but disagreed with the Third Circuit's reasoning. What do you glean is the main difference in the scope of the Supreme Court's holding versus the Third Circuit's?
> 2. The Supreme Court is careful not to articulate a general rule regarding the First Amendment implications of off-campus speech, but what takeaways do you discern from its identification of "three features of off-campus speech that often, even if not always, distinguish schools' efforts to regulate that speech from their efforts to regulate on-campus speech"?

B.H. EX REL. HAWK v. EASTON AREA SCHOOL DISTRICT

United States Court of Appeals for the Third Circuit
April 10, 2012, Argued; August 16, 2012, Rehearing En Banc Ordered;
February 20, 2013, Argued En Banc; August 5, 2013, Opinion Filed
No. 11-2067
Reporter: 725 F.3d 293 *

Judges: Before: McKee, Chief Judge, Sloviter, Scirica, Rendell, Ambro, Fuentes, Smith, Fisher, Chagares, Jordan, Hardiman, Greenaway, Jr., Vanaskie, and Greenberg, Circuit Judges. Hardiman, Circuit Judge, dissenting with whom Chagares, Jordan, Greenaway, Jr., and Greenberg, join. Greenaway, Jr., Circuit Judge, dissenting, with whom Chagares, Jordan, Hardiman and Greenberg, join.

Opinion by: Smith

Opinion (Edited for Content)

[*297] SMITH, Circuit Judge, with whom MCKEE, Chief Judge, SLOVITER, SCIRICA, RENDELL, AMBRO, FUENTES, FISHER, and VANASKIE, Circuit Judges join.

Once again, we are asked to find the balance between a student's right to free speech and a school's need to control its educational environment. In this case, two middle-school students purchased bracelets bearing the slogan "I ♥ boobies! [*298] (KEEP A BREAST)" as part of a nationally recognized breast-cancer-awareness campaign. The Easton Area School District banned the bracelets, relying on its authority under *Bethel School District No. 403 v. Fraser*, 478 U.S. 675, 106 S. Ct. 3159, 92 L. Ed. 2d 549 (1986), to restrict vulgar, lewd, profane, or plainly offensive speech, and its authority under *Tinker v. Des Moines Independent Community School District*, 393 U.S. 503, 89 S. Ct. 733, 21 L. Ed. 2d 731 (1969), to restrict speech that is reasonably expected to substantially disrupt the school. The District Court held that the ban violated the students' rights to free speech and issued a preliminary injunction against the ban.

We agree with the District Court that neither *Fraser* nor *Tinker* can sustain the bracelet ban. The scope of a school's authority to restrict lewd, vulgar, profane, or plainly offensive speech under *Fraser* is a novel question left open by the Supreme Court, and one which we must now resolve. We hold that *Fraser*, as modified by the Supreme Court's later reasoning in *Morse v. Frederick*, 551 U.S. 393, 127 S. Ct. 2618, 168 L. Ed. 2d 290 (2007), sets up the following framework: (1) plainly lewd speech, which offends for the same reasons obscenity offends, may be categorically restricted regardless of whether it comments on political or social issues, (2) speech that does not rise to the level of plainly lewd but that a reasonable observer could interpret as lewd may be categorically restricted as long as it cannot plausibly be interpreted as commenting on political or social issues, and (3) speech that does not rise to the level of plainly lewd and that could plausibly be interpreted as commenting on political or social issues may not be categorically restricted. Because the bracelets here are not plainly lewd and because they comment on a social issue, they may not be categorically banned under *Fraser*. The School District has also failed to show that the bracelets threatened to substantially disrupt the school under *Tinker*. We will therefore affirm the District Court.

I.

A. Factual Background

As a "leading youth focused global breast cancer organization," the Keep A Breast Foundation tries to educate thirteen- to thirty-year-old women about breast cancer. Br. of Amicus Curiae KABF at 13. To that end, it often partners with other merchants to co-brand products that raise awareness. And because it believes that young women's "negative body image[s]" seriously inhibit their awareness of breast cancer, the Foundation's products often "seek[] to reduce the stigma by speaking to young people in a voice they can relate to." *Id.* at 14-15. If young women see such awareness projects and products as cool and trendy, the thinking goes, then they will be more willing to talk about breast cancer openly.

To "start a conversation about that taboo in a light-hearted way" and to break down inhibitions keeping young women from performing self-examinations, the Foundation began its "I ♥ Boobies!" initiative. *Id.* at 20-21. Part of the campaign included selling silicone bracelets of assorted colors emblazoned with "I ♥ Boobies! (KEEP A BREAST)" and "check y♥urself! (KEEP A BREAST)." *Id.* at 21-22. The Foundation's website address (www.keep-a-breast.org) and motto ("art. education. awareness. action.") appear on the inside of the bracelet. *Id.*

As intended, the "I ♥ Boobies" initiative was a hit with young women, quickly becoming one of the Foundation's "most successful and high profile educational campaigns." *Id.* at 20-21. Two of the young women drawn to the bracelets were middle-school students B.H. and K.M. They **[*299]** purchased the bracelets with their mothers before the 2010-2011 school year—B.H. because she saw "a lot of [her] friends wearing" the bracelets and wanted to learn about them, and K.M. because of the bracelet's popularity and awareness message. App. 72, 92, 106, 442.

But the bracelets were more than just a new fashion trend. K.M.'s purchase prompted her to become educated about breast cancer in young women. The girls wore their bracelets both to commemorate friends and relatives who had suffered from breast cancer and to promote awareness among their friends. Indeed, their bracelets started conversations about breast cancer and did so far more effectively than the more-traditional pink ribbon. App. 73-74. That made sense to B.H., who observed that "no one really notices" the pink ribbon, whereas the "bracelets are new and . . . more appealing to teenagers." App. 74.

B.H., K.M., and three other students wore the "I ♥ boobies! (KEEP A BREAST)" bracelets at Easton Area Middle School during the 2010-2011 school year. A few teachers, after observing the students wear the bracelets every day for several weeks, considered whether they should take action. The teachers' responses varied: One found the bracelets offensive because they trivialized breast cancer. Others feared that the bracelets might lead to offensive comments or invite inappropriate touching. But school administrators also believed that middle-school boys did not need the bracelets as an excuse to make sexual statements or to engage in inappropriate touching. *See, e.g.*, Viglianti Test., App. 196, 198 (testifying that such incidents "happened before the bracelets" and were "going to happen after the bracelets" because "sexual curiosity between boys and girls in the middle school is . . . a natural and continuing thing").

In mid- to late September, four or five teachers asked the eighth-grade assistant principal, Amy Braxmeier, whether they should require students to remove the bracelets. The seventh-grade assistant principal, Anthony Viglianti, told the teachers that they should ask students to remove "wristbands that have the word 'boobie' written on them," App. 343, even though there were no reports that the bracelets had caused any in-school disruptions or inappropriate comments.[1]

With Breast Cancer Awareness Month approaching in October, school administrators anticipated that the "I ♥ boobies! (KEEP A BREAST)" bracelets might reappear.[2] The school was scheduled to observe Breast Cancer Awareness Month on October 28, so the day before, administrators publicly announced, for the first time, the ban on bracelets containing the word "boobies." Using the word "boobies" in his announcement, Viglianti notified students of the ban over the public-address system, and a student did the same on the school's television station. The Middle School still encouraged students to wear the traditional pink, and it provided teachers who donated to Susan G. Komen for the Cure with either a pin bearing the slogan "Passionately Pink for the Cure" or a T-shirt reading "Real Rovers Wear Pink."

[*300] Later that day, a school security guard noticed B.H. wearing an "I ♥ boobies! (KEEP A BREAST)" bracelet and ordered her to remove it. B.H. refused. After meeting with Braxmeier, B.H. relented, removed her bracelet, and returned to lunch. No disruption occurred at any time that day.

The following day, B.H. and K.M. each wore their "I ♥ boobies! (KEEP A BREAST)" bracelets to observe the Middle School's Breast Cancer Awareness Day. The day was uneventful—until lunchtime. Once in the cafeteria, both girls were instructed by a school security guard to remove their bracelets. Both girls refused. Hearing this encounter, another girl, R.T., stood up and similarly refused to take off her bracelet. Confronted by this act of solidarity, the security guard permitted the

---

1. In mid-October before the ban was publicly announced, school administrators received some unrelated reports of inappropriate touching, but neither the word "boobies" nor the bracelets were considered a cause of these incidents.

2. The Middle School permits students to wear the Foundation's "check y♥urself (KEEP A BREAST)" bracelets.

girls to finish eating their lunches before escorting them to Braxmeier's office. Again, the girls' actions caused no disruption in the cafeteria, though R.T. told Braxmeier that one boy had immaturely commented either that he also "love[d] boobies" or that he "love[d] her boobies."

Braxmeier spoke to all three girls, and R.T. agreed to remove her bracelet. B.H. and K.M. stood firm, however, citing their rights to freedom of speech. The Middle School administrators were having none of it. They punished B.H. and K.M. by giving each of them one and a half days of in-school suspension and by forbidding them from attending the Winter Ball. The administrators notified the girls' families, explaining only that B.H. and K.M. were being disciplined for "disrespect," "defiance," and "disruption."

News of the bracelets quickly reached the rest of the Easton Area School District, which instituted a district-wide ban on the "I ♥ boobies! (KEEP A BREAST)" bracelets, effective on November 9, 2010. The only bracelet-related incident reported by school administrators occurred weeks after the district-wide ban: Two girls were talking about their bracelets at lunch when a boy who overheard them interrupted and said something like "I want boobies." He also made an inappropriate gesture with two red spherical candies. The boy admitted his "rude" comment and was suspended for one day.[3]

This was not the first time the Middle School had banned clothing that it found distasteful. Indeed, the School District's dress-code policy prohibits "clothing imprinted with nudity, vulgarity, obscenity, profanity, and double entendre pictures or slogans."[4] Under the policy, seventh-grade students at the Middle School have been asked to remove clothing promoting Hooters and Big Pecker's Bar & Grill, as well as clothing bearing the phrase "Save the ta-tas" (another breast-cancer-awareness slogan). Typically, students are disciplined only if they actually refuse to remove the offending apparel when asked to do so.

B. Procedural History

Through their mothers, B.H. and K.M. sued the School District under 42 U.S.C. § 1983.[5] Compl., ECF No. 1 ¶ 3, B.H. v. [*301] Easton Area Sch. Dist., No. 5:10-CV-06283-MAM (E.D. Pa. Nov. 15, 2010). They sought a temporary restraining order allowing them to attend the Winter Ball and a preliminary injunction against the bracelet ban. *B.H. v. Easton Area Sch. Dist.*, 827 F. Supp. 2d 392, 394 (E.D. Pa. 2011). At the District Court's urging, the School District reversed course and

---

3. After the district-wide ban was in place, there were several incidents of middle-school boys inappropriately touching girls, but they were unrelated to the "I ♥ boobies! (KEEP A BREAST)" bracelets.
4. B.H. and K.M. do not assert a facial challenge to the constitutionality of the dress-code policy.
5. The District Court had both federal-question jurisdiction under 28 U.S.C. § 1331 and § 1983 jurisdiction under 28 U.S.C. § 1343(a)(3). *See Max v. Republican Comm. of Lancaster Cnty.*, 587 F.3d 198, 199 n.1 (3d Cir. 2009).

permitted B.H. and K.M. to attend the Winter Ball while retaining the option to impose a comparable punishment if the bracelet ban was upheld. *Id.* The District Court accordingly denied the motion for a temporary restraining order. *Id.*

The District Court conducted an evidentiary hearing on the request for a preliminary injunction. It soon became clear that the School District's rationale for disciplining B.H. and K.M. had shifted. Although B.H.'s and K.M.'s disciplinary letters indicated only that they were being disciplined for "disrespect," "defiance," and "disruption," the School District ultimately based the ban on its dress-code policy[6] together with the bracelets' alleged sexual innuendo. According to the School District's witnesses, the Middle School assistant principals had conferred and concluded that the bracelets "conveyed a sexual double entendre" that could be harmful and confusing to students of different physical and sexual developmental levels. Sch. Dist.'s Br. at 9. And the principals believed that middle-school students, who often have immature views of sex, were particularly likely to interpret the bracelets that way. For its part, the Foundation explained that no one there "ever suggested that the phrase 'I (Heart) Boobies!' is meant to be sexy." App. 150. To that end, the Foundation had denied requests from truck stops, convenience stores, vending machine companies, and pornographers to sell the bracelets.

After the evidentiary hearing, the District Court preliminarily enjoined the School District's bracelet ban. According to the District Court, B.H. and K.M. were likely to succeed on the merits because the bracelets did not contain lewd speech under *Fraser* and did not threaten to substantially disrupt the school environment under *Tinker*. The District Court could find no other basis for regulating the student speech at issue. The School District appealed, and the District Court denied its request to stay the injunction pending this appeal.

II.

Although the District Court's preliminary injunction is not a final order, we have jurisdiction under 28 U.S.C. § 1292(a)(1), which grants appellate jurisdiction over "[i]nterlocutory orders of the district courts . . . granting, continuing, modifying, refusing, or dissolving injunctions." *See Sypniewski v. Warren Hills Reg'l Bd. of Educ.*, 307 F.3d 243, 252 n.10 (3d Cir. 2002). We review the District Court's factual findings for clear error, its legal conclusions *de novo*, and its ultimate decision

---

6. Even the Middle School administrators seemed unsure which words would be prohibited by the dress code. When deposed, Viglianti and principal Angela DiVietro testified that the word "breast" (as in apparel stating "keep-a-breast.org" or "breast cancer awareness") would be inappropriate because the word "breast" "can be construed as [having] a sexual connotation." App. 490, 497. At the District Court's evidentiary hearing, they reversed course. Viglianti stated that "keep-a-breast.org" would be appropriate "[i]n the context of Breast Cancer Awareness Month," and DiVeitro no longer believed the phrase "breast cancer awareness" was vulgar to middle-school students.

to grant the preliminary injunction [*302] for abuse of discretion. *Id.* at 252. Four factors determine whether a preliminary injunction is appropriate:

> (1) whether the movant has a reasonable probability of success on the merits; (2) whether the movant will be irreparably harmed by denying the injunction; (3) whether there will be greater harm to the nonmoving party if the injunction is granted; and (4) whether granting the injunction is in the public interest.

Id. (quoting *Highmark, Inc. v. UPMC Health Plan, Inc.*, 276 F.3d 160, 170 (3d Cir. 2001)). The District Court concluded that all four factors weighed in favor of B.H. and K.M. In school-speech cases, though, the first factor—the likelihood of success on the merits—tends to determine which way the other factors fall. *Id.* at 258. Because the same is true here, we focus first on B.H. and K.M.'s burden to show a likelihood of success on the merits. *Id.*

III.

The School District defends the bracelet ban as an exercise of its authority to restrict lewd, vulgar, profane, or plainly offensive student speech under *Fraser*. As to the novel question of *Fraser*'s scope, jurists seem to agree on one thing: "[t]he mode of analysis employed in *Fraser* is not entirely clear." *Morse*, 551 U.S. at 404.[7] On this point, we think the Supreme Court's student-speech cases are more consistent than they may first appear. As we explain, *Fraser* involved only *plainly* lewd speech. We hold that, under *Fraser*, a school may also categorically restrict speech that—although not *plainly* lewd, vulgar, or profane—could be interpreted by a reasonable observer as lewd, vulgar, or profane so long as it could not also plausibly be interpreted as commenting on a political or social issue. Because the "I ♥ boobies! (KEEP A BREAST)" bracelets are not plainly lewd and express support for a national breast-cancer-awareness campaign—unquestionably an important social issue—they may not be categorically restricted under *Fraser*.

A. The Supreme Court's Decision in *Fraser*

"[A]s a general matter, the First Amendment means that government has no power to restrict expression because of its message, its ideas, its subject matter, or its content." *Ashcroft v. ACLU*, 535 U.S. 564, 573, 122 S. Ct. 1700, 152 L. Ed.

---

7. The rest of the Supreme Court's student-speech jurisprudence might fairly be described as opaque. *See Morse*, 551 U.S. at 418 (Thomas, J., concurring) ("I am afraid that our jurisprudence now says that students have a right to speak in schools except when they do not...."); *id.* at 430 (Breyer, J., concurring in part and dissenting in part) ("[C]ourts have described the tests these cases suggest as complex and often difficult to apply."); *see, e.g., Doninger v. Niehoff*, 642 F.3d 334, 353 (2d Cir. 2011) ("The law governing restrictions on student speech can be difficult and confusing, even for lawyers, law professors, and judges. The relevant Supreme Court cases can be hard to reconcile, and courts often struggle with which standard applies in any particular case."); *Guiles ex rel. Guiles v. Marineau*, 461 F.3d 320, 326, 331 (2d Cir. 2006) (acknowledging "some lack of clarity in the Supreme Court's student-speech cases" and stating that the "exact contours of what is plainly offensive [under *Fraser*] is not so clear").

2d 771 (2002). Of course, there are exceptions. When acting as sovereign, the government is empowered to impose time, place, and manner restrictions on speech, *see Ward v. Rock Against Racism*, 491 U.S. 781, 791, 109 S. Ct. 2746, 105 L. Ed. 2d 661 (1989), make reasonable, content-based decisions about what speech is allowed on government property that is not fully open to the public, *see Ark. Educ. Television Comm'n v. Forbes*, 523 U.S. 666, 674-75, [*303] 118 S. Ct. 1633, 140 L. Ed. 2d 875 (1998), decide what viewpoints to espouse in its own speech or speech that might be attributed to it, *see Johanns v. Livestock Mktg. Ass'n*, 544 U.S. 550, 560, 125 S. Ct. 2055, 161 L. Ed. 2d 896 (2005), and categorically restrict unprotected speech, such as obscenity, *see Miller v. California*, 413 U.S. 15, 23, 93 S. Ct. 2607, 37 L. Ed. 2d 419 (1973).[8]

Sometimes, however, the government acts in capacities that go beyond being sovereign. In those capacities, it not only retains its sovereign authority over speech but also gains additional flexibility to regulate speech. *See In re Kendall*, 712 F.3d 814, 825, 58 V.I. 718 (3d Cir. 2013) (collecting examples). One of those other capacities is K-12 educator. Although "students do not 'shed their constitutional rights to freedom of speech or expression at the schoolhouse gate,'" the First Amendment has to be "applied in light of the special characteristics of the school environment" and thus students' rights to freedom of speech "are not automatically coextensive with the rights of adults in other settings." *Morse*, 551 U.S. at 396-97 (internal quotation marks and citations omitted).

The Supreme Court first expressed this principle nearly a half century ago. In 1965, the United States deployed over 200,000 troops to Vietnam as part of Operation Rolling Thunder—and thus began the Vietnam War. That war "divided this country as few other issues [e]ver have." *Tinker*, 393 U.S. at 524 (Black, J., dissenting). Public opposition to the war made its way into schools, and in one high-profile case, a group of high-school and middle-school students wore black armbands to express their opposition. *Id.* at 504 (majority opinion). School officials adopted a policy prohibiting the armbands and suspending any student who refused to remove it when asked. *Id.* Some students refused and were suspended. *Id.* The Supreme Court upheld their right to wear the armbands. *Id.* at 514. *Tinker* held that school officials may not restrict student speech without a reasonable forecast that the speech would substantially disrupt the school environment or invade the rights of others. *Id.* at 513. As nothing more than the "silent, passive expression of opinion, unaccompanied by any disorder or

---

8. Other examples of categorically unprotected speech include child pornography, *see New York v. Ferber*, 458 U.S. 747, 764-65, 102 S. Ct. 3348, 73 L. Ed. 2d 1113 (1982), advocacy that imminently incites lawless action, *see Brandenburg v. Ohio*, 395 U.S. 444, 447-48, 89 S. Ct. 1827, 23 L. Ed. 2d 430 (1969) (per curiam), fighting words, *see Chaplinsky v. New Hampshire*, 315 U.S. 568, 571-72, 62 S. Ct. 766, 86 L. Ed. 1031 (1942), true threats, *see Watts v. United States*, 394 U.S. 705, 708, 89 S. Ct. 1399, 22 L. Ed. 2d 664 (1969) (per curiam), commercial speech that is false, misleading, or proposes illegal transactions, *see Cent. Hudson Gas & Elec. Corp. v. Pub. Serv. Comm'n of N.Y.*, 447 U.S. 557, 562, 566-67, 100 S. Ct. 2343, 65 L. Ed. 2d 341 (1980), and some false statements of fact, *see United States v. Alvarez*, 567 U.S. 709, 132 S. Ct. 2537, 2546-47, 183 L. Ed. 2d 574 (2012).

disturbance on [the students'] part," the students' armbands were protected by the First Amendment. *Id.* at 508.

Under *Tinker*'s "general rule," the government may restrict school speech that threatens a specific and substantial disruption to the school environment or that "inva[des] . . . the rights of others."[9] **[*304]** *Saxe v. State College Area Sch. Dist.*, 240 F.3d 200, 211, 214 (3d Cir. 2001) (citing *Tinker*, 393 U.S. at 504). Since *Tinker*, the Supreme Court has identified three "narrow" circumstances in which the government may restrict student speech even when there is no risk of substantial disruption or invasion of others' rights. *Id.* at 212. First, the government may categorically restrict vulgar, lewd, profane, or plainly offensive speech in schools, even if it would not be obscene outside of school. *Fraser*, 478 U.S. at 683, 685. Second, the government may likewise restrict speech that "a reasonable observer would interpret as advocating illegal drug use" and that cannot "plausibly be interpreted as commenting on any political or social issue." *Morse*, 551 U.S. at 422 (Alito, J., concurring); *see also id.* at 403 (majority opinion) ("[T]his is plainly not a case about political debate over the criminalization of drug use or possession.").[10] And third, the government may impose restrictions on school-sponsored speech that are "reasonably related to legitimate pedagogical concerns" — a power usually lumped together with the other school-specific speech doctrines but that, strictly speaking, simply reflects the government's more general power as sovereign over government-sponsored speech.[11] *Hazelwood Sch. Dist. v. Kuhlmeier*, 484 U.S. 260, 273, 108 S. Ct. 562, 98 L. Ed. 2d 592 (1988).

The first exception is at issue here. We must determine the scope of the government's authority to categorically restrict vulgar, lewd, indecent, or plainly

---

9. We have not yet decided whether *Tinker* is limited to on-campus speech. *See J.S. v. Blue Mountain Sch. Dist.*, 650 F.3d 915, 926 & n.3 (3d Cir. 2011) (en banc) (declining to reach this issue); *see also id.* at 936 (Smith, J., concurring) ("I write separately to address a question that the majority opinion expressly leaves open: whether *Tinker* applies to off-campus speech in the first place.").

10. As we explain in Part III.B(2), the limitations that Justice Alito's concurrence places on the majority's opinion in *Morse* are controlling.

11. *Compare Pleasant Grove City, Utah v. Summum*, 555 U.S. 460, 468, 129 S. Ct. 1125, 172 L. Ed. 2d 853 (2009) (discussing the government-speech doctrine and explaining that "[a] government entity may exercise this same freedom to express its views when it receives assistance from private sources for the purpose of delivering a government-controlled message" (citing *Johanns*, 544 U.S. at 562)), *with Kuhlmeier*, 484 U.S. at 271, 273 (reaffirming the government's same authority to control speech that might be "reasonably perceive[ed] to bear the imprimatur of the school" in its role as K-12 educator); *see also* Eugene Volokh, *The First Amendment and the Government as K-12 Educator*, The Volokh Conspiracy (Oct. 31, 2011, 6:26 PM), http://www.volokh.com/2011/10/31/the-first-amendment-and-the-government-as-k-12-educator/ ("[*Kuhlmeier*] generally reflects broad government-as-speaker law, and not special rules related to the government as K-12 educator."); Michael J. O'Connor, Comment, *School Speech in the Internet Age: Do Students Shed Their Rights When They Pick Up a Mouse?*, 11 U. Pa. J. Const. L. 459, 469 (2009) ("*Hazelwood* . . . simply illustrates the idea that the school speech arena is not isolated from developments in wider First Amendment jurisprudence. . . . *Hazelwood* recognizes that schools are government actors and therefore are entitled to control speech that could be reasonably viewed as originating with them."); Gia B. Lee, *First Amendment Enforcement in Government Institutions and Programs*, 56 UCLA L. Rev. 1691, 1711-12 (2009) (similar).

offensive speech under *Fraser*. *Fraser* involved a high-school assembly during which a student "nominated a peer for class office through an 'an elaborate, graphic, and explicit sexual metaphor.'" *Saxe*, 240 F.3d at 212 (quoting *Fraser*, 478 U.S. at 677). Fraser's speech "glorif[ied] male sexuality":

> I know a man who is firm—he's firm in his pants, he's firm in his shirt, his character is firm—but most . . . of all, his belief in you, the students of Bethel, is firm. . . . Jeff Kuhlman [the candidate] is a man who takes his point and pounds it in. If necessary, he'll take an issue and nail it to the wall. He doesn't attack things in spurts, he drives hard, [*305] pushing and pushing until finally—he succeeds. . . . Jeff is a man who will go to the very end—even the climax, for each and every one of you. . . . So vote for Jeff for A.S.B. vice-president—he'll never come between you and the best our high school can be.

Fraser, 478 U.S. at 687 (Brennan, J., concurring). In response, "[s]ome students hooted and yelled; some by gestures simulated the sexual activities pointedly alluded to in [Fraser's] speech." *Id.* at 678 (majority opinion). Still "[o]ther students appeared to be bewildered and embarrassed by the speech." *Id.* The school suspended Fraser and took him out of the running for graduation speaker. *Id.*

The Supreme Court upheld Fraser's suspension. *Id.* at 683. Rather than requiring a reasonable forecast of substantial disruption under *Tinker*, the Court held that lewd, vulgar, indecent, and plainly offensive student speech is categorically unprotected in school, even if it falls short of obscenity and would have been protected outside school. *Saxe*, 240 F.3d at 213 (discussing *Fraser*); *Morse*, 551 U.S. at 405 ("Had Fraser delivered the same speech in a public forum outside the school context, it would have been protected."); *Fraser*, 478 U.S. at 688 (Blackmun, J., concurring) ("If [Fraser] had given the same speech outside of the school environment, he could not have been penalized simply because government officials considered his language to be inappropriate."). For this proposition, the Court relied on precedent holding that the government can restrict expression that would be obscene from a minor's perspective—even though it would not be obscene in an adult's view—where minors are either a captive audience or the intended recipients of the speech. *See Fraser*, 478 U.S. at 684-85 (relying on *Ginsberg v. New York*, 390 U.S. 629, 635-37, 88 S. Ct. 1274, 20 L. Ed. 2d 195 & nn.4-5 (1968) (upholding criminal punishment for selling to minors any picture depicting nudity); *Bd. of Educ., Island Trees Union Free Sch. Dist. No. 26 v. Pico*, 457 U.S. 853, 870, 102 S. Ct. 2799, 73 L. Ed. 2d 435 (1982) (plurality opinion) (acknowledging that the Free Speech Clause would allow a local board of education to remove "pervasively vulgar" books from school libraries); and *FCC v. Pacifica Found.*, 438 U.S. 726, 749-50, 98 S. Ct. 3026, 57 L. Ed. 2d 1073 (1978) (rejecting a Free Speech Clause challenge to the FCC's broad leeway to regulate indecent-but-not-obscene material on broadcast television during hours when children were likely to watch)).

Fraser did no more than extend these obscenity-to-minors[12] cases to another place where minors are a captive audience—schools. Indeed, as the Court explained, schools are tasked with more than **[*306]** just "educating our youth" about "books, the curriculum, and the civics class." *Id.* at 681. Society also expects schools to "teach[] students the boundaries of socially appropriate behavior," including the "fundamental values of 'habits and manners of civility' essential to a democratic society." *Id.* at 681, 683 (citation omitted). Consequently, Fraser's "sexually explicit monologue" was not protected. *Id.* at 685.

It is important to recognize what was not at stake in *Fraser*. *Fraser* addressed only a school's power over speech that was plainly lewd—not speech that a reasonable observer could interpret as either lewd or non-lewd. *See, e.g., Doninger v. Niehoff*, 527 F.3d 41, 49 (2d Cir. 2008) ("[*Fraser*'s] reference to 'plainly offensive' speech must be understood in light of the vulgar, lewd, and sexually explicit language that was at issue in [that] case."); *Chandler v. McMinnville Sch. Dist.*, 978 F.2d 524, 530 (9th Cir. 1992) (interpreting *Fraser* as limited to "per se vulgar, lewd, obscene, or plainly offensive" school speech). After all, the Court believed Fraser's speech to be "plainly offensive to both teachers and students—indeed to any mature person."[13] *Fraser*, 478 U.S. at 683.

And because it was plainly lewd, the Court did not believe that Fraser's speech could plausibly be interpreted as political or social commentary. In hindsight, it might be tempting to believe that Fraser's speech was political because it was made in the context of a student election. *Cf. Citizens United v. FEC*, 558 U.S. 310, 130 S. Ct. 876, 898, 175 L. Ed. 2d 753 (2010) (describing the importance of political speech as the "means to hold officials accountable to the people"). But that kind of revisionist history is belied by both the logic and language of *Fraser*. "*Fraser* permits a school to prohibit words that 'offend for the same reasons that obscenity offends.'" *Saxe*, 240 F.3d at 213 (quoting *Fraser*, 478 U.S. at 685).

---

12. *See Brown v. Entm't Merchs. Ass'n*, 564 U.S. 786, 131 S. Ct. 2729, 2735, 180 L. Ed. 2d 708 (2011) (describing *Ginsberg* as regulating "obscenity for minors"); *Reno v. ACLU*, 521 U.S. 844, 869, 117 S. Ct. 2329, 138 L. Ed. 2d 874 (1997) (reaffirming the government's power under *Pacifica* and *Ginsberg* to "'protect[] the physical and psychological well-being of minors' which extended to shield them from indecent messages that are not obscene by adult standards" (quoting *Sable Comm'cns of Cal., Inc. v. FCC*, 492 U.S. 115, 126, 109 S. Ct. 2829, 106 L. Ed. 2d 93 (1989))); *Pacifica Found.*, 438 U.S. at 767 (Brennan, J., dissenting) (agreeing with the majority that the government could regulate "variable obscenity" or "obscenity to minors" on broadcast television, but disagreeing with the majority that the Carlin monologue met that standard); *Erznoznik v. City of Jacksonville*, 422 U.S. 205, 213 n.10, 95 S. Ct. 2268, 45 L. Ed. 2d 125 (1975) (describing *Ginsberg* as involving "obscenity as to minors"); *Ginsberg*, 390 U.S. at 635 n.4 (using the label "variable obscenity").

13. Of course, Fraser's speech might "seem[] distinctly lacking in shock value" today, especially "from the perspective enabled by 25 years of erosion of refinement in the use of language." *Zamecnik v. Indian Prairie Sch. Dist. No. 204*, 636 F.3d 874, 877 (7th Cir. 2011); *see also Fraser*, 478 U.S. at 691 (Stevens, J., dissenting) (noting that Clark Gable's famous use of the word "damn" in "Frankly, my dear, I don't give a damn" "shocked the Nation" when Justice Stevens was a high school student but had become "less offensive" by the time of *Fraser*). Any such change in perspective, however, is irrelevant to our examination of the Court's interpretation of Fraser's speech and its reasoning.

Obscenity, in turn, offends because it is "no essential part of any exposition of ideas, and [is] of such slight social value as a step to truth that any benefit that may be derived from [it] is clearly outweighed by the social interest in order and morality." *Fraser*, 478 U.S. at 683 (quoting *Pacifica Found.*, 438 U.S. at 746 (plurality opinion)). In other words, obscenity and obscenity to minors, like "other historically unprotected categories of speech," have little or no political or social value. *United States v. Stevens*, 559 U.S. 460, 130 S. Ct. 1577, 1585, 176 L. Ed. 2d 435 (2010). By concluding that Fraser's speech met the obscenity-to-minors standard, the Court necessarily implied that his speech could not be interpreted as having "serious" political value. *Miller*, 413 U.S. at 24.

In fact, the majority in *Fraser* made this explicit. "[T]he *Fraser* [C]ourt distinguished its holding from *Tinker* in part on the absence of any political message in Fraser's speech." *Guiles ex rel. Guiles v. Marineau*, 461 F.3d 320, 326, 328 (2d Cir. 2006). In the Court's own words, there [*307] was a "marked distinction between the political 'message' of the armbands in *Tinker* and the *sexual* content of [Fraser's] speech." *Fraser*, 478 U.S. at 680 (emphasis added); *see also Defoe ex rel. Defoe v. Spiva*, 625 F.3d 324, 332 (6th Cir. 2010) ("*Tinker* governs this case because by wearing clothing bearing images of the Confederate flag, Tom Defoe engaged in 'pure speech,' which is protected by the First Amendment, and thus *Fraser* would not apply."). Several courts of appeals have similarly interpreted *Fraser*. *Guiles*, 461 F.3d at 326, 328; *Newsom ex rel. Newsom v. Albemarle Cnty. Sch. Bd.*, 354 F.3d 249, 256 (4th Cir. 2003) (explaining that *Fraser* "distinguish[ed] *Tinker* on the basis that the lewd, vulgar, and plainly offensive speech was 'unrelated to any political viewpoint'" (quoting *Fraser*, 478 U.S. at 685)); *Chandler*, 978 F.2d at 532 n.2 (Goodwin, J., concurring) (concluding that *Fraser* does not apply because "this case clearly involves political speech"). And the Supreme Court later characterized *Fraser*'s reasoning the same way. *Morse*, 551 U.S. at 404 (noting that *Fraser* was "plainly attuned" to the sexual, non-political "content of Fraser's speech"). In fact, *Morse* refused to "stretch[] *Fraser*" so far as to "encompass any speech that could fit under some definition of 'offensive'" out of a fear that "much political and religious speech might be perceived as offensive to some." *Id.* at 409. *Fraser* therefore involved plainly lewd speech that did not comment on political or social issues.

B. How Far Does a School's Authority Under *Fraser* Extend?

The School District asks us to extend *Fraser* in at least two ways: to reach speech that is ambiguously lewd, vulgar, or profane and to reach speech on political or social issues.[14] The first step is justified, but the second is not.

---

14. *Fraser* differs from this case in a third way: *Fraser* involved speech at an official school assembly, whereas the School District's bracelet ban extends to the entire school day, not just school-sponsored functions. But like other courts of appeals, we do not think that this difference matters. *See, e.g., R.O. ex rel. Ochshorn v. Ithaca City Sch. Dist.*, 645 F.3d 533, 542 (2d Cir. 2011) ("[W]e have not interpreted *Fraser* as limited either to regulation of school-sponsored speech or to the spoken word."); *Chandler*, 978 F.2d at 529 (concluding that restriction of vulgar, lewd, and plainly offensive speech under *Fraser* is

[*308] 1. Under *Fraser*, schools may restrict ambiguously lewd speech only if it cannot plausibly be interpreted as commenting on a social or political matter.

Although *Fraser* involved plainly lewd, vulgar, profane, or offensive speech that "offends for the same reasons obscenity offends," *Saxe*, 240 F.3d at 213 (quoting *Fraser*, 478 U.S. at 685), student speech need not rise to that level to be restricted under *Fraser*. We conclude that schools may also categorically restrict ambiguous speech that a reasonable observer could interpret as lewd, vulgar, profane, or offensive — unless, as explained below, the speech could also plausibly be interpreted as commenting on a political or social issue. After all, *Fraser* made clear that "the determination of what manner of speech in the classroom or in school assembly is inappropriate properly rests with the school board." 478 U.S. at 683. The Supreme Court's three other student-speech cases suggest that courts should defer to a school's decisions to restrict what a reasonable observer would interpret as lewd, vulgar, profane, or offensive. *See Morse*, 551 U.S. at 403 (explaining that, under *Tinker*, courts determine whether school officials have "reasonably conclude[d]" that student speech will substantially disrupt the school); *id.* at 405 (explaining that, under *Kuhlmeier*, courts uphold a school's reasonable, pedagogically related restrictions on speech that an observer could reasonably attribute to the school); *id.* at 422 (Alito, J., concurring) (explaining that schools may restrict student speech that could "reasonably be regarded as encouraging illegal drug use" and that could not plausibly be interpreted as commenting on a political or social issue). This makes sense. School officials know the age, maturity, and other characteristics of their students far better than judges do. Our review is restricted to a cold and distant record. And we must take into

---

not limited to speech "given at an official school assembly"); Bystrom by and through *Bystrom v. Fridley High Sch., Indep. Sch. Dist. No. 14*, 822 F.2d 747, 753 (8th Cir. 1987) ("It is true that [*Fraser*] involved a speech given before a student assembly.... [But] [t]his possible difference, in our view, does not amount to a legal distinction making the *Bethel* rule inapplicable here."). As we explained, *Fraser* reflected an extension of the Court's obscenity-to-minors jurisprudence, which permits the government to restrict lewd speech to children where children are either a captive audience or the intended recipients of the speech. Children are just as much of a captive audience in the hallways, cafeteria, or locker rooms as they are in official school assemblies and classrooms. Naturally, then, we have never described a school's authority under *Fraser* as being limited to official school functions and classrooms. *See, e.g., J.S.*, 650 F.3d at 927 ("The first exception is set out in *Fraser*, which we interpreted to permit school officials to regulate "'lewd,' 'vulgar,' 'indecent,' and 'plainly offensive' speech *in school*." (emphasis in original) (quoting *Saxe*, 240 F.3d at 213)). Although Justice Brennan's concurrence and Justice Stevens's dissent in *Fraser* suggested that this difference might matter, nothing in the majority opinion endorsed their distinction. *See Fraser*, 478 U.S. at 689 (Brennan, J., concurring) (opining that Fraser's "speech may well have been protected had he given it in school but under different circumstances, where the school's legitimate interests in teaching and maintaining civil public discourse were less weighty"); *id.* at 696 (Stevens, J., dissenting) ("It seems fairly obvious that [Fraser's] speech would be inappropriate in certain classroom and formal social settings. On the other hand, in a locker room or perhaps in a school corridor the metaphor in the speech might be regarded as rather routine comment."). Indeed, if *Fraser* were so limited, then a school's authority under *Fraser* would largely merge with *its* power to reasonably regulate school-sponsored speech under *Kuhlmeier*, yet we have always viewed *Fraser* and *Kuhlmeier* as separate exceptions to *Tinker*. *See, e.g., J.S.*, 650 F.3d at 927.

account that these same officials must often act "suddenly and unexpectedly" based on their experience. *Id.* at 409-10 (majority opinion); see, e.g., *Walker-Serrano ex rel. Walker v. Leonard*, 325 F.3d 412, 416-17 (3d Cir. 2003) ("There can be little doubt that speech appropriate for eighteen-year-old high school students is not necessarily acceptable for seven-year-old grammar school students. Human sexuality provides the most obvious example of age-sensitive matter . . . ." (citing *Fraser*, 478 U.S. at 683-84)); *Sypniewski*, 307 F.3d at 266 ("What is necessary in one school at one time will not be necessary elsewhere and at other times.").

It remains the job of judges, nonetheless, to determine whether a reasonable observer could interpret student speech as lewd, profane, vulgar, or offensive. *See Morse*, 551 U.S. at 402 (taking the same approach with respect to the message of drug advocacy on Frederick's banner); *see also Christian Legal Soc'y Chapter of the Univ. of Cal. v. Martinez*, 561 U.S. 661, 130 S. Ct. 2971, 2988, 177 L. Ed. 2d 838 (2010) ("This Court is the final arbiter of the question whether a public university has exceeded constitutional constraints, and we owe no deference [*309] to universities when we consider that question."). Whether a reasonable observer could interpret student speech as lewd, profane, vulgar, or offensive depends on the plausibility of the school's interpretation in light of competing meanings; the context, content, and form of the speech; and the age and maturity of the students. *See, e.g., Chandler*, 978 F.2d at 530 (analyzing the word "scab" on buttons worn by students during a teacher strike to determine whether it was a vulgar, offensive epithet or just "common parlance" and concluding that, at the motion-to-dismiss stage, *Fraser* did not apply).

Although this is a highly contextual inquiry, several rules apply. A reasonable observer would not adopt an acontextual interpretation, and the subjective intent of the speaker is irrelevant. *See Morse*, 551 U.S. at 401-02 (explaining that Frederick's desire to appear on television "was a description of [his] *motive* for displaying the banner" and "not an interpretation of what the banner sa[id]"); *see also Saxe*, 240 F.3d at 216-17 (noting that students' intent to offend or disrupt does not satisfy *Tinker*). And *Fraser* is not a blank check to categorically restrict any speech that touches on sex or any speech that has the potential to offend. *See Morse*, 551 U.S. at 401, 409 (refusing to "stretch[] *Fraser*" so far as "to encompass any speech that could fit under some definition of 'offensive' and rejecting the argument that the "BONG HiTS 4 JESUS" message on Frederick's banner could be banned under *Fraser*, even though it "is no doubt offensive to some"); *accord* Eugene Volokh, *May 'Jesus Is Not a Homophobe' T-shirt Be Banned From Public High School As 'Indecent' And 'Sexual'?*, The Volokh Conspiracy (Apr. 4, 2012, 3:36 PM), http://www.volokh.com/2012/04/04/may-jesus-was-not-a-homophobe-T-shirt-be-banned-from-public-high-school-as-indecent-and-sexual/ ("But *Fraser* . . . hardly suggested that all speech on political and religious questions related to sexuality and sexual orientation could be banned from public high school."). After all, a school's mission to mold students into citizens capable of engaging in civil discourse includes teaching students of sufficient age and maturity how to navigate debates touching on sex.

2. *Fraser* does not permit a school to restrict ambiguously lewd speech that can also plausibly be interpreted as commenting on a social or political issue.

A school's leeway to categorically restrict ambiguously lewd speech, however, ends when that speech could also plausibly be interpreted as expressing a view on a political or social issue. Justices Alito and Kennedy's concurrence in *Morse* adopted a similar protection for political speech that could be interpreted as illegal drug advocacy. Their narrower rationale protecting political speech limits and controls the majority opinion in *Morse*, and it applies with even greater force to ambiguously lewd speech . . . .

[*315] Consequently, we hold that the *Fraser* exception does not permit ambiguously lewd speech to be categorically restricted if it can plausibly be interpreted as political or social speech.

3. Under *Fraser*, schools may restrict plainly lewd speech regardless of whether it could plausibly be interpreted as social or political commentary.

As the Supreme Court made clear in *Fraser*, though, schools may restrict plainly lewd speech regardless of whether it could plausibly be interpreted to comment on a political or social issue. *Fraser*, 478 U.S. at 682 ("[T]he First Amendment gives a high school student the classroom right to wear Tinker's armband, but not Cohen's ["Fuck the Draft"] jacket."). That is true by definition. [*316] Plainly lewd speech "offends for the same reasons obscenity offends" because the speech in that category is "no essential part of any exposition of ideas" and thus carries very "slight social value." *Id.* at 683 (quoting *Pacifica Found.*, 438 U.S. at 746 (plurality opinion)). As with obscenity in general, obscenity to minors, and all other historically unprotected categories of speech, "the evil to be restricted so overwhelmingly outweighs the expressive interests, if any, at stake, that no process of case-by-case adjudication is required" because "the balance of competing interests is clearly struck." *Stevens*, 130 S. Ct. at 1585-86 (quoting *New York v. Ferber*, 458 U.S. 747, 763-64, 102 S. Ct. 3348, 73 L. Ed. 2d 1113 (1982)). In other words, we do not engage in a case-by-case determination of whether obscenity to minors—and by extension, plainly lewd speech under *Fraser*—carries social value. As a result, schools may continue to regulate plainly lewd, vulgar, profane, or offensive speech under *Fraser* even if a particular instance of such speech can "plausibly be interpreted as commenting on any political or social issue." *Morse*, 551 U.S. at 422 (Alito, J., concurring).

In response, the School District recites a mantra that has *Fraser* providing schools the ultimate discretion to define what is lewd and vulgar. It relies on the Supreme Court's sentiment that schools may define their "basic educational mission" and prohibit student speech that is inconsistent with that mission. *Kuhlmeier*, 484

U.S. at 266-67.[21] Indeed, before *Morse*, some courts of appeals adopted that broad interpretation of the Supreme Court's student-speech cases. *See, e.g., LaVine v. Blaine Sch. Dist.*, 257 F.3d 981, 988 (9th Cir. 2001) ("[A] school need not tolerate student speech that is inconsistent with its basic educational mission."); *Boroff v. Van Wert City Bd. of Educ.*, 220 F.3d 465, 470 (6th Cir. 2000) ("[W]here Boroff's T-shirts contain symbols and words that promote values that are so patently contrary to the school's educational mission, the School has the authority, under the circumstances of this case, to prohibit those T-shirts [under *Fraser*].").

Whatever the face value of those sentiments, such sweeping and total deference to school officials is incompatible with the Supreme Court's teachings. In *Tinker*, *Hazelwood*, and *Morse*, the Supreme Court independently evaluated the meaning of the student's speech and the reasonableness of the school's interpretation and actions. There is no reason the school's authority under *Fraser* should receive special treatment. More importantly, such an approach would swallow the other student-speech cases, including *Tinker*, effectively eliminating judicial review of student-speech restrictions. *See Guiles*, 461 F.3d at 327 (making this point). That is precisely why the Supreme Court in *Morse* explicitly rejected total deference to school officials:

> [*317] The opinion of the Court does not endorse the broad argument advanced by petitioners and the United States that the First Amendment permits public school officials to censor any student speech that interferes with a school's "educational mission." . . . The "educational mission" argument would give public school authorities a license to suppress speech on political and social issues based on disagreement with the viewpoint expressed. The argument, therefore, strikes at the very heart of the First Amendment.

Morse, 551 U.S. at 423 (Alito, J., concurring).

Instead, *Morse* settled on a narrower view of deference, deferring to a school administrator's "reasonable judgment that Frederick's sign qualified as drug advocacy" only if the speech could not plausibly be interpreted as commenting on a political or social issue. *Morse*, 551 U.S. at 441 (Stevens, J., dissenting); *see also id.* at 408 (majority opinion) ("[S]chools [may] restrict student expression that they reasonably regard as promoting illegal drug use."); *id.* at 422 (Alito, J., concurring) ("[A] public school may restrict speech that a reasonable observer would interpret as advocating illegal drug use . . . ."). Our approach to lewd

---

21. *See also Fraser*, 478 U.S. at 683 ("[T]he determination of what manner of speech in the classroom or in school assembly is inappropriate properly rests with the school board."); *Pico*, 457 U.S. at 864 ("[F]ederal courts should not ordinarily 'intervene in the resolution of conflicts which arise in the daily operation of school systems.'" (quoting *Epperson v. Arkansas*, 393 U.S. 97, 104, 89 S. Ct. 266, 21 L. Ed. 2d 228 (1968))); *Wood v. Strickland*, 420 U.S. 308, 326, 95 S. Ct. 992, 43 L. Ed. 2d 214 (1975) ("It is not the role of the federal courts to set aside decisions of school administrators which the court may view as lacking a basis in wisdom or compassion."); *see also Kuhlmeier*, 484 U.S. at 273 ("[T]he education of the Nation's youth is primarily the responsibility of parents, teachers, and state and local school officials, and not of federal judges.").

speech provides the same degree of deference to schools as the Court did in *Morse*. We defer to a school's reasonable judgment that an observer could interpret ambiguous speech as lewd, vulgar, profane, or offensive only if the speech could not plausibly be interpreted as commenting on a political or social issue.

The School District invokes a parade of horribles that, in its view, would follow from our framework: protecting ambiguously lewd speech that comments on political or social issues — like the bracelets in this case — will encourage students to engage in more egregiously sexualized advocacy campaigns, which the schools will be obliged to allow. *See* Pa. Sch. Bd. Ass'n Amicus Br. in Supp. of Appellant at 19 (listing examples, including "I ♥ Balls!" apparel for testicular cancer, and "I ♥ Va Jay Jays" apparel for the Human Papillomaviruses); App. 275-76 (raising the possibility of apparel bearing the slogans "I ♥ Balls!" or "I ♥ Titties!"). Like all slippery-slope arguments, the School District's point can be inverted with equal logical force. If schools can categorically regulate terms like "boobies" even when the message comments on a social or political issue, schools could eliminate all student speech touching on sex or merely having the potential to offend. *See* Frederick Schauer, *Slippery Slopes*, 99 Harv. L. Rev. 361, 381 (1985) ("[I]n virtually every case in which a slippery slope argument is made, the opposing party could with equal formal and linguistic logic also make a slippery slope claim."). The ease of turning a slippery-slope argument on its head explains why the persuasiveness of such a contention does not depend on its logical validity. *Id.* Instead, the correctness of a slippery-slope argument depends on an empirical prediction that a proposed rule will increase the likelihood of some other undesired outcome occurring. *Id.* ("To some people, one argument will seem more persuasive than the other because the underlying empirical reality . . . makes one equally logical possibility seem substantially more likely to occur than the other."); *see also* Eugene Volokh, *The Mechanism of the Slippery Slope*, 116 Harv. L. Rev. 1026, 1066-71 (2003) (making a similar point in the context of extending precedent). Because courts usually lack the data necessary for such a prediction, "fear of . . . what's at the bottom of a long, slippery slope is not a good reason for **[*318]** today's decision." *Marozsan v. United States*, 852 F.2d 1469, 1499 (7th Cir. 1988) (en banc) (Easterbrook, J., dissenting). "The terror of extreme hypotheticals produces much bad law," and so our answer to the School District's "extreme hypothetical[s]" is that we will "cross that bridge when we come to it." *Id.*

To make matters worse, the School District has greased the supposedly slippery slope by omitting any empirical evidence. We have no reason to think either that the parents of middle-school students will be willing to allow their children to wear apparel advocating political or social messages in egregious terms or that a student will overcome the typical middle-schooler's embarrassment, immaturity, and social pressures by wearing such apparel. And many of the School District's hypotheticals pose no worries under our framework. A school could categorically restrict an "I ♥ tits! (KEEP A BREAST)" bracelet because, as the Supreme Court explained in *Pacifica*, the word "tits" (and also presumably the diminutive "titties") is a patently offensive reference to sexual organs and thus obscene to minors. *See Pacifica Found.*, 438 U.S. at 745-46 (plurality opinion) (explaining that the comedian George Carlin's seven "dirty" words, which includes "tits," "offend for the same reasons that obscenity offends"); *see also LaVine*, 257 F.3d at 989 (concluding that a poem "filled with imagery of violent death and suicide" was not "vulgar, lewd, obscene, or plainly offensive" because it was "not 'an elaborate, graphic, and explicit sexual metaphor' as was the student's speech in *Fraser*, nor [did] it contain the infamous seven words that cannot be said on the public airwaves"); *cf. FCC v. Fox Television Stations, Inc.*, 556 U.S. 502, 517-18, 129 S. Ct. 1800, 173 L. Ed. 2d 738 (2009) (concluding it was not arbitrary or capricious for the FCC to regulate even "isolated uses of sexual and excretory words," including Carlin's seven "dirty" words, because "[e]ven isolated utterances can be made in pander[ing], . . . vulgar and shocking manners" and can thus "constitute harmful first blow[s] to children" (alterations in original)). The same is true of a student's drawings of stick figures in sexual positions, even if used to promote contraceptive use. *Cf. R.O. ex rel. Ochshorn City Sch. Dist.*, 645 F.3d 533, 543 (2d Cir. 2011). And even if students engage in more questionable speech, the school retains the government's normal sovereign authority to regulate speech as well as its additional powers as educator to restrict speech under *Tinker, Kuhlmeier*, and *Morse*. *See, e.g., Hardwick v. Heyward*, 711 F.3d 426, 440 (4th Cir. 2013) (holding that a school's prohibition on wearing T-shirts depicting the Confederate battle flag was permissible under *Tinker* because of a history of racial tension and disruptions related to the Confederate flag).

By contrast, there is empirical support for the opposite worry. Some schools, if empowered to do so, might eliminate all student speech touching on sex or merely having the potential to offend. Indeed, the Middle School's administrators seemed inclined to do just that. They initially testified that they could ban the word "breast," even if used in the context of a breast-cancer-awareness campaign, because the word, by itself, "can be construed as [having] a sexual connotation." App. 490, 497. If anything, the fear of a slippery slope cuts against the School District.

In a similar vein, we need not speculate on context-dependent hypotheticals to give guidance to schools and district courts. The fault lines of our framework are adequately mapped out in the rest of First Amendment jurisprudence. The Supreme Court's obscenity-to-minors [*319] case law marks the contours of plainly lewd speech. *See, e.g., Brown v. Entm't Merchs. Ass'n*, 564 U.S. 786, 131 S. Ct. 2729, 2735, 180 L. Ed. 2d 708 (refusing to extend the categorical nonprotection for obscenity to minors to speech that is violent from a minor's perspective); *Ginsberg*, 390 U.S. at 638 (approving a state prohibition on selling minors sexual material that would be obscene from the minor's perspective). Those contours necessarily admit of some flexibility and can be "adjust[ed] . . . 'to social realities by permitting the [sexual] appeal of this type of material to be assessed'" from the minors' perspective. *Id.; see also Fox Television Stations, Inc.*, 556 U.S. at 520 (explaining that based on the obscenity-to-minors case law, the FCC properly "dr[aws] distinctions between the offensiveness of particular words based upon the context in which they appeared" on case-by-case basis without having to rely on empirical evidence as to the degree of offensiveness). And the government is not a stranger to determining whether speech plausibly comments on a political or social issue. For that, we look to case law on whether speech involves a matter of public concern. *See, e.g., Garcetti v. Ceballos*, 547 U.S. 410, 418, 126 S. Ct. 1951, 164 L. Ed. 2d 689 (2006) ("*Pickering* and the cases decided in its wake identify two inquiries to guide interpretation of the constitutional protections accorded to public employee speech. The first requires determining whether the employee spoke as a citizen on a matter of public concern. . . . If the answer is yes, then the possibility of a First Amendment claim arises."). Of course, these rules lack "perfect clarity"—just as every legal rule contains fuzzy borders. *Brown*, 131 S. Ct. at 2764 (Breyer, J., dissenting); *cf. United States v. Williams*, 553 U.S. 285, 304, 128 S. Ct. 1830, 170 L. Ed. 2d 650 (2008) ("[P]erfect clarity and precise guidance have never been required even of regulations that restrict expressive activity."). Even so, just because a "precise standard" for political speech or plain lewdness (obscenity to minors) "proves elusive," it is still "easy enough to identify instances that fall within a legitimate regulation." *Brown*, 131 S. Ct. at 2764 (Breyer, J., dissenting). Over time, the fault lines demarcating plainly lewd speech and political or social speech will settle and become more rule-like as precedent accumulates.

To recap: Under the government's sovereign authority, a school may categorically ban obscenity, fighting words, and the like in schools; the student-speech cases do not supplant the government's sovereign powers to regulate speech. *See, e.g., Doe v. Pulaski Cnty. Special Sch. Dist.*, 306 F.3d 616, 626, 626-27 (8th Cir. 2002) (en banc) (holding that the government, as K-12 educator, could punish a student for making a true threat); *Cuff ex rel. B.C. v. Valley Cent. Sch. Dist.*, 677 F.3d 109, 118 (2d Cir. 2012) (Pooler, J., dissenting) ("Indeed, despite the expansion of school-specific exceptions to the First Amendment's general prohibition against government restrictions on speech, certain well-settled rules apply to adults and adolescents alike."). Under *Fraser*, a school may categorically restrict plainly lewd, vulgar, or profane speech that "offends for the same reasons obscenity offends" regardless of whether it can plausibly be interpreted as commenting on social or political issues. *Saxe*, 240 F.3d at 213 (quoting *Fraser*, 478 U.S. at 685). As we have explained, see *supra* at 20-21, plainly lewd speech cannot, by definition, be plausibly interpreted as political or social commentary because the speech offends for the same reason obscenity offends and thus has slight social value. *Fraser* also permits [*320] a school to categorically restrict ambiguous speech that a reasonable observer could interpret as having a lewd, vulgar, or profane meaning so long as it could not also plausibly be interpreted as commenting on a social or political issue. But *Fraser* does not permit a school to categorically restrict ambiguous speech that a reasonable observer could interpret as having a lewd, vulgar, or profane meaning and could plausibly interpret as commenting on a social or political issue. And of course, if a reasonable observer could not interpret the speech as lewd, vulgar, or profane, then *Fraser* simply does not apply. As always, a school's other powers over student speech under *Tinker, Kuhlmeier,* and *Morse* remain as a backstop.

C. The Middle School's Ban on "I ♥ Boobies! (KEEP A BREAST)" Bracelets

Under this framework, the School District's bracelet ban is an open-and-shut case. The "I ♥ boobies! (KEEP A BREAST)" bracelets are not plainly lewd. The slogan bears no resemblance to Fraser's "pervasive sexual innuendo" that was "plainly offensive to both teachers and students." *Fraser*, 478 U.S. at 683. Teachers had to request guidance about how to deal with the bracelets, and school administrators did not conclude that the bracelets were vulgar until B.H. and K.M. had worn them every day for nearly two months. In addition, the Middle School used the term "boobies" in announcing the bracelet ban over the public address system and the school television station. What's more, the bracelets do not contain language remotely akin to the seven words that are considered obscene to minors on broadcast television. *Pacifica Found.*, 438 U.S. at 745-46 (plurality opinion); *LaVine*, 257 F.3d at 989 (concluding that speech was not vulgar, lewd, obscene, or plainly offensive because it was "not 'an elaborate, graphic, and explicit sexual metaphor' as was the student's speech in *Fraser*, nor [did] it contain the infamous seven words that cannot be said on the public airwaves" under *Pacifica*). Indeed, the term "boobie" is no more than a sophomoric synonym for "breast." And as the School District also concedes, a reasonable observer would plausibly interpret the bracelets as part of a national breast-cancer-awareness campaign, an undeniably important social issue. Oral Arg. Tr. at 10:11-16; *see also K.J. ex rel. Braun v. Sauk Prairie Sch. Dist.*, No. 11-CV-622, 2012 U.S. Dist. LEXIS 187689, at *18 (W.D. Wis. Feb. 6, 2012) ("When one reads the entire phrase, it is clearly a message designed to promote breast cancer awareness."). Accordingly, the bracelets cannot be categorically banned under *Fraser*.[22]

IV.

Fraser, of course, is only one of four school-specific avenues for regulating student speech.[23] The parties rightly agree [*321] that *Kuhlmeier* and *Morse* do not apply: no one could reasonably believe that the Middle School was somehow involved in the morning fashion decisions of a few students, and no one could reasonably interpret the bracelets as advocating illegal drug use.

---

22. Because we conclude that the slogan is not plainly lewd and is plausibly interpreted as commenting on a social issue, the bracelets are protected under *Fraser*. As a result, we need not determine whether a reasonable observer could interpret the bracelets' slogan as lewd.

23. As the Supreme Court has recently reaffirmed, there *might* be other exceptions to *Tinker* that have not yet been identified by the courts. See *Morse*, 551 U.S. at 408-09 (identifying a new exception to the *Tinker* framework for speech that is reasonably interpreted as advocating illegal drug use and that is not plausibly interpreted as commenting on any political or social issue). *Compare id.* at 405 ("*Fraser* established that the mode of analysis set forth in *Tinker* is not absolute."), *and id.* at 406 ("And, like *Fraser*, [*Kuhlmeier*] confirms that the rule of *Tinker* is not the only basis for restricting student speech."), *with id.* at 423 (Alito, J., concurring) ("I join the opinion of the Court on the understanding that the opinion does not hold that the special characteristics of the public schools *necessarily* justify any other speech restrictions." (emphasis added)). Here, however, the School District relies solely on the existing school-speech framework and does not propose any new bases for restricting student speech.

That leaves only *Tinker* as possible support for the School District's ban. Under *Tinker*'s "general rule," the government may restrict school speech "that threatens a specific and substantial disruption to the school environment" or "inva[des] . . . the rights of others." *Saxe*, 240 F.3d at 211 (citing *Tinker*, 393 U.S. at 504). "[I]f a school can point to a well-founded expectation of disruption—especially one based on past incidents arising out of similar speech—the restriction may pass constitutional muster." *Id.* at 212; *J.S. v. Blue Mountain Sch. Dist.*, 650 F.3d 915, 928 (3d Cir. 2011) (en banc) ("[T]he School District need not prove with absolute certainty that substantial disruption will occur."). The School District has the burden of showing that the bracelet ban is constitutional under *Tinker*. *See J.S.*, 650 F.3d at 928. That it cannot do.

Tinker meant what it said: "a specific and significant fear of disruption, not just some remote apprehension of disturbance." *Id.* Tinker's black armbands did not meet this standard, even though the armbands "caused comments, warnings by other students, the poking of fun at them, . . . a warning by an older football player that other, nonprotesting students had better let them alone," and the "wreck[ing]" of a math teacher's lesson period. *Tinker*, 393 U.S. at 517 (Black, J., dissenting).

Here, the record of disruption is even skimpier. When the School District announced the bracelet ban, it had no more than an "undifferentiated fear or remote apprehension of disturbance." *Sypniewski*, 307 F.3d at 257. The bracelets had been on campus for at least two weeks without incident. *B.H.*, 827 F. Supp. 2d at 408; *see also* App. 13 ("[N]one of the three principals had heard any reports of disruption or student misbehavior linked to the bracelets. Nor had any of the principals heard reports of inappropriate comments about 'boobies.' "). That track record "speaks strongly against a finding of likelihood of disruption." *Sypniewski*, 307 F.3d at 254.

The School District instead relies on two incidents that occurred after the ban. In one, a female student told a teacher that she believed some boys had remarked to girls about their "boobies" in relation to the bracelets—an incident that was never confirmed. *B.H.*, 827 F. Supp. 2d at 408. In the other, two female students were discussing the bracelets during lunch, and a boy interrupted them to say "I want boobies" while "making inappropriate gestures with two spherical candies." *Id.* The boy was suspended for a day. *Id.*

Even assuming that disruption arising after a school's speech restriction could satisfy *Tinker*—a question we need not decide today—these two isolated incidents hardly bespeak a substantial disruption caused by the bracelets. "[S]tudent expression may not be suppressed simply because it gives rise to some slight, easily overlooked disruption, including but not [*322] limited to 'a showing of mild curiosity' by other students, 'discussion and comment' among students, or even some 'hostile remarks' or 'discussion outside of the classrooms' by other students." *Holloman ex rel. Holloman v. Harland*, 370 F.3d 1252, 1271-72 (11th Cir. 2004) (internal quotation marks and citations omitted). Given that Tinker's black armband—worn to protest a controversial war and divisive enough to prompt reactions from other students—was not a substantial disruption, neither is the "silent, passive expression" of breast-cancer awareness.[24] *Tinker*, 393 U.S. at 508. If anything, the fact that these incidents did not occur until *after* the School District banned the bracelets suggests that the ban "*exacerbated* rather than contained the disruption in the school." *J.S.*, 650 F.3d at 931 (drawing this same conclusion on a similar record).

Undeterred, the School District invokes the other half of *Tinker*'s general rule, arguing that the bracelets invade other students' Title IX rights to be free from sexual harassment. *See Tinker*, 393 U.S. at 513. Under Title IX, students may sue federally-funded schools that "act[] with deliberate indifference" to "harassment that is so severe, pervasive, and objectively offensive . . . that the victim students are effectively denied equal access to an institution's resources and opportunities." *Saxe*, 240 F.3d at 205-06 (quoting *Davis ex rel. LaShonda D. v. Monroe Cnty. Bd. of Educ.*, 526 U.S. 629, 651, 119 S. Ct. 1661, 143 L. Ed. 2d 839 (1999)). According to the School District, the "I ♥ boobies! (KEEP A BREAST)" bracelet was "deemed inappropriate for school due to the likelihood of a resultant increase in student-on-student sexual harassment." Sch. Dist.'s Br. at 54.

That argument suffers from several flaws, not the least of which is the School District's failure to raise it in the District Court and that Court's consequent failure to address it. *Freeman v. Pittsburgh Glass Works, LLC*, 709 F.3d 240, 249 (3d Cir. 2013) ("We generally refuse to consider issues that the parties have not raised below." (citing *Singleton v. Wulff*, 428 U.S. 106, 120, 96 S. Ct. 2868, 49 L. Ed. 2d 826 (1976))). But there is an even more basic reason why the School District's invocation of Title IX is not the shield it claims to be. Even assuming that protecting students from harassment under Title IX would satisfy *Tinker*'s

---

24. According to B.H. and K.M., *Tinker*'s substantial-disruption standard does not permit a school to restrict speech because of the heckler's veto of other students' disruptive reactions. *See* Appellees' Br. at 35 (emphasis added). Because no forecast of substantial disruption would be reasonable on this record under any meaning of that term, we need not determine the precise interplay between the anti-heckler's veto principle present elsewhere in free-speech doctrine and *Tinker*'s substantial-disruption standard in public schools. *Compare Zamecnik*, 636 F.3d at 879 (noting that *Tinker* endorsed both the heckler's veto doctrine and the substantial-disruption test and concluding that other students' harassment of "Zamecnik because of their disapproval of her ['Be Happy, Not Gay' T-shirt] is not a permissible ground for banning it"), *and Holloman*, 370 F.3d at 1275-76 (interpreting *Tinker* as endorsing an anti-heckler's veto principle, concluding that "[w]hile the same constitutional standards do not always apply in public schools as on public streets, we cannot afford students less constitutional protection simply because their peers might illegally express disagreement through violence instead of reason"), *with Taylor v. Roswell Indep. Sch. Dist.*, 713 F.3d 25, 38 (10th Cir. Apr. 8, 2013) ("Plaintiffs note that most disruptions occurred only because of wrongful behavior of third parties and that no Plaintiffs participated in these activities. . . . This argument might be effective outside the school context, but it ignores the 'special characteristics of the school environment.'" (quoting *Tinker*, 393 U.S. at 506)).

rights-of-others [*323] prong,[25] the School District does not explain why the bracelets would breed an environment of pervasive and severe harassment. *See, e.g., DeJohn v. Temple Univ.*, 537 F.3d 301, 320 (3d Cir. 2008) ("[U]nless harassment is qualified with a standard akin to a severe or pervasive requirement, [an anti-]harassment policy may suppress core protected speech."); *Saxe*, 240 F.3d at 217 (rejecting a school district's similar argument that it could ban speech creating a "hostile environment" without showing that the particular speech covered by the policy would create a severe or pervasive environment); *see also Nuxoll ex rel. Nuxoll v. Indian Prairie Sch. Dist. No. 204*, 523 F.3d 668, 676 (7th Cir. 2008) ("[I]t is highly speculative that allowing the plaintiff to wear a T-shirt that says 'Be Happy, Not Gay' would have even a slight tendency to provoke such incidents [of student-on-student harassment], or for that matter to poison the educational atmosphere.").

The bracelet ban cannot be upheld on the authority of *Tinker*.

V.

Because the School District's ban cannot pass scrutiny under *Fraser* or *Tinker*, B.H. and K.M. are likely to succeed on the merits. In light of that conclusion, the remaining preliminary-injunction factors also favor them. The ban prevents B.H. and K.M. from exercising their right to freedom of speech, which "unquestionably constitutes irreparable injury." *K.A. ex rel. Ayers v. Pocono Mountain Sch. Dist.*, 710 F.3d 99, 113 (3d Cir. 2013) (quoting *Elrod v. Burns*, 427 U.S. 347, 373, 96 S. Ct. 2673, 49 L. Ed. 2d 547 (1976) (plurality opinion)). An after-the-fact money judgment would hardly make up for their lost opportunity to wear the bracelets in school. *See Elrod*, 427 U.S. at 374 n.29 ("The timeliness of political speech is particularly important.").

And the preliminary injunction does not "result in even greater harm to" the School District, the non-moving party. *Allegheny Energy, Inc. v. DQE, Inc.*, 171 F.3d 153, 158 (3d Cir. 1999). The School District complains that unless the bracelet ban stands, it "has no clear guidance" on how to enforce its dress code. Appellant's Br. at 60. But the injunction addresses only the School District's ban of the "I ♥ boobies! (KEEP A BREAST)" bracelets. It does not enjoin the School District's regulation of other types of apparel, such as the "Save the ta-tas"

---

25. As we have repeatedly noted, "the precise scope of *Tinker*'s 'interference with the rights of others' language is unclear." *Saxe*, 240 F.3d at 217 (quoting *Tinker*, 393 U.S. at 504); *DeJohn v. Temple Univ.*, 537 F.3d 301, 319 (3d Cir. 2008). And the Supreme Court has "never squarely addressed whether harassment, when it takes the form of pure speech, is exempt from First Amendment protection." *Saxe*, 240 F.3d at 207. We need not address either of these points today. Even if *Tinker* permits school regulation of pure speech that would constitute "harassment" under Title IX, the School District has not offered any explanation or evidence of how passively wearing the "I ♥ boobies! (KEEP A BREAST)" bracelets would create such a severe and pervasive environment in the Middle School. *Cf. Saxe*, 240 F.3d at 204 (Alito, J.) ("There is no categorical 'harassment exception' to the First Amendment's free speech clause."); *Rodriguez v. Maricopa Cnty. Cmty. College Dist.*, 605 F.3d 703, 708 (9th Cir. 2010) (agreeing with *Saxe*'s statement).

T-shirt or testicular-cancer-awareness apparel bearing the phrase "feelmyballs. org." Whether the injunction stays or goes, the School District will have to continue making individualized assessments of whether it may restrict student speech consistent with the First Amendment, just as school administrators [*324] have always had to do. *See, e.g., Castorina ex rel. Rewt v. Madison Cnty. Sch. Bd.*, 246 F.3d 536, 543 (6th Cir. 2001) ("The foregoing discussion of the three Supreme Court . . . cases demonstrates the importance of the factual circumstances in school speech cases . . . ."). The District Court's injunction against the bracelet ban does not change that.

Lastly, granting the preliminary injunction furthers the public interest. The School District argues that the injunction eliminates its "authority to manage its student population" and thus harms the public. Appellant's Br. at 61. Again, that hyperbolic protest ignores the narrow breadth of the injunction, which addresses only the constitutionality of the bracelet ban under the facts of this case. More importantly, allowing a school's unconstitutional speech restriction to continue "vindicates no public interest." *K.A.*, 710 F.3d 99, 2013 WL 915059, at *11 (citation omitted). For these reasons, the District Court did not abuse its discretion by enjoining the School District's bracelet ban.

* * *

School administrators "have a difficult job," and we are well-aware that the job is not getting any easier. *Morse*, 551 U.S. at 409. Besides the teaching function, school administrators must deal with students distracted by cell phones in class and poverty at home, parental under- and over-involvement, bullying and sexting, preparing students for standardized testing, and ever-diminishing funding. When they are not focused on those issues, school administrators must inculcate students with "the shared values of a civilized social order." *Fraser*, 478 U.S. at 683; *see also McCauley v. Univ. of the V.I.*, 618 F.3d 232, 243, 54 V.I. 849 (3d Cir. 2010) (quoting *Brown v. Bd. of Educ.*, 347 U.S. 483, 493, 74 S. Ct. 686, 98 L. Ed. 873 (1954)) ("Public elementary and high school education is as much about learning how to be a good citizen as it is about multiplication tables and United States history.").

We do not envy those challenges, which require school administrators "to make numerous difficult decisions about when to place restrictions on speech in our public schools." *Morgan v. Swanson*, 659 F.3d 359, 420 (5th Cir. 2011) (en banc) (majority opinion of Elrod, J.). And the School District in this case was not unreasonably concerned that permitting "I ♥ boobies! (KEEP A BREAST)" bracelets in this case might require it to permit other messages that were sexually oriented in nature. But schools cannot avoid teaching our citizens-in-training how to appropriately navigate the "marketplace of ideas." Just because letting in one idea might invite even more difficult judgment calls about other ideas cannot justify suppressing speech of genuine social value. *Tinker*, 393 U.S. at 511 ("The classroom is peculiarly the 'marketplace of ideas.' The Nation's future depends upon leaders trained through wide exposure to that robust exchange of ideas which discovers truth 'out of a multitude of tongues,' (rather) than through any kind of authoritative selection." (quoting *Keyishian v. Bd. of Regents of Univ. of State of N.Y.*, 385 U.S. 589, 603, 87 S. Ct. 675, 17 L. Ed. 2d 629 (1967))); *see id.* at 511 ("[S]chool officials cannot suppress 'expressions of feelings with which they do not wish to contend.'" (citation omitted)).

We will affirm the District Court's order granting a preliminary injunction.

Dissent by: Hardiman; Greenaway, Jr.

Dissent (Edited for Content)

HARDIMAN, Circuit Judge, dissenting, with whom CHAGARES, JORDAN, GREENAWAY, JR., and GREENBERG join.

Today the Court holds that twelve-year-olds have a constitutional right to wear in [*325] school a bracelet that says "I ♥ boobies! (KEEP A BREAST)." Because this decision is inconsistent with the Supreme Court's First Amendment jurisprudence, I respectfully dissent.

I [OMITTED]

[*334] II

As noted, the Majority holds that "*Fraser* . . . permits a school to categorically restrict ambiguous speech that a reasonable observer could interpret as having a lewd, vulgar, or profane meaning," but only "so long as it could not also plausibly be interpreted as commenting on a social or political issue." Maj. Typescript at 61. It is important to emphasize here that, despite my disagreement with the second part of the Majority's formulation, I agree fully with its understanding of the objective-reasonableness inquiry compelled under *Fraser*. *See* Maj. Typescript 32-35 (discussing why "courts should defer to a school's decisions to restrict what a reasonable observer would interpret as lewd, vulgar, profane, or offensive").[5]

---

5. Though I believe an objective-reasonableness test is the correct interpretation of *Fraser*, its level of generality leaves something to be desired, particularly when one considers that the lower courts will look to our decision for guidance. The Majority states that "[i]t remains the job of judges . . . to determine whether a reasonable observer could interpret student speech as lewd, profane, vulgar, or offensive." Maj. Typescript at 33-34. But who is this "reasonable observer"? The Majority gives us clues: he "would not adopt an acontextual interpretation" and would consider "the plausibility of the school's interpretation in light of competing meanings; the context, content, and form of the speech; and the age and maturity of the students." Maj. Typescript at 34. I would add several more considerations. Most importantly, evolving societal norms counsel that what is "objectively" considered "lewd, profane, vulgar, or offensive" one day may not be so the next. *See, e.g., Fraser*, 478 U.S. at 691 (Stevens, J., dissenting) ("'Frankly, my dear, I don't give a damn.' When I was a high school student, the use of those words in a public forum shocked the Nation. Today Clark Gable's four-letter expletive is less offensive than it was then."). Furthermore, given the diversity of opinions and perspectives across our country, the type of speech that may reasonably fall into one of the proscribable categories would vary widely from one community to the next. These considerations highlight the importance of ensuring that "the determination of what manner of speech in the classroom or in school assembly is inappropriate properly rests with the school board." *Fraser*, 478 U.S. at 683.

The Majority did not find that the school's interpretation of the bracelets' message as lewd was objectively unreasonable. **[*335]** *See* Maj. Typescript at 63 n.22 ("[W]e need not determine whether a reasonable observer could interpret the bracelets' slogan as lewd."). Thus, had the Majority not engrafted Justice Alito's concurrence in *Morse* onto the *Fraser* standard, my colleagues might agree that the school did not violate the First Amendment when it proscribed the bracelet. Because the Majority chose not to analyze whether the school was reasonable in determining that the bracelet could be proscribed under *Fraser*, however, I will briefly discuss why that is so.

In this close case, the "I ♥ boobies! (KEEP A BREAST)" bracelets would seem to fall into a gray area between speech that is plainly lewd and merely indecorous. Because I think it objectively reasonable to interpret the bracelets, in the middle school context, as inappropriate sexual innuendo and double entendre, I would reverse the judgment of the District Court and vacate the preliminary injunction.

The District Court correctly ascertained the standard of review to apply in a case that arises under *Fraser*, but proceeded to misapply that standard. First, by emphasizing whether Plaintiffs *intended* a vulgar or sexual meaning in their "I ♥ boobies!" bracelets and determining that a non-sexual, breast-cancer-awareness interpretation of the bracelets was reasonable, the Court inverted the proper question. Instead of asking whether it was reasonable to view the bracelets as an innocuous expression of breast cancer awareness, the District Court should have asked whether the school officials' interpretation of the bracelets—*i.e.*, as expressing sexual attraction to breasts—was reasonable. So long as the School District's interpretation was objectively reasonable, the ban did not contravene the First Amendment or our school-speech jurisprudence.

Second, in its substantive conclusion that "I ♥ boobies!" cannot reasonably be regarded as lewd or vulgar, the District Court highlighted the bracelets' social value while disregarding their likely meaning to immature middle-schoolers.[6]

---

6. In fact, we have questioned the applicability of the Supreme Court's student speech jurisprudence in the elementary and middle school settings:

> [A]t a certain point, a school child is so young that it might reasonably be presumed the First Amendment does not protect the kind of speech at issue here. Where that point falls is subject to reasonable debate.
>
> In any event, if third graders enjoy rights under *Tinker*, those rights will necessarily be very limited. Elementary school officials will undoubtedly be able to regulate much—perhaps most—of the speech that is protected in higher grades. When officials have a legitimate educational reason—whether grounded on the need to preserve order, to facilitate learning or social development, or to protect the interests of other students—they may ordinarily regulate public elementary school children's speech.

Walker-Serrano ex rel. Walker v. Leonard, 325 F.3d 412, 417-18 (3d Cir. 2003); *see also Walz ex rel. Walz v. Egg Harbor Twp. Bd. of Educ.*, 342 F.3d 271, 276 (3d Cir. 2003) (noting that "the age of the students bears an important inverse relationship to the degree and kind of control a school may exercise: as a general matter, the younger the students, the more control a school may exercise"). Other appellate courts share our misgivings, noting that "the younger the children, the more latitude

As the [*336] School District argues, the fact that Plaintiffs' laudable awareness message *could* be discerned from the bracelets does not render the School District's ban unconstitutional. "I ♥ boobies!" not only expresses support for those afflicted with breast cancer, but also conveys a sexual attraction to the female breast.

Notwithstanding the facts supporting Plaintiffs' case, I conclude that "I ♥ boobies!" can reasonably be interpreted as inappropriate sexual double entendre. In the middle school context, the phrase can mean both "I support breast-cancer-awareness measures" and "I am attracted to female breasts." Many twelve- and thirteen-year-old children are susceptible to juvenile sexualization of messages that would be innocuous to a reasonable adult. Indeed, at least one bracelet-wearer acknowledged that "immature" boys might read a lewd meaning into the bracelets and conceded that she understood why the school might want to ban the bracelets, *B.H.*, 827 F. Supp. 2d at 399, and other students parroted the phrase on the bracelets while conveying sexual attraction to breasts. Another school administrator has concluded that the bracelets at issue here "elicit attention by sexualizing the cause of breast cancer awareness." *Sauk Prairie*, No. 11-cv-622, at 4. And as Judge Crabb, the only other federal judge to consider these bracelets, put it in *Sauk Prairie*, "hints of vulgarity and sexuality" in the bracelets "attract attention and provoke conversation, a ploy that is effective for [KABF's] target audience of immature middle [school] students." *Id.* at 15. Finally, as the Gender Equality amicus brief points out, breasts are ubiquitously sexualized in American culture.

It is true that certain facts indicate that a sexual interpretation of the "I ♥ boobies!" bracelets may be at the outer edge of how a reasonable observer would interpret speech. Most obviously, the bracelets always modify the "I ♥ boobies!" phrase with "(KEEP A BREAST)" or other breast-cancer-awareness messages. "When one reads the entire phrase, it is clearly a message designed to promote breast cancer awareness." *K.J. v. Sauk Prairie Sch. Dist.*, No. 11-cv-622, 2012 U.S. Dist. LEXIS 187689, at *18 (W.D. Wis. Feb. 6, 2012). Additionally, school administrators did not immediately recognize the bracelets as vulgar or lewd; students had been wearing the bracelets for two months before they were banned, and teachers had to request guidance on whether and how to deal with the bracelets. Moreover, the school itself was compelled to use the word "boobies" over the public address system and school television station in order to describe the proscribed bracelets, which suggests that the word alone is not patently offensive.

---

the school authorities have in limiting expression." *Zamecnik*, 636 F.3d at 876 (citing *Muller ex rel. Muller v. Jefferson Lighthouse Sch.*, 98 F.3d 1530, 1538-39 (7th Cir. 1996)); *see also Nuxoll*, 523 F.3d at 673 (when a school regulates the speech of children that are "very young . . . the school has a pretty free hand"); *Morgan*, 659 F.3d at 386 ("[I]n public schools, the speech appropriate for eighteen-year-old high school students is not necessarily acceptable for seven-year-old grammar school students. Indeed, common sense dictates that a 7-year-old is not a 13-year-old, and neither is an adult." (alterations, citations, and internal quotation marks omitted)).

The Easton Area Middle School principals' willingness to say "boobies" to the entire school audience does not imply that the word does not have a sexual meaning; it merely suggests that "boobies" is not plainly lewd. Moreover, although KABF's decision not to market its products through porn stars and at truck stops is laudable, the interest such organizations have shown in the bracelets is further evidence that the bracelets are read by many to contain a sexual meaning. And the "I ♥ boobies!" bracelets' breast cancer message is not *so* obvious or overwhelming as to eliminate the double entendre. For one thing, the bracelets come in many colors other than the shade of pink widely associated with the fight against breast cancer.

Additionally, although Plaintiffs and their amici argue that the casual language of the "I ♥ boobies!" bracelets is intended [*337] to make breast cancer issues more accessible and less stigmatized for girls and young women, that purpose does not undermine the plausibility of a sexual interpretation of the bracelets. Nor does the fact that these Plaintiffs' mothers were happy not only to purchase the bracelets for their teenage daughters but also to wear them render the bracelets immune from school regulation. The mothers' intent that the bracelets convey a breast-cancer-awareness message, like Plaintiffs' own subjective motive, is irrelevant to interpreting the meaning of the speech.

Likewise, the School District administrators' subjective beliefs, expressed at the time of the ban and later during this litigation, do not affect my determination of whether it is objectively reasonable to infer a sexualized meaning from the bracelets. Their failure to use the words "lewd," "vulgar," "indecent," or "plainly offensive" is not fatal to their claim of regulatory authority. Similarly, some principals' inconsistent testimony regarding what other breast-cancer-related phrases they might censor does not make the phrase at issue here more or less vulgar. Therefore, it is not probative that administrators intermittently indicated that they thought the word "breast" by itself has an impermissible sexual connotation.

Plaintiffs rely on the initial statements by teachers at the middle school that the word "breast" alone in any context and the phrases "breast cancer awareness" and "keep-a-breast.org" could also be banned to argue that the School District has left them no other means to convey their breast-cancer-awareness message. But those words were not banned—indeed, students are permitted to wear KABF's "check y♥urself!! (KEEP A BREAST)" bracelets—and the administrators changed their position prior to the evidentiary hearing, opining that such phrases would *not* be inappropriate at school. Also significant is the fact that the Easton Area Middle School has not stifled the message of breast cancer awareness; in the course of a robust breast cancer awareness campaign it merely imposed a permissible restriction on the *way* in which that message may be expressed. See *Saxe*, 240 F.3d at 213 ("*Fraser* speaks to the form and manner of student speech, not its substance. It addresses the mode of expression, not its content or viewpoint." (citation omitted)).

Nor is Plaintiffs' position saved by the fact that the "I ♥ boobies!" phrase was "chosen to enhance the effectiveness of the communication to the target audience." *B.H.*, 827 F. Supp. 2d at 406. The District Court's focus on the strategic purpose of the words and format used in the bracelets was misguided. If indecency were permitted in schools merely because it was intended to advance some laudable goal, Matthew Fraser's speech would have been constitutionally protected insofar as he intended to win the attention of his classmates while advocating the election of his friend.

Finally, if we were to hold that the breast cancer message here makes any sexual reading of the bracelets unreasonable, schools would be obliged to permit more egregiously sexual advocacy messages. As Ms. DiVietro acknowledged, "other bodily parts in the human anatomy . . . can get cancer and . . . other types of slang terms" would have to be condoned. App. 275. DiVietro raised the specter of an "I ♥ Balls" slogan to support testicular cancer awareness. *Id*. at 275-76. These examples are not speculative. The Testicular Cancer Awareness Project sells "feelmyballs" bracelets to encourage male self-examinations and general awareness. *See* Testicular Cancer Awareness Project, **[*338]** http://www.feelmyballs.org/shop/front.php (last visited June 3, 2013). If middle school students have a constitutional right to wear "I ♥ boobies!" bracelets, it would be difficult to articulate a limiting principle that would disallow these other catchy phrases, so long as they were aimed at some socially beneficial objective.

Simply stated, the District Court correctly articulated the proper standard of review to be applied in cases that implicate *Fraser* (such as this one), but it strayed from that standard when evaluating the reasonableness of Plaintiffs' intended meaning. For that reason, and because the School District's reading of "I ♥ boobies!" as inappropriate sexual double entendre was a reasonable interpretation in the middle school context, I would hold that Plaintiffs cannot demonstrate a likelihood of success on the merits of their claim. Accordingly, the District Court abused its discretion in granting a preliminary injunction.

* * *

As this case demonstrates, running a school is more complicated now than ever before. Administrators and teachers are not only obliged to teach core subjects, but also find themselves mired in a variety of socio-political causes during school time. And they do so in an era when they no longer possess plenary control of their charges as they did when they acted *in loco parentis*. *See, e.g., Morse*, 551 U.S. at 413-16 (Thomas, J., concurring). The decisions school administrators must make regarding the deportment of their students—what they say, what they wear, or what they do—require common sense and good judgment. Many of those decisions will involve matters about which reasonable people can disagree. In the close cases, such as this one, there is virtue in deferring to the reasonable judgments of those responsible for educating our nation's youth. With respect, I dissent.

GREENAWAY, JR., Circuit Judge, dissenting, with whom CHAGARES, JORDAN, HARDIMAN and GREENBERG join.

My colleagues have determined today that "I ♥ boobies" is an ambiguous phrase that may connote an attraction to female breasts, but which falls under the protection of the First Amendment in the middle school context because it may plausibly be interpreted as commenting on a political or social issue. Reasonable minds may come to varying conclusions on this test, but one thing is not open to debate: a school district faced with the same dilemma in the coming weeks, months, or years is given no greater guidance regarding its ability to determine whether a particular message may be proscribed than before the Majority opinion issued.

The Majority lauds the intent of the two middle schoolers responsible for introducing "I ♥ boobies! (KEEP A BREAST)" bracelets into their school, which encouraged serious discussion regarding a medical issue of increasing social import. Appellees' actions may or may not reflect an admirable maturity, but the intent of Appellees is not at issue. In many cases, when the First Amendment is implicated, the intent of the speakers will be admirable or at worst benign. The Majority concludes that, as long as the ambiguous speech may be interpreted by a reasonable person as plausibly related to a political or social issue, it is protected. Despite its express disavowal of intent as a consideration, the Majority inadvertently re-injects the students' intent into the fray by mandating an analysis of whether a political or social issue is addressed by the speech. This is improper but it is not my sole criticism.

[*339] The Majority's test leaves school districts essentially powerless to exercise any discretion and extends the First Amendment's protection to a breadth that knows no bounds. As such, how will similarly-situated school districts apply this amorphous test going forward? The Majority's test has two obvious flaws. First, what words or phrases fall outside of the ambiguous designation other than the "seven dirty words"? Second, how does a school district ever assess the weight or validity of political or social commentary? The absence of guidance on both of these questions leaves school districts to scratch their heads.

Practical problems with the Majority's test abound. Where and how do school districts line-draw regarding the nouns used to describe the subject matter of the particular awareness campaign? The Majority has established that at opposite ends of the spectrum are "boobies," on the one hand, and "tits," one of the "seven dirty words," on the other hand. What lies between those two extremes and how a school district is to make a principled judgment going forward remain open questions. No doubt, there are some words and phrases that all would agree should be afforded no protection in the middle school context, despite their use in promoting an important social issue. My recalcitrance to extend First Amendment protection to the slogan at hand is simple—why is this word, "boobies," different? Why does it deserve protection? Is "boobies" a term that is inherently innocuous or sophomoric, as the Majority asserts? As noted in the Majority, "ta tas" is used as the descriptive term in some breast cancer awareness campaigns. The ambiguity of "ta tas" in this context is beyond question. What also seems beyond question is that the school district, according to the Majority, must lay dormant to a student's use of "ta tas" or any synonym of "breast" (other than "tits") as long as the student is commenting on a political or social issue, here, breast cancer awareness. The lack of certitude or a workable parameter unnecessarily handcuffs school districts.

What of the circumstance when an anatomically correct term is used in an awareness campaign? Applying the Majority's test, "I ♥ penises," "I ♥ vaginas," "I ♥ testicles," or "I ♥ breasts" would apparently be phrases or slogans that school districts would be powerless to address. Would the invocation of any of these slogans in a cancer awareness effort fail to garner protection under the Majority's test? It would appear not. What of the other slogans that the Majority mentions in its opinion that are sufficiently ambiguous? The Majority blithely states that "it does not enjoin the School District's regulation of other types of apparel, such as the 'Save the ta-tas' T-shirt or testicular-cancer-awareness apparel bearing the phrase 'feelmyballs.org.'" (Maj. Op. 71.) This is exactly my concern. What may a school district do? These phrases are both ambiguous and speak to political and social issues. How is a school district now better able to discern when it may exercise its discretion to impede the use of a particular slogan, as it relates to an awareness program, than before the issuance of this opinion?

The other practical problem which arises from application of the Majority's test is judging the validity of political and social comment. In the context of these social awareness campaigns, when would the students' involvement not invoke political or social comment? The constriction of "plausibly be interpreted as" adds little to our discourse. For instance, when would a student using a term that is admittedly ambiguous not be able to assert that the use of the offending word, term, or phrase is speech that is commenting on a political [*340] or social issue? What is the balancing that a school district can/should/may engage in to determine the merit or value of the proposed political or social comment? The unabashed invocation of a lewd, vulgar, indecent or plainly offensive term is not what is at issue here; what is at issue is the notion that we have established a test which effectively has no parameters. The political or social issue prong entirely eviscerates the school district's authority to effectively evaluate whether the student's speech is indeed protected. This shortcoming in the application of the test exemplifies its inherent weakness—a failure to resolve the conundrum school districts face every day.

In light of the Majority's approach, school districts seeking guidance from our First Amendment jurisprudence in this context will find only confusion. I cannot adhere to this approach. I respectfully dissent.

> **Questions Regarding *B.H. ex rel. Hawk v. Easton Area School District***
>
> 1. Under the majority's holding in *Easton Area School District*, what does it mean for speech to be "ambiguously lewd"?
> 2. What qualifies something as a political or social issue?
> 3. In analyzing political/social issues, does the court look to the speaker's intent or to the relevant audience's perception of the speech? Why?

> **Tips for First Amendment Rights at Morning Glory High Memorandum**
>
> 1. The affirmative arguments for Maya Smoot are limited (e.g., students retain First Amendment rights in school under *Tinker*; off-campus speech is generally afforded more protection than on-campus speech under *Mahanoy*); the arguments under disruption and lewdness are the *school's* arguments, which Smoot must rebut. You should keep this in mind as you decide how to structure your memorandum.
> 2. When arguing foreseeable substantial disruption, be specific about the kinds of disruption you anticipate. The same goes for political/social purpose. It's not enough just to claim that disruption would occur or that a social purpose would be perceived. Explain what kind of disruption you anticipate. Explain what purpose would be perceived by the speech and why.
> 3. Don't be shy about explaining lewdness. A judge may be unfamiliar with certain slang terms, so it's your job to educate them on that as much as it's your job to educate them on the relevant law.
> 4. Treat each piece of speech as its own separate case as opposed to four parts of one large First Amendment case. It's entirely possible that a court will find punishment for certain pieces of speech permissible under the First Amendment and other pieces impermissible.

ASSIGNMENT 9: FIRST AMENDMENT RIGHTS AT KINNEAR HIGH

Learned Foot, LLP

Memorandum

To: Associates
From: [Your Professor/Supervising Partner]
Subject: First Amendment Rights at Kinnear High

Background:

We represent Giorgio Bankard and Elise Condon, two juniors at Kinnear High School (KHS) in the Jeevers Independent School District (JISD) in Jeevers,

Delaware. Both students were suspended for on-campus and off-campus speech related to a faculty member, film teacher Roderick Davidson.

Last month, Bankard discovered that Davidson, now in his early forties, had starred in a trio of pornographic films while in his early twenties going by the name of Scout Mercer. The films were:

- *The Ass Menagerie,* starring Dame Judi Drench as a faded southern belle and Legs Magee as her HPV-afflicted daughter. Mercer plays the gentleman caller.
- *Saving Ryan's Privates,* starring Fellatio Del Toro and Mercer as World War II soldiers in Normandy, desperately searching for companionship while in the throes of war.
- *Peeing on John Malkovich,* starring Mercer and John Malkovich in a surrealist fetish piece about a Hollywood actor obsessed with golden showers.

At the time of Bankard's discovery, he was a student in Mr. Davidson's Introduction to Cinema class. He was shocked to learn that mild-mannered Mr. Davidson had this alternate identity, and one afternoon during the school day (as confirmed by the tweet's date and timestamp), he tweeted the following:

Mr. Davidson = Scout Mercer. Seriously, look it up!

Bankard's Twitter account was private, but he was followed by over 300 fellow students at Kinnear High School.

Later that day, Bankard's classmate, Elise Condon, replied to Bankard's tweet (again, during the school day based on the tweet's date and timestamp) with the following:

to Mr. Davidson! I hope he gets ed!

Later that evening, upon seeing Condon's Twitter reply, Bankard fired back:

Lighten up. Davidson's a good guy. I just thought it was funny.

An hour later, Condon replied:

Nothing funny about lust, Whore-gio. It's one of the seven deadly sins and any man who could do what he did shouldn't be teaching in a school.

Other classmates—over two dozen—weighed in on the exchange that night on Twitter, divided evenly between supporting Bankard's defense of Davidson and supporting Condon's campaign to have him removed from Kinnear High. The next morning at school, Giorgio Bankard and three of his friends came to school with socks stuffed into the crotches of their pants, purportedly to show their support and admiration for Mr. Davidson and to encourage "open discussions of sexuality in school."

The same morning, Condon went to Mr. Davidson's classroom, where it was well known that Davidson kept a small whiteboard with the words: "What I'm watching" above. The board, viewable from the hallway, would contain the title of whatever film Davidson was currently watching in case other students wanted to view it as well to discuss. On the morning in question, the board featured Merchant Ivory's *Howards End*. Ms. Condon erased that title and wrote the three entries from Davidson's/Mercer's filmography: "*The Ass Menagerie, Saving Ryan's Privates, Peeing on John Malkovich.*"

The school principal, Lexi Shaw, was immediately informed about the Twitter war, the sock stunt and the whiteboard incident. Both students were called into her office; both were given three-day suspensions for lewd and disruptive conduct. Bankard and Condon, whose parents each contacted our firm independently, now want to sue the Jeevers Independent School District for violations of their First Amendment rights. Our initial determination is that there is no conflict of interest in representing both students against the school (despite the fact that neither student has a high opinion of the other).

It is worth noting that Mr. Davidson has shown support for both Bankard and Condon and did not wish either to be suspended for their actions. He claims that he has not suffered because of the revelations and in fact felt relieved to have his secret unearthed. He is still employed by Kinnear High School, which determined that Davidson had not committed a fireable offense, though his hallway whiteboard has been removed.

Applicable Law:

The relevant statutory and constitutional provisions are below:

42 U.S.C. § 1983: Civil action for deprivation of rights

Every person who, under color of any statute, ordinance, regulation, custom, or usage, of any State or Territory or the District of Columbia, subjects, or causes to be subjected, any citizen of the United States or other person within the jurisdiction thereof to the deprivation of any rights, privileges, or immunities secured by the Constitution and laws, shall be liable to the party injured in an action at law, suit in equity, or other proper proceeding for redress, except that in any action brought against a judicial officer for an act or omission taken in such officer's judicial capacity, injunctive relief shall not be granted unless a declaratory decree was violated or declaratory relief was unavailable. For the purposes of this section, any Act of Congress applicable exclusively to the District of Columbia shall be considered to be a statute of the District of Columbia.

U.S. Const. amend. I.

Congress shall make no law respecting an establishment of religion, or prohibiting the free exercise thereof; or abridging the freedom of speech, or of the press; or the right of the people peaceably to assemble, and to petition the government for a redress of grievances.

In terms of case law, you can isolate your analysis to five cases: *Tinker v. Des Moines Indep. Cmty. Sch. Dist.*, 393 U.S. 503 (1969), *Bethel Sch. Dist. No. 403 v. Fraser*,

478 U.S. 675 (1986), *Wisniewski ex rel. Wisniewski v. Bd. of Educ. of the Weedsport Cent. Sch. Dist.*, 494 F.3d 34 (2d Cir. 2007), *Mahanoy Area Sch. Dist. v. B.L.*, 2021 U.S. LEXIS 3395 (2021), *B.H. ex rel. Hawk v. Easton Area Sch. Dist.*, 725 F.3d 293 (3d Cir. 2013).

Issues Presented:

Given the recent media attention on this matter, this case is high priority. Accordingly, the senior partnership would like a memorandum of law laying out arguments for both Bankard and Condon as well as the JISD's likely counterarguments in the District of Delaware. You should also opine on each client's prospective likelihood of success for each piece of speech.

Tips for First Amendment Rights at Kinnear High Memorandum

As with the Morning Glory High memorandum, the following tips apply:

1. The affirmative arguments for Bankard and Condon are limited (e.g., students retain First Amendment rights in school under *Tinker*; off-campus speech is generally afforded more protection than on-campus speech under *Mahanoy*); the arguments under disruption and lewdness are the school's arguments and both students must rebut those. You should keep this in mind as you decide how to structure your memorandum.

2. When arguing foreseeable substantial disruption, be specific about the kinds of disruption you anticipate. The same goes for political/social purpose. It's not enough just to claim that disruption would occur or that a social purpose would be perceived. Explain what kind of disruption you anticipate. Explain what purpose would be perceived by the speech and why.

3. Don't be shy about explaining lewdness. A judge may be unfamiliar with certain slang terms, so it's your job to educate them on that as much as it's your job to educate them on the relevant law.

4. Treat each piece of speech as its own separate case as opposed to four parts of one large First Amendment case. It's entirely possible that a court will find punishment for certain pieces of speech permissible under the First Amendment and other pieces impermissible.

chapter 11

Workshopping Legal Writing

The most intimidating room I've ever walked into was not a conference room or courtroom; it wasn't one of the sprawling lecture halls at Yale Law, either. It was Room 222 on 236 Bay State Road at Boston University, the place where all BU graduate fiction workshops took place. There were only ten seats in the class, only ten seats in the fiction program in any given year, and the nine authors by my side were some of the smartest and most talented writers I'd ever met. Class sessions lasted about two to two and a half hours, and in each session, we reviewed the works of two authors. That meant that when it was your week to be on the hot seat, you'd have to listen quietly for over an hour while your professor and fellow graduate students picked apart your story or novella.

As one can imagine, this is not an easy process, but it's hard to deny its utility. To have your work read, analyzed and critiqued by a room full of serious-minded writers is a gift. As an author, you naturally are so close to your work that it's often difficult to see its flaws. You see what you meant to write instead of what you did write. A thoughtful writing workshop tells you exactly what's on the page, how it can be improved and how you can improve as a writer.

Criticism is never easy to hear, and many undergraduates haven't had their writing seriously scrutinized beyond an English teacher's handwritten comment at the end of an essay. The first step in properly utilizing a writing workshop is removing one's ego from the equation. A writing workshop isn't about separating good writers from bad. As the name suggests, it's a place where authors bring works-in-progress and invite fellow authors to share their perspectives on the quality of the argumentation and prose. A workshop filled with nothing but compliments may boost an author's self-esteem, but it will do little to actually make them a sharper or more thoughtful writer. It's fair to want one's strengths recognized, but understand that most of the focus will inevitably be on perceived flaws. You don't have to agree with every criticism, but you should be grateful to those who articulate perceived weaknesses in your prose. Those kinds of comments can help a writer grow.

A well-executed workshop will encourage you to learn, not just from the critiques of your own work, but through offering constructive feedback to others and through seeing inspiring examples from your fellow classmates. When you see a technique or strategy from a peer that you wish you'd employed, integrate it into your next piece of writing or into your revision of the workshopped essay.

When offering feedback on your peers' work, be thoughtful and timely. Point out strengths (authors do need to hear what they're doing well so they can lean into those qualities) but be honest about what parts of the paper you didn't understand. The key to success in any workshop is that every participant takes their job seriously. This isn't some wan peer review, where you offer some nebulous advice and point out a typo or two. A workshop is only helpful if everyone in it agrees to be honest with one another and to critique with vigor. It might feel odd, playing critic in a genre that you yourself are just learning. But the point isn't about feigning an authority you don't possess. Rather, you're sharing with a writer your experience of reading their prose.

One final note on workshopping: some authors are more sensitive than others, and it's important for discussions about student writing to feel safe and civil. There may be pushback from some of your critiques, and you yourself may disagree with some of the advice you're given. Try not to take any of this process personally. Also, before discarding or discounting any unwanted piece of criticism, give yourself a day or two to absorb all the comments. If only one person out of ten takes issue with your counterargument on special relationship, maybe it's fair to consider that an idiosyncratic take. But if seven people point to the same issue, maybe you should reconsider that part of the work.

Below is some guidance on how to craft useful critiques:

ASSIGNMENT 10: PEER CRITIQUE

Purpose. No pedagogical tool will prove more powerful at improving your writing than the workshop/peer critique process. Invariably, it's easier to see the flaws and opportunities for improvement in *other* people's writing; the point of workshop is to offer authors a set of fresh eyes to help them revise their pieces. There are advantages to the critic as well: ideally, with practice, you'll one day be able to turn your refined critical eye toward your own work.

Audience. Your audience for each critique is the author of the workshopped essay. You may write in letter form or essay form, but you're writing directly to the author (and at the end of each workshop, you will hand the author your critique for their essay as well as a marked copy of their manuscript).

Assignment. For every essay in your workshop group, you must compose a one-page single-spaced critique, commenting on both macro- and micro-issues in the document and offering potential solutions to problems where appropriate. Macro-issues include:

- **Issues Presented and Answers:** Does the memo clearly lay out issues/questions responsive to the assignment and provide clear answers to those questions?

- **Statement of Facts:** Is the statement of facts sufficiently abbreviated, only including the facts necessary to the analysis that follows? Conversely, are any facts missing that are later revealed in the discussion? Are the facts presented in a logical order?
- **Discussion:** Is the discussion organized in a way that makes sense? Does it sufficiently explain the reasoning behind the memo's answers? Are there clear and cogent statements of the applicable law? Are they followed by a logical application of the law to the case's facts? Has the author followed IRAC? Has the author thoughtfully considered counterarguments?
- **Conclusion:** Does the author provide a satisfying and clear summary of the memo's findings? If not, what is missing?
- **Structure:** Did the organization of the memo make sense given its objectives? Are there any transitions that feel startling or abrupt? Bear in mind that abrupt transitions usually point to a larger problem with argumentation: the author needs to clarify the relationship between example X and example Y, showing how these ideas build on each other and relate to the main points of the memo. Does the piece feel unnecessarily repetitive at times?

Micro-issues include the following and should be attached to cited examples from the text:

- **Style:** Choose a sampling of sentences/phrases that are awkward, wordy or confusing and explain to the writer what feels off and why.
- **Mechanics:** Have you noticed any consistent or distracting errors? Look out for common mistakes, such as comma splices, subject/verb disagreement, weak verbs and citation errors.
- **Formatting:** Could the document be more reader-friendly and/or more clearly laid out?

Tips for Peer Critiques and Workshopping

1. Don't be afraid to compliment! Though the bulk of your analysis will more than likely be critical, you should also take time to praise the author for whatever they are doing well.
2. Be specific: vague criticisms are almost always useless without examples to make them clear. Every time you point out an issue, cite an example of that issue from the text and provide page numbers.
3. Mark manuscripts thoroughly with comments and grammatical corrections and suggestions. If someone has gone to the trouble of printing out a copy of their essay for you to review, don't hand them a clean copy back.

> 4. Conclude your written critique with suggestions for how to improve the paper.
> 5. Don't be afraid to be wrong. It might feel uncomfortable critiquing someone for writing in a genre you are only just learning, too. As a student-critic, your job isn't to be an authority on the subject or style but to share how you as an intelligent reader understood your peer's writing.
> 6. As the workshopped student, take notes during your workshop and ask questions when your time comes to speak. Remember that the comments you receive are intended to improve your writing. Please do not view them as personal criticisms. Be prepared to receive contradictory advice, and understand that at the end of the day, you have the final say on what ends up on a page representing you.

Below is an example of a peer critique of a First Amendment memorandum written by a student:

Sample Student Peer Critique

Dear R—,

Strengths

Overall, your paper was a pleasure to read because of your concise writing and clear formatting. The introductory section of the paper, in particular, was easy to understand. You made clear what laws were applicable and what questions needed to be answered. Similarly, in your discussion, I liked your structure: organizing by issue, then piece of speech, then stakeholder, then conclusion. I wish I had written mine like this.

Macro Trends

For both substantial disruption and lewdness, I felt that you could have found better quotes to use from the case law to establish clear guidelines and requirements. For *Tinker* especially, you could have done a better job capturing the true essence and implications of this landmark case. To this end, instead of quoting from cases cited within our main cases, you could have spent more time unpacking the standards from the actual main cases.

For your discussion section on foreseeable substantial disruption, your argument would have been stronger if you spent more time discussing how the state might interpret the situation at the time of the suspension as foreseeably dangerous. Keep in mind, not all the facts of the case—for example, Davidson's testimony—had happened at the time of the suspension, so they can't be used as evidence that the environment wasn't foreseeably disrupted.

For your discussion section on lewdness, I encountered multiple instances when you mentioned that the speech wasn't a political or social commentary and thus was plainly lewd. This argument failed to apply the *B.H.* guidelines correctly because political or social commentary is only necessary in cases where the speech is ambiguously lewd. When the speech is plainly lewd, it's irrelevant whether or not the speech had a sociopolitical purpose. I found this same confusion in the Brief Answer, where you say that "Condon's speech could not be plausibly interpreted as commenting on a political and social issue, in which case the School District would not be violating Condon's First Amendment rights by suspending her since her speech is plainly lewd." I think you should instead address plain lewdness and ambiguous lewdness separately.

Finally, some small areas for improvement: the statement of facts seemed to be almost an identical copy and paste from the memo. While this is allowed, you could have cut out a few sentences here and there to make it flow better, save length in the paper (12 pages), and make the statement of facts more tailored to Condon's case specifically. Also, there was no overall conclusion to the paper, which I think would have helped wrap everything up nicely.

<u>Grammar/Syntax</u>

I noticed some small grammatical and punctuation errors here and there. "Id." wasn't italicized, "Tinker" wasn't italicized on page 4, you used commas in several places where they weren't needed, and several sentences were awkwardly phrased. An example of this is on page 7: "The lack of disobedience from other students" (p. 7). Couldn't you just point to the student body's obedience?

Overall, I thought this was a strong effort and a definite improvement over your last memorandum.

Best,
T—

chapter 12

Basic Legal Research

Up to this point, you've been given closed universes of law to apply to your assignments. But in the real world, lawyers must find the law applicable to their issue and make sure that law has not been overturned. This section breaks down the basics of legal research into three objectives:

- Familiarizing Oneself with an Area of Law
- Confirming the Currency and Validity of Particular Laws
- Searching for Specific Law in Targeted Jurisdictions

FAMILIARIZING ONESELF WITH AN AREA OF LAW

Part of what makes law so daunting is its breadth. There's criminal law and civil law. There's federal law and state law. There are countless divisions and gradations within each. In practice, most lawyers specialize in a particular area. A family law attorney would most likely not take on the appeal of a death penalty case, for example. But as a student, you will often shift between many different areas of law from one class to the next. You'll have professors and carefully curated textbooks to guide you. But for someone outside of law school, figuring out where to start to understand an unfamiliar doctrine can be difficult without some assistance.

If you're new to an area of law in which you'd like some grounding, you might find it useful to consult a secondary source such as a legal encyclopedia, a treatise or a law review article. For beginning legal writers, it probably makes sense to start with a legal encyclopedia. Legal encyclopedias provide broad summaries of legal subjects and explain relevant terms of art. They also cite to relevant statutes and cases for further research. The two main legal encyclopedias for U.S. law nationally are *American Jurisprudence* and *Corpus Juris Secundum,* available both in print and online. Some states also have their own legal encyclopedias, which can provide the equivalent start on state law issues.

If you're looking for more than just a bird's-eye view of an area of law, a treatise might be the best place to look. A treatise is a single or multi-volume summary of a particular area of law. These are in-depth, scholarly works detailing

TABLE 12.1. SECONDARY SOURCES IN LAW

Secondary Source	Coverage	Examples
Legal Encyclopedias	Provide broad summaries of legal subjects and explain relevant terms of art	*American Jurisprudence, Corpus Juris Secundum, Georgia Jurisprudence*
Treatises	Provide in-depth, scholarly treatments of specific areas of law	*Tax Practice & Procedure, Price on Contemporary Real Estate Planning*
Law Reviews/ Journals	Provide detailed arguments on emerging and specific areas of law	*The Yale Law Journal, Michigan Law Review*

areas like Education Law, Labor and Employment Law, Sports Law and Products Liability. Since treatises cover their area with significantly more depth than a legal encyclopedia, you should use the table of contents and index to locate the relevant sections. Also make sure you're viewing the most current version of the treatise, as laws are constantly changing. As with legal encyclopedias, treatises are available both in print and online.

Law reviews (or law journals) are scholarly publications, often edited by law students, that contain articles and essays of varying length by law professors, lawyers and law students. Law review articles are particularly useful for exploring emerging areas of law. They also tend to be less objective than a legal encyclopedia or treatise. These articles often offer critiques of the law, so while they are excellent sources of legal foundations, you should keep in mind the author's ultimate objectives. They are available both in print and online as well, but given that individual law review issues often contain a hodgepodge of subject matters, it would be more efficient to search for relevant article titles online.

CONFIRMING THE CURRENCY AND VALIDITY OF PARTICULAR LAWS

In your legal studies and in your legal practice, your research more often will start with a specific piece of law: a statute or a case, for example. Perhaps you're curious as to how a statute's language has been interpreted in courts. Or maybe you want to see how lower courts have interpreted a standard from higher courts over the years.

Legal databases like LexisNexis and Westlaw make this process easy. Many college libraries allow students access to one or both of these online databases free of charge. Say, for example, that you wanted to delve deeper into 42 U.S.C.S. § 2000cc-1, the "Protection of religious exercise of institutionalized persons" statute from the Rusty Doucet memo in Chapter 8 (Assignment 5). Running a simple search using the section number above would pull up the current text of the statute. But after the text, you will also see the section's history (which will include any amendments since its original passage) as well as annotations linking to court cases interpreting the statute. There may also be a secondary sources section in the annotations that will link to related legal encyclopedia entries, treatises and law review articles.

You'll also see the option to Shepardize the document in Lexis or to KeyCite it in Westlaw. This process will extract a more exhaustive list of cases and secondary sources that have cited your statute, dividing the case citations into negative analyses (where, for example, a court might question the constitutionality of the statute) and positive analyses (where, for example, a court might uphold the constitutionality of the statute).

You can use the same process for checking case law. In LexisNexis or Westlaw, enter the citation for *DeShaney v. Winnebago Cnty. Dep't of Soc. Servs.*: 489 U.S. 189. Accompanying the opinion will be references to relevant secondary sources such as legal encyclopedias or treatises. Shepardizing or KeyCiting the case will reveal positive and negative treatments of *DeShaney* in multiple jurisdictions. Has the case been questioned or overruled? Has it been distinguished from other cases? Has it been criticized or limited? Has it been followed by courts in other cases? You can search through the citations by court. For example, you can find every case citing *DeShaney* in the Eighth Circuit or in the state of Iowa. You can also limit the search findings by date: for example, you could pull only cases decided after 2018.

Starting with a statute or case in your research rather than a general area of law can help anchor your search. Narrowing your search by jurisdiction or level of court (e.g., only searching Circuit Court cases or above) will refine your results and make the task of reviewing your findings less overwhelming.

On the opposite end of the writing process, though—far beyond the initial research phase and after you've drafted and revised your legal writing—you'll want to do one final cite check. In law firms, these are often done by someone other than the original author of the document. The cite checker goes through every citation to a statute, a case, an administrative regulation, etc. and makes sure:

1. That the citation itself is properly formatted. This textbook has focused on case citations specifically, but lawyers use a style manual called *The Bluebook: A Uniform System of Citation* that provides citation instructions for any kind of document that could be cited in a piece of legal writing;
2. That the language paraphrased or quoted from the cited source is accurate; and
3. That the cited law remains valid law and hasn't been overturned, overruled or deemed unconstitutional.

Shepardizing and KeyCiting are instrumental for performing task 3, though do remember that not every negative treatment of a statute or case is equivalent to an actual overturning of the law. Even if there's a negative treatment of a law that points to a court or multiple courts deeming the law unconstitutional, make sure (1) that citing court is binding on your jurisdiction and (2) that the part it's deeming unconstitutional is the part that's relevant to whatever you're arguing.

SEARCHING FOR SPECIFIC LAW IN TARGETED JURISDICTIONS

If secondary sources and starting point primary sources (such as statutes and cases) are not available or if you've exhausted all the above, you may want to try a targeted database search. A word of caution on targeted searches: there is a lot of case law in the world and if you search for a common legal term (e.g., "due process") in all federal cases in America, you're going to get thousands of results.

The first step in targeting a search is being as specific as possible in terms of (1) court(s) (federal or state jurisdiction? which specific court within that jurisdiction?) and (2) date range.

Both Lexis and Westlaw allow you to search for primary law using Natural Language (where you just enter your terms without any connectors) or Terms & Connectors (where you include connectors to establish relationships between terms). Terms & Connectors searching allows you to create more precise searches. With both methods, you can look for exact phrases by putting the phrases in quotation marks, e.g., "substantive due process." With Terms & Connectors, you can also use the following connectors:

- OR: Lexis and Westlaw will search for cases with either word/phrase on both sides of OR (e.g., liberty OR freedom)
- Proximity connectors:
  - Use w/p to find two words or phrases within the same paragraph (e.g., pharmacy w/p liability)
  - Use w/s to find two words or phrases within the same sentence (e.g., forfeiture w/s "property rights")
  - Use w/# to find two words or phrases within a certain number of words from one another (e.g., leave w/5 absence)
- AND: Lexis and Westlaw will search for cases that contain both words/phrases (e.g., criminal AND trespassing)
- AND NOT (Lexis) or BUT NOT (Westlaw): Lexis and Westlaw will look for cases with the word or phrase before the connector and exclude any results that have the word or phrase after the connector (e.g., catfish AND NOT water)

One other hint: if you want to capture multiple variations of the same root word, use the !. For example, a search for regulat! will capture results including "regulate," "regulates" and "regulator." On Lexis, you can use the ! for both Natural Language and Terms & Connectors searches.

SOME FINAL ADVICE ON THE RESEARCH PROCESS

In the course of your research, you may find it useful to craft a research outline where you curate all the potentially useful language you unearth. You can then cross-reference that outline to your writing/argument outline and match the research pieces to the relevant parts of your argument. Make sure your research outlines include full citations as well as pincites so you don't have to keep going back to the referent statute or case.

Finally, understand that research and writing are always intertwined. In the course of writing and rewriting any legal document, you will find gaps in your argument or the need for further clarification. Even the most well-prepared legal writer will move back and forth between research and writing. This is a natural part of the process, and it's why you must budget your time wisely.

> **Tips for Basic Legal Research**
>
> 1. Download any useful documents you pull from an online database as Word documents that you can mark and highlight. Highlight all important language from the statute or case. Then save all the downloaded, marked documents in a folder.
> 2. If you have trouble finding sources or are unsure whether your sources are correct for your task, consult a librarian, preferably a law librarian, for additional aid.

chapter 13

Introduction to Appellate Briefs

In the hierarchy of legal writing, the appellate brief stands at or near the very top, both in terms of its importance and of the wide range of skills required to craft an effective one. When a case in a lower court has been decided and that judgment is appealed, an appellant or petitioner will file a petition with the appropriate higher court asking for review of the opinion below. For example, if a party lost a federal case in district court, the appellant can appeal that case to the governing Circuit Court. If the same party loses at the Circuit Court, the petitioner can appeal that decision to the U.S. Supreme Court.

When a party appeals a decision, they are not asking the court to rehear the entire case. If, for example, a federal district court decided a kidnapping matter at trial, the relevant Circuit Court wouldn't put on the entire case—with witness testimony and opening and closing statements—a second time. Rather, the appellant would claim that the trial court made an error of law (such as misapplying a clause from the federal kidnapping statute) that requires the district court's decision to be reversed or vacated. The party opposing the appeal—the appellee or respondent—would then ask the same court to affirm the decision of the court below.

An appellate brief is not objective; you are writing on behalf of one side or another, and while you might choose to make certain strategic concessions, you should not concede any argument that is necessary for a positive outcome for your side. Embrace arguing in the alternative. If there are multiple ways for your side to win the case, start with the most straightforward path to victory, then posit other avenues in the event the court disagrees with the first.

GETTING STARTED

When crafting an appellate brief, regardless of which side you're on, you should start by carefully combing the opinion of the case being appealed. For example, if a Ninth Circuit decision is being appealed to the U.S. Supreme Court, your first frame of reference is that underlying Ninth Circuit opinion (and the district court opinion below that). You should also check to see what specific issues from the court below the higher court has agreed to hear. For example, if a given case involved seven issues and the Ninth Circuit decided all seven of them, the U.S. Supreme Court may only agree to hear an appeal on one of those issues. If that's the case, that one issue is the exclusive scope of the appeal and of the brief.

When starting to plan an appellate brief, it's not a bad idea to first summarize/brief the decision you are appealing, with an emphasis on the specific issues that have been preserved for appeal. What facts did the court use to arrive at its decision? What was its legal reasoning? What cited law supports that reasoning?

CONDUCTING RESEARCH

If you're unfamiliar with the area of law governing the case, you might find it useful to consult a legal encyclopedia, a treatise or a law review article to give you a general foundation. Once you have a grounding in the applicable doctrines, you should then read all the cited support for the lower court's reasoning. Did the lower court interpret its cited cases correctly? Are those cited cases still good law? You can determine the answer to the latter by researching the subsequent history (or Shepardizing or KeyCiting) those cases. Have any of the cases been overturned? Even if they haven't, have other courts criticized the reasoning or distinguished the matter from other cases?

Perusing the subsequent treatments of cited cases may reveal other useful decisions for your appellate brief. But you should also run targeted searches about the area of law, starting with binding jurisdictions (e.g., if the underlying appealed case was in the Ninth Circuit, start by searching for other Ninth Circuit cases and U.S. Supreme Court cases) but then expanding to other jurisdictions that would serve only as persuasive authority if the law isn't clear using binding authority alone.

Keep a list of all the cases you read. For the cases with some potentially useful language, save a copy, highlighting that language. You might then create a research outline: a set of notes with the citations for the cases you've pulled followed by excerpted quotes with pincites. For example:

DeShaney v. Winnebago Cnty. Dep't of Soc. Servs., 489 U.S. 189 (1989).

- "[N]othing in the language of the Due Process Clause requires the State to protect life, liberty, and property of its citizens against invasion by private actors." 195.
- "Its purpose was to protect the people from the State, not to ensure that the State protected them from each other." 196.

OUTLINING YOUR ARGUMENT

Again, you should start with the specific questions the appellate court has certified. Everything you write should be tailored toward answering those questions in your favor. Start with your strongest arguments, keeping in mind that a judge's attention will always be sharpest at the beginning of your presentation and that you shouldn't waste any opportunity to frame the case in a way that benefits you. Be thoughtful about your order of operations, though: make sure that any threshold or foundational propositions (like standards of review) precede arguments that necessarily build upon those foundations.

Standards of review dictate how much deference a court affords the decisions of the court below or the legislature (when determining the constitutionality of a statute). Generally, questions of law are reviewed *de novo*, or as if the appellate court is hearing the issue anew and independently, regardless of the conclusions of the lower court. By contrast, questions of fact might be reviewed under a clearly erroneous standard, requiring the appellate court to afford substantial deference to the lower court and to only overturn that court's finding if it has a firm conviction that a mistake has been committed. The way you argue necessarily shifts with different standards of review, so bear this in mind as you outline your strategy.

As stated above, you should be prepared to argue in the alternative if there is more than one way toward a favorable outcome. For example, if the best standard of review for your client is rational basis (a relatively permissive standard and easy threshold to meet), then argue for that first and show how you'd meet it. But if your opponent will likely argue that intermediate scrutiny (a more rigorous standard) is the proper standard of review, show how you could win under that standard as well.

When the constitutionality of a law is challenged, courts will typically analyze the law under one of the following levels of judicial scrutiny, ordered here from the highest to lowest level of scrutiny:

- *Strict scrutiny*, which requires the government to prove the law in question is narrowly tailored to achieve a compelling government interest. Strict scrutiny is applied when a law infringes upon a fundamental right (such as the right to marry) or discriminates against a class of individuals who have been historically subject to discrimination (on the basis, for example, of race, religion, national origin or alienage).
- *Intermediate scrutiny*, which requires the government to prove the law in question is substantially related to achieving an important government objective. Intermediate scrutiny has been applied, for example, when a law discriminates on the basis of gender.
- *Rational basis review*, where the government only has to show that the law in question is rationally related to a legitimate state interest. Generally, when a law doesn't involve a fundamental right or discriminate against a suspect class, courts will apply this much more deferential standard.

Arguments in an appellate brief should follow the CRAC structure:

1. Conclusion
2. Rule
3. Application
4. Conclusion

CRAC is similar to IRAC (Issue → Rule → Application → Conclusion) but instead of framing the issue as a neutral question, you begin right away with the ultimate conclusion you want your reader to come to. So instead of an open issue question like "Does X's work meet the elements of copyright infringement?" you'd start with your ultimate conclusion: "X's work infringes on Y's copyright." Your argument outline should include every necessary conclusion for your side. Underneath each conclusion, provide whatever relevant law applies (the Rule) and the facts relevant to that applicable law (the Application). With that raw material, you can craft the arguments and counterarguments for the rest of the Application in your CRAC.

Each major conclusion from your outline can convert into an argument heading in the body of your brief. The argument headings, in turn, would populate the line references in your Table of Contents.

FORMATTING YOUR BRIEF

Different courts will have different rules for formatting briefs. The following comes from the 2019 Rules of the Supreme Court of the United States.[1]

The cover page of the brief must include the following in order (see the following page for a sample cover page):

1. Docket number (e.g., No. 12-345)
2. Name of the court (e.g., "**In the Supreme Court of the United States**")
3. Caption of the case (e.g., "Shauli Bar-On, Petitioner v. Daniel Toomey, Respondent")
4. Nature of the proceeding and the name of the court from which the action is brought (e.g., "ON WRIT OF CERTIORARI TO THE UNITED STATES COURT OF APPEALS FOR THE NINTH CIRCUIT")
5. Title of document (e.g., "**BRIEF FOR THE PETITIONERS**")
6. Names of the attorneys of record for the filing party

---

1. https://www.supremecourt.gov/ctrules/2019RulesoftheCourt.pdf, Rules 34 and 24.

No. 12-345

In the Supreme Court of the United States

SHAULI BAR-ON, PETITIONER

v.

DANIEL TOOMEY, RESPONDENT

ON WRIT OF CERTIORARI TO THE UNITED STATES COURT OF APPEALS FOR THE NINTH CIRCUIT

BRIEF FOR THE PETITIONER

CYRUS MANN,
    Counsel of Record
MICHAEL JEUNG
GRACE MCMAHON
BEN ROSENTHAL
KASIA RUDNICKI
EVAN WALIKE
ADRIKA YOUSUF
VIBHAV LAUD
TRENTON STONE
    Attorneys

MANN & MCMAHON
123 Justice Street
Washington, D.C. 20004

(123) 456-7890

The cover page should be followed by:

1. **The questions presented for review.** The phrasing of the questions presented does not need to be identical to the questions from the petition for writ of certiorari or the jurisdictional statement, but the brief may not raise new questions or change the substance of the questions presented in those documents. Keeping this caveat in mind, use this opportunity to phrase the questions in your favor.

   In 2021, the California Supreme Court heard an appeal on a case called *Smith v. LoanMe*, where the central question, according to the court, was: "Does Penal Code section 632.7 prohibit only third-party eavesdroppers from recording calls involving a cellular or cordless telephone, or does it also prohibit participants in calls from recording them without the other participants' consent?"

   I had two teams of students representing both sides of this matter in an Advanced Legal Writing class, and they each framed the question presented differently:

   The team representing LoanMe, who argued that the law should only apply to eavesdroppers, crafted the following question: "Does California Penal Code section 632.7 apply to individuals participating in a telephone call or does it apply solely to eavesdroppers?"

   The team representing Smith, who argued that the law should apply to eavesdroppers *and* participants on a phone call, crafted this question: "Does California Penal Code section 632.7, which prohibits the intentional recording of wireless phone calls 'without the consent of all parties,' prohibit one wireless phone call communicant from intentionally recording other communicants without their consent?"

   Notice how the LoanMe team made the argument about whether a penal code section applied to "individuals participating in a telephone call" or whether it applied to "eavesdroppers." In that framing, "eavesdroppers" seem like the more probable target of a criminal statute. The Smith team, however, doesn't even mention eavesdroppers in their question. Instead, they draw attention to the specific language of the penal code as well as instances when someone on a call records that call without the other party's consent. Both articulations represent a fair reframing of the California Supreme Court's question, but the subtle changes in the focus of each question make you more inclined to answer that question in favor of the party posing it.

2. **A table of contents.** The Argument portion of your brief should roughly align with the flow of major points in your outline. Try to frame these headings as affirmative conclusions in your favor (e.g., "The Act's funding conditions may constitutionally be applied to foreign entities."). Each heading will then be a separate line reference in your table of contents.

3. **A table of cited authorities.** Reference the pages in the documents where the authorities are cited. Categories of authorities should be handled in the following order, and items within each category should be alphabetized:
    a. Cases
    b. Constitutional provisions, statutes and regulations
    c. Other cited documents, including, e.g., treatises and legislative histories
4. **Opinions below.** Provide citations of the official and unofficial reports of the prior opinions and orders in the case by courts and administrative agencies.
5. **Basis for jurisdiction.** Offer a concise statement of the basis for jurisdiction by the court, including relevant statutory provisions and the dates when the petition for *writ of certiorari* (the order by which an appellate court decides to review a lower court's decision) was filed and when the petition was granted.
6. **Constitutional provisions, treaties, statutes, ordinances and regulations involved.** Set out verbatim with proper citations. If a provision is lengthy, citation alone is sufficient as long as the pertinent text is included in an appendix to the brief.

A respondent's brief can exclude the following items from the list above unless the respondent is dissatisfied with the opposing party's presentation: (1) questions presented, (4) opinions below, (5) basis for jurisdiction and (6) constitutional provisions, treaties, statutes, ordinances and regulations involved.

After the cover page and the six sections listed above, the real meat of the brief begins.

CRAFTING THE STATEMENT OF THE CASE

In the Statement of the Case, you will recite the facts relevant to the questions presented. Explain the who, what, when, where, why and how of the case. Depending on the complexity of the matter, you may need to break the Statement into parts (e.g., Factual Background and Procedural History).

While you don't want to be overtly argumentative, how you present the relevant events can have a significant effect on how the reader interprets those events. All material facts—meaning facts that are relevant in determining the case's outcome—must be included. Any references to the appendix or to the factual record of the case must be cited.

Below is an example of a Statement of the Case, taken from the student team representing Petitioner Smith in the *LoanMe* matter discussed above.

STATEMENT OF THE CASE

A. Facts

Respondent LoanMe is a lender that offers personal and small business loans to qualified customers. Clerk's Transcript on Appeal, Vol. I ("CTA"), at 073. LoanMe offered Appellant Jeremiah Smith's wife a loan. *Id.* In October 2015, LoanMe called Smith's wife to discuss the specifics of the loan. *Id.* Smith answered the call on a cordless telephone and informed LoanMe that his wife was not home and ended the call. *Id.*

Unbeknownst to Smith, LoanMe recorded that entire phone conversation. *Id.* When Smith was on that call, LoanMe did not inform him that the call might be recorded for quality assurance purposes—as other businesses often do. Nor did Smith express on his own accord any permission for LoanMe to record him. Instead, three seconds into the call, LoanMe played a "beep tone" that—unlike the beep tones many are accustomed to hearing before leaving someone a voicemail—was not preceded by an oral instruction. This "beep tone" simply played in the background every 15 seconds, curiously without explanation. *Id.*

B. Procedural History

Within a year, Smith filed a civil class action complaint against LoanMe for violating P.C. § 632.7. While 632.7 imposes criminal penalties, Plaintiffs can also recover civil damages for each violation. *See* § 637.2. The parties agreed to a bifurcated bench trial to decide whether LoanMe's intermittent beep tones provided Smith sufficient notice that they were recording their call with him. LoanMe's argument was that, since Smith had notice that he was being recorded, and Smith stayed on the line, he implicitly consented to LoanMe recording him. By contrast, Smith's position was that he did not consent to being recorded because the beep tones by themselves were not sufficient notice, and that a verbal explanation was necessary. The trial judge found that the beep tones were sufficient notice and that Smith implicitly consented to being recorded—meaning that there was no violation of 632.7.

Smith appealed. Rather than consider the merits of the beep tone argument, the Court of Appeal—for reasons unclear—ordered that the parties provide supplemental briefing on an unrelated issue: whether 632.7 should be interpreted as only applying to the recording of a wireless communication that was "hacked" or "pirated" by someone who was not a party to the communication. Order Pursuant to Gov. C. Section 68081 (June 25, 2019) at p. 1. At the end of 2019, the Court of Appeal held that 632.7—which prohibits the intentional recording of a wireless communication "without the consent of all parties"—did not prohibit LoanMe from recording Smith without his consent. Within a month, Smith petitioned this Court for review—which was granted in early April 2020.

CRAFTING THE SUMMARY OF THE ARGUMENT

The Summary of the Argument is your opportunity to frame the meaning and significance of the case. It is not just a repetition of the argument headings, but a clear and concise condensation of your holistic argument. Think about a theme for your side ("This case is about X"). Think about the stakes to the relevant jurisdiction (e.g., the state, the country, the legal system). Break your argument down to the most compelling reasons that your side should prevail. And if possible, try to defang your opponent's anticipated case. You may be tempted to avoid tackling your opponent's strongest arguments head-on, but putting forward your own framing of the case only matters if you can keep the court from buying in to your opponent's framing.

Below is an example of a Summary of the Argument, again taken from the student team representing Petitioner Smith in the *LoanMe* matter.

SUMMARY OF THE ARGUMENT

This case is about upholding the long precedent in California of protecting telephone privacy rights. 50 years ago, the Legislature passed the California Invasion of Privacy Act § 630 *et seq.* ("CIPA") — an effort to protect privacy in the face of evolving technology. More than anything, CIPA guarantees Californians the expectation that their phone conversations won't be recorded unless *all* parties consent. As part of that scheme, the law in question — § 632.7 — prohibits *anyone* from "intercepting or receiving" and recording a wireless call "without the consent of all parties." Yet, in its decision, the Court of Appeal flipped that concept on its head, granting LoanMe the ability to record its clients despite the lack of affirmative consent.

When this Court has to determine the meaning of a statute, there are two steps. First, this Court has to determine whether the plain meaning of the law is clear and unambiguous. If it is, then the analysis stops here and that interpretation controls. But if the language of the statute permits more than one reasonable interpretation, this Court moves to the second step — which is to consider the statute's intent and public policy. Here, Smith prevails because the plain text of the law clearly and unambiguously supports his reading: that the law prohibits wireless call participants and eavesdroppers from recording. But even if this Court disagrees that Smith's reading is clear and unambiguous, the Legislature's intent and public policy tip the scales in his favor.

Plain Text Argument
The language and construction of § 632.7 makes its meaning clear and unambiguous; the law prohibits both eavesdroppers and call participants from recording a wireless call without the consent of all parties. Subsection A of § 632.7 reads, "Every person who, without the consent of all parties to a communication, intercepts or receives and intentionally records . . . a communication transmitted between two cellular radio telephones . . . shall be punished by a fine . . . or by imprisonment . . . or by both that fine and imprisonment."

§ 632.7 states that **all** parties to a communication must give their consent both to participate in the call and for the call to be recorded. Thus, § 632.7 applies both to parties who failed to receive consent from the other party to record the call, as well as to third parties who intercepted the call and recorded it without consent from any party. As a participant in the call, Mr. Smith falls under the category of all parties, but he never granted permission for LoanMe, or any other party, to record the call. That Mr. Smith, as a party to the call, did not give his permission to have the call recorded is not changed by **who** recorded the call.

But even if this Court is inclined to find that the law is subject to more than one reasonable interpretation, this Court should still side with the interpretation that § 632.7 applies to both third-party interlopers and call participants because both the Legislature's intent and public policy support that interpretation.

Intent Argument
The Legislature's intent behind 632.7 supports Smith's reading. Put simply: the statute was intended to extend landline privacy protections to wireless phone calls. Under 632—an original part of the 1967 CIPA legislation—recording a confidential communication without the consent of *all* parties is prohibited. Before 632.7 was passed, however, that protection was only extended to landline phone calls. That's because, the Legislature determined, while landline calls that travel by wire have an expectation of privacy that comes with them, wireless calls that travel through the air do not. This meant that while a participant to a landline call could not record without the consent of all parties, a participant to a wireless phone call could. The goal of the Legislature was to close this loophole. In his statement of intent, the author of 632.7—Lloyd Connelly—outright said that the purpose of the law was to extend to wireless calls the same protection from recording that landline calls enjoyed.

Public Policy Argument
The Court of Appeal guts California's reputation as an all-party consent state. Instead of Californians affirmatively giving their consent to being recorded, the Court of Appeal equated remaining on a call with consent to record. The danger is three-fold. Californians, who fear that their privacy has been violated, will turn to the California Constitution's affirmative guarantee of privacy. Businesses that record their customers will face a flood of litigation by Californians who no longer sue under § 632.7, but find alternative causes of action, such as the privacy torts. As an unintended consequence, the judicial system will have to bear the brunt of providing the infrastructure for the influx of litigation. In today's COVID-19 era, telephone and video calls are becoming more commonplace and personal, compounding the violations of privacy. Yet the issue of Californians' privacy is unlikely to go away after the coronavirus has been defeated. Rather, as businesses realize that they can save money by hiring remote employees, it is likely that the practice of holding most meetings over Zoom will continue. Even though the Legislature 50 years ago did not envision their statute's application in the middle of a global pandemic, preventing companies from unilaterally recording Californians in a phone conversation is exactly what legislators feared and worked to prevent. Today and into the future, Californians need their privacy protections more than ever.

CRAFTING THE ARGUMENT

The organizing theme or theory of the case should inform the structure and content of your argument. With that in mind:

- Consider a summary or umbrella paragraph(s) before launching into your individual arguments
- Remember to address necessary threshold issues first when appropriate (e.g., standard of review before applying that standard of review)
- Remember to argue in the alternative where necessary (e.g., even if the court doesn't accept your desired level of scrutiny, you would still win applying any scrutiny)
- Open with your strongest argument, and as long as logic would not dictate otherwise (see the second bullet point above regarding threshold issues), present your arguments from strongest to weakest
- Utilize headings and subheadings, and bullets and numbered lists to make your analysis as clear as possible
- Use transitions to make logical relationships clear

As mentioned in the Outlining section above, CRAC should be your default analytical model. The components of the analysis are almost identical to IRAC, discussed in depth in Chapters 6 and 7, but instead of starting with an open question, you start (and end) with a conclusion of law in favor of whatever side you're arguing.

1. **Conclusion:** Summarize how the law applies to your facts; this should be a proposition you want the court to accept.
2. **Rule:** Explain and cite the relevant legal propositions upon which you rely. Quote the law if necessary. Keep in mind the hierarchy of law and start with law that has the most binding authority (e.g., statutes before case law; Supreme Court cases before district court cases).
3. **Application:** Explain how the legal propositions above apply to the facts of the case. Repeat the language of the legal test to aid in clarifying the link between law and fact.
    a. You may also want to draw factual comparisons between your case and precedent cases (the latter of which might not have been included in the Rule section above, which generally only encompasses the basic standard). Analogize your client's facts to facts from favorable case law.
    b. You should also make counterarguments: summarize how the opposing party will likely apply the law to the facts, then counter that argument. Distinguish your client's facts from facts within unfavorable case law.
4. **Conclusion:** After rebutting your opponent's likely stance on your argument, reiterate the legal conclusion for which you advocate.
    a. To emphasize the importance of a conclusion in your party's favor, you may then contemplate the undesirable consequences—both from an individual case and a broader policy standpoint—should the court find against you.
    b. Conversely, you might posit any desirable anticipated outcomes if the court finds in your favor.

CONCLUDING THE BRIEF

Your conclusion to the brief can be as short as a sentence or two. You've already summarized your argument above, so all you must do now is specify with particularity the relief you are seeking (e.g., For the foregoing reasons, the judgment below should be affirmed/reversed.).

After your conclusion, you should then include the name of the counsel of record and other such counsel, as identified on the cover page.

ATTACHING APPENDICES

Craft a new table of contents for the appendix that provides a description of each document in the appendix. Renumber pages in the appendix (e.g., A1-A45).

Below is a rubric for evaluating appellate briefs:

APPELLATE BRIEF RUBRIC

Category	Accomplished	Competent	Beginning
Presentation and Professionalism			
· Writes in clear and accessible prose			
· Employs proper organization, including adherence to CRAC			
· Shows command of grammar, syntax and citation			
Substantive Argument			
· Question presented is clearly and strategically crafted			
· Statement of case is logically presented and properly curated			
· Summary of argument forecasts the argument effectively			
· Rule discussions are complete and accurate			
· Application analysis is focused, persuasive and clear			
· Application covers both argument and counterargument			
· Conclusions are clear and supported by argument			
General Comments and Suggestions for Improvement:			
			Grade: _____

Below is a more complete excerpt of the student-written appellant brief in the *LoanMe* case referenced above. The fuller treatment below should give you a better sense of how the pieces of a brief work together and how the argument is constructed. Notice the detailed Table of Contents that outlines the entire brief. And as complicated and multifaceted as the argument is, note how the prose is clear and accessible.

No. S260391

In the Supreme Court of California

JEREMIAH SMITH, PLAINTIFF AND APPELLANT,

v.

LOANME, INC., DEFENDANT AND RESPONDENT

After a Decision by the Court of Appeal
Fourth Appellate District, Division Two (Case No. E069752)
On Appeal from the Riverside County Superior Court
(Case No. RIC1612501; Hon. Sharon J. Waters)

APPELLANT'S OPENING BRIEF ON THE MERITS

Student G—
Student L—
Student M—
    Attorneys

G—, L— & M—, LLP
1880 Freedom Way
Los Angeles, CA 90007
(310) 123-0027

ISSUE PRESENTED

Does California Penal Code section 632.7, which prohibits the intentional recording of wireless phone calls "without the consent of all parties," prohibit one wireless phone call communicant from intentionally recording other communicants without their consent?

TABLE OF CONTENTS

ISSUE PRESENTED	277
TABLE OF AUTHORITIES	279
STATEMENT OF THE CASE	281
SUMMARY OF THE ARGUMENT	281
ARGUMENT	283
I. § 632.7 clearly and unambiguously applies to participants in a wireless phone conversation, not just third parties.	284
A. § 632.7 requires that both third parties and call participants obtain the consent of *all* call participants to record a call.	284
B. § 632.7 purposely uses *both* "intercepts" and "receives" to prohibit *both* third parties and call participants from recording without consent.	284
C. Consent cannot be implicitly given under § 632.7.	284
D. The grammatical construction of the statute supports the interpretation that § 632.7 applies both to third parties and call participants.	285
E. The Court of Appeal erred by applying the language of § 632.5 and § 632.6 to determine that § 632.7 applies only to third parties.	286
IV. The Court of Appeal's interpretation of § 632.7 has negative policy implications.	286
A. The Court of Appeal's interpretation revokes California's status as an all-party consent state and instead unilaterally changes it to a one-party consent state.	286
B. The Court of Appeal's interpretation will increase privacy violations under the California Constitution, leading to a flood of litigation.	287
C. Due to COVID-19, the use of telephone and video calls have become more pervasive and personal. A ruling for LoanMe would gut any semblance of societal privacy norms.	287
CONCLUSION	288

TABLE OF AUTHORITIES

CASES:

Ades v. Omni Hotels Mgmt. Corp. (C.D. Cal. 2014) 46 F. Supp. 3d 999 18
Brinkley v. Monterey Fin. Svcs. (S.D. Cal. 2018) 340 F. Supp. 3d 1036 19
Brown v. Defender Sec. Co. (C.D. Cal. Oct. 22, 2012) No. CV 12-7319-CAS
    (PJWx), 2012 WL 5308964 17
Burkley v. Nine W. Holdings Inc. (Cal. Super. Los Angeles County Sept. 5,
    2017), No. BC641730, 2017 35WL 4479316 .... passim
California Emp. Stabilization Commission v. Payne, 31 Cal. 2d 210 (1947) 27
Carrese v. Yes Online, Inc. (C.D. Cal. Oct. 13, 2016) No. CV 16-05301 SJO
    (AFMx), 2016 WL 6069198 19
Flanagan v. Flanagan (2002) 27 Cal. 4th 766 25
Forest E. Olson, Inc. v. Superior Court (1976) 63 Cal. App. 3d 188 26
Gamez v. Hilton Grand Vacations, Inc. (C.D. Cal. Oct. 22, 2018) No.
    18-cv-04803 GW (JPRx), 2018 WL 8050479 20
Granina v. Eddie Bauer LLC (Cal. Super. Los Angeles County Dec. 2, 2015), No.
    BC569111, 2015 WL 9855304 22, 23, ... 24
Horowitz v. GC Services Limited P'ship (S.D. Cal. Dec. 12, 2016) No. 14cv2512-
    MMA RBB, 2016 WL 7188238 17, ... 18
Kuschner v. Nationwide Credit, Inc. (E.D. Cal. 2009) 256 F.R.D. 684 17
Lal v. Capital One Fin. Corp. (N.D. Cal. Apr. 12, 2017) No.
    16-cv-06674-BLF, 2017 WL 1345636 18, ... 20
Lerman v. Swarovski North America Ltd. (S.D. Cal. Sept. 10, 2019) No.
    19cv638-LAB (BLM), 2019 WL 4277408 21
Maghen v. Quicken Loans, Inc. (C.D. Cal. 2015) 94 F. Supp. 3d 1141 21
McCabe v. Intercontinental Hotels Group Res., Inc. (N.D. Cal. Dec. 18,
    2012) No. 12-cv-04818 NC, 2012 WL 13060326 20
McEwan v. OSP Grp., L.P. (S.D. Cal. July 2, 2015) No. 14-cv -2823-
    BEN (WVG), 2015 WL 13374016 21
Meza v. Portfolio Recovery Associates, LLC (2019) 6 Cal. 5th 844 .... passim
Montantes v. Inventure Foods (C.D. Cal. July 2, 2014) No.
    CV-14-1129-MWF (RZx), 2014 WL 3305578 17
Mt. Hawley Ins. Co. v. Lopez, 215 Cal. App. 4th 1385, 1408 (Cal. App. Ct. 2013) ... 27
Portillo v. ICON Health & Fitness, Inc. (C.D. Cal. Dec. 16, 2019) 2019
    WL 6840759 20
Raffin v. Medicredit, Inc. (C.D. Cal. Jan. 3, 2017) No. CV 15-4912-
    GHK (PJWx); 2017 WL 131745 18
Ramos v. Capital One, N.A. (N.D. Cal. 2017) No. 17-cv-00435-BLF,
    2017 WL 3232488 19
Rezvanpour v. SGS Auto. Services, Inc. (C.D. Cal. July 11, 2014)
    No. 14-cv -00113-ODW(JPRx), 2014 WL 3436811 18
Ronquillo-Griffin v. TELUS Communications, Inc. (S.D. Cal. June 27,
    2017) No. 17cv129 JM (BLM), 2017 WL 2779329 18
Sentz v. Euromarket Designs, Inc. (C.D. Cal. May 16, 2013) No. EDCV
    12-00487-VAP (SPx), 2013 WL 12139140 21
Simpson v. Best Western Intern., Inc. (N.D. Cal. Nov. 13, 2012) No.
    12-cv-04672-JCS, 2012 WL 5499928 17
Simpson v. Vantage Hospitality Grp., Inc. (N.D. Cal. Dec. 4, 2012) No.
    12-cv-04814-YGR, 2012 WL 6025772 7
Smith v. LoanMe, Inc. (2020) 43 Cal. App. 5th 844 12

STATUTES:
Cal. Penal C. § 632 .... passim
Cal. Penal C. § 632.5 .... passim
Cal. Penal C. § 632.6 .... passim
Cal. Penal C. § 632.7 .... passim
Cal. Penal C. § 633.5 ....25, 27, 28
Cal. Penal C. § 637.2 7
California Invasion of Privacy Act, Penal Code § 630, et seq. 9, 25

CONSTITUTIONAL PROVISIONS:
Cal. Const. Art. I § 1 31

OTHER AUTHORITIES:
AB 2465 Author's File Materials, Statement of Intent 10
Black's Law Dictionary Eighth Edition 23
Clerk's Transcript on Appeal, Vol. I 7
Committee Report for 2015 California AB 925 (May 5, 2015) 29
Order Pursuant to Gov. C. Section 68081 (June 25, 2019) 8
Legislative Counsel of California Analysis re: Invasion of Privacy
    (December 17, 1991) 26
Letter from Gene Erbin, Counsel for Lloyd G. Connelly, regarding AB
    2465 (February 6, 1992) 28

STATEMENT OF THE CASE

A. Facts

Respondent LoanMe is a lender that offers personal and small business loans to qualified customers. Clerk's Transcript on Appeal, Vol. I ("CTA"), at 073. LoanMe offered Appellant Jeremiah Smith's wife a loan. *Id.* In October 2015, LoanMe called Smith's wife to discuss the specifics of the loan. *Id.* Smith answered the call on a cordless telephone and informed LoanMe that his wife was not home and ended the call. *Id.*

Unbeknownst to Smith, LoanMe recorded that entire phone conversation. *Id.* When Smith was on that call, LoanMe did not inform him that the call might be recorded for quality assurance purposes — as other businesses often do. Nor did Smith express on his own accord any permission for LoanMe to record him. Instead, three seconds into the call, LoanMe played a "beep tone" that — unlike the beep tones many are accustomed to hearing before leaving someone a voicemail — was not preceded by an oral instruction. This "beep tone" simply played in the background every 15 seconds, curiously without explanation. *Id.*

B. Procedural History

Within a year, Smith filed a civil class action complaint against LoanMe for violating P.C. § 632.7. While 632.7 imposes criminal penalties, Plaintiffs can also recover civil damages for each violation. *See* § 637.2. The parties agreed to a bifurcated bench trial to decide whether LoanMe's intermittent beep tones provided Smith sufficient notice that they were recording their call with him. LoanMe's argument was that, since Smith had notice that he was being recorded, and Smith stayed on the line, he implicitly consented to LoanMe recording him. By contrast, Smith's position was that he did not consent to being recorded because the beep tones by themselves were not sufficient notice, and that a verbal explanation was necessary. The trial judge found that the beep tones were sufficient notice and that Smith implicitly consented to being recorded — meaning that there was no violation of 632.7.

Smith appealed. Rather than consider the merits of the beep tone argument, the Court of Appeal — for reasons unclear — ordered that the parties provide supplemental briefing on an unrelated issue: whether 632.7 should be interpreted as only applying to the recording of a wireless communication that was "hacked" or "pirated" by someone who was not a party to the communication. Order Pursuant to Gov. C. Section 68081 (June 25, 2019) at p. 1. At the end of 2019, the Court of Appeal held that 632.7 — which prohibits the intentional recording of a wireless communication "without the consent of all parties" — did not prohibit LoanMe from recording Smith without his consent. Within a month, Smith petitioned this Court for review — which was granted in early April 2020.

SUMMARY OF THE ARGUMENT

This case is about upholding the long precedent in California of protecting telephone privacy rights. 50 years ago, the Legislature passed the California Invasion of Privacy Act

§ 630 *et seq.* ("CIPA") — an effort to protect privacy in the face of evolving technology. More than anything, CIPA guarantees Californians the expectation that their phone conversations won't be recorded unless *all* parties consent. As part of that scheme, the law in question — § 632.7 — prohibits *anyone* from "intercepting or receiving" and recording a wireless call "without the consent of all parties." Yet, in its decision, the Court of Appeal flipped that concept on its head, granting LoanMe the ability to record its clients despite the lack of affirmative consent.

When this Court has to determine the meaning of a statute, there are two steps. First, this Court has to determine whether the plain meaning of the law is clear and unambiguous. If it is, then the analysis stops here and that interpretation controls. But if the language of the statute permits more than one reasonable interpretation, this Court moves to the second step — which is to consider the statute's intent and public policy. Here, Smith prevails because the plain text of the law clearly and unambiguously supports his reading: that the law prohibits wireless call participants and eavesdroppers from recording. But even if this Court disagrees that Smith's reading is clear and unambiguous, the Legislature's intent and public policy tip the scales in his favor.

Plain Text Argument

The language and construction of § 632.7 makes its meaning clear and unambiguous; the law prohibits both eavesdroppers and call participants from recording a wireless call without the consent of all parties. Subsection A of § 632.7 reads, "Every person who, without the consent of all parties to a communication, intercepts or receives and intentionally records . . . a communication transmitted between two cellular radio telephones . . . shall be punished by a fine . . . or by imprisonment . . . or by both that fine and imprisonment."

§ 632.7 states that **all** parties to a communication must give their consent both to participate in the call and for the call to be recorded. Thus, § 632.7 applies both to parties who failed to receive consent from the other party to record the call, as well as to third parties who intercepted the call and recorded it without consent from any party. As a participant in the call, Mr. Smith falls under the category of all parties, but he never granted permission for LoanMe, or any other party, to record the call. That Mr. Smith, as a party to the call, did not give his permission to have the call recorded is not changed by **who** recorded the call.

But even if this Court is inclined to find that the law is subject to more than one reasonable interpretation, this Court should still side with the interpretation that § 632.7 applies to both third-party interlopers and call participants because both the Legislature's intent and public policy support that interpretation.

Intent Argument

The Legislature's intent behind 632.7 supports Smith's reading. Put simply: the statute was intended to extend landline privacy protections to wireless phone calls. Under 632 — an original part of the 1967 CIPA legislation — recording a confidential communication without the consent of *all* parties is prohibited. Before 632.7 was passed, however, that protection was only extended to landline phone calls. That's because, the Legislature determined, while landline calls that travel by wire have an expectation of privacy that come with them, wireless calls that travel through the air do not. This meant that while a participant to a landline call could not record without the consent of all parties, a participant to a wireless phone call could. The goal of the Legislature was to close this loophole. In his statement of intent, the author of 632.7—Lloyd Connelly—outright said that the purpose of the law was to extend to wireless calls the same protection from recording that landline calls enjoyed.

Public Policy Argument

The Court of Appeal guts California's reputation as an all-party consent state. Instead of Californians affirmatively giving their consent to being recorded, the Court of Appeal equated remaining on a call with consent to record. The danger is three-fold. Californians, who fear that their privacy has been violated, will turn to the California Constitution's affirmative guarantee of privacy. Businesses that record their customers will face a flood of litigation by Californians who no longer sue under § 632.7, but find alternative causes of action, such as the privacy torts. As an unintended consequence, the judicial system will have to bear the brunt of providing the infrastructure for the influx of litigation. In today's COVID-19 era, telephone and video calls are becoming more commonplace and personal, compounding the violations of privacy. Yet the issue of Californians' privacy is unlikely to go away after the coronavirus has been defeated. Rather, as businesses realize that they can save money by hiring remote employees, it is likely that the practice of holding most meetings over Zoom will continue. Even though the Legislature 50 years ago did not envision their statute's application in the middle of a global pandemic, preventing companies from unilaterally recording Californians in a phone conversation is exactly what legislators feared and worked to prevent. Today and into the future, Californians need their privacy protections more than ever.

ARGUMENT

Background—Analytical Framework for Statutory Interpretation

When interpreting a statute, this Court must "first examine the statutory language, giving it a plain and commonsense meaning." *Meza v. Portfolio Recovery Associates, LLC* (2019) 6 Cal. 5th 844, 856. If the language of the statute is clear and unambiguous, this Court is bound by its plain meaning "unless a literal interpretation would result in absurd consequences the Legislature did not intend." *Id.* Here, the language of § 632.7 is clear and unambiguous: parties of a wireless phone conversation cannot record each other without consent. If however, the § 632.7 language permits more than one reasonable interpretation, this Court "may consider other aids, such as the statute's purpose, legislative history, and public policy" to determine which interpretation is binding. *Id.* In this case, the purpose, history, and policy reasons behind § 632.7 undermine the Court of Appeal's reading and support Smith's position.

I. § 632.7 clearly and unambiguously applies to participants in a wireless phone conversation, not just third parties.

A. § 632.7 requires that both third parties and call participants obtain the consent of *all* call participants to record a call.

Subsection A of § 632.7 reads, "Every person who, without the consent of all parties to a communication, intercepts or receives and intentionally records . . . a communication transmitted between two cellular radio telephones . . . shall be punished by a fine . . . or by imprisonment . . . or by both that fine and imprisonment."

§ 632.7 states that **all** parties to a communication must give their consent both to participate in the call and for the call to be recorded. Thus, § 632.7 applies both to parties who failed to receive consent from the other party to record the call, as well as to third parties who intercepted the call and recorded it without consent from any party. As a participant in the call, Mr. Smith falls under the category of all parties, but he never granted permission for LoanMe, or any other party, to record the call. That Mr. Smith, as a party to the call, did not give his permission to have the call recorded is not changed by **who** recorded the call.

B. § 632.7 purposely uses *both* "intercepts" and "receives" to prohibit *both* third parties and call participants from recording without consent.

§ 632.7 includes both the words "intercepts" and "receives," meaning that they are not synonymous and therefore describe different actions. Had the legislators intended "intercept" and "receive" to have the same meaning, both words would not have been included in the statute. The definition of the word intercept is "to see or overhear (a message, transmission, etc.) intended for another." Because the word intercept describes hearing a communication that was intended for someone other than yourself, it is used in the statute to refer to third parties. But just because "intercept" describes third parties, that does not mean that "receive" does as well. To intercept something is necessarily surreptitious, while the word receive is not. The word receive means only "to take delivery of something." Therefore because the word receive is not surreptitious and because it means simply to take delivery of, the action of receiving in the statute describes participants in the call, not third parties. A participant in the call receives a communication when the other party speaks to them. And so, because the word intercept describes the action done by third parties and the word receive describes the action done by call participants, the statute applies both to parties to a call and interlopers.

C. Consent cannot be implicitly given under § 632.7.

§ 632.7 requires that all parties to a call give their consent for that call to be recorded. To consent to something is to give permission for that thing to happen. LoanMe never asked Mr. Smith for his permission to record the call, nor did he ever provide it. LoanMe therefore violated the statute. The Court of Appeal claimed that because Mr. Smith answered the call, he implicitly consented to having the call recorded as well. *Id.* at 852. But this contradicts the very definition of the word consent. Consent cannot be implicitly given because to consent to something is to affirmatively and specifically allow it. Additionally, while Mr. Smith did consent to participating in the call, it was not true, informed consent because he had not been apprised of all the circumstances surrounding the call—that LoanMe was recording the call. Mr. Smith may not have consented to remaining on the call if he had known that LoanMe was recording it. For those reasons, Mr. Smith could not, nor did he, implicitly consent to LoanMe recording their wireless phone conversation. Because LoanMe recorded the call without Mr. Smith's consent, as required by the statute, they violated § 632.7.

D. The grammatical construction of the statute supports the interpretation that § 632.7 applies both to third parties and call participants.

The prepositional phrase "without the consent of all parties" modifies the entire clause "intercepts or receives and intentionally records" in §632.7. Grammatically, the phrase cannot modify only part of the clause. All parties have to give consent **both** for the call to take place and for the recording of the call. The plain language and construction of the statute binds these two actions together. By the word "or," the statute makes clear that if someone either "intercepts" a call or "receives" it, and then records it, they must do so with the consent of all parties. The statute applies both to people who "intercept and intentionally record" a wireless phone conversation—third parties—and to people who "receive and intentionally record" a wireless phone conversation: participants on the call. Please see the following chart for further clarification on how the construction of the statute affects its meaning:

Part of the statute in question	How it functions in the sentence	Why	How that translates into the meaning of the statute
"Without the consent of all parties"	Serves to modify the entire clause "intercepts or receives and intentionally records"	When a prepositional phrase precedes a clause, it modifies the entire clause	All parties need to grant their consent for a conversation to be heard and recorded
"Intercepts or receives and intentionally records"	This clause describes the actions regulated by the statute: (1) either intercepting OR receiving a call AND (2) recording it	The use of the conjunctions "or" and "and" means that if a party takes either of the two actions (intercept; receive), as well as the action of recording, the statute regulates their behavior	Every person who intercepts and intentionally records OR every person who receives and intentionally records can be liable under 632.7 if they fail to receive consent from all parties of the conversation

Because § 632.7 applies to people who "receive and intentionally record," LoanMe was obligated under the statute to ask Mr. Smith for his permission to record their phone conversation with him. And since LoanMe failed to do so, they violated § 632.7.

E. The Court of Appeal erred by applying the language of § 632.5 and § 632.6 to determine that § 632.7 applies only to third parties.

The Court of Appeal erred in interpreting § 632.7 as applying to just third-party eavesdroppers. The Court of Appeal applied the language and meaning of § 632.5 and § 632.6 in their interpretation of § 632.7; it was incorrect of them to do so. *Smith v. LoanMe, Inc.* (2019) 43 Cal. App. 5th 844, 853. § 632.7 differs from § 632.5 and § 632.6 in two significant aspects, which makes them impossible to use as a framework for interpreting § 632.7. First, and most importantly, neither § 632.5 nor § 632.6 regulate recording, the central behavior regulated by § 632.7. California Penal Code, § 632. §§ 632.5 and 6 cannot be extrapolated to § 632.7, as § 632.5 and § 632.6 deal only with the action of intercepting communications, which is both a different action than recording and an action that cannot be performed by participants to a call. But recording, the central action of § 632.7, can be performed both by third-party interlopers and call participants.

Secondly, § 632.7 removes the element of malice that is a necessary threshold under § 632.5 and § 632.6. California Code, Penal Code, section 632. While § 632.5 and § 632.6 stipulate that an interception of a phone call has to be done with a malicious intent to be penalized, § 632.7 makes no such requirement. § 632.7 prevents unauthorized recordings for any purposes, which is important for protecting the privacy rights of all participants. Because of these two major differences between § 632.7 and § 632.5 and § 632.6, the meaning of § 632.7 necessarily must be evaluated independently of § 632.5 and § 632.6. For that reason, § 632.7 must be understood through its plain language meaning. The purpose of California Penal Code § 632.7 is to prevent anyone, whether that be a party to the call or a third party, from recording the call without the consent of all parties to the call; the plain language of the text of the statute supports this.

Sections II. and III. omitted for content
IV. The Court of Appeal's interpretation of § 632.7 has negative policy implications.
A. The Court of Appeal's interpretation revokes California's status as an all-party consent state and instead unilaterally changes it to a one-party consent state.

California is seen as the golden standard for privacy in the United States. Among all 50 U.S. states, California has the most stringent privacy protections for citizens, among them § 632. Sarah Rippy, *US State Comprehensive Privacy Law Comparison*, International Association of Privacy Professionals (2021), https://iapp.org/resources/article/state-comparison-table/. § 632 establishes California as an all-party consent state, so a call can only be recorded by anyone with the permission of all parties within the call. But the Court of Appeal's interpretation revokes California's status as an all-party consent state. In essence, the Court of Appeal's holding conflates consent to being on a call with consent to record. Parties in a call no longer need to ask for everyone's permission before recording the call; they would already have implicit permission to record them.

This principle both violates the definition of consent (that it must be affirmatively, not implicitly, given) and turns California into a one-party consent state. The Supreme Court should correct the Court of Appeal's interpretation of § 632.7.

B. The Court of Appeal's interpretation will increase privacy violations under the California Constitution, leading to a flood of litigation.

Among California's stringent privacy protections is an "inalienable right" of "privacy." Cal. Const. art. I, § 1. If the Court of Appeal's interpretation of § 632.7 is left to stand, this case would be resolved, and § 632.7 could no longer be used to hold parties who record a call without the permission of all parties criminally or civilly responsible. But § 632.7 is not the only legal avenue for litigants to sue for an infringement of privacy. Lawsuits under privacy torts such as inclusion upon seclusion or publication of private fact (if any of the information that was recorded on the call is leaked to the public) will become increasingly common. Departing from the precedent that § 632.7 applies to both parties to a conversation and third parties will only lead to an overwhelming of the judicial system as malicious actors exploit their newfound ability to record without explicit consent.

C. Due to COVID-19, the use of telephone and video calls have become more pervasive and personal. A ruling for LoanMe would gut any semblance of societal privacy norms.

Because of COVID-19, telephone and video calls have become more and more commonplace and personal. Conversations that once took place in the confidential contexts of doctors' offices, psychologists' offices, and lawyers' offices are now increasingly done over video-conferencing software. Before the Court of Appeal's decision, each patient or individual has expected that their privacy will be upheld and that their private conversations will not be recorded without their explicit consent. The Court of Appeal's decision has a precarious consequence: it will make it harder for patients or individuals to be frank with their doctors or attorneys. Apart from privileged contexts, it will also chill speech; because of the imposed social distancing guidelines, people cannot meet up in person to have conversations in person. If the Court of Appeal's interpretation of § 632.7 is left in place, people will be more hesitant to share information over the telephone and video calls.

The increasing use of video conferencing technology is expected to last even after the vaccine for COVID-19 has been widely distributed, meaning that the violation of privacy will be compounded even more. Since the beginning of the COVID-19-imposed shutdowns, many businesses have successfully made the transition to remote jobs. As those companies realize that they can cut costs by eliminating most brick and mortar office spaces and instead use work-from-home initiatives, the dependence on platforms such as Zoom and Google Meet is not expected to plunge. Therefore, the policy implications — lack of privacy on confidential calls, chilled speech, increased privacy litigation, and invasion of privacy by malicious actors — will only increase immensely.

CONCLUSION

For the reasons stated above, Smith requests that this Court reverse the Court of Appeal's decision and hold that Penal Code § 632.7 applies to both third-party interlopers and parties to a phone conversation.

DATED: February 15, 2021

Respectfully submitted,
G—, L—& M—, LLP
Student G—
Student L—
Student M—
Attorneys for Plaintiff and
Appellant Jeremiah Smith

Tips for Appellate Briefs

1. After you've finished outlining and start writing the brief, it might make sense to draft in the following order:
   a. Statement of the Case/Facts
   b. Argument
   c. Conclusion
   d. Summary of Argument: Do this last (even though it will ultimately be presented early in your brief) because it's easier to summarize an argument you've already crafted
2. Avoid accurate but irrelevant arguments. Make sure that every part of your brief answers the questions you have been asked to answer.
3. As with all types of legal writing, clarity is key. Legal arguments are almost always complex, so keep the prose as simple and efficient as possible.
4. When plotting your time for tackling your brief, aim to have all research completed and a rough draft written by halfway to your final deadline (e.g., if you have four weeks to complete the brief, aim to have your first draft written by the two-week mark). Writing is rewriting, and this kind of scheduling will give you the best opportunity to submit your strongest work.
5. When you've gotten the language in the brief just as you like it, the last step is a cite check. Go through every legal citation in your brief and cross-reference each one to the underlying cases or statutes (this will be much faster if you've printed or downloaded all cited authority and highlighted the relevant sections).

APPELLATE-STYLE ORAL ARGUMENT

Along with drafting a brief for your next assignment, you'll also be responsible for engaging in an appellate-style oral argument. Appellate oral arguments are not legal speeches — they're not like the opening or closing statement of a trial. Instead, it's best to think of oral arguments as conversations where judges get some necessary clarification on the arguments you've proffered in your brief as well as your reaction to your opponent's arguments.

Judges will have read all briefs ahead of time, so while you may want to spend some time summarizing your main arguments, you'll want to devote at least some time to confronting your opponent's best arguments. During the argument, you will be asked questions by your professor and potentially a panel of other judges, so be flexible and don't get thrown if you don't get to present all the arguments you wanted to. This isn't like a policy debate where arguments you don't get to are treated as concessions. Have a general plan about what you want to cover, but understand that that plan may get waylaid early on. That's okay. Your job during argument is to provide whatever answers the judges request. Though fielding judges' questions on the spot can be daunting (and certain judicial panels might be more aggressive than others), it's important not to view the judges as adversaries. You should be eager to answer their questions, not defensive.

It's important to answer direct questions with direct answers, but keep in mind what is necessary for you to win your case. Appellate brief writing and appellate oral arguments are not objective endeavors; your job isn't to give the court your honest and unbiased view of the law. You're zealously representing a side, so while strategic concessions are expected (and can even be beneficial), you must be careful not to concede any point that is necessary for your side to prevail.

Generally speaking, you should have a set opening statement with a thematic introduction (e.g., "This case is about _____"). You should also have a set closing statement that you can quickly revert to when your time is almost up. Don't waste the opportunity represented by the last words of your argument. In between, you should have an outline of your basic arguments and the factual and legal points that support them as well as refutations to your opponent's strongest arguments. Try to winnow your presentation to two to four main arguments, depending on the time you're allotted for argument. Below is a rubric I use for evaluating oral arguments:

ORAL ARGUMENT RUBRIC

Category	Accomplished	Competent	Beginning
Presentation and Professionalism			
· Is appropriately attired			
· Maintains eye contact			
· Speaks at an effective volume and speed			
· Exhibits proper posture and body language			
· Engages with optimal energy (neither overly emphatic nor apathetic)			
· Demonstrates sufficient preparation			
Substantive Argument			
· Introduces self/party and begins with a thematic introduction			
· Incorporates cases into arguments			
· Explains relevant analogies and distinctions			
· States facts accurately and shows knowledge of the record			
· Answers questions directly and effectively			
· Shows awareness of strongest and weakest arguments			
· Concludes effectively			

General Comments and Suggestions for Improvement:

Grade: _____

Tips for Oral Arguments

1. The first time you speak in an oral argument, say: "May it please the court, my name is _____ and I'm representing _____."
2. Your tone should be conversational. You're not lecturing the court, and appeals to pathos rarely succeed at this stage of argument. Note, however, that conversational is not the same as informal. Your goal should be to make your position understandable to the

panel while still adhering to the norms of professional respect and discourse that apply in any court.
3. After your thematic introduction, signpost the two to four (depending on the time you have to argue) main arguments you're planning to present for your side.
4. Speak slowly. Judges get annoyed when advocates speak too quickly. Speaking slowly shows the judge that you're comfortable, not nervous.
5. For every legal proposition you advance, cite an authority. For factual propositions, cite the record.
6. Be courteous to opposing counsel. There's a line between zealous advocacy and unprofessional rudeness, and with a panel of judges scrutinizing your every word, you won't get much leeway for unwarranted bluster.
7. When a judge asks a question, don't tell them that you'll answer it later. You are not obligated to follow your own argument outline. You *are* obligated to satisfy a judge's curiosity. If they ask a question now, it's fair to assume they want the answer now.
8. If a judge asks a yes-or-no question, answer directly: "Yes, because . . ." or "We respectfully disagree because . . ." as opposed to launching straight into your explanation. You don't want to come across as if you're dodging the question or hedging.
9. Avoid prefacing your legal arguments with qualifying statements like "I think" or "I believe"—again, hedging makes you seem less certain and less persuasive.
10. Know the case law and facts or at least have them in an easily accessible form. Oral argument time is limited. No judge wants to watch you spend 40 seconds rifling through binders.
11. Pay attention to the time. Before your time is up, try to get to your concluding statements. If you're in the middle of answering a judge's question, ask for a few additional seconds or up to one minute if you need the time to complete your reply.

ASSIGNMENT 11: *IN RE GALLAGHER* APPELLATE BRIEF

This is the final assignment in this textbook, a test of the analytical skills you've practiced throughout this text as well as an opportunity to not just posit the best arguments in a case but to actually argue as a lawyer would. The goal isn't to predict what a court will or should do. The goal is to win for your side. Zealous advocacy is a cornerstone of the American justice system. It's not the advocate's job to decide what's right; it's the advocate's job to represent one's client fully so that judges can make an informed decision. In the clash of two opposing sides overseen by a neutral arbiter, the hope is that truth will emerge.

Applicable Law

What follows is a real California Supreme Court decision (*In re Taylor*, 60 Cal. 4th 1019 (2015)) and a fictitious appellate opinion (*In re Gallagher*) that bases its logic on *Taylor*. The pair of opinions will provide the foundation for your analysis, but you are encouraged to do some light research and find other precedent cases to apply to our fact pattern.

Assignment

You will be assigned a side—either representing Gallagher or the state of California—and will then draft a brief to the California Supreme Court arguing that *Gallagher* ought to be either affirmed or reversed. Once the writing is complete, you will exchange briefs with opposing counsel. You will then be scheduled for a mock oral argument.

IN RE TAYLOR

Supreme Court of California
March 2, 2015, Filed
S206143

Reporter: 60 Cal. 4th 1019 *
In re William Taylor et al. on Habeas Corpus.

Judges: Opinion by Baxter, J.,* with Cantil-Sakauye, C.J., Werdegar, Chin, Corrigan, Liu, JJ., and Grover, J.,† concurring.

Opinion by: Baxter

Opinion

BAXTER, J.—On November 7, 2006, the voters enacted Proposition 83, The Sexual Predator Punishment and Control Act: Jessica's Law (Prop. 83, as approved by voters, Gen. Elec. (Nov. 7, 2006); hereafter Proposition 83 or Jessica's Law). "Proposition 83 was a wide-ranging initiative intended to 'help Californians better protect themselves, their children, and their communities' (*id.*, § 2, subd. (f)) from problems posed by sex offenders by 'strengthen[ing] and improv[ing] the

---

* Retired Associate Justice of the Supreme Court, assigned by the Chief Justice pursuant to article VI, section 6 of the California Constitution.

† Associate Justice of the Court of Appeal, Sixth Appellate District, assigned by the Chief Justice pursuant to article VI, section 6 of the California Constitution.

laws that punish and control sexual offenders' (*id.*, § 31)." (*In re E.J.* (2010) 47 Cal. 4th 1258, 1263 [104 Cal. Rptr. 3d 165, 223 P.3d 31] (*E.J.*).)

Among its proponents' objectives, Jessica's Law sought to "prevent sex offenders from living near where our children learn and play" by creating "predator free zones around schools and parks" (Voter Information Guide, Gen. Elec. (Nov. 7, 2006) argument in favor of Prop. 83, p. 46, capitalization & italics omitted) through the enactment of mandatory residency restrictions in the form of an amendment to Penal Code section 3003.5.[1] Section 3003.5, a preexisting law codified among statutes dealing with parole, already [set] forth certain restrictions on where and with whom certain paroled registered sex offenders may live. The initiative added a new subdivision (b) to section **[*1023]** 3003.5, making it "unlawful for any person for whom registration is required pursuant to Section 290 to reside within 2000 feet of any public or private school, or park where children regularly gather." (§ 3003.5, subd. (b), added by Prop. 83, § 21, subd. (b) (section 3003.5(b) or, generally, residency restrictions); see *E.J.*, *supra*, 47 Cal. 4th at p. 1266.) Subsequently, as relevant here, the Department of Corrections and Rehabilitation (CDCR) began enforcing the residency restrictions as a mandatory parole condition for all registered sex offenders on parole in San Diego County.

Petitioners in this consolidated habeas corpus proceeding were registered sex offenders on active parole in San Diego County against whom section 3003.5(b) was enforced. Petitioners alleged the residency restrictions, as applied to them, are unconstitutional. At the conclusion of an evidentiary hearing ordered by this court, the trial court agreed with petitioners' arguments, finding the mandatory residency restrictions unconstitutional as applied to all registered sex offenders on parole in San Diego County, and enjoining enforcement of the statute in the county. At the same time, however, the trial court concluded parole authorities retain the statutory authority to impose special parole conditions on sex offender parolees, including residency restrictions, as long as they are based on the specific circumstances of each individual parolee. The Court of Appeal affirmed.

As will be explained, we agree that section 3003.5(b)'s residency restrictions are unconstitutional as applied across the board to petitioners and similarly situated registered sex offenders on parole in San Diego County. Blanket enforcement of the residency restrictions against these parolees has severely restricted their ability to find housing in compliance with the statute, greatly increased the incidence of homelessness among them, and hindered their access to medical treatment, drug and alcohol dependency services, psychological counseling and other rehabilitative social services available to all parolees, while further hampering the efforts of parole authorities and law enforcement officials to monitor, supervise, and rehabilitate them in the interests of public safety. It thus has infringed their liberty and privacy interests, however limited, while bearing no rational relationship to advancing the state's legitimate goal of protecting children from sexual

---

1. All further statutory references are to the Penal Code.

predators, and has violated their basic constitutional right to be free of unreasonable, arbitrary, and oppressive official action.

Nonetheless, as the lower courts made clear, CDCR retains the statutory authority, under provisions in the Penal Code separate from those found in section 3003.5(b), to impose special restrictions on registered sex offenders in the form of discretionary parole conditions, including residency restrictions that may be more or less restrictive than those found in section 3003.5(b), as long as they are based on, and supported by, the particularized circumstances of each individual parolee.

[*1024]

Accordingly, we will affirm the judgment of the Court of Appeal.

PROCEDURAL AND FACTUAL BACKGROUND

A. The Habeas Corpus Proceedings Initiated in *E.J.*

In *E.J.*, *supra*, 47 Cal. 4th 1258, four registered sex offenders on parole in various counties for offenses committed before the passage of Proposition 83, but who were thereafter released on parole, filed a unified petition for habeas corpus challenging the constitutionality of section 3003.5(b)'s residency restrictions when enforced as a mandatory parole condition by CDCR. (*E.J.*, at pp. 1263-1264.) After issuing orders to show cause, we rejected two facial challenges to the constitutionality of the statute, finding that the residency restrictions, when so enforced, were neither impermissibly retroactive nor in violation of the state or federal constitutional prohibitions against ex post facto laws. (*Id.* at pp. 1264, 1272, 1280.)[2]

The *E.J.* petitioners further claimed that "section 3003.5(b) is an unreasonable, vague and overbroad parole condition that infringes on various state and federal constitutional rights, including their privacy rights, property rights, right to intrastate travel, and their substantive due process rights under the federal Constitution." (*E.J.*, *supra*, 47 Cal. 4th at p. 1280.) In support of these claims, they appended declarations and various materials as exhibits to their petition in an effort to establish a factual basis for each claim. CDCR, in its return, denied many of the allegations advanced in the petition in reliance on such exhibits, and disputed the authentication of several of the petitioners' exhibits. In their traverse, the petitioners alleged the new residency restrictions made entire cities off-limits to registered sex offenders on parole, and that the restrictions were "'so unreasonably broad' as to leave those to whom [they apply] 'with no option but prison or homelessness.'" (*E.J.*, *supra*, at p. 1281.)

We observed in *E.J.* that the petitioners were "not all similarly situated with regard to their paroles," as they had been "paroled to different cities and counties within

---

2. The further question whether section 3003.5(b) also creates a separate misdemeanor offense subject to violation by registered sex offenders who are not on parole was not before us in *E.J.* (*E.J.*, *supra*, 47 Cal. 4th at p. 1282, fn. 10) and is likewise not before us here.

the state," and that "the supply of housing in compliance with section 3003.5(b) [and] available to them during their terms of parole—a matter critical to deciding the merits of their [claims]—[was] not sufficiently established" by the declarations and materials to permit this court to decide the claims. (*E.J.*, *supra*, 47 Cal. 4th at p. 1281.)

[*1025]

The *E.J.* petitioners also alleged that the *manner* in which CDCR had enforced Jessica's Law constituted further evidence that the law was operating against registered sex offender parolees in an unconstitutional way. The matter of whether CDCR and, in particular, its Division of Adult Parole Operations (DAPO), are obligated by law to identify "compliant housing" for the petitioners or otherwise assist them in locating and securing such housing was sharply disputed in the parties' pleadings. (*E.J.*, *supra*, 47 Cal. 4th at p. 1282.) In support of their allegation that "'[r]espondent has provided little to no assistance to individual parolees attempting to find compliant housing'" (*id.* at p. 1283), the petitioners pointed to the initial CDCR policy statement (CDCR, Policy No. 07-36: Implementation of Prop. 83, also known as Jessica's Law (Aug. 17, 2007); hereafter Policy No. 07-36) that provided "'[t]he responsibility to locate and maintain compliant housing shall ultimately remain with the individual parolee through utilization of available resources'" (*E.J.*, at p. 1283). The petitioners asserted that they, and other parolees, "'ha[d] not been informed of areas in their counties where compliant housing [might] be found.'" (*Ibid.*) CDCR, in turn, denied "'the allegation that it provides "little to no assistance to individual parolees attempting to find compliant housing," [claiming] it does provide such assistance.'" (*Ibid.*)

We noted that these claims, unlike the retroactivity and ex post facto contentions, were "considerably more complex 'as applied' challenges" to the residency restrictions (*E.J.*, *supra*, 47 Cal. 4th at p. 1281), and that the evidentiary record before us was insufficient to decide them. Accordingly, we remanded the cases for evidentiary hearings in the trial courts of the various counties to which the *E.J.* petitioners had been paroled. (*Id.*, at p. 1284.) We further outlined an agenda for finding the relevant facts necessary to decide the petitioners' claims at these hearings. The issues, we stated, should "include, but . . . not necessarily [be] limited to, establishing each petitioner's current parole status; the precise location of each petitioner's current residence and its proximity to the nearest 'public or private school, or park where children regularly gather' (§ 3003.5(b)); a factual assessment of the compliant housing available to petitioners and similarly situated registered sex offenders in the respective counties and communities to which they have been paroled; an assessment of the way in which the mandatory parole residency restrictions are currently being enforced in each particular jurisdiction; and a complete record of the protocol CDCR is currently following to enforce section 3003.5(b) in those respective jurisdictions." (*E.J.*, *supra*, at pp. 1283-1284.)

Two of the four petitioners in *E.J.* were from San Diego County; the remand of their cases to that county for an evidentiary hearing gave rise to the instant consolidated habeas corpus proceeding. By May 2010, however, the two San Diego *E.J.* petitioners had been discharged from parole and their [*1026] cases dismissed as moot. Meanwhile, more than 150 other registered sex offender parolees filed habeas corpus petitions in the San Diego County Superior Court, and were granted temporary stays of the enforcement of section 3003.5(b) as to them pending resolution of this matter. The parties agreed that the petitions of four of these parolees—William Taylor, Stephen Todd, Jeffery Glynn, and Julie Briley—would serve as the representative cases for purposes of the evidentiary proceedings contemplated in *E.J.*, *supra*, 47 Cal. 4th 1258.

On February 18, 2011, the evidentiary hearing commenced in the San Diego County Superior Court. The following facts, drawn in large part from the opinion of the Court of Appeal, were established with regard to the circumstances of the four representative petitioners, the manner in which CDCR was enforcing the statute in San Diego County, and the general unintended and socially deleterious effects of such enforcement in that county.

B. Petitioners' Respective Parole and Residential Statuses

1. William Taylor

William Taylor was paroled in January 2008 after serving a sentence for failing to register as a sex offender. (§ 290.) He is required to register as a result of his conviction of sexual assault in Arizona in 1991, which was determined to be the equivalent of a rape conviction under California law. (§§ 261, subd. (a)(2), 290.005.) The victim in that case was an adult woman. Although Taylor has a long criminal history, he has never been convicted of another sex crime or a crime involving a child victim.

Taylor suffers from numerous illnesses, including throat cancer, AIDS, and diabetes. He has had a heart attack and several strokes, suffers from chronic depression and paranoid schizophrenia, and is addicted to cocaine. He had planned to live in Spring Valley with relatives, one of whom is a health care professional, but could not do so because the location of their residence is not compliant with the residency restrictions of section 3003.5(b). Taylor's parole agent was unable to obtain financial assistance for his housing. Subsequently, he slept outside in an alley behind the parole office, a location pointed out to him by his parole agent, and remained homeless for a month until arrested for using cocaine. Upon his rerelease on parole, he was admitted to the Etheridge Center, a residential drug treatment program near downtown San Diego and near the clinic where he was receiving treatment for AIDS. However, the location of the Etheridge Center is not compliant with the residency restrictions of section 3003.5(b). Taylor's application for a waiver of the 2,000-foot restriction was denied by CDCR, whereafter, on October 2, 2009, the court [*1027] issued him an emergency 120-day stay, enjoining CDCR from requiring him to leave the Etheridge Center unless alternative accommodations for medical treatment could be arranged.

Shortly thereafter Taylor was suspended from the Etheridge Center for nonsexual misconduct, was rearrested for another parole violation, was rereleased on parole and remained homeless for several weeks, and was then placed in a boarding house in Vista by CDCR, which was a three-hour bus ride from his parole office, his outpatient clinic, and the medical facility that agreed to provide his medical care. While in the Vista facility, Taylor collapsed and was hospitalized in the intensive care unit. His parole agent warned Taylor he would be arrested if he did not register the hospital address with local authorities within five days. Taylor's parole was revoked for not registering the hospital address and for possession of drug paraphernalia. Upon his rerelease on parole, Taylor lived in a compliant hotel with the CDCR paying the rent for 60 days. At the time of the evidentiary hearing, Taylor was living in the hotel.

2. Jeffrey Glynn

In 2009, Jeffrey Glynn was released on parole after serving a sentence for a theft-related crime. He is required to register as a sex offender due to his conviction, in 1989, of misdemeanor sexual battery (§ 243.4) committed against an adult woman. That conviction is his only sex crime, although he has numerous convictions for theft-and drug-related offenses.

Glynn planned to live with his wife and their children when he was paroled, but the location of the family's residence was not compliant with the residency restrictions of Jessica's Law. Glynn's wife did not want to move, and he was unable to find compliant housing in the area, so he purchased a van and lived in it as a transient. In December 2009, the court granted Glynn's motion for a temporary injunction enjoining enforcement of the residency restrictions against him. However, one week earlier, Glynn had committed a burglary. When Glynn was paroled again in August 2010, he moved into the family's noncompliant apartment under the previously issued injunction and was living there at the time of the evidentiary hearing.

3. Julie Briley

In April 2009, Julie Briley was released on parole after serving a prison term for failing to register as a sex offender. She is required to register due to her conviction, in 1988, of committing a lewd and lascivious act on a child under the age of 14 years. (§ 288, subd. (a).) The victim was Briley's daughter and the crime occurred inside the family residence. Since then, [*1028] Briley has suffered no new sex offense convictions, but has numerous convictions for drug offenses and failing to register as a sex offender.

Briley had planned to live with her sister upon her release, but the location of her sister's residence is not compliant with the 2,000-foot residency restrictions.[3] The

---

3. Briley would not have been able to live with her sister in any event because a different condition of her parole prohibits her from having contact with children and Briley's nephew, a minor, lives with her sister.

restrictions also prevented Briley from living with her sister-in-law or in any of the shelters or sober living houses for women with an available bed. After learning from a parole agent that other homeless parolees slept in an alley near the parole office, Briley began sleeping there, along with 15 to 20 other persons. Briley, who has hepatitis C, high blood pressure, thyroid problems and osteoarthritis that is aggravated by exposure to cold temperatures, lived there for approximately one and one-half years.

In July 2009, the court granted Briley a temporary injunction against enforcement of the residency restrictions as a condition of her parole, but she was unable to find affordable housing until November 2010. At the time of the evidentiary hearing, Briley lived in a recreational vehicle parked at a noncompliant location in return for five hours of work each week. She has two other part-time jobs, which together pay her approximately $250 a month.

4. Stephen Todd[4]

In June 2008, Stephen Todd was released on parole after serving a prison term for drug possession. He is required to register as a sex offender after the juvenile court found, in 1981, when he was 15 years old, that he committed a lewd and lascivious act with a child under 14 years old by molesting his 10-year-old sister. (§§ 288, subd. (a), 290.008.) Todd does not have any other sex crime convictions or convictions of crimes involving children, although his lengthy criminal history includes convictions for assault with a deadly weapon, burglary, vehicle theft, receiving stolen property and drug offenses. Todd suffers from bipolar disorder, is diabetic and subject to seizures, is a recovering heroin addict, and has been addicted to methamphetamine for 18 years. Upon his release on parole he planned to stay with a friend at the Plaza Hotel in downtown San Diego, the location of which was not compliant with the residency restrictions. Unable to find compliant housing, Todd followed his parole agent's suggestion that he live in the riverbed of the San Diego [*1029] River. Over the next one and one-half years, Todd was arrested and his parole revoked numerous times for violating various parole conditions. Throughout that time, Todd was homeless except for the periods he was in custody. By the time of the evidentiary hearing, Todd had suffered another drug conviction and had been returned to prison.

C. The Availability of Compliant Housing in San Diego County

In June 2006, Julie Wartell, a contract crime analyst for the San Diego County District Attorney's Office, used an automated mapping program to prepare an electronic map depicting the expected effect of the residency restrictions of Jessica's Law on available housing in San Diego County. Wartell mapped the

---

4. At the time of the evidentiary hearing, Todd was no longer on parole, as he had been returned to prison following his conviction for a new drug offense. The court and parties agreed his petition should not be dismissed as moot because of the original agreement to hear the four cases as a representative range of cases in San Diego County.

location of all public and private schools, kindergarten through 12th grade, and all active parks (see San Diego County, Code of Reg. Ords., tit. 8, div. 10, ch. 1, § 810.102, subd. (a)) in the county. Then, using data from the tax assessor's office showing the location of residential land parcels throughout the county, she drew shaded circles around each school and park on the map to reflect the 2,000-foot buffer zones around each such location. Thus, Wartell's map showed locations that were not compliant with the residency restrictions; residences within the shaded circles or buffer zones were noncompliant and unavailable to paroled registered sex offenders.

In 2010, Wartell twice updated her analysis and map to reflect recent additions of parks and schools in the county. Two analysts with the San Diego County Department of Planning and Land Use then refined Wartell's work into a 288-page map book and an online map application, both of which allow a person to view specific areas in much greater detail. In its statement of decision, the trial court stated the map "graphically show[s] huge swaths of urban and suburban San Diego, including virtually all of the downtown area, completely consumed by the [residency] restrictions."

The trial court further found that sex offender parolees are unlikely candidates to rent single-family homes and are most likely to seek out housing in apartments or low-cost residential hotels. Wartell's research showed that if single-family residences are eliminated from all the compliant residential parcels in San Diego County, the percentage of multifamily parcels that are compliant with the residency restrictions is less than 3 percent (2.9 percent). David Estrella, then the director of the San Diego County Department of Housing and Community Development, testified that at the time of the evidentiary hearing the countywide vacancy rate for low-income rental housing was approximately 5 to 8 percent. The trial court found that, as a practical matter, not all of the 2.9 percent of multifamily parcels located outside the buffer zones around schools and parks was necessarily available for rent to parolees due to the demand for low-cost housing in San Diego County, which had more than doubled in recent years.

[*1030]

Petitioners' counsel also enlisted the assistance of four investigators from the San Diego County Public Defender's Office to identify the potential number of compliant multifamily rental units that might reasonably be located and secured by registered sex offender parolees looking for such housing. Various factors were considered that could make it difficult for such persons to secure compliant housing, including the parolees' limited financial resources that typically made rent exceeding $850 per month[5] prohibitive; whether a criminal background check was required; whether a credit history check was required; whether a deposit

---

5. The $850 figure was chosen because it is within the range of $800 to $1,000 that Social Security Disability Income and Supplemental Security Income recipients in San Diego typically receive per month.

of more than two months' rent or income of more than two and one-half times the rent were required; and access to available public transportation. The investigators deemed otherwise compliant housing unsuitable if it met any of these exclusionary criteria. Limiting their search to compliant multifamily parcels with at least five units due to time constraints, the investigators found that only one-quarter of the 54 apartment complexes containing more than 60 units in the county rented units for $850 or less per month, with none available in downtown San Diego, and that of the 57 apartment complexes with between 15 and 60 units, only nine had units that rented for $850 or less per month.

D. CDCR's Statewide Protocol for Enforcing the Residency Restrictions

Upon their release from prison on parole, parolees are informed of their parole conditions and are further notified of the availability of social services, medical and psychological treatment resources, drug and alcohol dependency services, job counseling, and services for obtaining a general equivalency certificate, all designed to assist their transition back into society at no cost to them. Registered sex offenders released on parole are additionally advised of their obligation to comply with the residency restrictions of Jessica's Law. They bear the responsibility for locating compliant housing, as reflected in CDCR's policy memoranda. Parole agents are not authorized to tell sex offender parolees where to live or to recommend areas where they should look for compliant housing. In some specified and limited circumstances, if the parolee cannot afford housing, CDCR will provide funds so that he or she can obtain temporary transitional housing. Such limited housing assistance is usually reserved for the mentally ill, or for those who require housing for their or the public's safety, and is usually limited to 60 days and $1,500.

Upon locating a particular residence where he or she would like to live, a registered sex offender parolee must disclose the address of the intended residence to the parole agent. The agent has six working days to verify whether the parolee's intended residence is compliant with section [*1031] 3003.5(b)'s residency restrictions, i.e., not within 2,000 feet of a school or park where children regularly gather. The parolee cannot move into the residence before the agent confirms it is compliant. A determination that a proposed residence is noncompliant may be administratively appealed. If the proposed residence is not compliant, the parolee must declare himself or herself "transient," and must register with the parole office and local law enforcement agency as such.[6] It is a parole violation for a transient parolee to be in a noncompliant residence except for up to two hours twice a day to charge his or her global positioning system (GPS) device. However, a transient parolee is allowed to be in a noncompliant residence for

---

6. "'[T]ransient'" for this purpose is defined as a registered sex offender parolee "who has no residence." (§ 290.011, subd. (g).) "'Residence'" is defined as an address "at which a person regularly resides, regardless of the number of days or nights spent there, such as a shelter or structure that can be located by a street address, including, but not limited to, houses, apartment buildings, motels, hotels, homeless shelters, and recreational and other vehicles." (*Ibid.*)

approved employment, to conduct legitimate business, or to obtain care and treatment from licensed providers.

As noted by the Court of Appeal, among other things, CDCR Policy No. 07-36 requires supervisors of parole agents who handle registered sex offender caseloads to "'continue to collaborate with community-based programs and local law enforcement to facilitate the identification of compliant housing for sex offender parolees.'" The Court of Appeal also noted the policy also requires supervisors to "'utilize all available resources to obtain a current listing of all public and private schools and parks within their communities,'" and to provide "'[u]pdated information'" from the list to parole agents at least once a month. CDCR also has a procedure for obtaining waivers of the residency restrictions for parolees who are mentally ill and are housed in a mental health facility, and for parolees who are in need of medical care in a licensed medical facility that provides 24-hour care.

E. Enforcement of Section 3003.5(b) in San Diego County and the Resulting Increased Homelessness Among Paroled Registered Sex Offenders

At the time of the evidentiary hearing there were 482 registered sex offenders on active parole in San Diego County who were not in custody or in parolee-at-large status. Of that group, 165 (34 percent) were registered as transient or homeless, and 317 had a residential address on file with their parole office. However, the latter group included 140 parolees who had sought habeas corpus relief and received a stay of enforcement of section 3003.5(b) pending resolution of the lead cases in this consolidated proceeding. The trial court found that some percentage of those 140 parolees may be [*1032] living in noncompliant but authorized housing as a result of their stays, and may too have to declare themselves transient and homeless if the stays are lifted.

Detective Jim Ryan, a supervisor in the San Diego Police Department's sex offender registration unit, testified to a dramatic increase in the number of sex offender parolees who registered as transient with his department in the two years after Jessica's Law took effect on November 7, 2006. Between September 2007 and August 2010, the number of registered sex offenders on active parole in the City of San Diego who registered as transient with the San Diego Police Department increased four- to fivefold. Prior to Jessica's Law, many registered sex offender parolees lived in residential hotels in downtown San Diego, a situation favored by law enforcement because it fostered better surveillance and supervision. Some of these hotels are not in locations compliant with the residency restrictions, while others have been since demolished as a result of redevelopment.

Evidence was also presented below attesting that, from a law enforcement perspective, homeless sex offender parolees are more difficult to supervise than those who have established residences. Parole Agent Maria Dominguez testified that before Jessica's Law was enacted, she did not allow sex offender parolees in her caseload to live "on the street." Many lived in residential programs or in downtown San Diego hotels, where they could be easily supervised. When her office began enforcing the residency restrictions of Jessica's Law in 2007, agents would show parolees areas they considered compliant or tell them about specific addresses. But when her supervisor was transferred, agents were no longer allowed to advise parolees about compliant areas. If a parolee asked where he or she could live, the agent was instructed to say: "I can't tell you where you could live, but if you bring me an address I will check it and make sure that it's compliant."

Parole Agent Manuel Guerrero, who for three and one-half years was the supervisor of one of the two San Diego County units that supervise sex offender parolees, testified that as of the time of the hearing CDCR had not issued a policy statement defining either "school" or "park" for purposes of enforcing Jessica's Law. Guerrero defined "school" as any public or private school from kindergarten through 12th grade, but acknowledged some sex offender parolees in San Diego County have received Jessica's Law parole conditions that extended the restrictions to daycare centers.[7] He defined "park" as an area "where kids would normally be at," explaining he would [*1033] look at whether the location contains, among other things, open grassy areas, playground equipment or soccer and baseball fields, and whether the area is designated as a park. Guerrero conceded the definition of park sometimes differs among parole agents depending on how an agent interpreted the word "park." He agreed that homeless sex offender parolees pose more of a risk to public safety than those with known residences.

Evidence was also presented showing that homelessness poses significant challenges to sex offender treatment professionals in their efforts to rehabilitate sex offenders. John Chamberlin was employed by CDCR to provide psychotherapy and counseling to paroled sex offenders at parole outpatient clinics. Chamberlin testified that homelessness among paroled sex offenders is both morally and psychologically destabilizing to the parolees, hindering the success of their therapy and rehabilitation. Similarly, Michael Feer, a clinical social worker previously employed by CDCR to provide group and individual counseling to sex offenders at a parole outpatient clinic, testified at least 50 percent of his patients were homeless, and that homelessness was a significant impediment to his patients' mental and physical health and stability.

Finally, the trial court took judicial notice of a CDCR report issued in October 2010 by the department's own sex offender supervision and GPS monitoring task force (Task Force), a multidisciplinary group comprised of CDCR staff, law enforcement personnel, and other outside participants charged with making recommendations to the CDCR on various sex offender issues. The Task Force studied the increased rate of homelessness among paroled sex offenders following

---

7. Since the evidentiary hearing was conducted in 2011, CDCR has promulgated new regulations regarding its implementation and enforcement of the residency restrictions, including defining a school for purposes of the statute as a "public or private school, kindergarten through 12th grade." (Cal. Code Regs., tit. 15, § 3571, subd. (c).)

the enactment of section 3003.5(b)'s residency restrictions and reported that between 2007 and 2010, the number of homeless sex offender parolees statewide reflected an alarming increase of "approximately 24 times." (CDCR Task Force, Rep. (Oct. 2010) pp. 4, 17.) A specific finding was made that "[h]omeless sex offenders put the public at risk. These offenders are unstable and more difficult to supervise for a myriad of reasons." (*Id.* at p. 17.) The Task Force further concluded that homelessness among sex offender parolees weakens GPS tracking, making it more difficult to monitor such parolees and less effective overall. Ultimately, the report recommended that "residence restrictions as set forth in Penal Code Section 3003.5(b) should be repealed in favor of targeted residence restrictions." (*Id.* at pp. 4, 17.)

F. The Trial Court's Findings of Fact

At the conclusion of the eight-day evidentiary hearing the trial court issued its statement of decision in which it made, among others, the following findings of fact:

[*1034]

(1) Despite certain imprecisions, the map book prepared by San Diego County crime analyst Julie Wartell is the most accurate assessment of housing that is reasonably available to registered sex offender parolees in San Diego County.

(2) Registered sex offender parolees are unlikely candidates to rent single-family homes; they are most likely to be housed in apartments or low-cost residential hotels.

(3) By virtue of the residency restrictions alone, registered sex offender parolees are effectively barred from access to approximately 97 percent of the existing rental property that would otherwise be available to them.

(4) The remaining 3 percent of multifamily rental housing outside the exclusion areas is not necessarily available to registered sex offender parolees for a variety of reasons, including San Diego County's low vacancy rate, high rents, and the unwillingness of some landlords to rent to such persons.

(5) In addition to CDCR's policy prohibiting parole agents from supplying registered sex offender parolees with specific information about the location of compliant housing, parole authorities in San Diego County have taken affirmative steps to prevent parole agents from helping parolees find compliant housing.

(6) Rigid application of the residency restrictions results in large groups of registered sex offender parolees having to sleep in alleys and riverbeds, a circumstance that did not exist prior to Jessica's Law.

(7) The residency restrictions place burdens on registered sex offender parolees that are disruptive in a way that hinders their treatment, jeopardizes their health and undercuts their ability to find and maintain employment, significantly undermining any effort at rehabilitation.

The trial court concluded the residency restrictions, enforced as a mandatory parole condition against the four petitioners (Taylor, Glynn, Briley, and Todd) in San Diego County, are "unconstitutionally unreasonable," and ordered CDCR to cease enforcing the restrictions against petitioners. The court subsequently issued a supplemental statement of decision ordering CDCR to cease enforcing section 3003.5(b) as a blanket parole condition against any registered sex offender on active parole in San Diego County. At the same time, however, the trial court concluded parole authorities retain the authority to impose special conditions on registered sex offender parolees that mirror the residency restrictions of section 3003.5(b), or are even more restrictive, as long as they are based on the specific circumstances of the individual parolee.

[*1035]

G. The Appeal

CDCR appealed the trial court's injunctive orders. The Court of Appeal affirmed, concluding that "the blanket enforcement of section 3003.5(b) as a parole condition in San Diego County has been unreasonable and constitutes arbitrary and oppressive official action." Like the trial court, the Court of Appeal concluded that "[p]arole agents retain *the discretion* to regulate aspects of a parolee's life, such as where and with whom he or she can live. (§§ 3052, 3053, subd. (a).) Agents may, after consideration of a [registered sex offender] parolee's particularized circumstances, impose *a special parole condition* that mirrors section 3003.5(b) or one that is more or less restrictive. It is only the *blanket* enforcement—that is, to all registered sex offender parolees without consideration of the individual case—that the trial court prohibited and we uphold." (First and second italics added.)

We granted CDCR's petition for review.

DISCUSSION

Petitioners in this consolidated habeas corpus proceeding sought writ relief on grounds that the residency restrictions in section 3003.5(b), as applied to them and similarly situated registered sex offenders on parole in San Diego County, are "unconstitutionally unreasonable." After an eight-day evidentiary hearing, the trial court concluded that the blanket application of the residency restrictions violates their constitutional rights by denying them access to nearly all rental housing in the county that would otherwise be available to them, and as a direct consequence, has caused a great many of them to become homeless, and has further denied them reasonable access to medical and psychological treatment resources, drug and alcohol dependency services, job counseling, and other social services to which parolees are entitled by law.

As a general matter, we review the grant of a writ of habeas corpus by applying the substantial evidence test to pure questions of fact and de novo review to questions of law. (*In re Collins* (2001) 86 Cal. App. 4th 1176, 1181 [104 Cal. Rptr. 2d 108].) "[W]hen the application of law to fact is predominantly legal, such as when it implicates constitutional rights and the exercise of judgment about the values underlying legal principles, [the appellate] court's review is de novo." (*Ibid.*) The Court of Appeal determined that the trial court's factual findings are supported by substantial evidence adduced at the evidentiary hearing. CDCR does not contest that conclusion. We therefore proceed with our de novo review of the constitutional legal questions in light of the factual record made below.

[*1036]

A. Standard of Review Applicable to Petitioners' Constitutional Challenges

We next consider what particular standard of review should be invoked to evaluate the constitutionality of section 3003.5(b)'s mandatory residency restrictions, as applied to petitioners in San Diego County, in light of the constitutional challenges they have raised.

(1) Petitioners alleged below that blanket enforcement of section 3003.5(b)'s mandatory residency restrictions violates their fundamental constitutional rights to intrastate travel, to establish and maintain a home, and to privacy and free association with others within one's home, and further effectively "banishes" them from establishing homes or residing anywhere in the county. The Fourteenth Amendment's due process clause "'forbids the government to infringe . . . "fundamental" liberty interests'" in any manner "'unless the infringement is narrowly tailored to serve a compelling state interest [(i.e., strict scrutiny review)].'" (*Washington v. Glucksberg* (1997) 521 U.S. 702, 721 [138 L. Ed. 2d 772, 117 S. Ct. 2258] (*Glucksberg*), quoting *Reno v. Flores* (1993) 507 U.S. 292, 302 [123 L. Ed. 2d 1, 113 S. Ct. 1439] (*Reno*).) Petitioners urge that the constitutionality of section 3003.5(b) must be evaluated under heightened strict scrutiny review.

CDCR in turn argues that while some of the constitutional rights petitioners assert—the right to intrastate travel, to establish and maintain a home, and to privacy and free association within one's home—may be considered fundamental rights when advanced by members of the general public, the liberty interests of registered sex offenders while on parole are necessarily lawfully circumscribed and protected to a lesser degree than those of ordinary citizens. CDCR argues that petitioners, while serving a term of supervised parole, do not enjoy the claimed fundamental constitutional rights and liberty interests in their fullest sense, and accordingly, rational basis review, rather than heightened strict scrutiny review, is the appropriate level of judicial scrutiny by which to gauge the constitutionality of section 3003.5(b). Generally speaking, when a facial constitutional challenge is raised, and the "threshold requirement" for strict scrutiny review, i.e., that "a challenged state action implicate a fundamental right," is not established with regard to the person or class of persons raising the constitutional challenge, all that is required is that "a reasonable relation to a legitimate state interest" (*Glucksberg, supra,* 521 U.S. at p. 722) (i.e., a rational basis) be shown in order to justify the state action or find the challenged statute constitutional (*Reno, supra,* 507 U.S. at p. 306).

(2) CDCR's threshold premise, that the liberty interests of parolees is not the same as those of ordinary citizens, finds support in the case law. The **[*1037]** United States Supreme Court has recognized that parolees enjoy fewer constitutional rights than do ordinary persons. (*Morrissey v. Brewer* (1972) 408 U.S. 471, 482 [33 L. Ed. 2d 484, 92 S. Ct. 2593].) This court likewise has observed that "[t]he interest in parole supervision to ensure public safety, which justifies administrative parole revocation proceedings in lieu of criminal trial with the attendant protections accorded defendants by the Bill of Rights, also permits restrictions on parolees' liberty and privacy interests." (*People v. Burgener* (1986) 41 Cal. 3d 505, 532 [224 Cal. Rptr. 112, 714 P.2d 1251] (*Burgener*), overruled on other grounds in *People v. Reyes* (1998) 19 Cal. 4th 743, 756 [80 Cal. Rptr. 2d 734, 968 P.2d 445].) "Parole is the conditional release of a prisoner who has already served part of his or her state prison sentence. Once released from confinement, a prisoner on parole is not free from legal restraint, but is constructively a prisoner in the legal custody of state prison authorities until officially discharged from parole." (*Prison Law Office v. Koenig* (1986) 186 Cal. App. 3d 560, 566 [233 Cal. Rptr. 590] (*Koenig*), citing *People v. Borja* (1980) 110 Cal. App. 3d 378, 382 [167 Cal. Rptr. 813]; *Burgener, supra*, 41 Cal. 3d at p. 531; § 3056 [prisoners on parole remain under the supervision of CDCR].) "Clearly, the liberty of a parolee is 'partial and restricted,' (*People v. Denne* (1956) 141 Cal. App. 2d 499, 508 [297 P.2d 451]; see *People v. Anglin* (1971) 18 Cal. App. 3d 92, 95 [95 Cal. Rptr. 588]), [and] not the equivalent of that of an average citizen (see *Morrissey v. Brewer*[, *supra*,] 408 U.S. [at p.] 482) . . . ." (*Koenig, supra*, at p. 566.) And with specific regard to the housing of parolees, "[c]ourts have traditionally recognized a state's right to require a parolee to live in a particular place. (See *Morrissey v. Brewer, supra*, 408 U.S. at p. 477; *In re Schoengarth* (1967) 66 Cal. 2d 295, 300 [57 Cal. Rptr. 600, 425 P.2d 200]; *In re Faucette* (1967) 253 Cal. App. 2d 338, 341 [61 Cal. Rptr. 97] [parolee has no right to choose residence].)" (*Id.* at p. 567.) This court too has explained that the parole authority may impose parole conditions that "'*govern a parolee's residence*, his associates or living companions, *his travel*, his use of intoxicants, and other aspects of his life.'" (*E.J., supra*, 47 Cal. 4th at p. 1283, fn. 10.)

(3) On the other hand, petitioners' assertion that parolees, although under the constructive custody and supervision of the parole authorities, nevertheless retain certain basic rights and liberty interests while on parole, finds support in the case law as well. "[T]he liberty of a parolee . . . includes many of the core values of unqualified liberty" and his or her "condition is very different from that of confinement in a prison." (*Morrissey v. Brewer, supra*, 408 U.S. at p. 482; see *Burgener, supra*, 41 Cal. 3d at p. 530.) As *Burgener*, quoting a commentator, observed, "'[I]n most cases the life of a parolee more nearly resembles that of an ordinary citizen than that of a prisoner. The parolee is not incarcerated; he is not subjected to a prison regimen, to the rigors of prison life and the unavoidable company of sociopaths. . . . The **[*1038]** parolee lives among people who are free to come and go when and as they wish. Except for the conditions of parole, he is one of them.' (Note (1969) 22 Stan. L. Rev. 129, 133; see also White, *The Fourth*

Amendment Rights of Parolees and Probationers (1969) 31 U. Pitt. L. Rev. 167, 177.)" (*Burgener, supra,* 41 Cal. 3d at p. 530.) Moreover, well-settled authority establishes that every parolee retains basic constitutional protection against *arbitrary and oppressive official action.* (*In re Stevens* (2004) 119 Cal. App. 4th 1228, 1234 [15 Cal. Rptr. 3d 168]; *Terhune v. Superior Court* (1998) 65 Cal. App. 4th 864, 874 [76 Cal. Rptr. 2d 841]; *Koenig, supra,* 186 Cal. App. 3d at pp. 566-567; see *People v. Reyes, supra,* 19 Cal. 4th at pp. 753-754 & cases cited [arbitrary and oppressive parolee searches].)[8]

In this case, however, we need not decide whether rational basis or heightened strict scrutiny review should be invoked in scrutinizing petitioners' constitutional challenges to section 3003.5(b). As we next explain, we are persuaded that blanket enforcement of the mandatory residency restrictions of Jessica's Law, as applied to registered sex offenders on parole in San Diego County, cannot survive even the more deferential rational basis standard of constitutional review. Such enforcement has imposed harsh and severe restrictions and disabilities on the affected parolees' liberty and privacy rights, however limited, while producing conditions that hamper, rather than foster, efforts to monitor, supervise, and rehabilitate these persons. Accordingly, it bears no rational relationship to advancing the state's legitimate goal of protecting children from sexual predators, and has infringed upon the affected parolees' basic constitutional right to be free of official action that is unreasonable, arbitrary, and oppressive.

B. Scrutiny of Petitioners' As-Applied Constitutional Challenges Under the Rational Basis Test

The habeas corpus claims before us do not present a facial challenge to the statute.[9] Instead, petitioners have pursued habeas corpus relief in the wake of [*1039] *E.J., supra,* 47 Cal. 4th 1258, by challenging the constitutionality of the residency restrictions *as applied* to them and other similarly situated registered sex offenders on supervised parole in San Diego County, based on evidence adduced at an eight-day evidentiary hearing ordered by this court. (*Id.,* at pp. 1281-1284.)

---

8. The rule that parolees retain constitutional protection against arbitrary and oppressive official action has led to the conclusion that *discretionary* parole conditions must be reasonable. (*In re Stevens, supra,* 119 Cal. App. 4th at p. 1234; *Terhune v. Superior Court, supra,* 65 Cal. App. 4th at p. 874; see *People v. Reyes, supra,* 19 Cal. 4th at pp. 753-754 & cases cited.) Logic further suggests that, even with regard to a *mandatory* condition imposed by law on a class of parolees, the agencies and officials charged with implementing it cannot apply it to individual cases in a wholly arbitrary, capricious, unjust, and oppressive manner.

9. "A facial challenge to the constitutional validity of a statute or ordinance considers only the text of the measure itself, not its application to the particular circumstances of an individual. (*Dillon v. Municipal Court* (1971) 4 Cal. 3d 860, 865 [94 Cal. Rptr. 777, 484 P.2d 945].)" (*Tobe v. City of Santa Ana* (1995) 9 Cal. 4th 1069, 1084 [40 Cal. Rptr. 2d 402, 892 P.2d 1145] (*Tobe*).) In *E.J., supra,* 47 Cal. 4th 1258, we rejected two such facial challenges to section 3003.5(b), concluding that the residency restrictions, when enforced as a mandatory condition of a registered sex offender's parole, are not impermissibly retroactive and do not violate the state or federal constitutional prohibitions against ex post facto laws. (*E.J.,* at pp. 1264, 1272, 1280.)

(4) "An as applied challenge [seeking] relief from a specific application of a facially valid statute . . . to an individual or class of individuals who are under allegedly impermissible present restraint or disability as a result of the manner or circumstances in which the statute . . . has been applied . . . *contemplates analysis of the facts of a particular case or cases* to determine the circumstances in which the statute . . . has been applied and to consider whether *in those particular circumstances* the application deprived the individual to whom it was applied of a protected right. (See, e.g., *Broadrick v. Oklahoma* (1973) 413 U.S. 601, 615-616 [37 L. Ed. 2d 830, 93 S. Ct. 2908]; *County of Nevada v. MacMillen* (1974) 11 Cal. 3d 662, 672 [114 Cal. Rptr. 345, 522 P.2d 1345]; *In re Marriage of Siller* (1986) 187 Cal. App. 3d 36, 49 [231 Cal. Rptr. 757].)" (*Tobe, supra,* 9 Cal. 4th at p. 1084, italics added.)

The United States Supreme Court has emphasized that consideration of as-applied challenges, as opposed to broad facial challenges, "is the preferred course of adjudication since it enables courts to avoid making unnecessarily broad constitutional judgments. *Brockett v. Spokane Arcades, Inc.*, 472 U.S. 491, 501-502 [86 L. Ed. 2d 394, 105 S. Ct. 2794] (1985); *United States v. Grace*, 461 U.S. 171 [75 L. Ed. 2d 736, 103 S. Ct. 1702] (1983); *NAACP v. Button*, 371 U.S. 415 [9 L. Ed. 2d 405, 83 S. Ct. 328] (1963)." (*Cleburne v. Cleburne Living Center, Inc.* (1985) 473 U.S. 432, 447 [87 L. Ed. 2d 313, 105 S. Ct. 3249].) More recently, in *Gonzales v. Carhart* (2007) 550 U.S. 124 [167 L. Ed. 2d 480, 127 S. Ct. 1610], the high court explained that "[i]t is neither our obligation nor within our traditional institutional role to resolve questions of constitutionality with respect to each potential situation that might develop. '[I]t would indeed be undesirable for this Court to consider every conceivable situation which might possibly arise in the application of complex and comprehensive legislation.' [Citation.] For this reason, '[a]s-applied challenges are the basic building blocks of constitutional adjudication.' [Citation.]" (*Id.* at p. 168.)

At the conclusion of the evidentiary hearing below, the trial court found that blanket enforcement of section 3003.5(b), on its express terms, effectively barred petitioners access to approximately 97 percent of the multifamily rental housing units in San Diego County that would otherwise be **[*1040]** available to them. The court further found the small percentage of remaining compliant housing was not necessarily available to paroled sex offenders due to a variety of factors, including low vacancy rates, high prices, and the unwillingness of some landlords to rent to them. In short, the record establishes that the residency restrictions have prevented paroled sex offenders as a class from residing in large areas of the county, including most of the downtown area in the City of San Diego, as well as almost all of the residential parcels in the Cities of Chula Vista, Vista, El Cajon, Lemon Grove and National City. The exclusionary restrictions may also impact the ability of some petitioners to live and associate with family members. They face disruption of family life because, although the restrictions do not expressly prohibit them from living with family members, if the family members' residence is not in a compliant location, petitioners cannot live there.

The record further reflects that blanket enforcement of the residency restrictions has had other serious implications for all registered sex offenders on parole in San

Diego County. Medical treatment, psychological counseling, drug and alcohol dependency services, and other rehabilitative social services available to parolees are generally located in the densely populated areas of the county. Relegated to less populated areas of the County, registered sex offender parolees can be cut off from access to public transportation, medical care, and other social services to which they are entitled, as well as reasonable opportunities for employment. The trial court specifically found that the residency restrictions place burdens on petitioners and similarly situated sex offenders on parole in the county that "are disruptive in a way that hinders their treatment, jeopardizes their health and undercuts their ability to find and maintain employment, significantly undermining any effort at rehabilitation."[10]

Perhaps most disturbing, the record reflects that blanket enforcement of section 3003.5(b) in San Diego County has led to greatly increased homelessness among registered sex offenders on parole in the county. According to CDCR's own uncontradicted parole database reports, of the 482 sex offender parolees on active parole at the time of the hearing, 165 of them (34 percent [*1041] or a full one-third) were registered as transient, i.e., homeless. Between September 2007 and August 2010, the number of registered sex offenders on active parole in the City of San Diego who registered as transient with the San Diego Police Department increased four- to fivefold. Detective Jim Ryan, a supervisor in the San Diego Police Department's sex offender registration unit, testified to a dramatic increase in the number of sex offender parolees who registered as transient with his department in the two years after the law took effect. The trial court specifically found that blanket enforcement of the residency restrictions in the County has "result[ed] in large groups of parolees having to sleep in alleys and riverbeds, a circumstance that did not exist prior to Jessica's Law."

The increased incidence of homelessness has in turn hampered the surveillance and supervision of such parolees, thereby thwarting the legitimate governmental objective behind the registration statute (§ 290) to which the residency restrictions attach; that of protecting the public from sex offenders. (See *Wright v. Superior Court* (1997) 15 Cal. 4th 521, 527 [63 Cal. Rptr. 2d 322, 936 P.2d 101].) The trial court took judicial notice of the final report issued in October 2010 by the CDCR Task Force, a multidisciplinary group comprised of CDCR staff, law enforcement personnel, and other outside participants charged with making recommendations to the CDCR on various sex offender issues. The Task Force's final report concluded that the Jessica's Law's residency restrictions failed to improve public safety, and instead compromised the effective monitoring and supervision of sex

---

10. The deleterious impact of blanket enforcement of the mandatory restrictions against registered sex offenders on parole in San Diego County further appears in direct contravention of the general legislative intent behind the parole laws. Section 3000, subdivision (a)(1), provides, in pertinent part, "The Legislature finds and declares that the period immediately following incarceration is critical to successful reintegration of the offender into society and to positive citizenship. It is in the interest of public safety for the state to provide for the effective supervision of and surveillance of parolees, including the judicious use of revocation actions, and to provide educational, vocational, family, and personal counseling necessary to assist parolees in the transition between imprisonment and discharge."

offender parolees, placing the public at greater risk. A specific finding was made that "[h]omeless sex offenders put the public at risk. These offenders are unstable and more difficult to supervise for a myriad of reasons." (Task Force, Rep., *supra*, p. 17.) The report further found that homelessness among sex offender parolees weakens GPS tracking, making it more difficult to monitor such parolees and less effective overall. CDCR has conceded in its briefs before this court that "[t]he evidence . . . demonstrated that the dramatic increase in homelessness has a profound impact on public safety," and that "there is no dispute that the residency restriction[s] [have] significant and serious consequences that were not foreseen when it was enacted."[11]

Last, the trial court agreed with petitioners that the manner in which CDCR has been implementing the residency restrictions in San Diego County has [*1042] subjected them to arbitrary and oppressive official enforcement action, thereby contributing to the law's unintended, unforeseen, and socially deleterious effects. Petitioners point to evidence that both CDCR and local San Diego County parole authorities have refused to assist registered sex offender parolees to find housing that complies with the statutory residency restrictions. CDCR's policy memoranda in effect at the time of the hearing reflect that registered sex offender parolees bear the responsibility for locating compliant housing, and that parole agents are not authorized to tell them where to look for or find compliant housing.

(5) The authorities we have cited above explain that all parolees retain certain basic rights and liberty interests, and enjoy a measure of constitutional protection against the arbitrary, oppressive and unreasonable curtailment of "the core values of unqualified liberty" (*Morrissey v. Brewer*, *supra*, 408 U.S. at p. 482), even while they remain in the constructive legal custody of state prison authorities until officially discharged from parole. We conclude the evidentiary record below establishes that blanket enforcement of Jessica's Law's mandatory residency restrictions against registered sex offenders on parole in San Diego County impedes those basic, albeit limited, constitutional rights. Furthermore, section 3003.5(b), as applied and enforced in that county, cannot survive rational basis scrutiny because it has hampered efforts to monitor, supervise, and rehabilitate such parolees in the interests of public safety, and as such, bears no rational relationship to advancing the state's legitimate goal of protecting children from sexual predators.

(6) Last, we agree with the observations of the Court of Appeal that CDCR retains the statutory authority, under provisions in the Penal Code separate from

---

11. It has further been suggested that increased homelessness resulting from the enforcement of Jessica's Law's residency restrictions thwarts the purpose and intent behind Megan's Law (Stats. 1996, ch. 908, § 3, p. 5125), which authorizes public disclosure of the residential addresses and notification of the whereabouts of registered sex offenders in California in the interests of public safety. (See §§ 290.45, 290.46.) It is more difficult to track paroled sex offenders who are transient and have no residential addresses, and to notify the public of their whereabouts.

those found in section 3003.5(b),[12] to impose special restrictions on registered sex offenders in the form of discretionary parole conditions, including residency restrictions that may be more or less restrictive than those found in section 3003.5(b), as long as they are based on, and supported by, the particularized circumstances of each individual parolee.

[*1043]

CONCLUSION

The judgment of the Court of Appeal is affirmed.

Cantil-Sakauye, C.J., Werdegar, J., Chin, J., Corrigan, J., Liu, J., and Grover, J.,[*] concurred.

IN RE GALLAGHER

CERTIFIED FOR PUBLICATION

IN THE COURT OF APPEAL OF THE STATE OF CALIFORNIA

THIRD APPELLATE DISTRICT

DIVISION TWO

In re HARRISON GALLAGHER on Habeas Corpus	G034589
	(Super. Ct. No. 11-2016-0023457)
Plaintiff and Appellant	O P I N I O N
	Cite as *In re Gallagher* (2022) 123 Cal. App. 3d 19

Appeal from a judgment of the Superior Court of Laird County, Erin Chack, Judge. Affirmed.

---

12. The Legislature has given CDCR and DAPO expansive authority to establish and enforce rules and regulations governing parole. (§§ 3052, 3053.) Additionally, state law provisions already imposing limitations on the places where registered sex offenders may visit and reside, include prohibitions against (1) entering while on parole any park where children regularly gather without the express permission of the offender's parole agent if the victim of the registerable offense was under 14 years of age (§ 3053.8); (2) residing with other registered sex offenders in a single-family dwelling while on parole (§ 3003.5, subd. (a)); (3) entering any school without lawful business and written permission from a school official (§ 626.81); (4) loitering about any school or public place where children congregate after being asked to leave by a school or law enforcement official (§ 653b, subd. (b)); and (5) entering a daycare or residential facility for elders or dependent adults without registering with the facility administrator if the victim of the registerable offense was an elder or dependent adult (§ 653c).

* Associate Justice of the Court of Appeal, Sixth Appellate District, assigned by the Chief Justice pursuant to article VI, section 6 of the California Constitution.

Thornton, Gill, Ota & Moore. Jonas W. Thornton and Alijah M. Case for Appellant.

Ariana Arzani, Attorney General, and Ted A. Steinberg, Chief Assistant Attorney General for Respondents the People.

* * *

In November 2006, California passed Proposition 83, the Sexual Predator Punishment and Control Act or Jessica's Law. The legislation was passed with the goal of helping Californians better protect themselves and their children from the myriad problems posed by sex offenders. Among its edicts, Jessica's Law sought to "prevent sex offenders from living near where . . . children learn and play" by creating "predator free zones around schools and parks" (Voter Information Guide, Gen. Elec. (Nov. 7, 2006) argument in favor of Prop. 83, p. 46, capitalization and italics omitted); the law sought to accomplish this through mandatory residency restrictions in the form of an amendment to Penal Code section 3003.5. This amendment (codified in 2006 as subdivision (b)) makes it "unlawful for any person for whom registration is required pursuant to Section 290 to reside within 2000 feet of any public or private school, or park where children regularly gather." § 3003.5, sub. (b), added by Prop. 83, § 21 subd. (b) (section 3003.5(b) or, generally, residency restrictions). The Department of Corrections and Rehabilitation (CDCR) accordingly began enforcing the residency restrictions as a mandatory parole condition for all registered sex offenders on parole in Laird County.

Appellant in this habeas corpus proceeding is a registered sex offender on parole in Laird County against whom section 3003.5(b) was enforced. Appellant alleges that the residency restrictions are unconstitutional as applied to him. Appellant relies almost exclusively on the California Supreme Court's 2015 decision, *In re William Taylor*, (2015) 60 Cal. 4th 1019, to support his claims.

For the reasons discussed below, we agree with the trial court that the *Taylor* case is distinguishable from this one and that the hardships in finding residency for the instant plaintiff pale in comparison to the hardships the *Taylor* plaintiffs faced. Accordingly, we affirm the judgment of the Superior Court.

FACTUAL BACKGROUND

Last fall, Harrison Gallagher was released on parole after serving a sentence for failing to register as a sex offender. He is required to register as a result of a rape conviction in Los Angeles County in 2010. The victim in that case was an adult woman with whom Gallagher was romantically involved at the time. This is the only crime for which Gallagher has ever been convicted.

Upon his release, Gallagher purportedly sought a new start, and it was recommended to him by one of his counselors that he settle in largely rural Laird County in central California. Gallagher got a job as a handyman for a collective of inns in the center of town; one of the perks of the position was a discounted room in one of the inns. Under the residency restriction of § 3003.5, sub. (b), however, Gallagher was unable to take the discounted room because of the inn's proximity to a local park.

Gallagher claims great hardship at finding suitable housing despite the size and relatively small population density of Laird County. He points to the numerous local schoolhouses, some of which teach as few as a dozen students at a time, and the county's numerous and liberally-labeled "parks," which include a skating park, a drama park (where once a year, elementary schoolchildren put on a Christmas pageant) and an ice cream park (a grassy square surrounded by three of the county's most popular ice cream parlors). Gallagher claims that his only options for meeting the residency requirement were to either (1) buy a plot and build on empty land (prohibitively expensive, according to him) or (2) live in three undesirable pockets of the county that he claims are filled with deviants and drug addicts. Gallagher has taken residence in one of these allegedly undesirable pockets, but he claims to worry daily about his safety and health in his current apartment complex. Gallagher believes that his rehabilitation is compromised by being forced to live among criminals. He further claims a stigma attached to his current place of residence and mentions protests over the course of many years by local church-going citizens trying to shut down the apartment complex.

TRIAL COURT FINDINGS OF FACT

After a three-day evidentiary hearing, the trial court made the following relevant findings of fact:

1. Registered sex offender parolees are unlikely to have the capital necessary to build new homes on unoccupied plots of land; most likely, they will be housed in apartment rentals or low-cost residential hotels.
2. The residency restrictions effectively bar registered sex offenders from 35% of existing rental property that would otherwise be available to them.
3. Of the 65% available, however, about half of these properties are run by co-op boards who have wide discretion in deciding to whom they can rent. That still leaves 32.5% of rental properties available in Laird County.
4. The residency restrictions have resulted in a significant number of registered sex offenders being diverted to three apartment complexes in Laird County. Cumulatively, these complexes have about 70% more parolees and ex-convicts in residence than in any other area in Laird County.
5. An organization in Laird called "Christian Crusaders" has targeted these complexes over the past five years with protests and rallies, inviting the inhabitants to, among other things, "repent or burn in Hell."

The trial court held that the residency restrictions, enforced as a mandatory parole condition against appellant Gallagher in Laird County, were not "unconstitutionally unreasonable" given the above circumstances and accordingly denied Gallagher's request for injunctive relief. The lower court found that the CDCR did not overstep its bounds in enforcing the restrictions against Gallagher.

APPEAL

Gallagher appeals the trial court's denial of injunctive relief. Appellant points specifically to an intervening decision by the California Supreme Court, *In re William Taylor*, (2015) 60 Cal. 4th 1019, holding that blanket enforcement of § 3003.5, sub. (b) in San Diego County was unconstitutional under the due process clause of the Fourteenth Amendment.

DISCUSSION

At trial and in the instant appeal, appellant continually points to the California Supreme Court's decision in *Taylor* as a compelling analogy—and binding precedent—applicable to this case. While *Taylor* may indeed provide the strongest argument in appellant's favor, we believe that the comparisons between that case and this one reveal more division than alignment.

According to the trial court in *Taylor*, for example, "by virtue of the residency restrictions alone, registered sex offender parolees [we]re effectively barred from access to approximately 97 percent of the existing rental property that would otherwise be available to them." *Id.* at 1034. Further, "the remaining 3 percent of multifamily rental housing outside the exclusion areas [was] not necessarily available to registered sex offender parolees for a variety of reasons, including San Diego's low vacancy rate, high rents, and the unwillingness of some landlords to rent to such persons." *Id.* As a result of the scant housing options available, the trial court accordingly found that "blanket enforcement of § 3003.5, sub. (b) in San Diego County has led to greatly increased homelessness among registered sex offenders on parole in the county." *Id.* at 1040.

By contrast, in this case, registered sex offender parolees are only barred from access to approximately 32.5% of existing rental property under § 3003.5, sub. (b) alone. As for the additional factors making housing more challenging in San Diego, the same factors either don't apply or don't apply with the same force as in Laird County. Specifically, Laird County reports a relatively high vacancy rate (nearly double that of San Diego); the average rent in Laird is half the average rent in San Diego. As for the third factor—"the unwillingness of some landlords to rent to such persons"—this does appear to apply with at least equal force in Laird, if not more. That said, appellant could produce no evidence at trial of a similar homelessness problem stemming from the blanket enforcement of § 3003.5, sub. (b).

It's important to note that the decision in *Taylor* ended with the following clarification: "CDCR retains the statutory authority, under provisions in the Penal Code separate from those found in section 3003.5(b) to impose special restrictions on registered sex offenders in the form of discretionary parole conditions, including residency restrictions that may be more or less restrictive than those found in section 3003.5(b), as long as they are based on, and supported by, the particularized circumstances of each individual parolee." *Id.* at 1042. Keeping this general directive in mind, the Court finds that the particularized circumstances of a registered sex offender seeking residence in Laird County are markedly distinct from the circumstances facing the same class of person seeking residence in San Diego County. The numbers alone show a stark difference in the opportunities available in Laird County. Even assuming that the apparently large number of co-op boards in Laird would automatically disapprove of any application from a registered sex offender, that still leaves over ten times as many available rental opportunities to Laird residents as San Diego residents.

Appellant has attempted to cast doubt on the accuracy of those numbers. He argues that the 32.5% of rental properties available fails to consider the influence of organizations like "Christian Crusaders," who exert influence even in non-co-op situations. It was established at trial that Christian Crusaders has, in fact, targeted the three primary complexes where registered sex offenders have come to reside over the past five years with protests and rallies. Appellant claims that efforts like these have essentially made his current situation "un-liveable."

While the Court does not doubt the embarrassment caused by such protests, there is a difference between an "un-liveable" situation and an uncomfortable one. In San Diego, registered sex offenders often find so few options for residence that they are forced to live on the streets. In Laird, it seems, the same offenders have comparatively more options—but with perhaps an additional risk of stigmatization.

Appellant points to the factual finding in *Taylor* that the restrictions were "disruptive in a way that hinder[ed] their treatment, jeopardize[d] their health and undercut[] their ability to find and maintain employment, significantly undermining any effort at rehabilitation." *Id.* at 1034. Gallagher believes that the demonstrations he constantly faces at his current home similarly hinder his treatment, jeopardizes his health and undermines his rehabilitation. Again, while the Court appreciates the burden Appellant must feel, we believe such an argument reflects a misreading of *Taylor*'s holding. *Taylor* did not stand for the proposition that any hindrance on rehabilitation can be grounds for lifting residency restrictions on registered sex offenders on parole. *Taylor* instead stood for the much narrower proposition that blanket enforcement of residency restrictions for all sex offender parolees in San Diego County, in particular, was improper. Even though, as Appellant points out, the *Taylor* court held against "*blanket* enforcement . . . without consideration of the individual case," we do not believe the California Supreme Court intended to eviscerate the wide reach of 3003.5(b), absent particularized findings that enforcement would be unduly onerous on plaintiffs. In this instance, we find that the residency restrictions at issue do not violate Appellant's due process rights under the Fourteenth Amendment.

Further, in response to Appellant's hyperbolic arguments about the "impossibility" of his situation and the "scourge of shame" he faces from Christian Crusaders, a group he calls "a terrorist organization": the Court feels compelled to remind Appellant of his original crime and the very pressing policy reasons for which he is now legally required to register in the state of California.

Appellant is a convicted rapist. Though he may be rehabilitated, though he may no longer be a threat to society, the fact of his awful crime—and the attached risk that often comes with perpetrators of such offenses—remains. The citizens of California passed a proposition to protect themselves and their children from sexual predators. There are, of course, limits to the restrictions that the government can reasonably place on such offenders once their criminal sentence has been served. But those limits have not been exceeded in this case. Appellant comes to this Court—not as a man without options—but as a man who wants to be like everyone else. The nature of his crime, however, makes it such that he can never be just another member of the general population. If that circumstance provides a challenge to his rehabilitative efforts, so be it. The point of this extended coda is not to be unsympathetic or callous toward his plight, but to put his "dilemma" into proper perspective. Shame is never desirable. But sometimes, it is deserved.

CONCLUSION

The judgment of the trial court is affirmed.

DeSilva, Elizabeth W., MacCabe, George F., Rawson, Nicole W. concur.

chapter 14

Getting into Law School

Now that you've completed all the legal writing tasks in this book, you should have a better idea as to whether law school is potentially in your future or not. If you're thinking of applying, these last two chapters are designed to help guide you through admissions as well as life in and beyond law school.

The two most important data points a law school will look at in your application are your LSAT score (or GRE) and your GPA. Law schools get so many applications that they have to cull some from the start. While the scores above can hardly tell the whole story of any prospective applicant, they do help narrow the pool. As a prospective student, the intersection of these scores will tell you whether you're comfortably within a school's target range or if you're a reach. Let's say your scores put you in the bottom 25th percentile of a school's typical accepted student pool. It's a definite reach school, but a chance is a chance, and when you're a stretch based on the numbers, it's even more critical that the other parts of your application—the personal statement, the letters of recommendation, the diversity statement and resume—are as well crafted as possible. Of these additional components, the personal statement is likely the most important. It serves as a test of your writing and argument skills (because make no mistake: this piece is closer akin to an argument grounded in life experience than a short memoir). It will also reveal to the admissions committee (which will include your future professors) whether you're a person they want populating their classrooms and participating in their Socratic dialogues.

ASSIGNMENT 12: PERSONAL STATEMENT

Your assignment is to compose a 2- to 3-page double-spaced, 12-point font personal statement. You can write the statement for law school, graduate school or your dream job (just specify the goal of the statement in your subtitle). There should also be an original title. The top of your essay should look something like this:

May It Please the Court
A Law School Personal Statement by John Doe

or

Consulting Greatness
A Personal Statement by Jane Doe for a Position at McKinsey & Co.

You have no restrictions in terms of the substance of your essay, although you should keep in mind the following criteria, which will be used to evaluate your essay:

PERSONAL STATEMENT GRADING RUBRIC

Category	Accomplished	Competent	Beginning
Presentation and Professionalism · Writes in clear and accessible prose			
· Employs a style appropriate for the purpose			
· Shows command of grammar and syntax			
Substantive Argument · Provides a coherent narrative			
· Focuses the statement to achieve depth over breadth			
· Grounds the piece in specifics rather than generalities			
· Relates the personal and particular to some larger idea			
· Reflects on experience cogently and meaningfully			
· Offers a unique and memorable reading experience			
General Comments and Suggestions for Improvement: Grade: _____			

Below are some common pitfalls that make for mediocre personal statements:

- *Offering nothing more than a prose version of your CV.* This relates to the coherence and focus criteria in the rubric. At the end of the day, law school applications aren't as involved as other graduate school applications. Don't waste an opportunity to do something distinct by treading over territory covered better in another part of your application. A CV or resume can

cover the breadth of your intellectual, athletic, social and philanthropic involvement. A personal statement is all about digging deep.
- *Covering so much ground that nothing sticks out in memory.* A two- to three-page essay about five things is actually about zero things. The committee reading your statement is also reading hundreds more; to stick out, you need to focus on one or two aspects of yourself and illuminate your point(s) in the most vivid way possible.
- *Telling an interesting story with no discernible relationship to why you want to go to law school.* This relates to the earlier point about personal statements really being arguments. It's good to stand out because of the fine yarn you're spinning, but that story needs to connect to the school (or job) for which you're applying.
- *Telling a sad story without extrapolating from it some net positive.* Many applicants have struggled in their lives leading up to law school. Talking about that struggle earnestly and sincerely can be very powerful. But be careful that the essay doesn't devolve into an invitation for pity. Anyone can suffer; extraordinary people persevere. You don't have to be over your life troubles before applying to school, but law schools are famously rigorous and no professional school wants to admit someone it doesn't consider ready for the curriculum's unique challenges. Use your personal challenges as an indication of what you can overcome.
- *Paying more attention to the prose than to the substance of the essay.* Students often make the mistake of believing that a fancy writing style or a creative way of expressing oneself is what law schools are seeking. As a result they decide to experiment with style: telling the story backwards, for example, or using a level of diction better suited to a Victorian or postmodern novel. The problem is: a personal statement is rarely the right place to try a new way of writing for the first time. Law schools are interested in *you*, and when the prose inhibits or masks the message of the statement, then you're writing counter to your own purposes.

Over the years, a number of personal statements have stood out in my memory as being particularly vivid. One involved a student whose hometown water supply was polluted so badly by a big corporation that she and her family had to spend months living in a hotel. The details of the story—walking to and from school, getting lunch out of vending machines—set an indelible scene. And the relationship to law was clear: she wanted to help bring greedy corporations like that one to justice.

Another story came from a student not destined for law school but for computer science graduate school. An undergrad professor had a simple assignment: break into the university-run website. The student at issue succeeded in his assignment, a bit too well. In the wee hours of the morning, he sent a frantic message to his professor because he'd shut down an entire part of the university's webpage. What I liked about this statement was that in one incredibly memorable story, he established both an explicit thesis—with great ability comes great responsibility—and an implicit one: only someone very skilled in his area of study could do what he did. The best arguments can function on multiple levels — think about text but also subtext.

If you're stuck trying to think of an approach to your personal statement, start by answering the following questions:

- Ideally, where do you see yourself in ten years?
- Why law school?
  - First, answer in a straightforward declarative sentence. I want to go to law school because _____.
  - Second, answer in the form of a narrative or memory.
- What value do you think you'll add to whatever law school you end up attending? You can answer generally but consider this more specifically for each law school application, especially your dream schools.

The answers to all these questions shouldn't be crammed into one statement, but hopefully at least one answer will bear fruit. To those who worry they lack that one killer narrative to really drive their argument home, no worries. That's not the only way to craft an effective statement.

Below is the personal statement I used to get into my Master of Fine Arts fiction writing program. While the purpose of the statement obviously is not to get into law school (if anything, it was to get out of the practice of law, at least temporarily), the same strategies applied:

> As I've grown older, I've noticed a change in the quality of time. Days go by slower as months and years race by. With each change of the calendar, I find myself increasingly stuck in smaller increments: pointless meetings, overlong dinner parties, overcrowded movies.
>
> It wasn't always like this. As a young boy in Port Neches and College Station, Texas, I constantly felt swept up by daily routines, packed schedules and carefully selected extracurriculars. And yet at every level of advancement, at the beginning of every new school year, I always had a sense of rebirth, renewal, reinvention. If I had to state in one phrase my purpose for applying to your program it would be to reclaim command over the smallness of time.
>
> The only time in my life when I felt like a full-time writer was my final year of college, my schedule filled with independent studies in prose and playwriting. Time moved slowly then as well, but not in the mechanical dance of corporate law (my current occupation) but in the intense and thoughtful scrutiny of small moments and large ideas.
>
> I wrote my first novel at the age of twenty. The project won first prize at Texas A&M's Student Research Week. At Yale Law, I wrote two additional novels for credit during my second and third years: *Private Gods* under the supervision of Harlon Dalton and *Mix* under the supervision of Deborah Cantrell. Both projects received an Honors distinction, the highest mark Yale Law offers. Since working at my law firm, Kaye Scholer LLP, I have continued writing, both plays and novels. I've most recently finished a series of short stories (two of which are serving as my writing sample) and a new play about the aftermath of a hurricane on an East Texas town.
>
> For years now, I have made writing an avocation, relegated to late night after work hours. It has not always been easy but a writer writes and I've never lacked

for discipline. But I have enough humility to realize that I am not nearly as good as I could be—with the aid of thoughtful instruction, constructive criticism and more than anything else—the luxury to reside and explore completely in a given moment; with a renewed sense of purpose and a little extra wisdom, to once again embrace the infinite within the infinitesimal.

Like my former computer science student, I'm saying multiple things at once:

1. I am persistent—though my resume shows a person who's done a lot of things other than write, I've always been a writer and always will be.
2. I am teachable—despite my fancy law degree, I know I can be better and that you can help me get there.

The best statements will use the limited space offered to maximum effect. They will answer the question of why you want to go to law school as well as how likely it is that you'll succeed there.

Below are some thoughts on the rest of the components of a typical law school application:

LETTERS OF RECOMMENDATION

Letters of recommendation give schools an objective and authoritative perspective on your potential as a prospective law student. You should have at least one academic reference, preferably two, and ideally they can speak to different aspects of your candidacy (i.e., a writing professor will likely identify different strengths than a math professor). If you have references from outside academia, make sure they can talk about you as specifically as possible, ideally grounding their observations in work you've accomplished that they've personally seen. Getting a vague form letter from the mayor of your hometown will not be as probative or convincing to an admissions committee as an honest assessment from a professor who's seen you grow in their class over the course of a semester.

Academic recommenders can come from any department and can teach any class; the content of the letter is more important than the content of the class itself (though be sensible: a letter from a neurochemistry professor is probably going to look weightier than one from the teaching assistant who led your improv workshop). Recommenders don't have to talk about your abilities in law specifically if they can talk about skills that matter to law schools, such as:

- Writing
- Critical thinking
- Problem solving
- Public speaking

Recommenders should be people who know you well, so target smaller classes and classes where the professor or teaching assistant has given you lots of feedback. That feedback will aid the recommenders in crafting a tailored letter. Develop relationships with professors early. Don't be the student who only comes to office hours at the end of the term to ask for a favor. If you want professors to know you and champion you, you need to give them the opportunity to do so. A lot of professors, me included, won't just write a letter based on the resume you hand me — what do I know, after all, about the volunteer work you did last summer in Montana? I want to talk about what I have actually observed — that's what makes sense and it will carry more weight with admissions committees.

DIVERSITY STATEMENTS

This is often an optional statement, but before you dismiss the option, remember that this is one of limited opportunities to advocate for yourself: to show your argumentative prowess, to reveal what makes your voice unique and to show your creativity. Keep in mind that there are many kinds of diversity. Race is where we often start the discussion, but you can also talk about socioeconomic status, geographical diversity or your unique area of study/expertise. A biochemistry major, for example, is going to stand out more in this applicant pool than a history major.

Ask yourself: what makes you unique? What makes your voice particularly vital or important to the conversation? How will your perspective enrich class conversations? If you have interesting answers to those questions, you should consider writing a diversity statement.

RESUMES/CVs

Don't throw in every single thing you've ever done. Be sensible and strategic. Remember that a resume is an argument, too, so make sure the formatting highlights what needs to be highlighted. Use templates and stylistic aids to make your resume look as sleek and professional as possible. If an item isn't self-evident, make clear the work you did with specifics.

ADDENDA

Addenda are typically used for one purpose and one purpose only: to explain a potentially problematic part of your application. The most common issues are low or disparate LSAT scores and low GPAs. For the LSAT, if there were particular circumstances that led to one low score, you may want to explain that. With GPAs, if your low grades were isolated to a particular semester (perhaps your first ever away from home, or perhaps during a time when you had unusual personal stressors), this would be your chance to explain that as well. The point of this isn't to make the committee feel sorry for you but to contextualize numbers that may raise red flags and to explain that you as a student are not represented accurately by those numbers.

chapter 15
Practical Advice for Law School and Beyond, or What I Wish I'd Known When I Started Law School

As I mentioned in the Preface, about a quarter to a third of the students I teach every semester at USC are not interested in law school or paralegal school. They're interested in the law generally or they foresee a basic command of its principles to be potentially useful in their future careers. So if your exploration of this subject matter ends here, I hope you leave this text feeling less intimidated by the law and its sometimes strange, archaic-sounding language. I hope you'll pore through the text of your next employment contract. And I hope you won't be afraid to defend your rights when they're violated and to demand fairness from those who would deny you.

For the rest of you for whom law school might be a possibility, I offer the following advice:

CHOOSING LAW AS A FIELD

Law can be a wonderful profession. At its best, a career in law will keep you intellectually stimulated and financially secure. Students often ask why I no longer practice law, assuming that I hated working as an attorney. But the assumption is not true. I very much enjoyed being a lawyer; I just found two things I enjoyed more: writing, which I've loved since I was a child, and teaching, a passion I discovered while I was getting my MFA at Boston University.

That said, choosing law as your profession is not a decision to be made lightly. Law school is expensive, and taking on significant debt is a risk in any economy. I see too many students default to the law for the wrong reasons: their parents want them to do it, or they can't think of anything better to do. Given the commitment and focus required to be both a good law student and a good lawyer, choosing law should be an affirmative choice, not a fallback. If you're not sure about the law, then wait. Entering law students vary widely in age; only a small fraction come to law school straight out of undergrad. Waiting to enter law school, in fact, actually helps your candidacy, as law schools view applicants who've had a little time away from school more favorably than those who go straight through. Gap years, in other words, aren't just good for your mental health — they improve your chances of getting into the law school of your dreams.

Students often think that gap years are only useful if they're actually doing work in the legal field, but again, I don't think this is true. If you want to work in a law firm post-undergrad, do so because you need the money or because you want to be in proximity to lawyers and paralegals to really see what their day-to-day life is like. Don't take a law job just to improve your law school applications. Work experience — other than meaningful work in another field (e.g., working for ten years as an electrical engineer) — factors very little into admissions decisions (which are determined largely by the intersection of one's GPA and LSAT score).

CHOOSING A LAW SCHOOL

Most of my students start the law school evaluation process by consulting national rankings, and I understand the reasons why. The advantage of a top-tier school is that it will have a national reputation, which offers you flexibility in terms of where you might want to practice post–law school. But beyond the top tier, look at where any given school's graduates are practicing. Most likely, they're in the state where the law school is. So if you want to practice in California, Pepperdine, Loyola or Southwestern may be a more logical choice than a higher-ranked school in Tennessee.

Visiting a school is a fine way to get a sense of how you'll fit in there. Admitted student weekends are nice, but those events, where you'll interact with carefully selected students and professors, are perhaps less revelatory than a visit on a random day. Sit in on a class or two and ask the students around you how they're enjoying their law school experience. A visit to the law school's placement office might also be useful. Does the school host an array of on-campus interviews each fall? What percentage of the law school's alums find employment within six months of graduation? Law school is a big decision, and you're likely going to be spending significant resources to go there. You owe it to yourself to deliberate as thoroughly as possible.

PREPARING FOR LAW SCHOOL

Students getting ready to enter law school always ask what to do in the summer leading up. "Is there a book I should read?" Well, now there is, but since you've already read it, my advice is to relax. Don't worry about learning law before law school. But you should get plenty of rest and quality time with family and friends. The first year of law school, especially the first semester, is an all-consuming time, and it will require almost your full attention. So if there's a trip you've always wanted to take, take it. Committing to professional school isn't just about committing three years of your life; it's committing several years after that as you pay off your loans and establish your career. If there's an adventure you've been itching to embark upon, don't waste time. Have fun, get lots of sleep and come to orientation week refreshed and ready.

STARTING LAW SCHOOL

When I started law school, I didn't know anything except where the law school was and how to walk there from my apartment. Here are some of the things I wish someone had told me when I started.

Understandably, your immediate concerns will be your first-semester class load. What makes law school so daunting and so different from undergrad isn't so much the difficulty of the material as the volume. You're going to have so many cases to read for so many different classes. It's vital that you keep up with the readings and don't get behind. Briefing cases is important, too (and now you know how!), because at the end of the term, when you're preparing for exams, it's much easier to wade through your own notes than it is to reread entire sections of your casebook. Putting in the work as you go along in the semester will make the end of the semester less fraught.

You're going to see a number of students in your classroom who will seek and relish the spotlight during Socratic dialogues. They will make you feel inadequate. They will send your imposter syndrome into overdrive. Know that even these students have their moments of doubt and that you were admitted into your school for a reason. Maybe you're not as polished in class discussions, but you're a better writer or better exam-taker. Those skills might actually be more important—they certainly affect your grade more.

At the end of your first semester or first year, typically, there will be a competition to join the law school's law review or law journal. Law reviews solicit, choose and then edit articles about contemporary law. To get chosen to be on a law review, you'll need to master the aforementioned *Bluebook*, which is a guide for citing every kind of legal source material. Having a law review on your resume is helpful when you're applying for a position at a firm but especially for clerkships and academic positions down the line.

A clerkship involves working for a judge—it can be in state or federal court or in a trial or appellate court—and helping them prepare for cases they're about to hear as well as helping them draft the opinions they'll issue. It's a labor-intensive job (how much labor is dependent on the judge) but incredibly rewarding as you get a front seat to the actual deliberative process. Clerkships are very prestigious positions, and while they won't pay as much as private work, firms and companies covet attorneys with clerking experience. In fact, many law firms will offer clerkship bonuses for any attorney who joins a firm post-clerkship; they will also often give you seniority credit for the time you were clerking. In other words, if you clerked for two years before starting at a law firm, you start at that firm as a third-year associate, not a first-year associate.

Clinics are also excellent opportunities to get practical, hands-on experience in law school. You get to take on real cases and advocate for clients under the supervision of a law professor. After a first year in which you'll be taking mostly big lecture courses, it's nice in one's second and third year to use your knowledge in the real world and to remind yourself what you're working toward.

WORKING DURING LAW SCHOOL

In a typical three-year law school progression, there are two summers in between the start of law school and graduation. In the fall or early spring of your 1L year, you'll interview for positions for the following summer. At this point, you might not even have grades back from your first semester, and plum positions — like judicial externships or law firm summer associate jobs — may be scarce. Cast a wide net, both in terms of types of positions and geography, and know that the most significant summer is still ahead.

Typically, the fall of your 2L year is when you'll interview for positions the following summer. By then, you'll have a full year of grades and perhaps a better sense as to what you want to practice and where. Your school may even have on-campus events where employers, often represented by alumni of your school, will come to interview prospective summer associates. This is the summer that really counts, as 2L summer associate positions are often the gateway to full-time post-graduation employment.

In terms of getting to your ultimate destination post–law school, I've already mentioned the utility of law reviews. But your professors are another excellent resource. You likely won't have your choice of classes or professors in your 1L year. But starting your second year, you'll have lots of electives and lots of choices. Certain professors may be known as being feeders to particular judges for clerkships or particular firms. Your best resource for finding out who can connect you to whom will be your school's upper-class students, especially the 3Ls.

WORKING AFTER LAW SCHOOL

Whether you end up getting a post-graduation clerkship or not, a law firm of some size may be in your future. Big firms with diverse practices will offer the most money right away (it makes paying off law school debt much easier); they also offer some of the most sophisticated on-the-job training that one can get. The disadvantage of places like these is that especially in your first years as an associate, your time (or at least most of your time) belongs to that firm. You will be expected to bill (as in keep track of your billable hours to clients) above a certain threshold. If you start teetering below that threshold, an assignment coordinator will hand you all sorts of tasks. Being on constant call can be exhausting, but it is the price for the high salary.

For the vast majority of lawyers, big-firm practice is not a sustainable lifestyle. The partnership track varies from state to state; when I was in New York, you were an associate for eight years before you were considered for promotion to either counsel (a kind of intermediate step) or partner. Even partners are sometimes tiered: there are equity partners (whose salary is tied to the firm's profits) and nonequity partners (whose salary is either not tied to the firm's profits or whose salary is considerably less tied to the firm's profits). By the time you're a mid-level associate, around year four, the firm will start to either groom you for promotion or encourage you to find other employment. But many associates leave before this point for smaller firms, different firms, in-house counsel positions or nonprofit or government jobs.

The advantage of starting at one of the above positions is that you'll likely get more responsibility right away. While the salary might not be as robust, especially if you're working for a nonprofit or the government, the quality of the work you're doing and the clientele you'll be helping may be the real reward.

Lawyers tend to be mobile; it's the rare attorney who works at the same place from law school graduation to retirement. Law is one of the few professions where you can change your specialty overnight. You could be a products liability litigator one day and then a real estate attorney the next. That's not to say the business transition isn't difficult, especially if you're working solo, but lawyers shift course all the time. As with appellate oral arguments and most of life, it's best to be flexible.

CLOSING STATEMENT

I hope this book has proven helpful at introducing you to the world of legal discourse and argument. Even though I'm no longer a practicing attorney, I wouldn't trade my legal training for the world. Whether you ultimately go on to law school or not, the law plays a big part in our lives, and learning how to navigate through it and how to advocate for yourself can be incredibly empowering. Whatever your future holds, I wish you the best of luck. Though when your reasoning is sound and your prose is clear, luck is a little less necessary.

All my best,
Antonio

Glossary

affirm: to uphold a lower court's ruling.

appellant or petitioner: the party who files or petitions an appellate court after losing in a lower court.

appellate court: court that determines whether the lower court committed an error significant enough to require the decision be reversed or modified or a new trial granted.

appellee or respondent: party defending the lower court's decision in an appeal.

as applied challenge: contention that a law is unconstitutional as applied to the particular litigant challenging it.

cause of action: combination of defined factual elements entitling one to a legal remedy.

civil action: lawsuit where one person files a complaint against another asking the court to order the other side to pay money or to stop doing something.

common law: legal system in the United States in which judges create their own body of law.

complaint: legal argument submitted to a court to commence a lawsuit.

concurrence: opinion of a judge or justice who agrees with the outcome of a case (meaning they agree on which party should prevail) but disagrees with at least part of the majority's reasoning. Concurrences often offer alternative logic for reaching the same outcome.

courts of inferior jurisdiction: courts that hear limited types of cases, including traffic, family law, small claims and juvenile court.

courts of original jurisdiction: trial courts where litigation often begins, usually courts of general jurisdiction (meaning they can hear cases of all subject matters: civil and criminal).

criminal action: proceeding where the plaintiff is a government prosecutor (the United States in federal cases and a state in state cases) asking the court to punish a defendant with jail time or a fine.

damages: an award of money for violating a law.

de novo: anew; when a court reviews an issue as if it were the first court to do so, giving no deference to the lower court's decision on the same issue.

defamation: a statement that injures another's reputation.

defendant: party that a lawsuit has been brought against (the party that has been sued by the plaintiff).

dicta: statement or observation that is not an essential part of the legal reasoning necessary to resolve a case.

discovery: process of finding answers about what happened between the parties in the case.

dissent: opinion of a judge or justice who disagrees with the outcome of a case. Dissents often offer alternative logic for reaching their different outcome.

en banc: case heard by the full court (or a critical mass) of all appeals judges in a given jurisdiction, as opposed to a smaller panel. En banc proceedings often occur when the court believes there is a particularly significant issue at stake.

facial challenge: contention that a law is unconstitutional as written, or on its face. The result of a successful facial challenge to a law is invalidation of that law for everyone.

holding: judge's ultimate decision in resolving a case or controversy and the reasoning that led to that decision.

injunction: an order to do something.

intermediate scrutiny: level of judicial scrutiny in which the government must prove that the law in question is substantially related to achieving an important government objective. Intermediate scrutiny has been applied, for example, when a law discriminates on the basis of gender.

interrogatories: sets of questions exchanged between opposing parties.

legislative history: committee reports, hearings and debates preceding a law's enactment.

material fact: fact relevant to the underlying legal claim.

moral reasoning: mode of constitutional interpretation using moral concepts and ideals to inform judges' interpretations.

motion to dismiss: request that a court end a lawsuit or part of a lawsuit.

order to show cause: demand from a judge for a party to prove why the court should not grant a particular motion.

originalism: mode of constitutional interpretation focusing on the intent of the framers of the Constitution. An originalist believes that the language of the Constitution had an objective meaning at the time it was crafted and that meaning should not change over time.

pincite: page number of a judicial opinion where the cited language can be found.

plaintiff: in a civil case, the party who initiates the lawsuit (or brings the matter before the court and seeks some remedy); in a criminal case, the plaintiff is the government (the United States in federal court and a state in state court).

pragmatism: mode of constitutional interpretation focusing on the probable practical consequences of those interpretations. A pragmatist selects the interpretation they believe would lead to the best outcome in the future.

preliminary injunction: order from a judge, typically granted before or during trial, with the goal of preserving the status quo before a final judgment.

prima facie: sufficient to establish a fact or raise a presumption. A prima facie *case* is a cause of action or defense that is proven by a party's evidence. Prima facie evidence and cases can be rebutted or disproved by an opposing party.

pro bono: work undertaken without charge.

procedural history: an account of how lower courts decided a particular case on appeal.

qualified immunity: legal immunity for government officials against lawsuits suing them as individuals as opposed to suing the government body for which they work.

rational basis review: deferential level of judicial scrutiny in which the government only has to show that the law in question is rationally related to a legitimate state interest. Generally, when a law doesn't involve a fundamental right or discriminate against a suspect class, courts will apply this level of review.

remand: an order to send a case back to a lower court for further proceedings, often with specific instructions or legal clarifications to guide the lower court.

reverse: to hold in favor of the losing party from a lower court proceeding.

stare decisis: principle that courts need to follow their own precedent and the precedent of courts higher than them in the hierarchy of law. Latin for "to stand by things decided."

statute: law passed by a legislature, either Congress or its equivalent on the state level.

statutory construction: process of determining what a statute means so that a court can apply it correctly.

strict scrutiny: level of judicial scrutiny in which the government has to prove that the law in question is narrowly tailored to achieve a compelling government interest. Strict scrutiny is applied when a law infringes upon a fundamental right (such as the right to marry) or discriminates against a class of individuals who have been historically subject to discrimination (on the basis, for example, of race, religion, national origin or alienage).

summary judgment: judgment as a matter of law, which resolves the matter in dispute without the benefit of a full trial. Summary judgments are only appropriate when a judge is convinced there is no genuine dispute as to any material fact in the case.

textualism: mode of constitutional interpretation focusing on the plain meaning of a legal document's text.

traverse: denial of a matter of fact alleged in an opposing party's pleadings.

vacate: to wipe out a lower court opinion's entirely, often necessitating a remand.

writ of certiorari: order by which an appellate court decides to review a lower court's decision.

writ of habeas corpus: petition to a court by a prisoner to determine the legality of their current detention, including the conditions of confinement.

Index

1L, 326.
2019 Rules of the Supreme Court of the United States, 268.
2L, 326.
3L, 326.

Addenda for law school applications, 322.
Admissions committee, 317, 321-322.
Advice letter, 14, 17, 97, 135.
American Jurisprudence, 259-260.
Answers, as memorandum section, brief answers or holdings, 21, 24, 29, 98, 103, 106, 108-110, 114, 121.
Appeal, 2-3, 6, 23, 265-289.
Appendix to appellate brief, 271, 276.
Application of law, 13-17, 101-102, 110-112, 114, 169, 255, 268, 275-276.
Arguing in the alternative, 17, 265, 267, 275.
Argument, legal argumentation, 97, 99-102, 107-108, 110-112, 114, 121, 161, 169, 253-255, 263, 267-268, 275-276, 288.
    as section of a brief, 275, 276, 283-288.
    counterargument, 102, 111-112, 114, 169, 171, 254-255, 268, 275-276.
As applied challenge, 123.
Associate at law firm, 325-327.
Attire for oral argument, 290.
Audience, in writing, 97, 106, 108, 135, 254.
    lay, 135.
    peer, 254.

Billable hours, billing hours, 105-106, 326.
Binding, in law, 4-5, 22, 25, 210, 262, 266, 275.
Body language in oral argument, 290.
Briefs, 19-29, 97, 112, 265-289, 325.
    appellate, 25, 97, 112, 265-289.
    case, 19-29, 44-47, 325.
Bulleting, bullets, 22-23, 100-101, 107, 275.
Burden of proof, 11, 17, 134, 161.

Caption of the case, 268.
Character and fitness test, 163.
Charts, 107.
Chronological order, timeline, 99, 109.
Citation errors, 255.
Citations, 20-22, 29, 101, 113-114, 121, 168, 261, 271, 276, 288. See also Pincites, 20-22, 24, 113, 168.
    cite check, 121, 261, 288.
    string cites, 101.
Civil action, 6.
Clerkship, 325-326.
Clinics, 325-326.
Closing statement, 265, 289.
Common law, 1.
Complaint, 6, 51.
Conclusion,
    in an appellate brief, 268, 275-276, 288.
    in a memorandum, 101-103, 106, 110, 112-114, 121, 169, 255.
Concurrences, 21, 25-26, 29, 47.
Confidential, 163.
Conflict of interest, 163.
Constitutional law,
    constitutionality, 261, 267.
    interpretation, 49.
    questions, 49.
Corpus Juris Secundum, 259-260.
Court system, 2-5.
    appellate, appeals, intermediate, circuit, 2-4.
    federal, 3.
    highest, last resort, 2-3.
    inferior jurisdiction, 2-3.
    lower, trial, district, 2-3.
    original jurisdiction, 2-3, 23.
    state, 3.
Cover page, 268-271, 276.
CRAC structure, 268, 275-276.

Credibility, 97, 112.
Cross-reference, 121, 263, 288.

Damages, 6.
De novo, 51, 267.
Defamation, 135.
Deference, 51, 267.
Dicta, 5–6, 101.
Discovery, 13–14.
    depositions, 13.
    interrogatories, 13.
Discussion, as memorandum section, 98, 103, 106, 109–113, 121, 255.
Dissents, 21, 25–26, 28–29, 47.
Diversity statement, 317, 322.
Docket number, 268.
Efficiency, in writing, 97, 102, 135.
En banc proceedings, 51.
Error of law, 265.
Ethical behavior, 163.
Eye contact, 290.

Facial challenge, 123.
Facts, 2–3, 6, 13–14, 21–23, 29, 44, 271–272.
    arbiter, 3.
    disputes, 23.
    finder, 13.
    issues, 13, 49.
    material, non-material, 13, 23, 102, 110, 271.
    questions, 3, 6, 267.
Focus, in writing, 97, 108, 110, 114, 171, 276, 318–319.
Formality, in writing, 97, 105–106.
Formatting
    appellate brief, 268–271.
    memorandum, 101–102, 106–107, 255.
    peer critique, 254–256.
Framers, of the Constitution, 49–50.
    See also Original intent, originalism, 9, 49–50.

Gap year, 324.
GPA, 317, 322, 324.
Grammar, 114, 276, 318.
    See also Mechanics, 255.
Graphs, 101, 107.
GRE, 317.

Headings, 106–107, 110, 268, 270.
Headnotes, 19.
Hedging, in discussion or argumentation, 291.
Hierarchy of law, 1–7, 49, 101, 110, 275.

Holding, 5–6, 21, 24, 27, 29, 46, 50, 101.

Imagery, 100.
In-house counsel, 327.
Injunction, 6, 135.
Interpret, judicial interpretation, 49–50, 95, 260–261, 266.
Interrogatories, 13.
IRAC structure, 101–102, 110–111, 114, 135, 171, 255, 268, 275.
Issues presented, questions presented
    in appellate brief, 270–271, 276.
    in case brief, 21, 23–24, 28.
    in memorandum, 97–98, 106, 108–109, 121.
Issues, in IRAC, 101–102, 110.

Judicial actions, case decisions,
    affirm, 6, 265, 276.
    remand, 6.
    reverse, 6, 265, 276.
    vacate, 6, 265.
Judicial panel, 19, 289.
Judicial parties, 6.
    defense, appellee, respondent, 6, 265.
    plaintiff, appellant, petitioner, 6, 265.
Judicial philosophy, 50.
Judicial scrutiny, 267.
    intermediate, 267.
    rational basis, 267.
    strict scrutiny, 267.
Jurisdiction, 2–4, 23, 51, 101, 106, 112, 163, 261–262, 266, 271, 273.
    diversity, 4.
Jurisdictional statement, basis for jurisdiction, 271.

KeyCite, 261.

Law firm, 98, 105, 320, 324–326.
Law journals, law reviews, 259–261, 266, 325.
Law types,
    civil, 2, 6, 259.
    criminal, 2, 6, 259.
Legal encyclopedia, 259–261, 266.
Legislative history, 9, 271. See also Statutory construction, 9, 11.
Letters of recommendation, 317, 321–322.
LexisNexis, 19–20, 260–261.
LSAT, 317, 322, 324.

Mechanics, 255. See also Grammar, 114, 276, 318.

Memorandum, 13, 14–17, 19, 97–98, 102–103, 105–121.
    client, 106, 112.
    interoffice, 106, 112, 123.
    predictive, 106.
Moral reasoning interpretation, 50.
Motions, 23, 51, 97, 112, 123.
    12(b)(6), 51.
    to dismiss, 23.

Natural language, 262.
Negative analyses, 261.
Negative expressions, 100.
Nominalizations, 100.
Numbered lists, 100, 108, 275.

On-campus interviews, 324.
Opening statement, 289.
Oral argument, appellate-style, 289–291, 327.
Order to show cause, 123.
Ordinances, 271. See also Statutes, 1, 2, 5, 9, 11, 101, 110–111, 113, 121, 259–263, 267, 270–271, 275, 288.
Organization, in writing, 97, 114, 171, 255, 276.
Original intent, originalism, 9, 49–50.
    See also Framers of the Constitution, 49–50.
Outline,
    for argument, 263, 268, 270, 289, 291.
    for research, 263, 266.
Parallel construction, 100.
Paraphrasing, 100, 111, 261.
Partners at a law firm, 98, 106, 327.
Pathos, 290.
Peer critique, 254–257. See also Writing workshop, 253–257.
Personal statement, 135, 317–321.
Persuasive authority, 4–5, 210, 266.
Pincites, 20–22, 24, 113, 168.
    See also Citations, 20–22, 29, 101, 113–114, 121, 168, 261, 271, 276, 288.
Positive analyses, 261.
Pragmatist, pragmatic interpretation, 50.
Precedent, 1–2, 4–6, 24–25, 49–50, 96, 100, 110–112, 171, 275.
Preliminary injunction, 135.
Prima facie, 123, 134.
Primary source, law, 262.
Pro bono work, 123.
Procedural history, procedural posture, 21–23, 26–27, 29, 45, 51, 271–272.
Professional writing, 97, 106, 114, 276.
Purpose, in writing, 97, 114, 254, 318, 320, 322.

Qualified immunity, 51.
Quote, quoting, 100, 261, 266, 275.

Reasoning, 5, 19, 21–22, 24–29, 44–47, 50, 95, 109, 255, 266.
Repetition, 97, 102–103, 110.
Reporters, 20–22, 113, 168.
    LexisNexis, LEXIS, 19–20, 260–261.
    Supreme Court Reporter, 20.
    United States Report, 20.
    United States Supreme Court Report, Lawyers' Edition, 20.
    Westlaw, 260–262.
Resume, CV, 317–319, 321–322, 325.
Revision, rewriting, 103, 254, 261, 263, 288.
Rubric, 114, 276, 290, 318.
Rule, in IRAC and CRAC, 101–02, 110–111, 114, 268, 275–276.

Secondary source, 259–262.
Sentence structure, 99–100.
    See also Syntax, 99, 114, 276, 318.
Shepardize, 261, 266.
Socratic dialogue, 22, 317, 325.
Speed, of speech, 290–291.
Standard of review, 267, 275.
Stare decisis, 4, 47, 95–96.
Statement of Facts, 99, 106, 108–110, 114, 121, 135, 255.
Statement of the Case, 271–272, 288.
Statutes, laws, 1, 2, 5, 9, 11, 101, 110–111, 113, 121, 259–263, 267, 270–271, 275, 288.
Statutory construction, 9, 11, 271.
    See also Legislative history, 9, 271.
Straw man arguments, 112.
Style of writing, 98, 255–256, 318–319.
Subheadings, subject headings, 22, 102, 110, 275.
Subject, of a memorandum, 107.
Subject/verb disagreement, 255.
Subtext, 320.
Summarization, summarizing, summary, 19, 29, 44–45, 100, 106, 113, 255, 259–260, 266, 275, 288–289.
Summary judgement, 23, 51, 135.
Summary of Argument, 272–274, 276, 281–283, 288.
Supremacy Clause, 1.
Supreme Court, 2–3, 20–21, 23, 29, 265–266, 268, 275.

Syntax, 99, 114, 276, 318. See also Sentence structure, 99–100.

Table of cited authorities, 271, 279–280.
Table of contents, 260, 268, 270, 276–278.
Template, guide, 102, 106, 322.
Terms & Connectors, 262.
Textualism, 49–50.
The Bluebook: A Uniform System of Citation, 261, 325.
Thesis, 97, 319.
Transitions, 255, 275.
Traverse, 123.
Treatise, 259–261, 266, 271.
Trial types, 2–3, 13.
    bench, 3, 13.
    jury, 2–3, 13, 23.

U.S. Constitution, 1, 2, 49–50, 101.

Visual aid, illustrations, 101, 107.
Volume, in books or journals, 20, 22, 113, 259.
Volume, in speech, 290.

Westlaw, 260–262.
Work product, 105–106.
Writ of certiorari, 270–271.
Writ of habeas corpus, 123.
Writing workshop, 253–257.
    See also Peer critique, 254–257.